Cases on Business and Management in the MENA Region:

New Trends and Opportunities

El-Khazindar Business Research and Case Center, Egypt

THE AMERICAN UNIVERSITY IN CAIRO
KCC SCHOOL OF BUSINESS
El-KHAZINDAR
Business Research
and Case Center

BUSINESS SCIENCE
Reference

Senior Editorial Director:	Kristin Klinger
Director of Book Publications:	Julia Mosemann
Editorial Director:	Lindsay Johnston
Acquisitions Editor:	Erika Carter
Development Editor:	Hannah Abelbeck
Production Editor:	Sean Woznicki
Typesetters:	Natalie Pronio, Jennifer Romanchak, Deanna Jo Zombro
Print Coordinator:	Jamie Snavely
Cover Design:	Nick Newcomer

Published in the United States of America by
Business Science Reference (an imprint of IGI Global)
701 E. Chocolate Avenue
Hershey PA 17033
Tel: 717-533-8845
Fax: 717-533-8661
E-mail: cust@igi-global.com
Web site: http://www.igi-global.com

Library of Congress Cataloging-in-Publication Data

Cases on business and management in the MENA region: new trends and opportunities / El-Khazindar Business Research and Case Center, editor.

p. cm.

Includes bibliographical references and index.

Summary: "This book presents a careful blend of conceptual, theoretical and applied research in regard to the relationship between the Middle East and North Africa region and business and management"--Provided by publisher.

ISBN 978-1-60960-583-4 (hbk.) -- ISBN 978-1-60960-584-1 (ebook) 1. Industrial management--Middle East--Case studies. 2. Industrial management--North Africa--Case studies. I. American University in Cairo. El-Khazindar Business Research and Case Center.

HD70.M628C37 2011

658.00956--dc22

2011001302

British Cataloguing in Publication Data

A Cataloguing in Publication record for this book is available from the British Library.

All work contributed to this book is new, previously-unpublished material. The views expressed in this book are those of the authors, but not necessarily of the publisher.

Table of Contents

Detailed Table of Contents

Section 1
Accounting

In today's computerized, interconnected, global business environment, the accounting profession has to deal with a host of complex issues; for instance, how to capture and record new business transactions and events, develop value-added business and information processes, create new value-chain opportunities, disseminate useful knowledge to a wide array of information consumers, and provide assurance services across the entire spectrum of economic activities. The cases in this section deal with technology, systems, change, and change management. The first case, "The Egyptian International Motor Company," deals with the use of automated accounting Information Systems in the context of global business operations. The case explores the company's strategic decisions regarding the implementation of computerized accounting Information System, problems met during the implementation process, and the actions taken to remedy these problems to gain the potential system redesign benefits. The second case, "The Maridive Company for Oil and Marine Services," presents the problems related to the application of the International Accounting Standards no 32 and 38 "Financial assets and Derivatives" and their Egyptian equivalent, the Egyptian Standards on auditing no 700 and 702. The third case, "Electronic Commerce and Management Accountants in Egypt," explores the process of change in the role of management accountants associated with the implementation of B-to-B e-commerce. The fourth case, "The Application of ABC in an Industrial Company," illustrates the application of ABC method in a single manufacturing organization operating in the metal industry and compares the results of ABC with the traditional, volume based costing method.

Section 3
Management

Organizations operating worldwide adopt different strategies and marketing techniques in various geographic areas, depending on the cultural perception of the country in which they are active. There are diverse reasons for implementing different management strategies, even under the same organizational umbrella. Responsiveness to customers, market adaptability, and competitiveness with other organizations operating in the same sector are some of the most important. The first case, "Innovative Managerial Approaches in MENA Countries," examines the management strategies of a leading furniture company that started off as a small business and rapidly expanded globally. The case highlights the company's flexibility in adapting its organizational structures to the nature of the market in different countries, and its reliance on a cross-cultural management approach to marketing in order to increase product acceptance by consumers across the world. In today's hyper-competitive environment, understanding factors that contribute to effective management of change, and achieving strategic competitive standing is critical. The second case, "Facing Organizational Change and Stress Management," explores the implementation of two electronic banking delivery systems, namely ATMs and Internet banking, in a leading bank in Egypt. The case identifies and describes the bank's approach to managing change through Information Technology with regards to leadership actions, overcoming resistance to change, personal and organizational attributes, strategies, structures, business processes, culture, as well as organizational commitment.

The case discusses the various reasons for implementing different organizational strategies, such as responsiveness to customers, adaptability to market, and competitiveness with other competitors. It explores the factors that encourage a company to diversify its organizational structure in different countries. Further, it highlights the important differences between organizational structure at headquarter as compared to that in foreign subsidiaries.

The case of First Commercial Bank provides a detailed exploration, description, and explanation of the implementation of two electronic banking delivery systems, namely ATMs and Internet banking. The case identifies and describes the bank's approach to managing change through Information Technology with regards to leadership actions, overcoming resistance to change, personal and organizational attributes, strategies, structures, business processes, culture, as well as organizational commitment.

Section 4
Management Information Systems

To compete successfully in today's retail business arena, senior management are often demanding fast and responsive Information Systems that enable the company not only to manage its operations, but to provide on-the-fly performance measurement through a variety of tools including ERP systems, data warehousing, and Business Intelligence (BI) applications. The focus of the first case, "Strategic Role for Management Information Systems in a Multinational Company," is on the strategic role that Information Technology (IT) plays in two subsidiaries of an international company, one located in Egypt and the other in Sweden. The case explores the importance of balancing business, information, and organizational strategy in a manner conducive to business-IT strategy alignment. The second case, "Business Intelligence Systems in the Dynamic Sales Environment of Beverage Distribution," deals with the application of ERP system as the backbone for BI tools designed to provide sales and marketing units in a transnational company subsidiary in Egypt to effectively respond to the demands for agile information services. The third case, "Ghabbour Group -- GB Auto," has gone through two ERP successive implementations. The driver for the most recent implementation was to secure all the necessary platforms and management tools for enabling growth and improving efficiency and effectiveness of the company's business operation and resources. Following its public offering and registration in the CASE and CMA, GB Auto was legally required to provide annual and quarterly audit reports of its varied LOBs performance. The trajectory of implementation of integrated Enterprise Information Systems at the group is reviewed to assess its effectiveness and appropriateness in response to CASE and CMA audit reports.

This case study examines the strategic role that Information Technology (IT) plays in the subsidiaries of a multinational company. The subsidiaries are located in Egypt and Sweden. The case explains the differences and similarities between the two subsidiaries of the same multinational company. The main two issues of this case are: a) how IT supports business and organizational strategy and b) how business-IT strategy is aligned. Moreover, this case study discusses the importance of achieving a balanced relationship among business, information, and organizational strategy.

Current severe competition in the market forced senior management to give much care to acquiring quick and efficient Information Systems that enable the company not only to manage its operations but to provide on-the-fly performance measurement through a variety of tools. This case study explains how the ERP system was used as the backbone by BI systems to help Sales and Marketing units in Transnational Company subsidiary in Egypt successfully meet the demands for nimble information services.

This case was developed for use as a teaching case for highlighting the fundamental impediments and obstacles in instituting cross-functional CBISs in business operations within the Egyptian business environment and culture. The executive management and the Board of Directors of a Egyptian large trading and manufacturing group, "GB Auto," in pursuit of securing all the necessary infrastructure platforms and management tools for enabling growth and improving efficiency and effectiveness of the group's business operation and resources, have thoroughly examined the status of the IS services and their impact on the quality of decision making at all levels of management. The extent of lack of control and effective utilization of the use of resources in the group has been cited by the top management. The reporting system was required to be responsive in order to provide the management with the necessary verifiable and comprehensive information services. Two implementations of ERP systems in the group were duly investigated and reviewed in this case to assess their respective effectiveness and appropriateness in serving these purposes. Various success and failure factors of these two implementations were reviewed, and actions in the post-implementation phase are being researched.

Section 5
Marketing

In a highly competitive and turbulent market environments, carefully formulated, orchestrated, and meticulously implemented marketing strategies are imperative for gaining and retaining market share and profitability. The first case, "Ariel in Egypt," examines the past and present challenges facing Ariel, a long-time market leader in the detergent sector in Egypt whose market share has started to slip. In particular, it examines the marketing strategies and performance of Ariel High Suds, which is witnessing a declining market share as well as a decline in the overall high-suds market due to fierce competition and the growing low-suds market in Egypt. The second case, "Social Marketing in Egypt," focuses on the application of social marketing by charity and development-focused Egyptian NGO called Nahdet El Mahrousa (NM). NM initiated a creative model, whereby individuals and institutions are encouraged to seek NM's support in the start-up of any developmental initiative in Egypt. One of the projects that NM is proud to support is the "Young Innovators Awards" (YIA) program. After several successful years, the managing team faced the challenge of finding alternative sources of support in a tight time frame to avoid halting stopping the program all together. The third case, "The International Commercial and Industrial Investment Company, S.A.E (ICII)," operates in the trading of high-end power products and construction equipments, with Honda power products taking up the majority of the company's portfolio. Since the introduction of Chinese products into the Egyptian markets, Honda sales have been increasing, however at a decreasing rate. ICII is facing a number of challenges commonly faced by companies that operate in a highly segmented markets targeted by a plethora of product assortments. The main question raised is: what marketing strategy should the company implement in order to ensure its success and sustainability?

The case discusses the dilemma that arises at P&G Egypt when the market of the Ariel Hand Wash detergent reached maturity and is going into decline. The fierce competition and the growing market of the automatic detergents negatively affected the sales of Ariel Hand Wash. Being positioned as "The Brand of the People," P&G needs to resolve this dilemma while maintaining the overall portfolio of the company. The case discusses the product life cycle of Ariel Hand Wash, which is shifting into being a cash cow instead of a star.

Nahdet El Mahrousa is a Non-Governmental Organization (NGO) that uses social marketing as an effective way to gathering funds needed for the sustainability of the organization. The Young Innovators Award (YIA), a program established by Nahdet El Mahrousa, benefited from the marketing strategies implemented by the organization. However, when funds suddenly stopped, the management was faced with the threat of cancelling the program. Nahdet El Mahrousa is facing the dilemma of finding different ways to market the program in an efficient way as to secure enough funds to execute the program on-time.

This marketing case describes the dilemma that the market leader of the power products' market in Egypt, Honda Power Products, is facing. The company is facing fierce competition from the Chinese competitors. Although the company's sales are increasing, the management is not happy because the market share is decreasing. The company is threatened to lose its position in the market; therefore, the management is seeking alternative solutions that would enforce its market position and strengthen its competitiveness against the Chinese products.

Section 6
Operations Management

Successful marketing starts with value creation, a joint responsibility of production/operations and marketing management. The coordination and integration of these silo business functions is often achieved through the design of business processes including demand management, demand fulfillment, customer service operation, to name a few. The first case, "Spinning Off the Supply Chain," examines the operation of a business in the food service industry. It demonstrates the importance of sound supply

Foreword

I am delighted to see the publishing of this book, which sees the production of cases that address the developments taking place in emerging economies with an emphasis on Egypt. Cases are important in linking industry, business, and academia, as well as blending educational content and in-class discussions with real-life market practices and emerging concepts and trends. According to multiple reports and studies published recently, emerging economies are going through rapid developments, and with a world constantly affected by innovative information and communication technology tools and applications, information sharing and knowledge dissemination is an invaluable mechanism for sharing expertise and lessons learnt. Respectively, case studies represent the ideal platform to report and document the successes and failures for different projects, initiatives, and companies operating in various sectors and disciplines.

Cases flourishing from emerging economies and addressing various developments represent an important part of the advancement of both the academic and professional disciplines. The need for local cases has become evidently critical since the desire of local knowledge pertaining Egyptian businesses have become increasingly necessary to better comprehend organizational performance, development, and growth. They reflect the implications of global market, economic, and development trends while catering for local conditions, cultural implications, and societal values and norms. For many decades, the literature addressing markets in developing and emerging economies had witnessed minimal coverage for complete field research-based cases. This book is the first of a book series to be published by IGI Global in collaboration with the School of Business of the American University in Cairo represented by its El-Khazindar Business Research and Case Center. The book series targets the production of an invaluable education element, case studies, which not only provides the basis for case-teaching methodologies, but also, more importantly, uses cases that are a reflection of local market conditions, challenges, and opportunities.

The book combines a variety of research-based cases in a number of diversified disciplines. One of the most notable aspects of the book is its broad coverage of challenges and opportunities involved from the local point of view. The book divides the cases into six business areas, including marketing, management of Information Systems, operations management, accounting, management, and finance. With at least two cases per area, readers are able to get a full glimpse of strategic, structural, and managerial issues that reflect the fabrics of the local society, the business practices, and the market developments. Providentially, this first volume of case studies is just the beginning of many more cases to come enriching the landscape of locally developed case studies. These research-cases are the basis of a new learning tool that would not just add value to the education field, but to the corporate world as well. Students, professors, and CEOs benefit from such real-life content in excelling their careers, improving their organizational performance, realizing their endeavors, and broadening their entrepreneurial mindset, innovative skills, and capacities.

Entrepreneurship and innovation are transforming individuals, organizations, and societies and I am confident that the content of this book will have an effective contribution to these influential trends on the society. I would like to seize the opportunity and thank all those who got involved in the development and production of this book as well as all the authors, reviewers, and editors whose expertise helped in delivering such important contribution.

It is my hope that this book will provide emerging economies and evolving organizations with good-practice principles for development, growth, policy, and regulatory and market frameworks in such evolving, dynamic, complex, and constantly changing marketplace. Eventually, sharing the lessons learnt and exchanging capacities and knowledge will allow newly growing and emerging economies and their start-up companies to leverage their entrepreneurial skills to create and sustain companies and to benefit from the opportunities constantly emerging in this global, interconnected, and dynamic market.

Sherif Kamel
School of Business, American University in Cairo, Egypt

Sherif H Kamel *is Dean of the School of Business at the American University in Cairo (AUC) since 2009 and Professor of Management Information Systems at the Department of Management. Kamel served as Associate Dean for executive education (2008-09). Prior to that, he was the director of the Management Center (2002- 08) and was the director of the Institute of Management Development (2002- 06). Before joining American University in Cairo, he was the director of the Regional IT Institute (1992-2001), and he co-established and managed the training department of the Cabinet of Egypt Information and Decision Support Centre-IDSC (1987- 92). He has accumulated experience in building and managing professional development institutions addressing management development and leadership aspects. He consults with government organizations and corporations addressing professional and executive development as well as IT transfer, management, and IT strategy deployment issues. Kamel is a co-founding member of the Internet Society of Egypt (1996). His research and teaching interests include management of Information Technology, Information Technology transfer to developing nations, electronic business, human resources development, and decision support systems, and he has published widely in the areas of IS and management. He taught for a number of universities in degree and non-degree programs in Egypt, the UK, the US, and the Netherlands. He was invited as a panelist in a variety of expert meetings including Asia-Middle East Dialogue, Microsoft Leaders Forum Arabia, AMIDEAST, ITU, UNECA, UNIDO, and the League of Arab States. Kamel serves on the editorial and advisory board of a number of IS journals and is the associate editor of the Journal of Cases on Information Technology, Journal of IT for Development, and the Electronic Journal of IS in Developing Countries. He is the editor of Electronic Business in Developing Countries: Challenges and Opportunities (2005) and Managing Globally with Information Technology (2003). Kamel served as VP for communications and member of the Executive Council of the Information Resources Management Association-IRMA (2002- 07). He is a member of the board of trustees of the Information Technology Institute since 2005 and was a member of the board of trustees of the Sadat Academy for Management Sciences (2006- 07). Kamel served as Chairman of the Chevening Association in Egypt (2004-09). He is an Eisenhower Fellow (2005) and a member of the Eisenhower Fellowships Alumni Advisory Council since 2008. Kamel has served as co-chair of the ICT committee at the American Chamber of Commerce since 2008. He served as judge in different IT competitions including the Stockholm Challenge (2008); Mtandao Africa (2004 and 2007); and the ThinkQuest challenge (1999 and 2001). Kamel won a number of organizational leadership awards for serving the IT community in 1999 (IRMA, USA), 2000 (BITWorld, Mexico), and 2009 (IBIMA, Egypt). He has served as treasurer and board member of the Friends of the Museum of Islamic Arts since 2004 and as a member of the Egyptian Council for Foreign Affairs since 2007. His general interests include history, sports, and music. He has been a member of the Rotary Organization since 2004. He holds a PhD from London School of Economics and Political Science (1994), an MBA (1990) and a BA in Business Administration (1987) from The American University in Cairo; currently he is pursuing an MA in Islamic Art and Architecture.*

Preface

It is with pleasure that I serve as Editor-in-Chief for the first volume of case studies written and published under the auspices of the El-Khazindar Business Research and Case Center at School of Business of the American University in Cairo. This volume fills a need that went unfulfilled for a stretch of decades going back to the 1960s. The need for endemic, relevant, and rigorous cases was recognized in Egypt as management development and executive education emerged in the 60s and flourished in the 70s, 80s, and beyond. The Institute for Management Development (IMD) then produced a number of field research cases written in Arabic. Albeit endemic to Egypt, these cases were written in a teaching note format. Eventually the cause was abandoned as the IMD evolved into Sadat Academy for Management.

The publication of this volume is significant in more than one respect. First, it fills the need for relevant, rigorous, research-based cases. Second, it signals the recognition of case research as a scholarly contribution. Such recognition is essential for sustaining the practice of case research and writing in Egypt. Mr. El-Khazindar's insightful contribution and American University in Cairo's initiative are laudable. This volume is just the beginning of a series. It features 17 cases covering a broad range of business functions, management processes, and related tools. Topics related to each are shown in Table 1. The cases involve B2C and B2B organizations that operate in the industrial, trade, and service sectors.

TEACHING WITH AND LEARNING FROM CASES

The cases present an opportunity to explore strategic, structural, and managerial issues that impact organizational performance. In order to reap the maximum learning benefits from teaching with cases, it is recommended that case data are sorted out in five categories:

Table 1. Case topic classification by business functions, management processes and tools

Functions	Marketing	Operations	Logistics	Finance
	Strategy Formulation & Implementation		Spinning the Supply Chain	Budgeting Value Based Management
Processes	Management			
	Innovative Approaches	Management of Change	Strategic Planning	
Tools	Accounting		Information System	Technology
	Accounting and Auditing Standards ABC Accounting		IICT Applications in Accounting Systems	E-Commerce Enterprise Resource Planning

1. **Performance:** data illustrative of the effectiveness and efficiency dimensions of organizational performance. This category reflects *symptoms* of problems endemic to the strategy, structure, and managerial practices of the subject organization. Inexperienced analysts often mistakenly diagnose these symptoms as problems.
2. **Environment:** data pertinent to situation analysis including industry and company analysis. This category reflects the *states of nature (SONs)*, i.e., the immediate, intermediate, and the macro environment in which the organization operates. Inexperienced analysts often mistakenly point to these SONs as problems or sources of problems.
3. **Strategy:** plans formulated and mechanisms designed to *relate and adapt the organization to its environment*. SWOT analysis is the most often used tool to match the strength of the organization to opportunities and ameliorate the threats facing the organization as it operates in the said environment. Effective strategies are designed to mitigate the weakness(es) of the organization in a manner conducive to minimizing their negative impact on organizational performance. Problems may emanate from errors of omission or commission in the design of the strategic plan. For example, while failure to differentiate the offer of a firm is an error of omission, selecting a Point of Parity instead of a Point of Difference constitutes an error of commission.
4. **Structure:** refers to the *internal and external organizational structures* through which the strategy is *implemented*. For example, delivering the value to the customers may require hiring and training a sales force, retaining wholesale and/or retail distributors, or both. Oftentimes, top management may concoct or redesign strategic plans without altering or redesigning the attendant structures in charge of their implementation. The untold power of organizational structures is that the *resources and capabilities* that reside in these structures are the engines that power the implementation of these plans. In essence, retaining the same organization structures to implement new or significantly modified strategic plan will render their implantation impossible, ineffective, or inefficient.
5. **Management:** refers to the *tactical decisions* that must be taken to implement the strategic plans. Problems may emanate mostly from errors of commission in tactical decision making. For example, in marketing decision making, faulty product design, mismatching message with media in advertising, selecting too high or too low pricing, and/or mismatching marketing channels with target markets all are errors of commission.

Attendant to each data category is an Axiom that may be helpful in guiding the analyst of business cases.

- **Axiom1:** Poor financial and marketing performance results are symptoms indicative of problem(s) emanating from the strategy, structure, and/or management practices.
- **Axiom 2:** Volatile States of Nature (SONs) are neither problems nor source of problems. These are mere conditions that dominate the environment in which the organization operates. Management failure to adjust the strategy, structure, and/or management practices to address volatility is the problem.
- **Axiom 3:** Errors of omission and commission in strategy development are the root causes of problems.
- **Axiom 4:** Structure must fit the strategy, not vice versa. Failure to redesign or configure organizational structures in response to new or redesigned strategies is the leading cause of failure in or poor implementation of the strategy.

Figure 1. A framework for case analysis

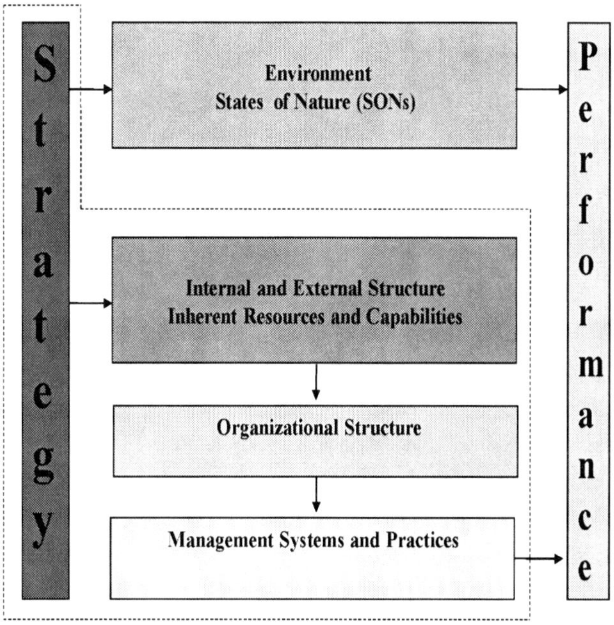

- **Axiom 5:** Tactical managerial decision making to implement the strategy is the "last mile," leading to organizational performance. Therefore, the best strategies and structures may sour as a result of poor implementation.
- **Axiom 6:** In problem solving, strategic design is the independent variable, performance is the dependent variable, and organization structure and managerial practices mediate the relationship between strategy formulation and performance results. These variables and their relationships are shown in Figure 1.

Adel El Ansary
University of North Florida , USA

Acknowledgment

El-Khazindar Business Research & Case Center (KCC) aims to build capacity in the development of quality case studies on businesses in the Middle East and North Africa region, and promote participant-centered learning technique in the region in a way that bridges the gap between theory and practice.

First of all, KCC would like to thank Dr. Mehdi Khosrow-Pour, President and CEO of IGI Global as well as all the IGI staff for their guidance, patience, professionalism, and dedication to produce a high quality casebook. Dr. Khosrow-Pour gave KCC the chance to develop this case book for the first time in Egypt. He also conducted a valuable presentation at American University in Cairo last March "*Preparing Acceptable Teaching Case Studies: Opportunities and Challenges*" to guide American University in Cairo faculty on writing publishable cases.

It is a great pleasure for us to send our heartfelt thanks to Dr. Adel El-Ansary, Donna L. Harper Professor of Marketing at the Coggin College of Business, University of North Florida, for his great effort and valuable time as the Editor- in-Chief of this case book. His expertise, guidance, and eye to detail and perfection have been invaluable to this project.

In addition, we would like to take this opportunity to thank all reviewers, English editors, and KCC team who contributed tremendously towards the successful completion of the manuscript. Reviewers and editors exerted great efforts to send us thorough feedbacks to produce high quality case studies.

Finally, we would like to thank Dr. Sherif Kamel, Dean of the School of Business at the American University in Cairo (AUC) for his continuous support and encouragement. He supported us since the first stages of developing this case book as he introduced KCC to IGI Global.

Ahmed Tolba, Director
El-Khazindar Business Research & Case Center (KCC)
School of Business, American University in Cairo (AUC), Egypt

Section 1
Accounting

In today's computerized, interconnected, global business environment, the accounting profession has to deal with a host of complex issues; for instance, how to capture and record new business transactions and events, develop value-added business and information processes, create new value-chain opportunities, disseminate useful knowledge to a wide array of information consumers, and provide assurance services across the entire spectrum of economic activities. The cases in this section deal with technology, systems, change, and change management. The first case, "The Egyptian International Motor Company," deals with the use of automated accounting Information Systems in the context of global business operations. The case explores the company's strategic decisions regarding the implementation of computerized accounting Information System, problems met during the implementation process, and the actions taken to remedy these problems to gain the potential system redesign benefits. The second case, "The Maridive Company for Oil and Marine Services," presents the problems related to the application of the International Accounting Standards no 32 and 38 "Financial assets and Derivatives" and their Egyptian equivalent, the Egyptian Standards on auditing no 700 and 702. The third case, "Electronic Commerce and Management Accountants in Egypt," explores the process of change in the role of management accountants associated with the implementation of B-to-B e-commerce. The fourth case, "The Application of ABC in an Industrial Company," illustrates the application of ABC method in a single manufacturing organization operating in the metal industry and compares the results of ABC with the traditional, volume based costing method.

Chapter 1
Blending Information and Communication Technology (ICT) with an Accounting System:
The Case of the Egyptian International Motors Company (EIM)

Khaled Dahawy
American University in Cairo (AUC), Egypt

Khaled Samaha
American University in Cairo (AUC), Egypt

EXECUTIVE SUMMARY

Rapid technological changes in the business world place immense pressure on business executives to stay ahead of the competition by dramatically and continually integrating Information and Communication Technology (ICT) in redesigning business processes and models, nevertheless accounting processes and models. In today's computerized, interconnected, global business environment, the accounting profession has to deal with a host of complex issues that never existed in the past—for instance, how to capture and record new business transactions and events, develop value-added business and information processes, create new value-chain opportunities, disseminate useful knowledge to a wide array of information consumers, and provide assurance services across the entire spectrum of economic activities. The use of automated accounting information system has become an integral part of accounting systems worldwide. An Accounting Information System (AIS) usually consists of integrated sets of components established to collect, store, and manage financial data, and provide useful information supporting managers in decision making. The AIS main goals would be the collation and processing of business activities data

DOI: 10.4018/978-1-60960-583-4.ch001

efficiently and effectively; processing data into accurate, timely, and useful information, nevertheless establishing adequate controls to ensure that data recorded and processed accurately. The presence of well designed automated AIS would lead to progressed efficiency through providing timely information; higher organization profit by progressing the efficiency and effectiveness of its supply chain; improved decision making by providing accurate information in a timely manner, in addition to easier sharing of knowledge and expertise. However, decisions relating to the choice and implementation of computerized accounting systems are very sensitive to cultural, economic, and environmental factors including IT skills, IT budgeting, and end users' resistance. Such factors differ dramatically between developed and developing nations. In addition, within the context of developing nations, the cultural, political, and economic realities of each country are often very different; therefore, automated accounting information systems decisions should be studied within the context of their own environments.

Improving our understanding of the accounting information system development in a specific Egyptian context, this case aims to investigate the development of a redesigned automated accounting system in a privately owned Egyptian company that was planning material changes in its accounting systems and organizational structure through integrating ICT systems. In other words, this case attempts to explore the company's strategic decisions regarding computerized accounting information system implementation choices, problems met during the implementation process, and the actions taken to takeover these problems to gain the potential accounting system redesign benefits. Tracking the automated accounting system redesign highlights some implementation success key factors and emphasizes that obtaining top management commitment to the process of an automated accounting system implementation is a prerequisite for success.

1- ORGANIZATION BACKGROUND

Egyptian International Motors Company (EIM) was established in 1979 as a main business unit within Alkan group. Its remarkable growth over the years has positioned it as a market leader in various business fields. The company activities include multinational enterprise representation, lease finance services and free zone storage and clearance. The company is categorized as a commercial company that is involved in various areas/ disciplines through the acquisition of licenses. This makes the company a unique company in the sense that each acquired license is treated as a separate line of business.

The company's description of line of businesses in its articles of incorporation states that it is a retail company that operates in: manufacturing, importation, export, distribution and acts as an agent of passenger cars, heavy equipment and agriculture equipment; importation of textile machinery and equipment for flour mills and crushing plants. Today the company is one of Egypt's most mature private sectors operations, exclusively distributing and servicing more than 25 world renowned brands in more than 7 business sectors, both in Egypt and in the Region (see Figure 1).

Each of the brands represented by EIM is a leader in its segment. These brands are served by a distribution network including EIM branches as well as extensive dealer networks and after-market services delivered through highly qualified and well trained technical staff in EIM workshops across the country or on-site wherever the customer is. EIM strives to make a distinct and profound positive difference in the trade industry in Egypt and the region by supplying the highest quality service, products and solutions to its customers.

Figure 1. EIM renowned brands

EIM has represented diverse multinational names over the years. EIM has created a very special position for itself in the market, serving a large number of clients of various sizes, ranging from major local and international contractors to individuals. What makes EIM unique are its strategic capabilities that allows it to pursue market opportunities in the best, most speedy manner. The company's deep local roots give it greater insight into what clients want and where opportunities for growth reside. The diversified range of businesses permits exposure to several fields of expertise, creating a knowledge base in the respective market sectors.

EIM Company has nationwide presence, ensuring full local market coverage that allows for unmatched distribution. The company's broad reach of experienced and qualified employees offers an ongoing renewal of ideas, strategies and new business acquisitions. Local presence and regional reach is made more powerful by the company's third competitive advantage; managing a portfolio of some of the most powerful brands worldwide.

EIM has a high dynamic operational structure (see Figure 2). Seven semi-independent business divisions organized mainly around the business sectors they serve, manage the company's different brands. EIM is able to offer its customers the superior levels of support they deserve as a result of a strong managerial and operational structure, powered by nearly 1500 employees.

The Information Systems (IS) department consists of 5 employees including the IS manager. During implementation of an IS project the IS manager usually undertakes any checks to ensure the organizational goals are being met, this includes regular assessment after project completion to ensure the IS is being used to maximum effectiveness. The IS manager still believes that there is room for improvement with regard to the knowledge of IT of employees within the organization, and believe this can be improved with regular up-to-date training, giving an opportunity for employees to gain the relevant knowledge.

EIM evidently has a good knowledge of Information and Communication Technology (ICT) and top management involvement is viewed as an important part of the process. The decision making usually lies with the IS manager, however major decision about the system must be discussed and verified with the board of directors. This shows

Figure 2. EIM operational structure

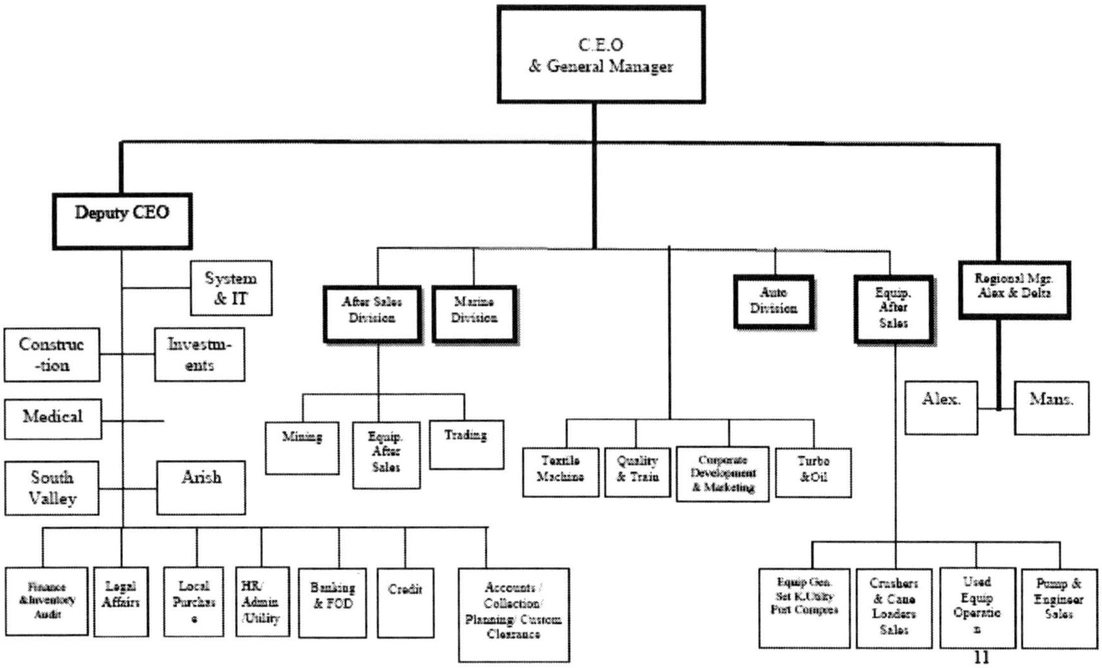

that top management involvement is seen as a major part of the IS strategy. It is important as they are aware of the significance of aligning all departments and the impact ICT has on the organization.

2- SETTING THE STAGE

The first experience that the company had with accounting computer software came in the mid 1990s when the company bought its first software that works on Vax/Vma and was installed on a mainframe and connected to a small number of terminals where the users only had a screen and a keyboard. The software was written in a language called Vax/Basic which is one of the oldest programming languages. The interface at the user terminals was text mode that was based on a question/answer interface with the user. The database depended on flat files without any relation so the integration exists in programs and not in the database. The main advantage of this software, that it was open source software, which meant that the program codes were available and could be tailored to accept the increases in the capacities of this program. However, this application was designed to work on one division, so it was very difficult to make suitable integration after the company's expansion. The database was very limited, where there was very limited configuration of the fields in the files. It was close to impossible to adjust the system to meet the needs of handling each license that the company used as a separate subsidiary within EIM. The IS department manager felt the dramatic need to change the accounting system to a more developed system to be installed as an isolated system in each division with some programs created to work as a middleware between the head office server and the subsidiaries offline database. As a result, the IS department sent a memo to the company's CEO that summarized the reasons for the needed change.

Having a meeting with the EIM CEO the IS department manger has more clearly explained the company's accounting system technical difficulties faced and how The applied software is ineffective to satisfy the increased management analytical requirements, reports, and analysis. The IS manager stated that

"……the current accounting system coding was very limited…The code of the branches was only 0-9 which meant that when the company had more than 10 branches they were unable to code them. In addition, the code of the customers only included 3 digits which meant that the company could not code more than 1,000 customers……."

Moreover the IS department manager expressed the inapplicability of the system adjustment to meet the increased company's managers information needs. The IS department manger said that " ………*The needed tools for this software were fading very quickly. Therefore, it was becoming prohibitively expensive to maintain the system. Moreover, The development of the IS education market made it very hard to find employees who know how to work on the aging software……….."*

The CEO commented "…….. *This would mean that our accounting system was not suitable to keep the company's competitive edge in the market and due to the expansion of the company there was an urgent need to have new software that provided more flexible, accurate and up to date information…*".

Consequently, the CEO agreed with the IS manager accounting system assessment. After getting the Board of Directors (BOD) approval to proceed developing a more advanced accounting system, the CEO contacted the IS department manger asking for a detailed analysis about the viable new accounting system implementation options that EIM had to proceed.

3- CASE DESCRIPTION

Outsourcing vs. In-House Development

To remain competitive and ever increasingly sophisticated in the marketplace, businesses must invest in automated accounting information system if they are to survive in the long-term, whether this is through outsourcing or internal solutions. However, Managers should not make a one-time decision whether to outsource or not.

Companies are increasingly outsourcing the development and management of information systems for reasons that include access to specialized skills, cost, staff utilization, reduced recruitment and training, high standards of control and security, and proliferation of information services (Udo, 2000). However, many reasons remain for developing information systems applications internally. These reasons include the need to accommodate customized products or services, confidentiality of business data, the desire to reduce vendor risk, ease of development, ease of internal adaptation of software, and the desire to develop leading-edge competence (Downing et al., 2003). Deciding between outsourcing and internal software development is problematic, principally as a result of the difficulties inherent in measuring the benefits and costs associated with such investments (Ballantine et al., 1998).

Searching the market, The IS department manager informed that the company can either: (1) Buy readymade software and he recommended Oracle Financials, which he believed was the strongest and most advanced software at that time, or (2) Use Oracle tools to tailor software suitable for the EIM company specific needs. Oracle Financials includes the (1) General Ledger, (2) Payables, (3) Assets, (4) Purchasing, (5) Receivables, (6) Cash Management, and (7) Inventory modules. In a meeting with the CFO and the accounting manager, the IS department manager pointed out that there will be a need to adjust some of these modules to meet the company's specific information needs. Further discussions indicated that in addition to the software package modules, the company needs to establish some other modules including: (1) Payroll, (2) human resources, (3) call center, and (4) workshop.

Presenting these two options to the EIM CEO the IS manager explained some of the benefits and costs associated with each choice stating that "........*getting a ready made software package would be cost expensive and required a detailed training programs to the IS personnel and the end users hereafter, however it save a lot of time consumed tailoring the software to the company's specific needs. However, for our company's competitive advantage and future expansion plans, it would be important to set software specifications very suitable for the company's emerging reporting and analysis needs, but this would require our IS personnel to gain an extensive knowledge and expertise in IS planning and designing which is not available at a point of time.........it was really a very critical to decide between the two choices*"

The CEO getting confused with the IS manager accounting system implementation choices discussions, had decided to have a meeting the company's CFO to understand how it would be feasible to use the ready made Oracle Financials software in regards to the emerging companies expansion and information needs. The CFO stated that "...... *Oracle Financials would seem suitable for the prevailing EIM position in the market. Oracle Financials included the General Ledger, Payables, Assets, Purchasing, Receivables, Cash Management, Inventory modules. However, there would be a need to adjust some of these modules to meet the company's specific information needs. Further, according to the company' branches and employees expansion, it would be a need to establish some other modules including Payroll, Human resources, Call center, and Workshop......etc*"

After having extensive meetings between the EIM CEO, CFO, and IS department manager they decided to combine the two choices getting the best of both. They decided on the new automated accounting system establishment to be as follows:

- Buying Oracle Financials package,
- Hiring Oracle Egypt company to administer the required gap analysis adjustments,
- Estimating the costs of the needed adjustments,
- Supporting the IS department personnel with the required training for the implementation, and finally
- Buying the license of Oracle tools and allow the company's IS department to build the needed modules that are missing from Oracle Financials.

At first, this plan seemed satisfactory and the company started implementing it. The company paid the first contractual installment of 10% of the Oracle Financials cost. The CEO then hired the Oracle engineers to apply gap analysis and assess the required adjustments. During this time the members of the IS department started taking extensive courses on how to implement, operate, and maintain the Oracle Financials software. Parallel to this the members of the IS department were also taking courses to develop their abilities in using Oracle tools to produce the missing modules that are needed.

However some irritating news occurred. Using Oracle in the financial analysis charged the company high hourly rates. In addition, the findings of the gap analysis indicated that the required adjustments would be very expensive. Further, the cost of training was very expensive. But the IS department personnel had proven their abilities and have produced the Human resources module and the Payroll module. These two designated modules implementation results were outstanding.

Facing these problems the CEO and IS department manager have decided to change their plan to building whole tailor made software using Oracle tools. By this time, The IS department personnel were ready to produce a tailor made program that has all the advantages of Oracle financials ready made software and at the same time specifically designed for the companies needs. This decision seemed feasible as the IS personnel have been trained very well in using the Oracle tools, further while being trained to use Oracle financials the IS personnel got highly accustomed to the design and interface of the ready-made program.

The New Tailor Made System Implementation: Obstacles and Benefits

To start establishing the new tailor made system the IS department manager was assigned by the CEO to lead a team of IS personnel in conjunction with an employees group from the various departments that would be affected. The new system implementation plan involved

1. Increasing the number of IT department personnel from 5 to 11,
2. Developing a comprehensive detailed study (by the Senior IT personnel) that includes the specific needs of the current situation in every department, putting solutions to the problems, and discussing these needs with the programmers,
3. Comparing the current status, the problems and the Oracle Financials design for the section that is studied. At that time the programmers had formulated the backbone of a system that is almost identical with the Oracle Financials and were ready to adapt it to the needed adjustments to solve the needs discovered from the analysis,
4. Establishing an organizational structure in a new manner that can accommodate the addition of any new company, license, department, and/or division, and finally
5. Scheduling the implementation of each system part in conjunction with the end users.

The CEO biggest concern was the employee resistance. Employees were afraid that the development of the software, would lead to more automation and less need for humans. This problem was intensified by the fact that many users had no experience with the basic knowledge of using Windows. Further, the new developed software impacted the power of balance in the company. Many of the more tenured employees who had long experience with company had little computer background, while many of the younger inexperienced employees had more computer knowledge and were able to understand the changes in the system more readily.

The CEO was keen that IS department made sure to involve the key new tailor made system users in their goals and vision. In one case the IS department prepared an International Computer Driving License (ICDL) training to the users by dividing them into groups. The aim was to raise the level of appreciation of the technology to a level that made the employees appreciate the new automated system as a benefit and not a threat. Moreover, the CEO was very careful in dealing with the employees and automated system issues as they had to assign a special secretary to the old employees to make sure that he/she can act as a facilitator between the manager and the automated system.

Along the implementation period any employee was offered detailed hands on session on how to use his/her division automated system part. He/she was allowed to freely state his/her remarks and/or comments on the software and the IS personnel were responsible to make the required adjustments if applicable. The implementation stage ended with the presence of the end user (employee) who would be actually using his/her division automated system part.

Another obstacle faced by the CEO was the need to change the whole environment, especially hardware. This turned out to be expensive and sometimes led to unpleasant confrontations. With the exception of some incidents the IS department was able to overcome this obstacle by preparing detailed budgets that included as much information as possible. In addition, the IS department manager tried as much as possible to meet with the BOD members every time to explain to them any changes in the budget and the reasons for the change.

Further, there was difficulty in the integration between the new accounting system development and implementation periods. The implementation could not be done at one time for all the diverse sections. Also, the implementation team could not shut the company during the implementation period. Instead, they implemented the software in what they called a "step by step way". For example the IS department started by the car maintenance department. When they migrated the maintenance department system to the new system, it was hard for the updated department data to be visible to the old system. However, the transactions performed in the maintenance department (for example a client brings his car for repair) would impact several other departments like client account, inventory, and treasury (cash). To overcome this problem the IS department had to create a middle-ware application to be able to keep the effect of the existing links between the new application and the old one. Second, the IS department recognized the need to deliver one report which includes the data from the old and the new software together. To overcome this problem the IS department created a data warehouse server and migrated daily batches from the two platforms and explored it by the Oracle discoverer tool.

Dealing with such obstacles, the new system implementation was successful taking place in full four months. The system was running within one year of the inception plan. The IS department employees spent many sleepless nights in the company making sure that the new automated accounting system was functional in the shortest period possible. They also had to work on daily problems. However, at the end the new automated accounting system was a great success with many benefits for management and users.

The most important benefit resulted from implementing the system is the ability to view the company information at different levels of integration on a timely basis. The new accounting system allows the information to be reported and updated instantaneously on line, with not lag time. The decision maker can receive his/her information on time when he/she needs it. Further, management was allowed full access to detailed information at different levels of aggregation, depending on the level that the decision maker needs. For example the decision maker can see financial information from a comprehensive picture, for the whole company as a whole. In the same time he/she can see the financial information by brand, site, geographical location, and/or any factor/characteristic that he/she deems necessary. The IS department is currently working on updating this feature by using the data warehouse to create Key Performance Indicators (KPIs). This will allow the decision maker to perform sensitivity analysis (What If analysis) that help him/her forecast the result of certain decision before proceeding. This will allow the decision maker to view the historical information, change any part of it, and view the impact of the change on the results in graphical, user friendly, and simple way

The new system established the ability to handle huge volumes of transactions without compromising speed or efficiency. This ability made employees more comfortable with the system as they started to view it as a friend and not an enemy. In informal surveys that the IS department applied one year after the system implementation, is found that the employees actually "highly like" the new system and that they find it "strongly" help them in their work. Furthermore, many employees found the training they received made them feel more valuable.

4- RESULTS OF THE SUCCESS: BROADER ICT INTEGRATION

The success of the system implementation generated so much interest and genuine momentum towards applying ICT in different fields in the company. The snowball effect of the success of automation of AIS at EIM resulted in five, until today, major projects that utilized ICT to upgrade and develop the company's abilities.

First, the company implemented a Customer Relation Management system (CRM). This system has helped the company in preparing important reports relating to its customers. These reports have allowed the company to better serve the customers and produce valuable information about how to target these customers. The IT department is currently working on transferring the CRM system into an e-CRM system to facilitate dealing with customer data through the internet.

Second, the company implemented a "Mobile-Commerce System", which is a system that is based on mobile service installed on handheld machines. This was applied in the service centers of the company. The receiving engineer can receive the equipment/car at the reception area by reading a bar code that is set on it which contains all the needed information about the equipment/car. This system has helped the company operations by reducing the wait time, and assuring the entry of correct equipment/car information when received. This system also allows the engineer to see if there was prior reservation or not and to access the history of the equipment/car, to see if there are any special notes that would help him/her. Furthermore, this system allows the information desk instantaneous information about the status of the equipment/car in repair and estimated time of end of task. As an end result this system also increased customers' satisfaction and trust.

Third, the company implemented a Voice Over Internet Protocol system (VOIP), which connects the many branches, sites, buildings, and offices that the company has. This development facilitates the ability to communicate between the different parts/employees of the company with zero cost. The speed of the connection also increases the speed of business between the different departments and branches of the company, while allowing faster transfer of data.

Fourth, the company initiated an SMS server that has the ability to send thousands of messages to the customers. This server is linked to the CRM system which allows the SMS to be sent to targeted customers depending on the included information in the SMS. This system allows the company to connect more efficiently with the customers, sending customized information and offers that meet the individual customer interests and needs.

And finally, the company linked the SMS service system with the after sales division. This link allows the creation of a report from the after sales division data that determines the needed maintenance appointment for each individual customer. This report automatically generates an individualized SMS that is sent to the customer to remind him/her of his next maintenance appointment and any needed information that he/she needs to know; like cost of the service.

REFERENCES

Ballantine, J., Levy, M., & Powell, P. (1998). Evaluating information systems in small and medium-sized enterprises: Issues and evidence. *European Journal of Information Systems*, *7*(4), 241–251. doi:10.1057/palgrave.ejis.3000307

Downing, C. E., Field, J. M., & Ritzman, L. P. (2003). The value of outsourcing: a field study. *Information Systems Management*, *20*, 86–91. doi:10.1201/1078/43203.20.1.20031201/40088.11

Udo, G. G. (2000). Using analytic hierarchy process to analyze the information technology outsourcing decision. *Industrial Management & Data Systems*, *100*(9), 421–429. doi:10.1108/02635570010358348

Chapter 2
Accounting and Auditing of Financial Derivatives:
The Case of Maridive & Oil Services (MOS)

Mohamed Hegazy
American University in Cairo (AUC), Egypt

Karim Hegazy
Crowe Dr A. M. Hegazy & Co, Egypt

EXECUTIVE SUMMARY

This case study discusses accounting and auditing implications resulting from the dispute among auditors and the management of Maridive & Oil Services Company (MOS) in the preparation of the company's financial statements at December 31, 2008. The dispute occurred for the accounting treatment of losses of $ 18 million dollars expected to be realized on the swap agreement made between MOS and a number of international banks during the period 2009-2018. MOS is a publicly traded company at both Cairo and Alexandria Stock exchanges, with total assets of more than $390 million dollars. The company entered into swap agreement with two international banks to minimize the risk associated with credit facilities received by the company to expand its marine services through the construction of a number of marine vessels. The dispute among the three international audit firms resulted in the issuance of two different sets of audit reports.

The Egyptian Capital Market Authority (CMA) examined the company's financial statements for the year ended on December 31, 2008, while the auditors' reports forced the company's management, despite the objection of two of the company's auditors, to restate its financial statements at December 31, 2008, and modify its profit appropriation statement after their publication to shareholders and the public. The research presents the problems related to the application of the International Accounting Standards no 32 and 38 "Financial assets and Derivatives," their Egyptian equivalents, and the Egyptian Standards on auditing no 700 and 702. Further, the research identifies the differences associated with auditors issuing contradictory audit reports for a company's single set of financial statements.

DOI: 10.4018/978-1-60960-583-4.ch002

INTRODUCTION

The following case is divided into three main sections. The first section provides a detailed background about Maridive & Oil Services Company, showing the development of the company from a medium size marine services company into an international company providing a variety of marine and oil support activities, including maintenance, installations, rescue aid, erections, towage whether above, outside, and/or under water, as well as land establishments. The same section also highlights the management structure and competitive strengths used to achieve the growth seen by MOS since 1978 and the company's future strategy that is required to maintain its competitive edge in the market for marine and oil services. The second section summarizes the financial information of the company for the period 2006-2008 showing its financial position, results of operations and elements of corporate governance applied to enhance MOS's management performance. While, the third section presents the nature of financial derivatives, mainly the characteristics of the swap agreements made between MOS and the two international banks and the dispute occurring between the Egyptian Capital Market Authority (CMA), management of MOS and its auditors. MOS management charged the effects of ineffective swap analysis into the company's special reserve for 18.6 million based on the Companies Act 159 for 1981 and the company's articles of incorporations. Also, the company capitalized 1.6 million representing the cost of obtaining a loan, without taking in consideration the requirements of the Egyptian Accounting Standards. Details about the accounting and auditing treatments of the swap losses and capitalization of the costs of obtaining the loan are presented. The question of whether the requirements of laws have a priority over the application of both the accounting and auditing standards is discussed showing the need for future research to investigate such issue in other accounting and auditing cases.

AN OVERVIEW OF THE DEVELOPMENT OF MARIDIVE AND OIL SERVICES

Maridive History and Main Activities

Maridive & Oil Services (MOS) was founded in 1978 as a free zone joint stock company, and now has its official headquarter in Port Said, Egypt, with offices in Cairo and Alexandria in Egypt and Abu Dhabi in the United Arab Emirates (UAE). With a history spreading over 31 years, the company is one of the leading and oldest companies in the Middle East and North Africa (MENA) region to provide offshore marine and oil support activities, including services, maintenance, installations, rescue aid, erections and towage whether above, outside and/ or under water. It also provides all activities related to the industrial services for maritime and land establishments such as cleaning, maintenance, erections, installations, transportation supply, as well as providing all necessary equipment and relevant spare parts. With the company being a highly integrated marine and offshore oil services company, it provides services to oil and gas exploration and production ("E&P") clients throughout the value chain:

- Oil and gas related Offshore Construction Services (OCS), such as pipe laying, platform installation as well as engineering, procurement and construction (EPC) for underwater projects. The OCS operates through the company's subsidiaries MOP and Valentine Maritime Ltd. (Valentine).
- Chartering Offshore Support Vessels (OSV) needed to tow offshore rigs, supply both rigs and production platforms with all material required and ensure their safety through fire-fighting and anti-pollution. The OSV segment is operated by MOS and the subsidiary Maritide Offshore Oil Services (Maritide).

- In addition, the company provides Diving Support Vessels (DSVs), as well as divers for sub-sea maintenance and repair operations.

Management expanded the business globally by winning contracts in the Persian Gulf area, Caspian Sea and Mexico, as well as Northern and Western African countries and Southeast Asia. The company's global business model is reflected in its revenue base, where more than 80% of 2008 revenues are being generated from outside Egypt. The company possesses a high reputation among numerous oil companies around the world. In 2008, the company owned and operated 43 vessels and 11 barges, making it the largest marine offshore oil and gas service provider based in Egypt and the Middle East and one of the largest in the world in this field in terms of fleet size. The company embarked on an aggressive expansion plan in 2004, contracting for 22 new vessels and two barges that are expected to be delivered by 2011. For the fiscal year that ended December 31, 2008, the operating revenue, gross profit and net profit were $257.7 million, $118.9 million, and $82.2 million, respectively.

Figure 1 illustrates the current legal structure of MOS as follows:

The names and registered offices of the subsidiary companies that form the MOS Group are listed in Table 1.

The key milestone in the development of the MOS Group can be summarized as follows:

- In 1978, MOS was established and started its first year of operations with three vessels and four mooring boats, and was awarded its first marine contract with the Western Desert Operating Petroleum Company.
- In 1980, Barclays Bank acquired a 10% stake in MOS and its management contacted G. Hitsler to build seven AHTS vessels. In 1987, Maridive entered into a joint venture agreement with Tidewater Marine Inc., the biggest U.S. oil and gas services company, and established Maritide Marine.
- In 1990, Valentine was incorporated to provide full services of EPC and management, and acquired its first pipe laying con-

Table 1.

Equity	Incorporated in	Ownership % at December 31, 2008
Valentine Maritime LTD	Liberia	75.00%
Valentine Maritime (Gulf) LLC	UAE	49.00%
Valentine Maritime (Mauritius) Ltd	Mauritius	100.00%
Ocean Marine FZC	UAE	100.00%
Maritide Offshore Oil Services S.A.E	Egypt	99.46%
Maridive Offshore Projects S.A.E	Egypt	100.00%

Figure 1. The legal structure of MOS

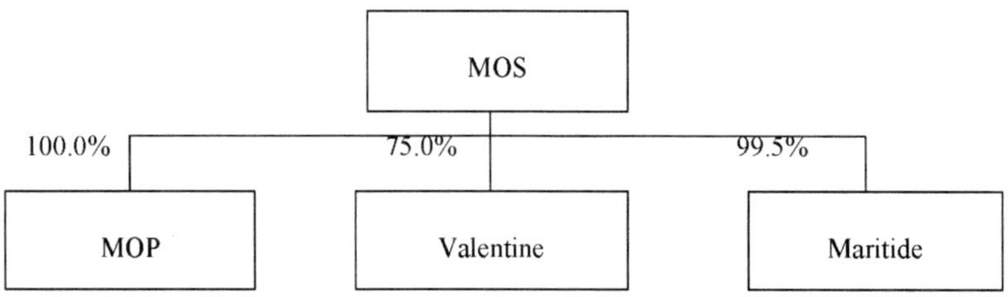

struction barge, "REGINA", with a crane capacity of 300 tons. In 1991, MOS established its first office in the region (Abu Dhabi) and started expanding regionally by commencing operations in the Gulf of Arabia as part of the Kuwaiti reconstruction efforts.

- In 1993, Maridive Offshore Projects (MOP) was established and wholly owned by the three founding families of MOS to offer a comprehensive and integrated range of marine construction, support and diving services. In 1996, MOS was awarded the first contract in West Africa, marking its first step in expanding operations beyond the region and ordered the first two advanced 6.000 brake horsepower ("BHP") vessels with Dynamic Positioning ("DP") systems. In 1998, Commercial International Bank S.A.E, one of the largest banks in Egypt, acquired a 10% stake in MOS.
- In 2004, Maridive Group initiated its first phase of the major expansion (22 vessels and two barges) and upgraded its strategy, ordering in that year six new vessels, one construction barge and upgrading five existing vessels with DP and fire fighting capabilities. In 2005, Valentine successfully signed its biggest EPC contract worth a total of $125 million in the Persian Gulf. In 2006, MOS received its first AHTS vessel from the new expansion project and was awarded its biggest series of OSV contracts from Aramco.
- In 2007, MOS received one AHTS vessels from the new expansion project. Barclays Bank divested its 10% stake in MOS and EFG-Hermes, through its asset management and private equity arms, acquiring a 13.4% stake in MOS. In January 2008, all shareholders of MOS approved the share swap between MOP and MOS, under which MOS would acquire all the outstanding shares of MOP. On April 13, 2008 the share swap was completed and consequently the restructuring plan was completed as MOP was swapped into MOS, in preparation for the Initial Public Offering (IPO), and received three new AHTS vessels as part of the expansion strategy which begun in 2004.

Management and the Company Competitive Strengths

The management of the company describes Maridive business as being characterized by a number of competitive strengths. First, by leveraging on the company's strong brand name in the market and experienced management, which successfully implemented an ambitious organic growth plan over the past 31 years, continuously expanding and upgrading the company's fleet to cater to clients' needs and markets dynamics. The fleet's size grew from 33 marine units in 2000 to 51 at the end of 2008, and is expected to reach 73 units by the end of 2011. Currently, the fleet size positions MOS as the largest player in Egypt and with the expected advanced new generation fleet, the company will be positioned as the largest marine and offshore oil services company in the MENA region. Management sees that the significant investments required in owning a fleet represents a significant barrier entry for competitors.

Second, the company operates in an attractive industry that benefit from high demand for oil, consequently driving up oil E&P activities, the main driver for the offshore oil industry. Oil and gas E&P spending grew by a compound annual growth rate (" CAGR") of 19% over the past five years, driven by increased exploration to satisfy current levels of demand, as well as the depletion of onshore oil supplies, forcing E&P companies to search for oil in offshore areas, and expecting that this trend will continue in the future. Management emphasizes that the location in the MENA region positions the company to benefit from this potential, as the region contains 70% of the world's oil reserves and 46% of the world's natural gas reserves.

Third, the management team of MOS has a strong track record with respect to the achievement and effective management of growth. In the past three years before 2008, management team of MOS has achieved a compound annual growth rate of revenues of 37.7%. Management team has also succeeded in diversifying and expanding the range of products and services offered to clients to include salvage operations and ship and port management. The Group management had the vision to expand internationally in several markets, such as Kuwait, UAE, India, Qatar, Southeast Asia, West Africa and the Gulf of Mexico, allowing the group to significantly diversify its clientele base and enhance profitability.

Fourth, MOS has a strong brand name and extensive client base. It benefits from good long-term relationships with its key clients, including shell, Petronas, British Petroleum (BP), British Gas, Adnoc, Bunduq, Kuwait Oil Company, Aramco, Pemex, Qatargas, Total, Egyptian Natural Gas Co., Suptec, Maersk Oil, Bechtel, and Petrobel. MOS presence in the sector for 31 years has placed it in a strong position to bid for and secure international tenders for marine offshore services. Management has been involved in projects in West Africa, Tunisia, Italy, India, Mexico and the Caspian Sea, and is in the process of submitting bids in other regions including Venezuela, Congo and Southeast Asia. The international operations of MOS generated an average of more than 80% of the combined revenues for the years 2006, 2007 and 2008 respectively.

Fifth, the management of MOS realizes that the group is one of the lowest costs marine offshore oil services providers worldwide due to several factors, including economies of scale, which give an advantage when negotiating with supplier and shipyards. Management also works to reduce the average age of MOS fleet through the current expansion program, thus reducing MOS average maintenance costs, as well as the average time when the fleet is out of services for maintenance and dry-docking.

Finally, MOS revenue, gross profit and net profit after tax grew from $139.3 million, $32.5 million and $ 19.2 million, respectively in 2005, to $ 257.7 million, $ 118.9 million and $ 82.2 million, respectively in 2008, with a compound annual growth of 84.9%, 265.84% and 328.1% from 2005 to 2008.

The Structure of MOS Management and their Remuneration

The board of directors of MOS is formed of five to fourteen members appointed for three years term, which may be renewed by a resolution adopted at the general shareholder's meeting. The current board of directors is formed of fourteen directors, the majority of which are non-executive members. The board of directors meets as needed (but in any case at least four times per financial year) at the request of the chairman or of one-third of the board of directors. Meetings of the board of directors may be held at company's headquarters or at any location within Egypt. The chairman of the board of directors will have a casting vote in case of a tie.

Pursuant to Maridive & Oil 's bylaws, the board of directors is entitled to 10% of the company's profits after: (i) first deducting 5% of the profits as a legal reserve (deduction to cease once legal reserve is equivalent to 50% of capital); (ii) deducting 10% of profits as the employees' share in the profits, with a cap equal to the employees' aggregate annual salary; and (iii) distribution of a first dividend of 5% of the company's paid-in capital. The distribution of the profit of MOS in accordance with the Egyptian Companies Act no 159 for the year ending December 31, 2008 was as shown in Table 2.

Table 2. Profit appropriation statement for the year ending December 31, 2008 (Amounts in U.S dollars)

Retained Earnings	1 504 262
Adjusted Profit of the year	62 479 052
Profit available for distribution	63 983 314
5% first Distribution to shareholders	(5 120 000)
10% distribution to	employees (5 886 331)
2nd & 3rd distribution to shareholders	(52 976 983)
Retained earnings for 2009	------

The Company Future Strategy

MOS strategic plans are to continue to expand, replace and upgrade the fleet and equipment. It will acquire 22 new vessels and two barges, which will allow MOS to operate in deeper waters and to undertake more EPC projects that generate higher revenue and profit margins. The new investments made by MOS shareholders are aimed at improving operating and cost analysis and control. These initiatives include:

- Focusing on securing long term contracts for vessels to ensure high utilization rates.
- Expanding and upgrading the fleet with technologically advanced and sophisticated marine units that will command higher daily rates.
- Reducing the average fleet age to control maintenance and dry-docking expenses.
- Continuing to attract, develop and retain high caliber personnel including senior managers by providing competitive salaries, bonus and benefits package such as an employee stock option plan.

MOS COMBINED FINANCIAL INFORMATION

This section summarizes the financial information for MOS Company and briefly presents the main corporate governance aspects complied with by the company. The combined financial statements are presented for the three years that ended on December 31, 2006, 2007 and 2008, and consist of the historical consolidated financial statements of MOS and its consolidated subsidiaries for the above years prepared in accordance with the Egyptian Accounting Standards (EAS). EAS differs in certain aspects from the International Financial Reporting Standards (IFRS). (see Tables 3 and 4)

MOS and Corporate Governance

The company complies with applicable corporate governance rules in effect in Egypt. An audit committee was established in 2008 comprised of three non-executive directors in compliance with article 7 of the Capital Authority Stock Exchange (CASE) listing rules. The audit committee is authorized to investigate any activity it deems appropriate to seek any information from any officer or employee of the Company, all of whom will be directed to cooperate with any request made by the audit committee, and to have recourse to seek independent counsel and advice. In addition to the general duties and obligations under Article 7 of the CASE listing rules, MOS audit committee is also responsible for:

- ensuring that there is an open avenue of communication between internal auditors, external auditors and the board of directors;
- considering, in consultation with the external auditors and the Internal Audit Director, the audit plans and scope of the external and internal auditors, ensuring that the coordination of audit effort is maximized;
- reviewing the financial statements with the Deputy General Manager and General

Table 3. Income statement years ended December 31

	2006 (U.S.S'000s)	2007 (U.S.S'000s)	2008 (U.S.S'000s)
Operating revenues	250,040	264,065	257,710
Cost of operations	(162,196)	(151,437)	(138,797)
Gross profit	**87,844**	**112,628**	**118,913**
General and administration expenses	(15,738)	(16,119)	(23,532)
Capital gain	432	248	9,456
Impairment of fixed assets	(4,157)	——	--
Operating profit	**68,381**	**96,758**	**104,837**
Other Income	574	509	1,078
Financing charges	(4,719)	(3,266)	(4,586)
Foreign exchange (loss) gain	(695)	(131)	(624)
Compensations	--	--	689
Interest income	110	206	794
Net profit for the year before tax	**63,652**	**94,067**	**102,188**
Change in fair value of cash flow Hedge	--	--	(18,602)
Income tax	(2,751)	(1,658)	(1,387)
Net profit for the year after tax	**60.901**	**92.418**	**82199**
Minority Interest:			
Valentine	7,439	12,332	13,183
Maritide	21	15	18
Net profit attributable to minority shareholders	**7,459**	**12,347**	**13,201**
Net profit attributable to equity shareholders	**53,441**	**80,071**	**68,998**

Manager for Finance at the completion of the annual examination;

- assessing with Internal Audit Directors significant risks or exposures and evaluating the steps to be taken to minimize such risks or exposures to the company as well as reviewing related party transactions;
- considering and reviewing with senior management and the Internal Audit Director significant violations of internal control systems, if any, during the year and the senior management's responses thereto;
- considering and reviewing the contents of the external auditors management letter, if any, together with the senior management's responses thereto.

The audit committee operates in accordance with charters approved by the board of directors, holds at least four ordinary meetings a year and may also hold additional meetings when deemed necessary.

Egyptian law requires that all relationships between the company and the board must be at arm's length. All contracts entered into with a board member or shareholder are considered related party transactions and must be authorized or approved by the general shareholders meeting; otherwise any such contract will be avoidable at the request of any shareholder if proven to be favoring or causing harm to a group of shareholders, or against the best interests of the company. Under the Egyptian law, members of the board of directors who have a conflict of interest with

Table 4. Balance sheet years ended at December 31

	2006 (U.S.$000s)	2007 (U.S.$000s)	2008 (U.S.$000s)
Non- current assets			
Property, plant and equipment	112,221	192,283	186,081
Goodwill	9,841	9,841	9,841
Loans to related parties	278	278	278
Other long term assets	——	137	6,128
Assets under construction			118,252
Total non- current assets	**122,340**	**202,539**	**320,580**
Current assets			
Inventories	3,958	5,815	5,584
Trade and notes receivables	88,305	90,935	72,417
Due from related parties	58	318	2,062
Prepaid expenses	891	1,595	2236
Due from customers	4.554	7,924	9,394
Cash in hand and at banks	15,193	9,451	78,100
Other receivables	42,537	39,145	6,339
Total current assets	**155,496**	**155,182**	**176,132**
Current liabilities			
Provisions	1,688	1,885	2,546
Bank credit facilities	7,290	24,516	11,791
Trade and note payables	20,275	40,818	17,837
Due to related parties	3.260	432	1
Short term loans installments	10,148	24,080	38,503
Dividends payable	56	330	8
Accrued expenses	18,052	6,652	16,404
Customer advanced payment	32,810	2,146	5,317
Other current liabilities	3,248	3,816	7,441
Total current liabilities	**96,826**	**104,674**	**99,848**
Working capital	**58,670**	**50,508**	**76,284**
Total investment	**181,010)**	**253,047**	**396,864**

continued on following page

the company are required to inform the board of directors of such conflict and may not vote on the subject matter of conflict. These matters are reported by the board of directors to the first general shareholder's meeting to be convened thereafter.

The law prohibits the company from providing cash loans to any members of the board of directors and expected to guarantee any loan such member takes from a third party. The board's members may not vote on any transaction related to the shareholders they represent.

During the course of its ordinary business in 2008, MOS made business transactions with MOP amounting to $4492893, in addition to consultancies and diving services for $ 4743129. Moreover, MOS rented marine units from Maritide

Table 4. continued

	2006 (U.S.$000s)	2007 (U.S.$000s)	2008 (U.S.$000s)
Financed as follows:			
Shareholder's equity			
Issued and paid up capital	65,000	85,000	102,400
Legal reserve	9,000	11,709	20,480
Special reserve			76,877
General reserve	24	24	
Consolidation reserve			(2,557)
Retained earnings (accumulated loss)	(3,885)	(10,514)	3,329
Minority interest	18,680	22,540	26,131
Net profit for the year	53,441	80,071	68,998
Total shareholder's equity	**142,268**	**188,830**	**295,658**
Non- current liabilities			
Long-term loans installments	38,742	64,217	82,605
Change in fair value of cash flow Hedge			18,601
Total non-current liabilities	**38,742**	**64,217**	**101,206**
Total finance of working capital and non-current assets	**181,010**	**253,047**	**396,864**

Table 5. A summary of swap agreements made by MOS as at December 31, 2008

	Type of Contract	Amount & Interest	Period of contract
Credit Agricole	Swap agreement Swap agreement	$ 30 million- 8.4% $ 30 million-3.825%	1/6/2008-1/9/2017 1/6/2008-1/3/2018
Citi Bank	Swap Agreement Swap Agreement	$ 44 million-2.9% to 5.8% $ 26.4 million-2.9% to 5.8%	30/5/2008-1/1/2013 30/5/2008-1/10/2013

Offshore Company for the amount of $ 5274890 in addition to providing technical consultancies of $ 60000. As to Valentine Company, there was a current balance owed to MOS for $ 102523. All the above transactions were made at arm's length.

Accounting and Auditing of MOS Derivative Swap losses

The management of MOS decided to minimize the risk of borrowings, associated with the acquisitions of the new vessels and barges, needed to achieve the objectives of the company future strategy and maintain its competitive edge in the marine and oil industry. Management entered into swap agreements with a number of international banks to minimize the likelihood of increase in interest rates for loans contracts taking into consideration that swap agreements are considered an example of cash flow hedging (Kasapi, 1999 and Kolb and Overdahl (2003). (see Table 5)

Paragraph 9 of International Accounting Standard No 39 defines a hedging instrument as "*a designated derivative or (for a hedge of the risk of changes in foreign currency exchange rates only) a designated non-derivative financial asset or non-derivative financial liability whose fair value or cash flows are expected to offset changes in the fair value or cash flows of a designated hedged item*". Under paragraph 9 of IAS 39, a hedged item is "*an asset, a liability, firm commitment, highly probable forecast transaction or net investment in a foreign operation that (a) exposes the entity to risk of changes in fair value or future cash flows and (b) is designated as being hedged*" (IASB, 2009, p 2001). While under paragraph 81 of IAS 39, if the hedged item is a financial asset or financial liability, it may be hedged with respect to the risks associated with only a portion of its cash flows or fair value provided that effectiveness can be measured (IASB, 2009, p 2020).

The IAS 39 defined cash flow hedge as "*a hedge of the exposure to variability in cash flows that (i) is attributable to a particular risk associated with a recognized asset or liability (such as all or some future interest payments on variable rate debt) or a highly probable forecast transaction and (ii) could affect profit or loss* "(IASB, 2009, p 2021). An example of a cash flow hedge is the use of a swap to change floating rate debt to fixed rate debt (i.e. a hedge of a future transaction where the future cash flows being hedged are the future interest payments - Ghosh, 2007). Trombley (2003, p 72) indicated that the hedging company enters the pay-fixed, receive-floating side of the swap, and the swap has the effect of converting floating-rate debt into fixed-rate debt. He added that this type of hedging is typically attractive to a company that has issued floating rate debt but does not have floating-rate interest-bearing assets, and is therefore concerned about cash flow variability from adverse changes in interest rates.

Management is required under IAS 39 to assess hedge effectiveness (i.e. swap effectiveness). Hedge effectiveness is the degree to which changes in the fair value or cash flows of the hedged item that are attributable to a hedged risk are offset by changes in the fair value or cash flows of the hedging instrument. Effectiveness is assessed whenever an entity prepares its annual or interim financial statements. A cash flow hedge is considered highly effective if both of the following conditions are met "*(a) at the inception of the hedge and in subsequent periods, the hedge is expected to be highly effective in achieving offsetting changes in cash flows attributable to the hedged risk during the period for which the hedge is designated, and (b) the actual results of the hedge are within a range of 80-125 per cent*" (IASB, 2009, p 2071). For example, if management decides that the total loss on hedging instrument is $100 and the gain on the cash instrument is $ 120, offset can be measured by 100/120, which is 83.33 per cent or by 120/100 which is 120 per cent. In such a situation, assuming that the hedge meets the condition stated in (a) above, the company would conclude that the hedge is highly effective.

The IAS 39 differentiated between the accounting treatments of the results of the assessment of effective versus ineffective cash flow hedges. IAS 39, in paragraph 95, indicated that the portion of the gain or loss on the hedging instrument, which is determined to be an effective hedge, shall be recognized in other comprehensive income; otherwise the ineffective portion of the gain or loss on any hedging instrument shall be recognized in the income statement.

MOS entered into four swap agreements totaling $130.4 million. The management of MOS performed the analysis of the effectiveness of the swap agreement made with the two banks (Credit Agricole and CitiBank) as at December 31, 2008. The results of such analysis were that this hedge instruments are ineffective with total losses of $18.6 million. The management prepared the company's financial statements for the year ending December 31, 2008 where they charged the effects of ineffective swap analysis into the company's special reserve for $18.6 million, in accordance with the requirements of the Egyptian Companies Act 159 for 1981. While, Article 57 of the Egyptian Law 159 for 1981 and its amendments allowed the management of companies to use the company's special reserve for purposes which may benefit the company's shareholders. Management decided that this is the time at which the special reserve should be used to offset losses resulting from the financial crisis. The accounting treatment proposed by the company was presented to the auditors Crowe Dr A.M.Hegazy & Co, RSM Magdi Hashish & Co and one of the big four CPA firms - Delloitte & Touch Kamel, Saleh and Barsom.

The big four CPA firms have total revenues exceeding $ 25 billion compared to maximum of $ 5 or 6 billion for non-big four. Also, the big four have a large number of partners and other members of staff including audit managers, supervisors and other auditors, many of whom are qualified CPA. The big four CPA firms cover almost every country in the world through their representative offices. Finally, the big four are capable of satisfying many of their clients' requests for assurance and other management advisory services, as a result of their diversified portfolio of clients, qualifications and experience of their large number of partners and managers.

For MOS swap agreements losses, auditors were in disagreement concerning the accounting treatment of such losses. Both Hegazy and Hashish firms agreed to the accounting treatment made by MOS management, whereas Deloitte objected and requested that the swap losses of $ 18.6 million be charged to the company's income statement, based upon the requirement of IAS no 32 & 39 and their equivalents in EAS. The auditors in favor of management treatment of the swap losses issued an unqualified audit report with explanatory paragraph "emphasis of matter", and the third auditor Delloitte & Touch issued a qualified report. A comparison between the financial statements of MOS as at December, 31, 2008 under each of the two possible accounting treatments of the swap losses is provided as shown in Tables 6 and 7.

The audited financial statements were sent to the Egyptian Capital Market Authority, (CMA-www.cma.gov.eg) the equivalence of SEC in the U.S.A, as required by the Capital Market Law no 95 for 1992. The Capital Market Authority issued an opinion in favor of the proposed treatment by Delloitte & Touch. The CMA justified its position based on the following justification.

1. The charging of the expected losses resulting from the application of the fair value of the swap agreement, which were considered ineffective on the owners' equity section, is considered in violation with the requirements of the Egyptian Accounting Standards No. 26 (equivalent to IAS 39), which charges such losses to the income statement for not having the effectiveness of the contract. In accordance with this treatment, one of the auditors reports was qualified while other auditors did issue unqualified reports, with explanatory paragraph for the same accounting treatment stating that "such losses were charged to the special reserve instead of charging it to the income statement, in accordance with the requirements of EAS No. 26. The board of directors of MOS decided to charge such losses to the special reserve due to the global financial crises". CMA felt that there is an agreement among all auditors for the non-compliance of such treatment with the requirements of the Egyptian Accounting Standards no. 21.
2. *The company in its decision to charge more losses to the special reserve account is in violation with article No. 39 of the Joint-Stock Companies Act No. 159 for 1981 and article 6 of the capital Market Law No. 95 for 1992 and article 58 of its executive regulations. The above articles require the company to prepare their financial statements in accordance with the Egyptian Accounting Standards, a matter which makes the company liable for penalties in accordance with article No. 60 of Capital Market Authority Law. Since the company has listed its shares by initial public offering the management insistence to apply such treatment would fall under non-compliance with the Egyptian Accounting Standards during the period of covering of such contracts until 2018* (MOS, 2009).

Table 6. Income statement years ended December 31 (U.S 000)

	2008 (Swap losses in Income Sta)	2008 (Swap losses in Balance Sheet)	Main Variance
Operating revenues	257,710	257,710	0
Cost of operations	(138,797)	(138,797)	0
Gross profit	**118,913**	**118,913**	**0**
General and administration expenses	(23,532)	(23,532)	0
Capital gain	9,456	9,456	0
Operating profit	**104,837**	**104,837**	**0**
Other Income	1,078	1,078	0
Financing charges	(4,586)	(4,586)	0
Foreign exchange (loss) gain	(624)	(624)	0
Compensations	689	689	0
Interest income	794	794	0
Net profit for the year before tax	**102,188**	**102,188**	**0**
Change in fair value of cash flow Hedge	(18,602)	0	18,602
Income tax	(1,387)	(1,387)	0
Net profit for the year after tax	**82,199**	**100,801**	**18,602**

The Capital Market Authority mandated that MOS should restate the financial statements for the year ending December 31, 2008 to comply with the Egyptian Accounting Standards and charge the losses to the income statement even if this results in net income reduction by 23% of the financial year's profits ended December 31, 2008 and the company is required to publish the adjusted financial statements in two widely distributed daily newspapers, at least one of which should be in Arabic. Also, the CMA noted that the company had capitalized $1.6 million as the net cost of obtaining loan No. 5 of the long-term loans on the loan's duration of 10 years without consideration of the Egyptian Accounting Standards. The company has to re-state the appropriate adjustment to charge such amount to the income statement for the year ending December 31, 2008.

At the same time, the CMA communicated its opinion to the two auditors who issued an unqualified report with explanatory paragraph objecting to such opinion and asking for a correction of the auditors' reports:

"*We noticed that your report on the financial statements of Maridive & Oil Services Co. included an explanatory paragraph violating the Egyptian Accounting Standards in light of the significant effects resulting from the accounting treatment applied in treating the losses of MOS financial swap contracts which represent 23% of the year's profits ended 31\12\2008, a matter which necessitated a qualification based on what was included in article No.16 of the Egyptian Accounting Standard No.1, the justification of the management treatment cannot be considered a correction to inaccurate and inappropriate accounting treatment*" (MOS, 2009).

Officials at the CMA asked for a meeting to discuss the disagreement occurring between the three auditors before the annual general meeting to approve MOS financial reports for 2008. The meeting was attended by the partners and managers from the three CPA firms, CFO and officials from MOS and from the Capital Market Authority. The following discussions occurred during the meeting:

Table 7. Balance sheet

	2008 (U.S.$000s)	2008 (U.S.$000s)	Variance (U.S.$000s)
Total non- current assets	**320,580**	**320,580**	**0**
Total current assets	**176,132**	**176,132**	**0**
Total current liabilities	**99,848**	**99,848**	**0**
Working capital	**76,284**	**76,284**	**0**
Total investment	**396,864**	**396,864**	**0**
Financed as follows:			
Shareholder's equity			
Issued and paid up capital	102,400	102,400	0
Legal reserve	20,480	20,480	0
Special reserve	76,877	58275	(18602)
Consolidation reserve	(2,557)	(2,557)	0
Retained earnings (accumulated loss)	3,329	3,329	0
Minority interest	26,131	26,131	0
Net profit for the year	68,998	87600	18602
Total shareholder's equity	**295,658**	**295,658**	**0**
Non- current liabilities			
Long-term loans installments	82,605	82,605	0
Change in fair value of cash flow Hedge	18,601	18,601	0
Total non-current liabilities	**101,206**	**101,206**	**0**
Total finance of working capital and non-current assets	**396,864**	**396,864**	**0**

Official CMA: What are the justifications that made MOS management and auditors agree not to charge the $18.6 million to the company's income statement at the end of December 2008?

The Auditors (Hegazy & Hashish): The decision of the board of directors to use the special reserve amount of $76.8 million on December 31, 2008 to cover losses resulting from future expectation of the swap agreement amounting to $18.6 million, instead of charging such losses to the income statement for the year 2008, was in accordance with the Companies Act 159 for 1981 and its executive regulations and the company article of incorporations as follows:

a. Article no 57 of the company's articles of incorporation refer to the special reserve as a last resort to help the company treat unusual circumstances. The board decision to use such account was for the benefit of the company. Therefore, the board exercised its authority mandated by the above article for the accounting treatment referred to and will present such treatment to the annual general meeting which will have the final decision concerning such issue, and

b. The decision to apply the wording of the company's articles of association quoted from the companies Act No. 159 for 1981 in reference to the special reserve account is in accordance with article 57 of the Companies Act and article 94 of its executive regulations superseded the requirements of the accounting standards. The board of MOS decision for the swap losses was in compliance with the wording of the above mentioned articles.

Officials of CMA: Deloitte's qualification explicitly stated that the accounting treatment of the swap losses is in violation with the requirements of the Egyptian Accounting Standards no 25 & 26 (the equivalent to IAS 32 & 39), so how the CFO of MOS did not restate the company's financial statements?

CFO of MOS: Article No. 39 of the Companies Act 159 for 1981 stated "the company will have a financial year specified by its articles of incorporation and financial statements will be prepared according to the accounting standards". Then Article 40 of the same law stated" it is possible to use the special reserve to cover the company's losses and to increase its capital… and if the special reserve is not identified for specific purposes included in the company's articles, the annual general meeting based upon recommendations of the board may use it for the benefit of the company and its shareholders". From the wording of the above article, MOS management, as well as Hegazy & Hashish auditors, are of the opinion that the Companies Act authorized the general meeting to use the special reserve in any form other than the distribution of profits. On the contrary, the law did exceptionally allow the use of reserves and give such decision to shareholders in relation to losses realized by the company. Thus, the accounting treatment of the general reserve to offset future expectation of unrealized losses for the swap agreement for the year 2009 – 2017 is the proper accounting treatment. As a matter of principle, the management can use the reserve to offset such future losses of the swap transaction rather than charging such losses to MOS income statement as of December 31, 2008. In addition, if the balance of the special reserve account is not used to offset future unrealized losses, what can those accounts are used for otherwise?

Hegazy & Hashish: Our opinion to treat the unrealized future losses of the swap agreement was made in order not to charge the income statement for the period 2009 – 2017 with the results of unstable and significant changes related to the forecast of interest rates and the offsetting of its related losses to the special reserve reflects the actual performance of the company's operations for the year 2008 and future periods.

Table 8.

Amount at 30 Sept. 2008	Amount at 31 Dec. 2008	Amount at 25 Feb. 2009
\$6,7 Million	\$18,6 Million	\$14,2 Million

Hegazy & Hashish: There is noticed subjectivity associated with the calculation of the expected losses resulting from such contracts due to the exceptional financial circumstances as the valuation of such contracts during the period September 30, 2008 until February 25, 2009 using the present value approach were as shown in Table 8.

From the above analysis, one cannot rely on the accuracy of such forecast in the light of the current financial circumstances and the right treatment of such losses or profit should be charged to the special reserve account.

Hegazy & Hashish: The report also took into consideration the uncertainty related to results of future expectation of the swap agreement. Moreover, we support MOS management accounting treatment of the results of the swap agreement because this complies fully with paragraph 5 of the Egyptian Standards on Auditing No. 701 which includes: "*In special circumstances, the auditor may modify his report by adding an explanatory paragraph for a special matter which may affect the financial statements and should be explained in details in the notes of these statements and such explanatory paragraph does show the auditor opinion not to be considered as a qualified one*".

Hegazy & Hashish: Our report complied fully with paragraphs 5 & 7 of the Egyptian Standards on Auditing No. 701 as the auditor may modify his report with the addition of an explanatory paragraph if there is fundamental uncertainty circumstances (other than the going concern) which are based on future events affecting the financial statements. The uncertainty is an issue where its results are based on future events, the company cannot control but which may affect the financial statements. The company's management decided to minimize the effects of such future expectation during the period 2009 until 2017 by charging these uncertain forecasts to the special reserve for the benefit of the company and its shareholders in accordance with article 57 of the articles and the Companies Act No. 159 for 1981 and its executive regulations.

Officials of CMA: What is the basis under which MOS capitalized the cost of the loan obtained by MOS?

MOS CFO: On April 2008, MOS has signed a medium-term joint financing contract with three banks for an amount of $ 133.6 million, to finance 80% of the total cost of construction of nine marine vessels. The cost of obtaining such loan amounted to $ 1691400. According to the guidelines of applying the international accounting standard No.39 of the financial instruments, the financial assets, which must be evaluated on the fair-value basis, shall appear in the revenues and loss, and the costs of obtaining such loan shall appear (in the net value after deducting the accumulated amortization) deducted from the balance of the obligation (loan) as issue fees. Moreover, according to the Egyptian accounting standard No.14 " the cost of borrowing " section 11, the company applied the alternative method in accordance with the Egyptian Accounting Standards which state that the costs of borrowing related to establishing and producing a specific asset should be capitalized on that asset, until such asset is used or sold.

MOS CFO: Also, the capitalization of the cost of acquiring the loan on the loan period was made in accordance with article 14 of the Egyptian Accounting Standards No. 14 which states: *"The amortization of other costs incurred by the company for borrowing ...."* The two auditors need to also emphasize that what is stated in the notes of the financial statements comply fully with what is contained in the standard as follows: *The amortization of the cost of acquiring the loan on the period of loan agreement, such amortization of the cost of borrowing will be charged to the income statement unless such borrowing is related to an asset susceptible for capitalization, at that time such costs should be capitalized on that asset.* The decision made by the board in its meeting dated February 23, 2009 is a recommendation to the annual general meeting and shareholders have the final decision.

Hegazy & Hashish: According to article 4.C in the Egyptian Accounting standard No 14, the cost of obtaining a loan includes other deductions occurring during the period of obtaining such loan which means that the company has the right to deduct the cost of obtaining the loan occurred during the time when the assets on marine vessels are being constructed instead of charging it as expenses. According to such method, the cost of obtaining the loan has been capitalized over the period of the loan and was deducted annually as follows:

1. The deducted amount for the period of constructing the assets has been capitalized on such assets as a part of the debts of obtaining the loan of marine vessels which amounted to $ 70476 and it has been postponed the deduction of the remaining part amounted to $ 1620924 as a deferred asset presented in the financial statements with the net value to be deducted from loans balance.
2. The remaining amount of the post-construction period will be realized on an annual-basis as an expense in the income statement, it will be considered as a settlement to loan interests. According to what is stated in the Egyptian accounting standard No. 14 that the cost of obtaining the loan depends on the loan period so it cannot be totally charged to the income statement for one year and it also cannot be fully capitalized on the assets.

The meeting between MOS's CFO, auditors and CMA officials was concluded and CMA officials promised to inform the company with their final decision concerning whether CMA would insist on the re-statement of MOS financial statements as at December 31, 2008. A few days later, the management of MOS received CMA's decision quoted as follows:

"Referring to the discussions at the meeting held at CMA Head office attended by the auditors and the management of the company concerning the financial statements of MOS as at December 31, 2008, the Capital Market Authority confirms the need to restate the financial statements of MOS as at December 31, 2008 due to the followings:

1. The accounting treatment that the company applied in charging the losses resulting from the recognition of the fair value of the obligations arising from the swap contracts which were considered ineffective to the owners' equity (special reserve), is considered a violation of the Egyptian Accounting Standards.
2. The authority did not assess the legality of using the special reserve and the responsible authority for that and the basis of its use.
3. There is general legal commitment to prepare the financial statements of the listed companies according to the Egyptian Accounting Standards, in accordance with the Companies Act no. 159 of 1981, and there is a legal commitment on the joint-stock companies whose shares are listed by initial public offering to comply with these standards in preparing their financial statements according to law No.95 of 1992.
4. According to the significant effects resulting from violating the standards, which represent 23% of the year's profits, the violation of the Egyptian accounting standard No.26 is considered a misleading presentation of the financial statements. According to the board's suggestion to distribute 25 cent on each share the company will distribute part of the special reserve used to cover the financial losses related to swap contracts – indirectly - because if the company charged such losses to the income statement the realized revenues will decrease to USD 62.5 million and the suggested distribution amounted to USD 64 million will not be met. It is illegal to use the special reserve formed from additional paid up capital balances in cash distribution.
5. In relation to the amortization of the cost of obtaining the loan on the duration of the loan, the company's accounting treatment did violate the requirements of the Egyptian Accounting Standard no 14 which allowed the capitalization of finance costs directly attributable to obtaining or producing an asset on the cost of such asset. Therefore, such cost is considered part of the cost of the asset being depreciated based upon the agreed upon depreciation rates, and not to be amortized over the duration of the loan".

In sum, the CMA is still of the opinion for the restatement of the company's financial statements of December31, 2008 after applying the appropriate changes to comply with the Egyptian Accounting Standards and MOS should publish the adjusted financial statements in two widely distributed daily newspapers at least one in Arabic (MOS, 2009). As to the type of the auditors' report issued by both Hegazy and Hashish CPA firms, the CMA confirms that the Egyptian Accounting Standard No.26 included only one accounting treatment and did not include any alternative treatment to agree upon it with the company's management. Accordingly, a qualified opinion should have been issued in light of the significant violations to the Egyptian Accounting Standards discovered.

Based upon the final decision of the Capital Market Authority, the management of MOS decided to restate the company's financial statements for the year ending December 31, 2008 and charged the losses of the swap agreements to the income statement and complied with CMA request for finance cost on borrowings related to acquiring assets. Auditors restated their audit opinion and the three auditors issued a single unqualified audit opinion.

CONCLUSION

The case study discussed points of strengths for a successful international company, "Maridive & Oil Services", in terms of its management structure, company strategies and competitive strengths, governance issues and other financial and non financial measures. The case also explained the nature of derivatives mainly swap agreements and the financial implications related to the assessment of such agreements as being ineffective. The case outlined the accounting and auditing treatments for losses computed for the swap agreements, with both Credit Agricole and Citi Bank, showing points of dispute between management and auditors on one side and government authority (CMA) on the other side. The case demonstrated the problems related to the auditors' independence, auditors' possible errors of judgments versus audit failures, accounting standards versus requirements of various laws and the company's articles of incorporation. The case emphasized the authority of the government supervisory board represented in the Egyptian Capital Market Authority, in forcing the management of MOS to restate its financial statements at December 31, 2008 despite the objection of two of its auditors and their issue of unqualified report with explanatory paragraph. There is still an unanswered question of whether the decision of CMA to restate the financial statements of MOS is the right decision giving the facts surrounding the swap agreements, the requirements of the accounting and auditing standards and the strong financial position of MOS.

The case also pointed out the need to undertake future research to solve points of conflicts between the requirements of local laws and International accounting and auditing standards. Such conflict needs to be assessed not in the light of the possible interpretation of the requirements of both the laws and the standards but in the light of what is considered beneficial to shareholders, investors and other users of MOS financial statements.

ACKNOWLEDGMENT

The authors acknowledge the professional opinion of Dr. Medhat Hassanein, Professor of finance and banking of the management Department of the school of business, the American University in Cairo and thank him for his insightful remarks regarding the impact of the right treatment of swap contracts of the financial results of corporations.

REFERENCES

Capital Market Authority. (2008). *The Egyptian standards on auditing, limited review and other assurance services*. The Capital Market Authority.

Ghosh, J. (2007). *Understanding financial instruments: A guide to IAS 32, IAS 39 and IFRS 7*. CCH-a Wolters Kluwer Business.

International Accounting Standards Board. (2009). *International financial reporting standards (IFRS)-official pronouncements as issued at 1 January 2009*. IASB.

Kasapi, A. (1999). *Mastering credit derivatives*. Prentice Hall.

Kolb., R., & Overdahl, J. (2003). *Financial derivatives*. Wiley & Sons, Inc.

Maridive & Oil Services. (2009). *Correspondences between management, auditors and the Egyptian capital market authority*. Maridive & Oil Services.

Trombley, M. (2003). *Accounting for derivatives and hedging*. McGraw-Hill Irwin.

Chapter 3
Electronic Commerce and Management Accountants in Egypt:
New Opportunities and Threats

Mayada Abd El-Aziz Youssef
UAE University, UAE

EXECUTIVE SUMMARY

This research reports on a longitudinal case study in an Egyptian organization (TexCo[1]) that implemented Business-to-Business (B-to-B) electronic commerce. The objective is to explore the process of change in the role of management accountants associated with the implementation of B-to-B e-commerce. TexCo was subject to a change in leadership; subsequently, their traditional means of operation was put into question. This process resulted in realizing issues related to planning and internal control within the company. The B-to-B system was chosen to introduce new control-based rules. Resistance to change was detected in the case. It is posited that various power strategies were used to ameliorate covert and overt resistance. Over time, the role of management accountants in TexCo changed towards greater decision support and control. B-to-B electronic commerce poses management accountants with new challenges in TexCo. As such, it represents both an opportunity and a threat.

ORGANIZATION BACKGROUND

TexCo is a company wholly owned by an Egyptian family. Established in 1950, by the grandfather of the current CEO, TexCo soon became one of the four leading companies operating in textile manufacture[2] in Egypt. It is primarily engaged in dyeing, printing and finishing textiles. According

DOI: 10.4018/978-1-60960-583-4.ch003

to a report (Textile Sector Report, 1999) prepared by SEAM, a project implemented by the Egyptian Environmental Affairs Agency and Entec UK Limited, the textile sector in Egypt consists of over 3,000, both public and private sector, companies. Seventy-seven of these are engaged in dyeing, printing and finishing textiles. TexCo's products are characterised by both high quality and high price. Consequently, most of its customers are from the upper class of the Egyptian society.

The CEO at TexCo is at the pinnacle of the organizational structure, which is divided into seven departments. A manager responsible directly to the CEO heads each department. The latter includes the outlets' department, the production department, the stores department, the projects' department, the export department, the general accounting department and the purchasing department.

The company sells its products through its own outlets as well as the outlets of its distributors in Egypt and abroad. The sales of the company are channeled through three departments; the outlets' department, the projects' department and the export department. The outlets' department deals with distributors besides TexCo's own outlets. The projects' department liaises with hotels, hospitals and other businesses throughout Egypt. The export department deals with the distributors and TexCo's outlets abroad.

After the death of the organization's founder in 1978, TexCo was passed on to his son, the previous CEO. In that period, TexCo had a 'production oriented' culture. There were shared assumptions, within the company, about the importance and priority of production quality. Although TexCo was profitable, this was mainly due to its excellent products and production systems rather than to its management and accounting controls. The role of accounting in TexCo during this period could best be described as 'ceremonial'. The previous CEO used to determine the production quantities depending on his personal experience, accounting was not an integral part of the management process, and cost accounting was only used for pricing decisions and financial statements' preparation.

SETTING THE STAGE

Previously, TexCo sold its products on consignment basis, where a large stock of its textile collection remained in the distributors' outlets. Based on the previous CEO's expectations, the production orders were sent to the production department. After production, the products were transferred to the stores department and then sent from there, on order, to TexCo's own outlets in addition to those of its distributors.

At the end of each week the outlets sent the invoices to the outlets' department in TexCo, where four accountants entered the invoices on a simple, locally produced accounting information system. At the end of each month, the accountants compared their records with those of the outlets from

Figure 1. Partial organizational chart of TexCo

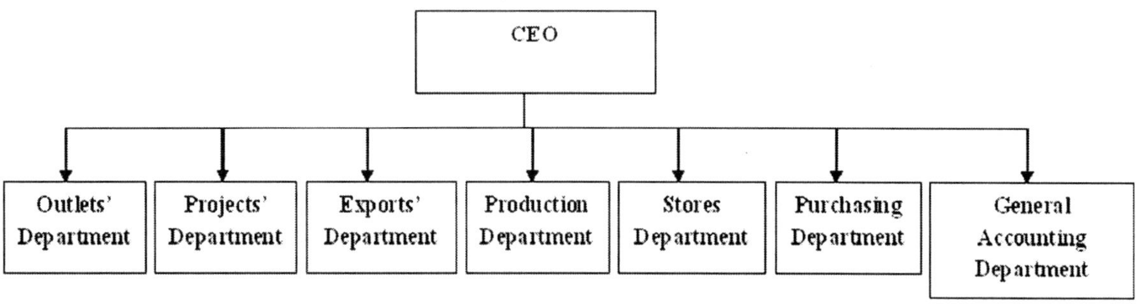

which the receivables were collected. Thereafter, the accountants prepared monthly accounting reports, relating to the balances of stock, sales, sales returns and cash collections. The reports were then passed to the CEO and the general accounting department.

In 1993, the previous CEO ceded all authority and responsibility of the management of TexCo to his son. Afterwards, it was recognized within TexCo that significant changes would have to take effect. The new CEO, then in his thirties and highly ambitious, appointed an IT manager and began to introduce computers in each and every department. A solitary computer existed in the company prior to this action located in the general accounting department.

CASE DESCRIPTION

The CEO, a business school graduate with limited experience, started using the accounting reports in decision-making processes, particularly in production planning. However, he realized that the company was facing some reporting problems. The outlets' department used to send 'out of date' accounting reports to the CEO and the general accounting department. Although these accounting reports became the main tool that was used in taking numerous decisions regarding production expectations, cash flow management, and purchases of raw materials besides the preparation of financial statements and budgets, they were usually based on old data. An accountant[3] explained:

"Top management had a problem in decision making as the reports were always late and out of date. We were busy in data entry and stocktaking ... " (Accountant 1).

Through analyzing the accounting reports, the CEO also realized that TexCo was facing some problems in inventory control. He concluded that there was a high degree of textile wastage, 7-8% of the stock balance. The accountants explained to him that the control over the huge stock that was kept in the distributors' outlets was largely ineffective and hence susceptible to theft and wastage. The CEO remarked:

Figure 2. The business process in TexCo before implementing the B-to-B e-commerce

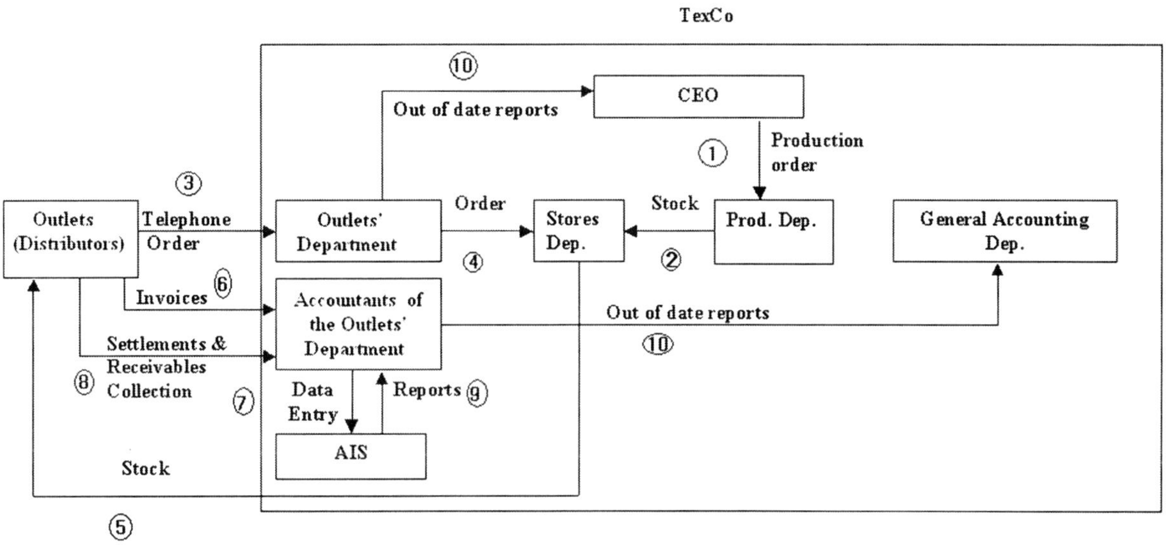

"Our main problem was that we used to deal with our distributors on consignment basis. Each distributor had a fixed stock of LE3-4 million and in case of its reduction; a reorder was made to reach this level again. Our stock balance was about LE100-150 million in the 35 outlets that we were dealing with. The wastage from textile [through cutting] was around 7-8% of this value, which was a very big burden on the company ..." (CEO).

Furthermore, through one of the meetings with the accountants of the outlets' department, the CEO discovered that TexCo was beset by invoicing control problems. This was due to the fact that the invoicing errors made by the bookkeepers in the outlets were not routinely detected. Even if a stock deficit was discovered, through stocktaking, they could not determine which transaction was mistakenly recorded. The deficit, which might have been due to recording mistakes, wastage, or even theft, was invariably recorded as wastage. The accountants' errors in entering the invoices on the AIS were not discovered until they made the settlement at the close of each month, when they compared the records of the outlet with those of the outlets' department.

We can safely state that the change in leadership at TexCo had created a general recognition that 'things would change'. Questioning of the company's traditional ways of doing things began, and it was acknowledged that the new CEO would inevitably make changes. There were some external factors that catalysed this "questioning" process. Those factors included firstly, the application of the GAAT[4] agreement in Egypt by 2005. The terms of said agreement meant that TexCo, along with Egyptian textile companies, was expected to face fierce competition from abroad. So, according to the CEO's words, TexCo 'had to be ready for that'. Secondly, the recession that the Egyptian market was experiencing at that stage, briefly mentioned by the outlets' department manager in one of the interviews, highlighted the problem of textile wastage. During that time, TexCo was driven to reduce their expenditure. Hence, solving the problem of textile wastage was brought out into the open and became an immediate priority. Thirdly, the political support and encouragement of the Egyptian government to telecommunication and IT activities encouraged the CEO to consider using an IT solution to resolve TexCo's difficulties. The CEO remarked:

"We have a lot of competitors inside Egypt and after applying the GAAT agreement in 2005, we will face competition from outsiders as well, so we have to be ready for that. We have to lead the Egyptian market in applying such a technology. There is a lot of information technology development in Egypt nowadays. We should put our feet on the beginning of this road and then we can make more improvements. IT is not a luxury; it is a prerequisite to competition and survival." (CEO).

This process, of questioning the taken-for-granted ways of thinking is what Burns et al. (2003) called "bursting the bubble". In other words the company's taken-for-granted assumptions, or institutions, were questioned and, as such, they could no longer be said to be taken-for-granted. Instead, they were exposed and were finally challenged. Following this, the CEO thought of introducing a new set of "control oriented" rules through keeping the stock in the factory under TexCo's control and sending the textiles to the distributors on order. To facilitate the ordering process, to solve both the invoicing control and the reporting problems and to lead the Egyptian market in applying the B-to-B electronic commerce, the CEO, in 1996, decided to use an extranet (online ordering system) linking the outlets' department in Cairo with TexCo's distributors and outlets worldwide.

CHALLENGES FACING THE ORGANIZATION

At the end of 1996, the CEO explained to the expected users of the new system the need for change. He organized a meeting with the IT manager and accountants in the outlets' department. The mobilisation of meanings, power over meaning, and the use of resources, resources power, were evident at that meeting. Hardy (1996) defined the power over meaning as "influencing actors' perceptions, cognitions and/or preferences in order that they accept the status quo (failing to recognize alternatives) or, rather, become convinced that change is desirable, rational and/or legitimate." The CEO discussed the difficulties that TexCo was encountering with the aforementioned staff. His discussion and comments caused the accountants to reflect more seriously upon TexCo's problems. During the meeting, he suggested utilising a B-to-B application, the extranet, to solve such problems. His aim was to clarify that the adoption of the B-to-B application did not merely imply a change in the IT application in use, but represented a highly desirable choice, as well as offering the best solution to TexCo's problems (power over meaning). The IT manager reacted very positively to this option and started explaining how the new system would streamline complex processes and improve the reporting facilities. However, the accountants, while being aware of TexCo's difficulties and becoming convinced that the B-to-B system might actually provide the solution, were anxious that the system would affect their work negatively or could cause them to be met by new and demanding challenges. An accountant remarked:

"At the beginning we were worried about using the new system. After our meeting with the CEO we were convinced that the new system might solve the company's problems. But we also thought that it might increase the work burden..." (Accountant 1).

We can interpret the accountants' anxiety in terms of what Burns and Scapens (2000) refer to as, a 'mental allegiance' to established ways of thinking and doing embodied in existing routines and institutions. This is what Hardy (1996) calls "power of the system". The accountants in the outlets' department had a stable, unquestioned behaviour and attitude, and they have been following a routine for a long period of time. Data entry and financial reporting formed their daily routine. Implementing the new system caused them to believe that it might alter such behaviour and lead them into unfamiliar territory. Clearly they were concerned about the consequences of change and it seems that the CEO's discussion and motivation was not enough to assuage their anxiety. However, their anxiety was not reflected in any kind of overt resistance. The accountant explained:

"We didn't make any objections... we are here working in a private entity. Our contracts are renewed every year based on our performances' evaluation. The CEO was supporting the change, so we could both accept it and develop our skills, or we could look for a job in another place..." (Accountant 1).

There were certain features that characterize the Egyptian labour market during that time. These features include the limited number of job opportunities, the spread of unemployment[5], the large number of qualified accountants[6], and the unavailability of unemployment benefits[7]. The accountants believed that resistance was an option they could not afford. For them, it meant that TexCo could swiftly find a qualified replacement for them and they could remain unemployed for an indefinite period without recourse to any form of income.

The CEO's status acted as a resources, hierarchical, power that prevented conflict from emerging in the first instance. Whilst he made no correlation between their acceptance of the system and retaining their positions, the accountants nevertheless believed that they could lose their jobs if they reacted negatively. His support to the system forced them to accept the change because they saw no alternative to it (power over meaning). Therefore, despite their anxiety, they acquiesced the CEO's suggestion regarding extranet implementation.

The more pressing problem that faced TexCo was convincing the distributors to adopt the new system. Initially, the distributors refused this, as they would have to bear some expenses associated with its usage. One of the distributors mentioned that these expenses included purchasing desktop computers, modifying the outlets' decorations to include samples and catalogues rather than textile rolls, and increasing the number of cashiers staffing their outlets. They were not convinced that there was any advantage to using the system and yet they would be expected to cover additional costs. At the same time, they were not confronting any visible challenge that could oblige them to adapt their ways of working, i.e. there was no motive for them to change. The outlets' department manager added:

"We faced a lot of problems in implementing the system. Each of our distributors had his interests; they were looking for any reason for not implementing the system. So, we had to face those problems firmly..." (Outlets' department manager).

SOLUTIONS AND RECOMMENDATIONS

The CEO and the IT manager, soon after to become the outlets' department manager, negotiated the issue of change with the distributors in a meeting. Again, power over meaning was brought into play. The CEO discussed the problems that TexCo was facing, and how introduction of the new system was expected to solve such matters. He and the IT manager attempted to motivate the distributors through explaining the benefits that they would enjoy by using the system. And, to facilitate matters for them, the CEO suggested implementing the change gradually over two years. But when the CEO failed to mobilise their meanings through the discussion, he informed them, unequivocally, that TexCo was committed to using the system in its own outlets either way and those who wished to continue to deal with TexCo had, therefore, to follow suit.

We can interpret the CEO's latter action in terms of the use of power over both meaning and resources. He employed TexCo's market status and prestige to influence the behaviour of the distributors coercively. The CEO knew as well as they did that TexCo's leading position in the Egyptian textile market meant that the distributors had little choice but to deal with them. It was widely acknowledged that the clients purchasing TexCo's products belonged to Egyptian society's elite, those able to afford premium rates to obtain their high quality products. By the end of the meeting he succeeded in gaining the acceptance of approximately 20% of the distributors to use the new system because they saw no other alternative. This percentage had reached 80% within the first year of using the system. One of the distributors explained:

"We achieved a lot of profit through working with TexCo. Their products attract the elite of the society. I am talking about those customers who change the decorations of their houses every year. Such customers can pay top price for TexCo's products. I agreed to use their extranet because I didn't want to lose my customers. I could cover these extra expenses [of implementing the system] from my profits sooner or later. However, if I lost my customers then I would lose everything..." (One of the distributors).

In 1997, the CEO, the accountants and the IT manager began an analysis of the system. They concurred that it should have extensive inventory control, invoicing control and reporting facilities. As a result, new 'control oriented' assumptions started to emerge at TexCo. By mid-1999[8], NetCo[9] took around six months to tailor the B-to-B system in line with TexCo's specifications. As a tailored system, the new B-to-B application included all the reports previously prepared by the accountants using Excel, plus others that they had insufficient time to cater for. In other words, the accountants drew upon the existing ways of doing things to determine the reporting needs of the new system. The accountant remarked:

"This is the advantage of a tailored system. When we designed the system, we took into consideration the specificity of the company. The system includes the same product codes and terminologies that we were using, the same reports that we were doing plus other reports that we didn't have time to do..." (Accountant 2).

The managing director of NetCo also explained:

"We went through a lot of details with the accountants and the outlets' department manager to settle some issues. There were some complexities regarding discount ranges for different distributors; how to deal with the invoices in the case of sales returns; also how to deal with pending invoices when the client makes down payment and pay the rest after a number of days..." (Managing director of NetCo).

Upon completion of the system's design, four modules were included: the branch module, the stock control module, the web-based administration module, and the real-time reporting module. Password protection was incorporated to increase security; monthly, quarterly, annual reports as well as graphical analysis for each branch/agent; online invoicing; sales returns handling; and different pricing/discount ranges for various branches/distributors. Accordingly, outlets were able to check item availability status and order items directly online; and management was able to monitor outlets' performance online.

When TexCo began implementing the system, they were faced with resistance from the distributors' bookkeepers. This was due to them having to alter their working practices from manual labour to computers. Some of the staff members were elderly and had not dealt with computers before so it became evident that they were apprehensive about such a radical shift. To ameliorate their resistance and familiarize them with the new application, the outlets' department manager organized a free training course for them, along with the accountants in the outlets' department. The training course took one day. It proved not to be onerous for any of the participants to comprehend. One of the bookkeepers explained:

"...I took some time, around two months, to get used to the new way of doing work. During that time, the outlets' department manager and the accountants in the factory were offering us help. Whenever we needed any query [answered], we called them and they were usually there to help..." (Distributor's bookkeeper).

Implementing the B-to-B e-commerce in TexCo was accompanied by redesigning the business process in the outlets' department. The B-to-B application assisted TexCo in maintaining the stock in its stores, and dispatching the products to distributors on order. Thus, instead of having immense stocks of textiles in their outlets, the distributors had a catalogue and a 'balance' that included textile samples. Each sample had a special card that included its code, specifications and price, which permitted the prospective customers all the requisite information concerning the samples.

The new business process can be summarized as follows. Once the customer has selected the desired product, the cashier checked stock availability and sent the order to the outlets' department via the extranet. In TexCo, an accountant from the outlets' department received the order and sent it to the stores. There the workers prepared all the orders and forwarded them to the outlets by the following day if it was in Egypt, or within two weeks if it was overseas. The accountant tracked the order to ensure that it was sent on time.

The order was rechecked in the outlet before the customer received it. The recheck was made to confirm that it was the same quantity, quality and degree of colour that was originally ordered. The accountant then entered the transaction on to the AIS. At the close of each week, another accountant made the settlements with the distributors using the systems' reporting facilities, and collected the receivables through either cheques or bank deposits. Each month end involved the CEO, the outlets' department manager and one of his accountants in scrutinising accurate and timely reports, retrieved from the system, for decision-making. Additionally, some of these reports were then sent to the general accounting department for budgetary and financial statements' preparation.

At that stage of implementing the new changes, the CEO delegated the authority of the outlets' department to the IT manager. He gave him, in association with one of the accountants, the responsibility of determining the production orders. Accordingly, the authority concerning what to produce and in what quantities shifted from the CEO to the outlets' department manager and one of the accountants. In doing so they drew on the reporting facilities provided by the new system. In this situation, we can see the CEO as using more than one power dimension. He offered the accountant a role in the decision-making process (decision-making power) to ensure his compliance and mobilise his meanings (legitimate power) in a manner that convinced them that change is "desirable". Such empowerment imbued the accountant with feelings of capability. Over time he became very satisfied with the system, and it seems that he accepted the changes and the additional commensurate responsibilities. The accountant remarked:

Figure 3. The business process in TexCo after implementing the B-to-B e-commerce

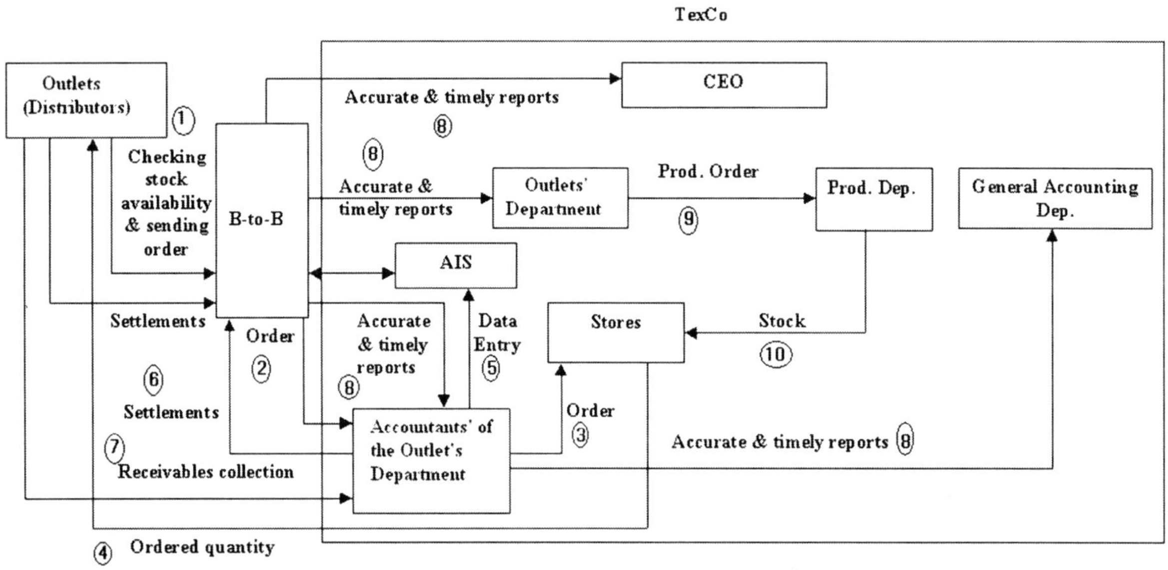

"...I was challenged when the CEO asked us to be responsible of determining the production orders. I wanted to prove to him that I am capable of doing this job perfectly.... Now I believe that the system developed my skills...It saves my time and effort and give me more time to analyze the reports and interpret the data ..." (Accountant 1).

Over the three-month enactment of the new rules, the repeated behaviour of the accountants led to reproduction of new routines. The accountants realized that they needed more reports to undertake their new role than what had already been provided by the system. Responding to their needs, the outlets' department manager asked NetCo to modify the system to embody the necessary reports. This event revealed the interaction between the users and the system and how the users affected (modified) the system. The managing director of NetCo explained:

"...There were a lot of modifications made in the first three months of implementing the system. Actually they needed extra reports. We designed them and now the system includes a reporting tool so that they can make any other reports they wish..." (Managing director of NetCo).

Over time, the newly imposed accounting practices at TexCo became routine. Using the new system, especially its reporting facilities, soon became a "programmatic" activity for the accountants. Through observation, we concluded that firstly, the B-to-B system became the sole tool to be used by the accountants to deal with their distributors. We could find no evidence of "work arounds". Secondly, the reporting facilities produced by the system became the key tool used by the outlets' department manager and the accountant to take decisions related to the production orders. These reporting facilities were explicitly interpreted as substantial advantages for the accountants. An accountant remarked:

"... Before using the new system we were busy in data entry and financial reports' preparation. We had no time for preparing reports about stock turnover on a regular basis and nobody was following up the stock turnover of the different products. This is because preparing those reports could take a lot of time and we had limited time to do that. However, after using the reporting facilities of the system we got to know the products that have high stock turnovers and those that have low ones. So we started to determine the production quantity depending on such reports. Before the new system determining the production quantity was based on personal expectations and out of date reports. But now it is based on the analysis of accurate and timely reports..." (Accountant 1).

The outlets' department manager also added:

"... The CEO used to determine the production quantity. When his decision was wrong he had to bear the results. However, now, I am responsible for such a decision in collaboration with the accountant. When the thing is revised twice, you usually have a better decision. Two people think better than one. By this discussion we usually reach the right decision...this has saved the time of the CEO and he is no more responsible for such business details..." (Outlets' department manager).

All the while, the introduced routines were the enactment of the rules established by the new CEO. Gradually, the routines were self-enforced, as the re-enactment and reflexive monitoring contributed to a burgeoning tacit knowledge for the accountants. The accountant remarked:

"... At the beginning I was worried about using the system. But after one month I get used to it and know all its details. I find it very easy and user friendly. ..." (Accountant 1).

We can see further use of power by the end of the first year of using the new system. The

CEO developed a team-based evaluation system, replacing a traditional reward system based on individual performance, to monitor the execution of the new routines. Under this system, the departmental managers became responsible for monitoring the execution of the introduced routines and the employees were rewarded for working as a team. These group-based rewards included salary increases, promotions and bonuses (resources). That is to say, the resources were again used to manage the meanings. They were used to manage the cross-functional groups' meanings towards operating as a team. It seems that the team-based evaluation system was constructive in "controlling" the execution of the new routines. The CEO stated:

"...The new team-based evaluation system was very useful in encouraging the cross functional teams to work collaboratively..." (CEO).

We can state here that the new "control oriented" assumptions became widely accepted in the company and they could be regarded as a new company culture. Following our observations and interviews with the stakeholders at various levels, we can remark that the B-to-B system was successfully implemented at TexCo. It is successful in the sense that both the users and top management are very satisfied with it (see Seddon, 1997; Seddon et al., 1999). In addition to being simple and user-friendly, the system solved any difficulties related to reporting, inventory control and invoicing control encountered by the company. The outlets' department manager remarked:

"...The new system has solved our problems. The success of the new system is that we are achieving profit and opening new outlets abroad at this time of recession that others are suffering from losses. We opened twelve new outlets in USA, Europe, Asia and Africa. Also the share of the outlets' department from the total sales of the company is raised from 10% in 1996 to around 50% in 2002..." (Outlets' department manager).

According to the outlets' department manager's claims, maintaining the stock in the factory under TexCo's control solved the inventory control problem. It resulted in reducing the textile wastage by about 6% of the stock balance. He remarked:

"...Now, the percentage of wastage is around 1-1.5%. The reduction in the wastage percentage has improved our profitability..." (Outlets' department manager).

One of the accountants additionally confirmed that the invoicing control problem ceased. He confirmed that he could now detect any recording error by the day's end, through comparing the orders entered on to the extranet by the bookkeepers (cashiers) with the invoices entered on to the AIS by himself. Any error made by the bookkeeper in entering the order would be detected by the next day on delivery. The accountant added:

"...Now the cashier in the outlet must enter the correct code and the correct quantity to the system. If there is any mistake, it is detected by the next day on delivering the order to the outlet. There is no way they could make deliberate mistakes now, as the distributor will bear them. Now the mistakes made by the cashiers do not exceed 0.5% and they are detected..." (Accountant 2).

From our observations we can state that the B-to-B application provides the company with accurate and timely information. For instance, it provides up to the minute reports including sales of each outlet, sales from each product, sales returns, stock turnover of each product, cash collections, pending invoices, the ten best outlets in terms of sales and their locations, the ten outlets with least sales, which outlets return most and the prime areas in sales. According to the CEO, these reporting facilities aid top management when making countless decisions related to sales, production, purchases, cash-flow management and determining the most suitable locations for opening new branches. It also facilitated the accurate and timely preparation of financial statements and budgets.

In addition to resolving the invoicing and reporting problems for management accountants, the B-to-B system altered their daily routine, authorities and responsibilities. The accountants in the outlets' department became more involved in the day-to-day operation of the business. An accountant is now responsible, as we previously mentioned, for co-ordinating production orders in tandem with the outlets' department manager via following up the reorder quantities of the various products and analysing the stock turnover using the system's reporting facilities. Another accountant is charged with tracking the orders sent through the extranet, sending a copy to the stores, entering them on to the AIS and providing feedback to the production department in case of sales returns. A third accountant is responsible for making the settlements with the outlets, using the system's reporting facilities, and tracking the cash collection. Finally, a fourth accountant is responsible for following up the accounts of other clients such as decorators. One of the accountants explained his new role as follows:

"...Now, my work is more dynamic. I become the link between the outlets and the production department; I am more involved in the operation of the company. My work now is communication and interpretation..." (Accountant 1).

In effect, by implementing the B-to-B in TexCo, the role of accountants has diversified from 'bean-counting'[10] towards 'business orientation' by allowing them to act more as business consultants rather than concentrating on financial reporting alone. Moreover, despite the reporting facilities offered by the B-to-B system, the accountant still has an important role within the organization. He is responsible for interpreting the accounting reports produced by the system. The outlets' department manager, from an IT background, displayed a high level of understanding of accounting information. Nevertheless, he still professed the need of the management accountant's services. In response to a question regarding the role of the accountant, he explained that he regarded him as necessary; this is because of his ability to interpret the accounting figures and to provide comprehensive understanding of the business. The outlets' department manager remarked:

"...The accountant is not a calculator. I believe that the accountant is a 'brain' that analyses and interprets the accounting figures and thinks with me. Anyone can make data entry but no one can interpret the accounting reports better than the accountant. He knows their meaning and can justify why figures have increased or decreased. His job is to help me in taking decisions and solve problems. He has to interpret the sales reports produced by the system, and prepare the production orders after assessing the consequences of the various courses of action. He has to find out the reasons of sales returns and feed back to the production department; find out why that outlet has low sales compared to others. He should follow up and try to solve the problems. The role of the accountant now is to answer those 'why' questions. It is the art of interpreting data that only the accountant can do...." (Outlets' department manager).

The new system has also facilitated the "settlement process" for the accountants. Prior to using the system, and in the situation of a conflict between the outlets' records and TexCo's records, they had to revise the transactions of the entire month to discover the fault, which occupied a great deal of time. However after implementing the system, as attested by the accountant, both the outlet's director and the accountant could log on and make the settlement for cash collection using the same report.

The system's reporting facilities offered the accountant and the outlets' department manager the necessary tools for evaluating the performance of the company's own outlets and controlling them. The accountant mentioned an interesting metaphor of the B-to-B application; he compared it to a camera that gave him a view of what passed at their outlets. He added:

"...I can now see each invoice on the screen at the moment it is made...now we could know their sales and sales returns moment by moment. Those reports also give us the opportunity to know their problems so that we could help them in solving it. For example, if the sales of an outlet decreases rapidly or is significantly less than other outlets, we could contact the outlet's director to find out the reason for that and try to find a solution..." (Accountant 1).

The reporting facilities also afford the accountants and the outlets' department manager a good instrument to control the collection of pending invoices. The outlets' department manager added:

"...Sometimes the customer makes down payment and pays the residual amount when he has the product. In some cases the customer could be late 2-3 days in receiving the order and thereby does not pay the residual amount. In such cases the outlet director must call him to find out the reason. If the director is late in collecting such invoices, we call him to investigate the issue. So this kind of report is a good tool to control the collection of pending invoices. Now the outlets' directors couldn't leave the pending invoices for a long time..." (Outlets' department manager).

Finally, having the stock in the factory resulted in saving the time and effort of the accountants during the stocktaking process[11]. The outlets' department manager added:

"...Before using the system the stocktaking is made at the end of each quarter, and it used to take a long time. This is because the outlets are scattered in different places and the stock balance was huge. However, now, we have the stock in one place, our stores. So this saved the time and effort of the accountants. They now make the stocktaking only once a year and in one place..." (Outlets' department manager).

In TexCo, B-to-B electronic commerce poses management accountants with new challenges. As such, it represents both an opportunity and a threat. CIMA in its Membership Survey (July 1998) suggests:

"Those who grasp the opportunity presented by the new technology and 'bend' it to their advantage may reap the benefits of a wider and more varied role, with greater management responsibilities, and perhaps greater rewards, and more involvement in business strategy. Those who resist the change will find themselves increasingly 'sidelined' as computers take over many of the more mundane tasks, and other managers are better able to access and understand basic financial information" (in Mathews, 1998, p. 68).

REFERENCES

Burns, J., Ezzamel, M., & Scapens, R. W. (2003). *The challenge of management accounting change: Behavioural and cultural aspects of change management*. London, UK: CIMA Publications.

Burns, J., & Scapens, R. (2000). Conceptualising management accounting change: An institutional framework. *Management Accounting Research, 11*(1), 3–25.

Chesher, M. (1999). *Electronic commerce and business communications*. London, UK: Springer-Verlag London Limited.

Hamilton, W. (1932). Institutions. In Seligman, E. R. A., & Johnson, A. (Eds.), *Encyclopedia of social science* (pp. 560–595).

Hardy, C. (1996). Understanding power: Bringing about strategic change. *British Journal of Management*, *7*, 3–16.

Horngren, C. T., Bhimani, A., Foster, G., & Datar, S. M. (1999). *Management and cost accounting*. London, UK: Prentice-Hall Europe.

Laudon, K. C., & Laudon, J. P. (2004). *Management Information Systems: Managing the digital firm*. New Jersey: Pearson Education, Inc.

Lyne, R. S., & Friedman, A. L. (1997). Activity-based techniques and the death of the beancounter. *European Accounting Review*, *6*(1), 2–20.

Mathews, S. (1998). The changing role of the management accountant: And its implications for qualification development. *Management Accounting*, *76*(8), 68–69.

Seddon, P. B. (1997). A respecification and extension of the Delone and Mclean model of IS success. *Information Systems Research*, *8*(3), 240–253.

Seddon, P. B., Staples, D. S., Patnayakuni, R., & Bowtell, M. J. (1999). Dimensions of Information Systems success. *Communications of the Association for Information Systems*, *2*(3).

Support for Environmental Assessment and Management Project. (1999). *Textile sector report, Egypt*. Retrieved on April 25, 2010, from http://www.eeaa.gov.eg/seam/Manuals/TextileSector-Report/Part%20A.PDF

Wilson, R. M. S., & Chua, W. (1994). *Managerial accounting: Method and meaning* (2nd ed.). London, UK: Chapman and Hall.

Zwass, V. (2003). Electronic commerce and organizational innovation: Aspects and opportunities. *International Journal of Electronic Commerce*, *7*(3), 7–37.

KEY TERMS AND DEFINITIONS

B-to-B E-Commerce: B-to-B e-commerce involves sales of goods and services among businesses (see Laudon and Laudon, 2004, p. 118). Many companies exchange business documents (purchase orders, invoices, remittance advice, etc.) with their trading partners using private Electronic Data Interchange (EDI) technology (Chesher, 1999, p. 41). However, the trend in business today is to use the public Internet and Web as the vehicle for B-to-B e-commerce. For Web-based B-to-B e-commerce, companies can sell to other businesses using their own Web sites as electronic storefronts or they can execute purchase and sale transactions through Net marketplaces or extranets.

Electronic Commerce: Zwass (2003, p. 8) refers to e-commerce as: "The sharing of business information, maintaining business relationships, and conducting business transactions by means of telecommunications networks."

Extranet: Extranets are considered the fastest growing segment of B-to-B e-commerce. The extranet permits the firm and its designated suppliers, distributors, and other business partners to share production scheduling, inventory management, and unstructured communication, including graphics and e-mail.

Institutions: A commonly used definition of 'institution' is, "a way of thought or action of some prevalence and permanence, which is embedded in the habits of a group or the customs of a people" (Hamilton, 1932, p. 84). It mirrors the notion of 'culture'.

Management Accountants: Wilson and Chua (1994, p. 7) stated that the job labeled 'management accountant' is not applied consistently in different organizations. Instead it is used to refer to a disparate range of jobs, types of task, level of seniority and responsibility. This breadth of tasks is partly a reflection of the sheer diversity of organizations that management accountants now work within. In a small family business, the management accountant may maintain all the bookkeeping and cost records and prepare the financial statements. In a large enterprise, there are likely to be several ranks of management accountants, each of which performs specific tasks.

Management Accounting: Horngren et al. (1999, p. 5) point out that "Management accounting measures and reports financial as well as other types of information that are primarily intended to assist managers in fulfilling the goals of the organization".

Power of the system: Involving the unconscious acceptance of the values, traditions, cultures and structures of a given organization. It captures all organizational actors in its web.

Power over decision-making: Exerting influence over subordinates' participation in decision–making processes.

Power over meaning: Influencing actors' perceptions, cognitions and/or preferences in order that they accept the status quo or, rather, become convinced that change is "desirable", "rational" and/or "legitimate".

Power over resources: Actors deploying (or restricting) key resources to modify the behavior of others.

Routines: Routines refer to practices actually in use.

Rules: By rules Burns and Scapens (2000) refer to the formally recognized way in which 'things should be done', being necessary to co-ordinate and give coherence to the actions of individuals or groups.

ENDNOTES

1 We conceal its true identity for confidentiality reasons.

2 The company is known as one of the major players in the Egyptian textiles market. However, the CEO is very sensitive about providing us with any information whatsoever related to its capital or profit.

3 He is one of the four accountants working in the outlets' department. He obtained a Bachelor of Commerce degree in 1993, and worked in TexCo soon after his graduation.

4 (GATT) stands for the General Agreement on Trade and Tariffs. GAAT 1994 agreement, on textiles and clothing, aims to liberalize trade through the elimination of trade barriers by the year 2005.

5 According to the Central Agency for Public Mobilization and Statistics (CAPMAS) the unemployment rates in Egypt in 1996-1998 (when the change in TexCo took place) was ranging between 7.9%-8.2%.

6 Due to free post-secondary education in Egypt, a large number of accounting students (around 15,000) are graduated each year from the Egyptian universities.

7 The Egyptian government does not offer any benefits for unemployed workers.

8 Preceding this time, in TexCo, new designs were produced and stored. Clearance of stock located in the outlets was made and the outlets re-decorated.

9 NetCo is a 100% Egyptian corporation that started working in the IS market in 1998. We conceal its true identity for confidentiality reasons.

10 Lyne and Friedman (1997) concluded that operational managers regard accountants as 'bean counters'. Operational managers used this term in order to show accountants as people who do not understand the business and whose only preoccupation is the mechanical execution of tasks, i.e., counting beans.

11 The production manager mentioned that the system encouraged them to reduce the stock balance from each product and increase their designs. He stated that they are now using their production capacity in producing many more design collections than before.

Chapter 4
A Comparative Analysis of Activity-Based Costing and Traditional Costing Systems:
The Case of Egyptian Metal Industries Company

Khaled Samaha
School of Business, AUC, Egypt

Sara Abdallah
British University in Egypt (BUE), Egypt

EXECUTIVE SUMMARY

Today, organizational environments are increasingly characterized by an expanding use of advanced technologies. A company's management accounting system should capture the underlying technology, be consistent with corporate commitment to total quality and increased automation, and promote its efforts to compete on the basis of cost, quality, and lead time. However, the recent literature reveals that traditional cost accounting systems systematically introduce serious product cost distortions, which lead to inappropriate strategic decisions. Activity-Based Costing (ABC) represents an alternative paradigm that is giving more accurate and traceable cost information. The objective of this case is to illustrate the application of ABC method in a single manufacturing organization operating in the metal industry and to compare the results of ABC with volume based costing (traditional costing) method. The results of the application highlight the weak points of volume based costing which assigns factory overhead costs using direct labor-hours or machine-hours as a cost driver. As a result, volume-based costing under-costs low-volume product (i.e. products requiring fewer direct labor hours in total), while it over-costs high-volume products (i.e. products requiring more direct labor-hours in total), and thus, a product is subsidized at the expense of others. In cost accounting this is called cross-subsidization. However, activity-based costing traces overhead consumption by each product and thus provides a more accurate per-unit overhead cost.

DOI: 10.4018/978-1-60960-583-4.ch004

1- ORGANIZATION BACKGROUND

Egyptian Metal Industries Co. (Metalco), an ISO 9002 certified company, was established in 1987 as the first Egyptian manufacturing company in the field of 'Hot Water Boiler and Radiators'. With headquarters in Egypt, Metalco provides superior quality products, serving both the domestic and international sectors. After over 20 years of long experience, and being always on top of all forms of new scientific improvement and technical developments, its research and development teams were able to further improve the production of hot water boilers to a more practical and higher efficient 'Hot Water Boilers', while maintaining the superior quality and designs that Metalco associates its name with. These new hot water boilers were given a new brand name "*Kinz*" which translates to the word "Treasure".

Heat exchangers are common components in many of the everyday devices. Central heating boilers and radiators all contain heat exchangers. Their purpose is to transfer heat from a hot liquid or gas to a colder one. In industry, steam is often used for heating and cold water for cooling. A variety of heat exchangers have been designed to suit the range of heating or cooling applications. Boiler and radiator heating systems are already green in many respects, since they are one of the cleanest heating systems around when it comes to fostering good indoor air quality - a big plus in green remodeling circles. Nevertheless, boiler or radiator heating system can still benefit from going green, especially when it comes to reducing the heating costs and improving the energy efficiency.

In 2005, the total world domestic boiler market was estimated at $ 10.9 billion and 10.46 million units, while it is expected to grow at a moderate rate over the next few years. The United Kingdom is the biggest market in both value and volume terms, followed by South Korea and Italy. Growth rates vary significantly between countries, with smaller markets generally offering higher growth potential. These are found in North Africa, the Middle East and Central Asia, with double-digit growth forecast in Kazakhstan, Tunisia, Morocco, Jordan and Turkey up to 2010. The growth expected in these markets occurs from a low base.

Today, Meltaco Company is one of Egypt's most mature manufacturing sectors operations, exclusively distributing and servicing more than 70,000 clients both in Egypt and in the world. Meltaco's goal is to exceed the expectations of every client by offering outstanding customer service, increased flexibility, and greater value, thus optimizing system functionality and improving operation efficiency. Meltaco associates are distinguished by their functional and technical expertise combined with their hands-on experience, thereby ensuring that our clients receive the most effective and professional service. Meltaco Company's policy is to provide a culture of continual improvement that is committed to exceed Customer expectations and requirements, by providing products and services of excellent quality. Customer support is number one at Meltaco Company

Meltaco Company is caring to develop its employee's staff and provide them with good work environment to achieve its goals and to maintain highly regarded performance level. Currently, it has a staff of 10 managers and 50 professionally trained maintenance personnel available 24 hours a day, 7 days a week to service all clients' needs. The company offers many different service plans. Meltaco's professional sales staff would assist the clients in choosing the best system of boilers or water heaters to meet their specific needs. The company warranties all its equipment, installation and spare parts. Customers are welcome to stop by the Spare Parts Department. While there, the company's professionally trained personnel will consult with each client to find the spare parts and equipment they need for their operation.

Meltaco produces a wide range of hot water boilers, including residential boilers, commercial boilers, swimming pool boilers, water heaters and laundry equipments. The most significant highly demanded product lines are Commercial Boiler (COM) and Residential Boiler (RES). Between those two products' lines, capacities range from 30,000 Kcal/hr up to 2,240,000 Kcal/hr. Each boiler type is produced in three types (1) Gas Boiler and (2) Oil Boiler and (3) Electric Boiler.

Seeking adequate operational information flow, the firm invests approximately 5% of their $30 million annual turnover in information systems adaptation. However, due to the information technology rapid advances, the company's management realizes the emerging need to update its current working systems. Top management support is imperative within this organization as they are the ones making the decisions. The organization seems to be under developed with regard to accounting information system (AIS) strategy planning; however they don't believe that it is a major problem. It is apparent that the president of the firm believes that investing in AIS will give a significant financial return. This shows a commitment by top management to forecast the long term benefits of AIS.

2- SETTING THE STAGE

Nour Khaled, the Factory Accountant, was sitting in a meeting with Glenn Hoddle, the General Manager of Egyptian Metal Industries Co. They were reviewing the March 2010 quarter's management accounts and discussing cost information on the company's two main product lines.

The general manager of the company was in full flight, frustrated as ever with the output from the company's costing system. 'How can it be? I just don't understand it. We've been losing business on the Residential Boilers line over the past quarter. Yet, your data indicates that it's our most profitable product. It doesn't seem logical to me.'

Glenn continued.........

Hisham Ibrahim (the Production Manager) insists that the Residential Boilers is so much harder to make than the commercial boilers range. How can it cost less to manufacture? Magda Khaled (the Sales Manager) is absolutely confident that, if they could reduce the commercial boilers selling price, they would see an even higher increase in sales. Are you sure that these costs are correct? How have you computed the overhead content of each product cost?'

Khaled had covered this ground on many previous occasions with Hoddle and, yet again, set out to explain the operation of the company's costing system. In particular, she detailed the different steps in the allocation of overhead to the two product lines.

The overhead allocation process involves two separate steps. General Factory Overhead is spread across the two production departments (Assembly and Test) on the basis of the direct labor cost incurred in each department. The relevant portions of General Factory Overhead are then added to the separate overhead costs of the Assembly and Test departments before being divided by the total amount of direct labor hours required in each department. This exercise produces an overhead rate per direct labor hour for each production department. We then determine factory overhead rate for the entire production (i.e. plant-wide rate). Finally, we go on to apply that overhead per direct labor hour to the individual product's usage of direct labor hours (see Figure 1). We have used the same approach for years - long before we introduced the current products. No one has ever queried it. It's always worked before,..'

Before Khaled could continue, Hoddle interrupted her. It was clear that Hoddle was far more than impressed with this detailed and complicated explanation.

'Hmmm... Nour, plain common sense tells me that it's time to look again at the way we

Figure 1. Current overhead allocation in Metalco: A single plant wide rate

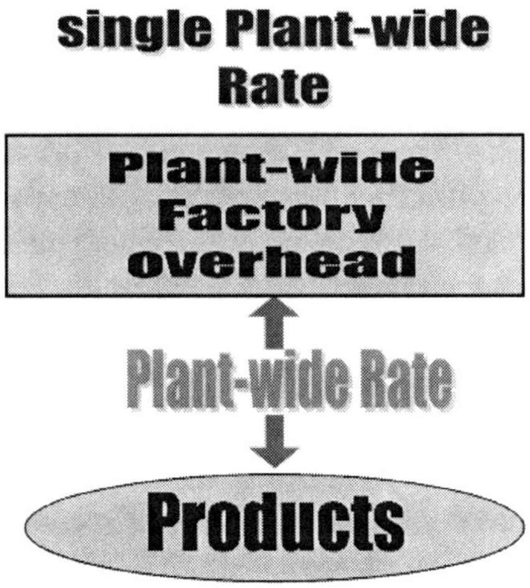

tackle costing. I was talking to Romani George at Liverpool Products limited last week and he said that his company had brought in something called XYZ, or was it ABC - some kind of new approach to costing. Would that be any simpler than that we do now? More important, do you think that it would produce any better quality cost data? Can you find out about it and let me know? We need fast answers on this - there are some good market opportunities out there, but we need to be in a position to respond to them. Come back to me as soon as you have had an opportunity to look into this.' In other words, the General Manager asked Khaled to provide a detailed analysis on *Overhead Allocation under the present costing system, and detailed computations on the effect of the implementation of an ABC approach on the allocation of total factory overhead.*

3- CHALLENGES FACING THE ORGANIZATION

A potential problem with this company's costing system is that overhead is calculated based upon direct labor cost, which is not the driving force behind the incurrence of the indirect costs in this company. Further, decision making regarding the company's product lines is not supported adequately to be of use to management.

Because volume-based costing uses an aggregate rate rather than a specific one, it loses a lot of information and control over product costs. A selected volume-based cost driver (e.g. direct labor-hours) might have little to do with how factory overhead costs accumulate. This can cause not only product price distortions, but it can also decrease the incentives for department managers to control product costs.

In traditional costing systems, direct materials and direct labor are the only cost components that can be traced directly to the product. Traditional costing systems were designed in the late nineteenth and early twentieth centuries, where the business environment was far less automated and the product line heterogeneity was less common. In this early era, the direct materials and direct labor truly reflect the primary components of the production costs, indirect overhead costs were relatively low, and the distortions arising from inappropriate overhead allocations were not significant. Information processing costs were high, and it was therefore difficult to justify more sophisticated overhead allocation (Xiong et al., 2008). However, today with far more automated production environment and companies produce a wide range of products, direct labor represents only a small fraction of total costs, and overhead indirect costs are far more of considerable importance. Such increase in indirect costs causes the overhead component to be the truly production prime costs. Simplistic overhead allocations using a declining direct labor base cannot be justified, particularly when information processing costs are no longer a barrier to introducing more sophisticated systems.

The increase in overhead cost portions distorts the product costing as traditional costing systems aggregate these overhead costs to product lines, and apply the aggregated overhead on a basis not necessarily consistent with the resources consumed by the product lines. Traditional overhead allocations are based on volume related bases (based on direct labor, direct materials, or machine hours), which may not be the driving force of the overhead activities. However, many organizational resources exist for activities that are unrelated to physical volume. Non-volume-related activities include probable support activities such as material handling, material procurement, set-ups, and production scheduling and first-item inspection activities. Also, the consumption of resources in production may differ extensively among product lines. Some costs or departmental cost pools may apply to a single or a few product lines, rather than to all products. Traditional product cost systems, which assume that products consume all resources in proportion to their production volumes, thus report distorted product costs (Hicks, 2006). Cooper and Kaplan (1988) claimed that the commonly used systematic overhead allocation methods distorts production costs, resulting in under-costing of low volume products and over-costing of high volume products, and thus, producing unreliable product costs to be utilized by management in attempt to control costs in the current highly competitive markets.

According to Cooper (1989), the traditional product costing misrepresentation could be regard to three prominent causes: (1) the failure to use direct costing where it is economically "feasible". In spite of the fact that advances in information technology have greatly reduced the costs associated with tracking and assigning costs to specific products and services, many companies under-utilize this technology. Rather than using meters to measure different products' energy consumptions, motion sensors to detect the amount of time employees spend at given tasks, and bar codes to help calculate the costs associated with moving specific materials and finished products, the majority of companies allow these costs to lapse into a general, catch-all category called 'overhead'; (2) the failure to segregate overhead costs into unique cost pools. All costs that cannot be classified as direct materials or direct labor the company categorizes into one cost pool, or at best a mere handful of cost pools. No attempt is made to separate overhead costs into common overhead cost categories. As a result, the company's ability to associate overhead costs with specific products, services, customers, or some other equally important attribute is blunted.(3) The failure to apply appropriate cost allocation bases. Just as there is often only one or a very limited number of overhead cost pools, so too there is often only one or a very limited number of cost drivers used to allocate the overhead costs. Frequently, direct labor hours or direct labor dollars are used to allocate the overhead costs. Critics have long charged that such a practice is antiquated and outmoded as labor costs as a percentage of product, and even service, are rapidly decreasing. For many of today's manufacturers direct labor costs represent less than 10 per cent of the product's total cost. Therefore, say these critics, the allocation of over-head based on direct labor is likely to result in distorted product costs.

In light of the above, Metalco Company may be operating with distorted product cost information, and thus likely to make incorrect pricing and product mix decisions. In particular, the company's general manager fears are stemming from the fact that the company may believe it is incapable of matching its competitors' prices on the high volume business, and thus likely to become increasingly committed to chasing the illusory profits that its cost accounting system suggests are available on the low volume business. Invariably the company ends up with low market share, high per unit overhead costs, and large losses. Ironically, therefore, it is often the company itself, or more precisely the accounting function, that strikes the mortal blow.

4- CASE DESCRIPTION

Nour left the General Manager's office, suppressing an inward groan. She had heard of ABC - activity based costing - but she was uncertain whether it would bring any benefits to the company's costing system.

Her main concern was that any change to the company's costing system would be painful to introduce and involve her in a considerable amount of extra work.

For the next month, Nour threw herself into acquiring as much knowledge as possible on ABC. She obtained copies of a couple of new text-books and scanned the ABC case study examples to see if they were relevant to the company. She contacted the accountant at Liverpool to learn from their experience in ABC implementation.

Nour noticed that an activity-based costing (ABC) system is a complex cost system that provides detailed and accurate information about each product's cost and thus each product's profitability. The ABC system is very expensive and time-consuming system to implement due to the high cost of collecting, measuring, and recording production information, especially for her company that is producing many different products that require hundreds of various activities. For a large company like Metalco, it might take millions of dollars and many years to develop and implement an ABC system. Despite its high cost, ABC systems have many benefits to offer.

The Advantages of an Activity-Based Costing System

An activity-based costing system has the following advantages:

Accurate product cost and product and customer profitability measurement: An ABC system provides accurate and detailed product information that can be utilized by management in decision making process. It can help to make better-informed management decisions concerning product pricing, product volumes, market segments, product lines, and target costing.

- Better-informed strategic decisions: The information about cost drivers for each activity enables management to make better-informed decisions concerning product design, customer support, etc.
- Production improvement: An ABC system provides information helpful in improving production processes.
- Better product cost information: An ABC system provides a lot of information necessary for strategic budgeting, planning, and product pricing decisions. It also takes into consideration cost of unused capacity and measures it at all levels (i.e. product, batch, and facility-levels).

Mechanics of ABC implementation

Nour recognized that there are five main steps involved in the implementation of ABC. These steps consist of:

1. identifying activities;
2. determining the costs of activities;
3. identifying cost drivers for each activity;
4. determining the annual capacity for the activity;
5. calculating the activity overhead rate.

The first step in implementing ABC is the identification of activities. Activities are best viewed as groupings of related actions. For example, the activity called 'machine set-up' is the outcome of a variety of individual actions. These actions might include cleaning or flushing the machine of any residue remaining from the previous batch that was run, adjusting the feed and speed of the machine for the new batch's requirements, and inspecting the first item produced to ensure that it conforms to the product's standards for fitness.

The second step in implementing ABC involves determining the costs of activities. Continuing with the machine set-up example used above, all the costs involved in executing machine set-ups need to be accumulated.

The third step in the implementation of ABC involves the selection of cost drivers. Actually, this third step consists of two sub stages.

The first-sub stage requires the identification of what are commonly called first-stage drivers. First-stage drivers trace the costs of inputs or resources into the cost pools that comprise each activity; remember an activity consists of a number of company-defined interrelated actions. It is possible, for instance, that a company may wish to include as a set-up cost the costs of moving material from inventory storage to the shop floor. Consequently, it is for this reason that an activity may consist of a number of cost pools. The appropriateness of these first-stage drivers has an important influence on the accuracy of the calculated product costs. Poorly chosen, first-stage drivers will likely jeopardize the usefulness and accuracy of the ABC system. The cost distortions that may arise will ripple through the ABC system and potentially be exaggerated by the more prone to error second-stage drivers. It is to this reason that companies may wish to trace the consumption of resources directly (as opposed to allocating them) to cost pools.

Second-sub stage drivers are used to allocate the cost pool overheads to products. The cost driver chosen should relate to the product's consumption of the particular activity's cost pool.

The fourth stage in the implementation of ABC requires the determination of the annual capacity for each activity. For example, if set-up hours are used as the cost driver for assigning the costs related to machine set-ups, then the company must determine the number of hours it has made available and therefore committed to this activity.

The fifth stage of ABC implementation involves the calculation of activity over-head rates. Let us say for the sake of illustration that 15,000 hours of machine set-up have been made available for the year at a cost of $ 600,000. Then the overhead rate for the set-up activity is $40 per set-up hour. This $40 rate will be used not only to cost products, but can also be used for the purpose of budgeting as well.

Activity-based costing focuses on the relative differences in assigning support costs. It uses the experience of operations people, and quantitative information, where available, to develop causal relationships between work drivers (what causes work to be done) and work to be done (activities). It allows the value of each activity to be assessed, identifies the factors that cause the activity to happen, and gives a true representation of the unit of measure of those activities (Figure 2).

5- COMPARATIVE ANALYSIS AND PRACTICAL INSIGHTS: TRADITIONAL VERSUS ABC

To better understand the differences between the traditional and activity-based costing and how those differences affect product profitability analysis as well as management decisions, we will look at the Egyptian Metal industries company (Metalco) which has the data shown in Table 1 for the two products.

Using a Volume-Based Costing System

Under traditional costing, the factory overhead cost is assigned based on direct labor-hours (DLH). The factory overhead rate is determined as follows:

Figure 2. ABC looks at what drives the cost

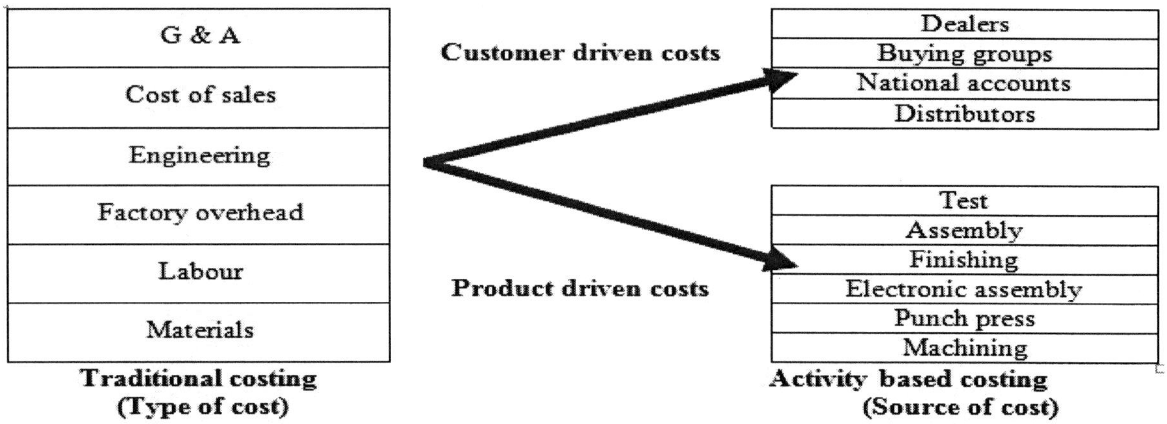

Factory Overhead Rate per DLH =

$$\frac{Total\ Factory\ Overhead}{Total\ DLH}$$

In this case, the factory overhead rate per DLH = $600,000 / 50,000 = $12 per DLH (i.e. plant-wide rate). Using this information, we can determine the total amount of factory overhead assigned to each product and the factory overhead cost per unit for both products (see Table 2).

Now we can calculate the unit margin profit for each product and determine how profitable the products are (see Table 3).

Table 1. Cost data for the two major products

	RES	COM
Production Volume	10,000	5,000
Selling Price	$78.00	$130.00
Unit prime cost	$21.00	$35.00
Direct labor-hours	30,000	20,000
Direct labor-hours per unit	3	4
Budgeted factory overhead	$600,000	
Budgeted direct labor-hours	50,000	

Therefore, using the volume-based costing we can see that the product COM is much more profitable than the product RES. However, let's use the activity-based costing and see if we can get the same or similar results.

Using an Activity-Based Costing (ABC)

Nour was able to gather some thoughts on other possible approaches to the apportionment of overheads. At last, she felt that he was ready for another meeting with the General Manager. Over the two weeks, Nour has assembled information which she believes will be relevant to the implementation of an ABC approach. In particular, she has reviewed

Table 2. Factory overhead cost per unit under traditional costing

	RES	COM
Factory overhead cost per DLH	$12.00 per DLH	
Direct labor hours	30,000	20,000
Factory overhead assigned	$360,000	$240,000
Production volume (in units)	10,000	5,000
Factory overhead cost per unit	***$36.00***	***$48.00***

Note: $360,000 = $12.00 x 30,000 and $240,000 = $12.00 x 20,000.

Table 3. Unit margin profit for each product under traditional costing

		RES	COM
Unit Selling Price	A	$78.00	$130.00
Less: Unit Prime Cost	B	($21.00)	($35.00)
Less: Unit Overhead Cost	C	($36.00)	($48.00)
Unit Margin	*D=A-B-C*	*$21.00*	*$47.00*
Unit Margin Percentage	*E=D/A × 100%*	*26.92%*	*36.15%*

Note C: $36.00 = $12.00 x 3 hrs and $48.00 = $12.00 x 4 hrs.

Table 4. Activities, costs, and activity consumption cost drivers

Activity	Budgeted Cost	Cost Driver
Machine set-ups	$100,000	Number of set-ups
Machine running	$400,000	Machine-hours
Inspection	$70,000	Inspection-hours
Packing	$30,000	Number of packing-orders
Total	*$600,000*	

Table 5. Activity data for each product

Cost Driver	RES	COM	Total
Number of set-ups	80	260	340
Machine-hours	18,000	36,000	54,000
Inspection-hours	3,000	4,000	7,000
Number of packing-orders	2,100	3,500	5,600

Table 6. Activity cost rate

Cost Driver	Cost ($)	Activity Amount	Activity Rate ($)
	A	B	C=A/B
Number of Set-ups	100,000	340	294.12
Machine-hours	400,000	54,000	7.41
Inspection-hours	70,000	7,000	10.00
Number of packing-orders	30,000	5,600	5.36

the content of total factory overhead (including Assembly and Test departments' overheads) and considered how to set up appropriate cost pools and identify cost drivers.

Nour has identified the activities, costs, and activity consumption cost drivers shown in Table 4.

Nour also collected the activity data for each product (see Table 5).

Using the total cost for each activity and the total amount of activity cost driver we can determine the activity cost rate (see Table 6).

As we can see from Table 6, one set-up costs $294.12, one machine-hour costs $7.41, one inspection-hour costs $10, and one packing order costs $5.36. Now, let's calculate the per-unit cost of each product manufactured by Metalco Company (see Table 7).

The allocation of factory overhead using activity-based costing is summarized in Figure 3.

Using the obtained data we can perform the product profitability analysis; that is, we will determine the unit margin profit of each product (see Table 8).

According to the data presented in Table 8, the COM product is actually $22.57 ($37.18−$14.61) less profitable than the RES product. The unit margin percentage for the COM product is lower than the one for the RES product when using the activity-based costing. Therefore, the management of Metalco Company might consider changing the production process of the COM product (e.g. increase batch-size to decrease the cost of machine set-ups per item produced) and increasing the selling price (i.e. as long as the increase in selling price would not substantially decrease product sales).

Using this example we can see that activity-based costing provides a lot of information about production activities and how they affect the cost of products, which the volume-based costing system does not explain.

Table 7. Per-unit cost of each product manufactured under ABC

RES (10000 units)				
Activity Cost Driver	**Activity Rate**	**Activity Amount**	**Total Overhead**	**Overhead per Unit**
	A	B	C=A x B	D = C /10,000
Number of Set-ups	$ 294.12	80	23,529.60	$ 2.35
Machine-hours	7.41	18,000	133,380.00	13.34
Inspection-hours	10.00	3,000	30,000.00	3.00
Number of packing-orders	5.36	2,100	11,256.00	1.13
Total				*19.82*
COM (5000 units)				
Activity Cost Driver	**Activity Rate**	**Activity Amount**	**Total Overhead**	**Overhead per Unit**
	A	B	C=A x B	D = C /5,000
Number of Set-ups	$ 294.12	260	$ 76,471.20	$ 15.29
Machine-hours	7.41	36,000	266,760.00	53.35
Inspection-hours	10.00	4,000	40,000.00	8.00
Number of packing-orders	5.36	3,500	18,760.00	3.75
Total				*80.39*

Table 8. Unit margin profit for each product under ABC

		RES	**COM**
Unit selling price	A	$78.00	$130.00
Less: Unit prime cost	B	($21.00)	($35.00)
Less: Unit overhead cost	C	($19.82)	($80.39)
Unit margin	*D = A-B-C*	*$37.18*	*$14.61*
Unit margin percentage	*E=D/A x 100%*	*47.67%*	*11.24%*

Table 9. Product profitability analyses under volume-based and activity-based costing

	Volume-based costing		**Activity-based costing**	
	RES	**COM**	**RES**	**COM**
Unit selling price	$78.00	$130.00	$78.00	$130.00
Less: Unit prime cost	($21.00)	($35.00)	($21.00)	($35.00)
Less: Unit overhead cost	($36.00)	($48.00)	($19.83)	($80.39)
Unit margin	*$21.00*	*$47.00*	*$37.18*	*$14.61*
Unit margin percentage	*26.92%*	*36.15%*	*47.67%*	*11.24%*

Figure 3. Factory overhead using activity-based costing

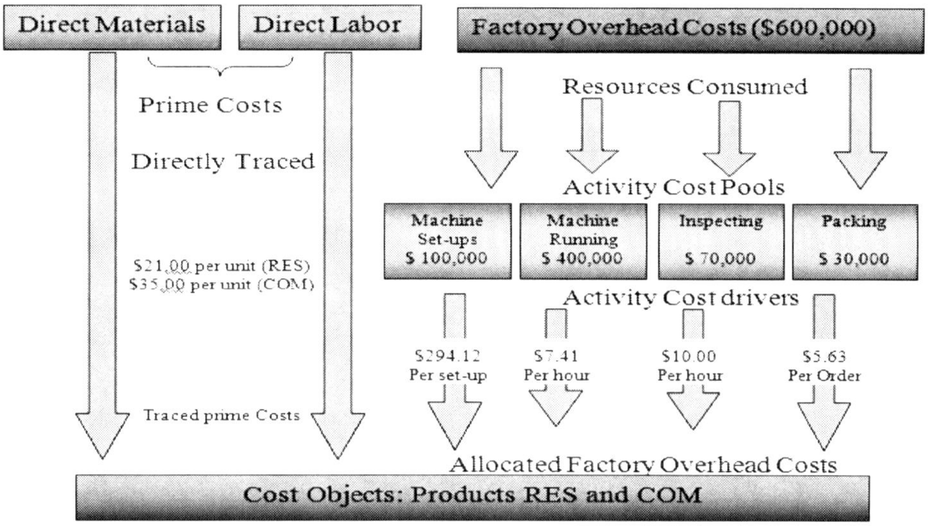

Let's compare the product profitability analyses under volume-based and activity-based costing (see Table 9).

As we can see from Table 9, the product per-unit cost and per-unit margin profit differ under the volume-based and activity-based costing. The reason is that activity-based costing traces overhead consumption by each product and thus provides a more accurate per-unit overhead cost.

On the other hand, volume-based costing assigns factory overhead costs using direct labor-hours or machine-hours as a cost driver. As a result, volume-based costing under-costs the low-volume products (i.e. products requiring fewer direct labor hours in total), while it over-costs high-volume products (i.e. products requiring more direct labor-hours in total). In our example, the production of RES product and COM product required 30,000 and 20,000 direct labor-hours, respectively. Therefore, the overhead per unit cost for products RES and COM were overstated and understated, accordingly.

Using the data obtained under the activity-based costing, for example, we can see that the overhead per-unit cost of product RES is overstated by $16.18 (i.e. $16.18 = $36.00 – $19.82) under the volume-based costing because the production of RES requires more direct labor-hours (in total). Thus, a product – COM in this case – is subsidized at the expense of others. In cost accounting this is called cross-subsidization.

REFERENCES

Cooper, R. (1989). You need a new cost system when.... *Harvard Business Review*, (Jan-Feb): 77–82.

Cooper, R., & Kaplan, R. S. (1988). How cost accounting systematically distorts product costs. *Management Accounting Quarterly*, 20-27. London.

Searcy, D. L. (2004). Using activity-based costing to assess channel/customer profitability. *Management Accounting Quarterly,* Winter, 51-60.

Thomas, M. F., & Mackey, J. (2006). Supply chain management: Monitoring strategic partnering contracts with activity-based measures. *Management Accounting Quarterly,* Fall, 1-10.

Thorne, H., & Gurd, B. (1999). Activity-based costing: Improved product costing or activity management? *Advances in Management Accounting*, *8*, 173–194.

Turney, P. B. B. (1992). What an activity-based cost model looks like. *Journal of Cost Management,* Winter, 54-60.

Xiong, Y., Su, W., & Lin, T. W. (2008). Activity-based costing popularity in China. *Cost Management,* May/June, 40-48.

KEY TERMS AND DEFINITIONS

Activity Cost Driver Rate: Is calculated by dividing activity expenses by the total quantity of the activity cost driver (e.g. machine set up expenses divided by total number of machine set up hours).

Activity-Based Costing (ABC): Is a product costing system when a company allocates factory overhead costs to activity centers (e.g. machine set ups, running machines) and then uses activity cost drivers to allocate factory overhead costs to individual products or services

Actual Costing: Is a product costing system when a company measures actual costs of direct materials, direct labor, and factory overhead. Actual costing system is rarely used because it does not provide accurate information on a timely basis: many costs can be measured only at the end of the production, and some actual costs fluctuate a lot leading to potential errors in price recording.

An activity Cost Driver: Is a quantity of activities needed to produce a product (e.g. 'machine set ups' activity center will have set-up hours as the activity cost driver).

Job Costing: Is a product costing system when costs are accumulated by specific job orders (e.g. Job Order XX2, Job Order 02357) and assigned to batches of products. In other words, manufacturing costs are assigned to specific jobs: specific customers, specific orders, specific projects, specific contracts, etc. Job costing is often used by small and medium-sized firms. Also, it is often used in the following industries: professional services (e.g. medical, legal), advertising agencies, construction, shipbuilding, custom equipment/furniture manufacturing, etc.

Normal Costing: Is a product costing system when a company measures the actual costs of direct materials and direct labor, but uses predetermined factory overhead rates to measure the factory overhead cost for a period. In other words, throughout the production time, the company measures and records the actual costs of direct materials and direct labor used, but it estimates a portion of factory overhead to be assigned to the product(s) (i.e. factory overhead applied). Normal costing system provides a timely cost estimate of a product or batch of products.

Process Costing: Is a product costing system when costs are accumulated by departments or processes (e.g. Printing Department, Assembling Department) and assigned to a large number of homogenous, identical products. In other words, manufacturing costs are assigned to each process in each manufacturing department: assembling costs (including direct materials, direct labor, and factory overhead) in the assembling department; cost of printing (direct labor, direct materials, and factory overhead) in the printing department, etc. Process costing is usually used by companies characterized by continuous mass production (i.e. firms that produce one or a few homogenous products). Process costing is often used in the following industries: textiles, food processing, automobile manufacturing, and electronics.

Standard Costing: Is a product costing system when a company measures all costs – direct materials, direct labor, and factory overhead – using standard quantities and costs.

Volume-Based Costing: Also called traditional costing, is a product costing system when a company allocates factory overhead costs to a single cost pool (e.g. factory overhead) and then uses volume based cost drivers to allocate factory overhead costs to individual products or services. The company uses volume-based cost drivers that depend on number of units manufactured. Cost bases (or drivers) often used are: labor hours, machine hours, labor costs, etc.

An easy way to remember the relationship between products: activity cost drivers, and resources, is to recall that products consume activities and activities consume resources.

Section 2
Finance

Change requires strategic response that may impact sources and allocation of funds. The first case, "Centralizing Long Range Planning and Budgeting at AUC," details the process and technical aspects of AUC's transition to a centralized and synchronized planning and budgeting cycle. The system is focused on determining appropriate workflows and leveraging database technologies to track planning initiatives throughout an approvals process. The second case, "Premium International for Credit Card Services," examines the concept of value-based management, and how applying it to the company's restructuring process would help PICS's management track its performance and make sound strategic decisions for the company. The third case, "Alexandria Minerals Oils Company," deals with the process and underlying motives for Initial Public Offerings (IPOs). AMOC, a government owned company, was seeking partial privatization through an IPO. The outcome of the IPO raised major concern because the resulting high P/E ratio was perceived as an obstacle to attracting strategic investors.

Chapter 5
Centralizing Integrated Long Range Planning and Budgeting

Taylor Valore
American University in Cairo (AUC), Egypt

EXECUTIVE SUMMARY

Upon relocation to a new, state-of-the-art, 260-acre campus outside of Cairo, Egypt, the American University in Cairo (AUC) sought to revamp its annual planning and budgeting processes to address several deficiencies. Primarily, long-range planning and annual budgeting were two independent events with little synchronization. This case study will detail the process and technical aspects of American University in Cairo's transition to a centralized and synchronized planning and budgeting cycle focused on determining appropriate workflows and leveraging database technologies to track planning initiatives throughout an approvals process. Readers will be able to weigh the drawbacks of centralization against the benefits of standardized budget review and planning.

ORGANIZATIONAL BACKGROUND

The American University in Cairo (AUC) is the Middle East's premier English-language university, serving more than 5,000 undergraduate and 1,000 postgraduate students. An independent and non-profit institution, American University in Cairo was founded in 1919 by Americans devoted to education and community service in the Middle East. It is fully accredited in Egypt and the United States and offers a liberal arts curriculum intended to build a culture of leadership, lifelong learning, continuing education and service among its graduates.

DOI: 10.4018/978-1-60960-583-4.ch005

Organizational Structure

More than 200 administrative and academic units make up American University in Cairo's organizational structure. Each is led by a director (in the case of administrative units) or department chair (in the case of academic units) who oversees the budget and operations of the given unit. This is the lowest level at which strategy and finances are formulated.

Generally, each administrative unit reports to an associate vice president and each academic unit to a dean. Each of these individuals is charged with formulating a strategic and financial plan for his or her set of units.

The next organizational level is the area head, to which all associate vice presidents or deans report. There are six areas: the President's area, Finance, Student Affairs, the Provost's area, Planning and Administration and Institutional Advancement. Area heads are the primary individuals charged with executing and synchronizing American University in Cairo's strategic and budgetary plans. They report directly to the President of the university, who, in turn, reports to the Board of Trustees.

As one might expect, thebulk of American University in Cairo's planning and budgeting units are in the academic field. Table one provides a breakdown of the total number of offices per area.

The Organization of Yearly Budgeting

Planning and budgeting is an annual process that begins with submissions from individual units in November and culminates in the submission of a proposed budget for the coming year to the university's Board of Trustees in May. This is an iterative process in which unit proposals are reviewed and endorsed by successive administrative levels and are finally examined by the university's budget committee before submission to the Board of Trustees.

The process begins with the issuance of a memorandum from the Vice President for Planning and Administration and the Vice President for

Figure 1. Partial organizational chart for the American University in Cairo (AUC)

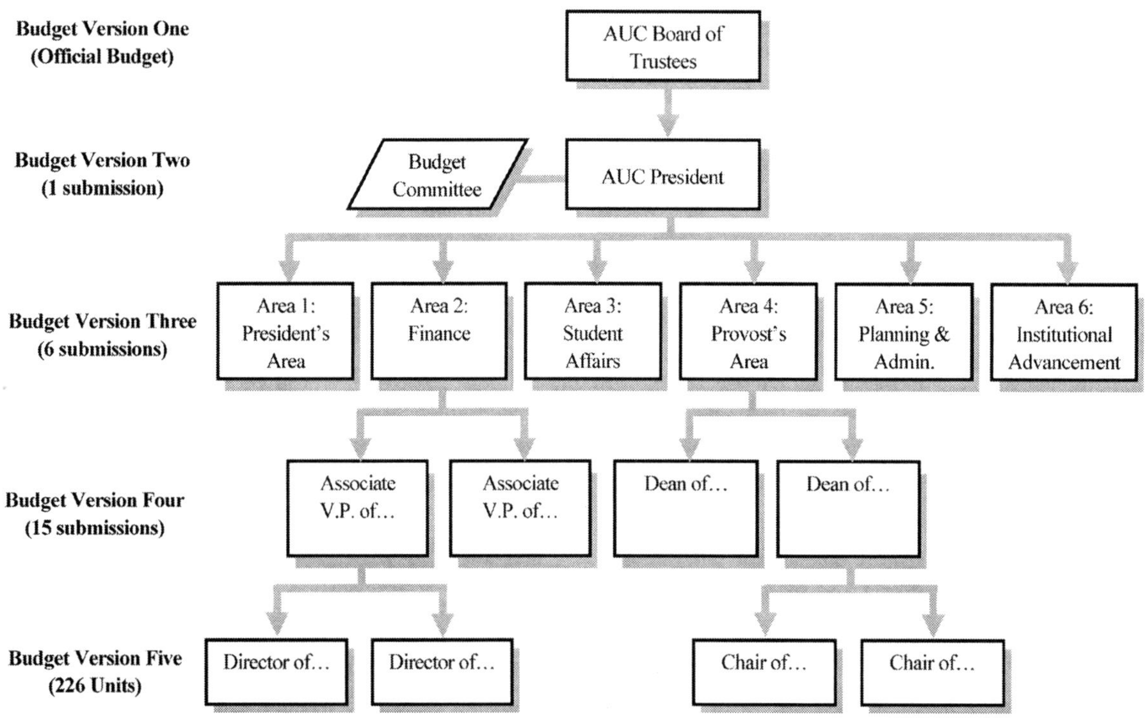

Table 1. Distribution of planning and budgeting units by area

Area	Units (% of Total)
One: President's Area	22 (9%)
Two: Finance	13 (5%)
Three: Student Affairs	19 (8%)
Four: Provost's Area	147 (60%)
Five: Planning and Administration	37 (15%)
Six: Institutional Advancement	8 (3%)
Total	246 (100%)

Finance to all units detailing the requirements and guidelines related to the construction of the next year's budget. The document details the inflation rate to be assumed, exchange rates, target areas for growth or reduction, and others.

Before pursuing the changes described in this case study, university administrators prepared budgets by using the university's enterprise resource planning software from SAP AG (SAP) to adjust allocations in each general ledger of the cost center. The base of each year's budget is the previous year's allocation. Thus, units wishing to pursue new initiatives in the coming year increased their allocation in the relevant general ledgers of the cost center. There was no standardized process for documenting how increases beyond the base budget would be used, and a common budget-cutting technique was to reduce specific types of funding (travel or hospitality, for example) by a fixed percentage across all cost centers

Development of the university's budget is divided into five distinct phases, each of which corresponds to a different administrative level. Each stage in the process is referred to by its SAP version number, decrementing from Version Five. In this version, individual units propose a budget allocation in SAP. The proposals are reviewed by deans and associate vice presidents, who engage in individual procedures for refining them. Once the revised proposals are endorsed, the budget becomes Version Four. At this stage, area heads carefully review submissions and make adjustments based on the goals and strategies of their respective area. The endorsed budget becomes Version Three.

Once area heads have approved and revised their budgets, American University in Cairo's budget committee is convened to review the university's budgetary and strategic standing for the coming year in light of the proposals made by the six area heads. This committee is chaired by American University in Cairo's President and includes all six area heads as well as administrators in finance, human resources and institutional planning.

The budget committee's mandate is to refine the budget so that it represents a responsible proposal to the Board of Trustees for advancing the university's strategic plans in the next fiscal year. The committee often iterates through several versions of this budget before it is suitable for presentation to the board.

The budget emerging from the committee becomes Version Two and is presented to American University in Cairo's Board of Trustees in May. After further consultation and revision with the board, a final budget is approved for the coming year, which becomes Version One.

The Organization of Planning

The long-range planning process varies significantly from unit to unit. Some departments in the academic area, for example, have detailed long-range plans that describe objectives, their budgetary requirements, and the projects being pursued to achieve those objectives. Others lack basic information such as a mission.

A concerted effort was made in 2006 to synchronize the university's long-range planning efforts by launching a process to develop a five-year plan with six strategic themes. Several dozen units participated in this process and each produced a strategic plan for the five-year period from 2007 to 2012. These plans varied significantly in quality, and many did not explicitly provide a link between planning and budgeting.

During that time, a significant amount of time was invested in defining American University in Cairo's strategic themes and goals and encouraging individual planning and budgeting units to develop strategies to advance six university-wide goals:

- Academic Excellence: Develop the curriculum, reward faculty, strengthen academic programming, and others.
- Institutional Effectiveness: Re-accreditation, outcomes assessment, enrollment management, and others.
- International Education: High-quality study abroad programs, international curriculum and student body, global visibility of research, and others.
- Service: Volunteer programs, continuing education programs, and others.
- Operational Excellence: Integrate technology capabilities, best practices in facilities management, career growth for managers and staff, and others.
- Student Experience: Improve course registration systems, first-year experience, extracurricular programming, and others.

In 2009, it was decided to shift away from a five-year planning window toward a three-year rolling strategic plan explicitly linked with budgets. The idea was that the strategic plans should be very practical and reflect current and upcoming efforts to achieve three-year goals. The previously developed five-year plans would serve to inform future three-year plans and the strategic themes would be maintained in a revised format.

A New Phase for American University in Cairo

In August 2008, AmericanUniversity in Cairo relocated from downtown Cairo to a new, state-of-the-art, $400 million, 260-acre campus in New Cairo. A primary goal in relocating to the new facility was to provide the physical groundwork for transforming American University in Cairo into a world-class institution of higher learning. The move was accompanied by the expansion and reorganization of several academic programs and some administrative units and set the stage for developing an institutional culture of continuous improvement, assessment and use of industry-standard processes.

Developing such practices across the institution would involve creating close linkages between strategic planning and yearly budgeting. Individual units would be encouraged to develop strategies that synchronize with the university's strategic goals and reflect awareness of American University in Cairo's mission, vision and values.

From a theoretic perspective, the idea of linking strategic planning and budgeting was about what is referred to in management literature as creating a strategy-focused organization. Pioneered by Kaplan and Norton (2001), the idea is to make strategy formulation interconnected with daily workflows and yearly budgets. Indeed, American University in Cairo could fall under Kaplan and Norton's statistic of more than half of the organizations surveyed indicating that "budgeting and performance review processes were done separately from the strategic planning process" (p. 279).

While American University in Cairo was not yet ready to take on the Balanced Scorecard approach advocated by Kaplan and Norton, the concept of bridging the gap between strategic planning and budgeting was precisely at the core of American University in Cairo's aspirations. The first iteration year sought to move toward this goal by establishing the processes and technical framework for a bottom-up approach to strategic planning, centralized in a single office charged with synchronizing American University in Cairo's strategic planning and budgeting efforts. Put another way, American University in Cairo sought to make operational the integration aspect of planning and budgeting advanced by Kaplan and Norton.

SETTING THE STAGE

The university sought to revamp its annual planning and budgeting processes to address several deficiencies. Primarily, long-range planning and short-term budgeting were two disparate events with little synchronization. Long-range plans often did not include detailed budgetary requirements, and yearly budget allocations did not systematically incorporate long-range strategic goals. Moreover, planning and budgeting were independently lacking in robustness and transparency.

The basis of the rolling three-year strategic plan would be the budgets and plans submitted by individual units. The goal was to produce a document that reflected a spirit of collaboration, transparency and accountability. Moreover, because the strategic plan was rolling, the first version produced would serve as the basis for the following year's planning and budgeting process.

At the outset of the project, eight problematic practices were identified, with a central goal of improvement.

1. Units requested additional funds without systematically or consistently specifying their usage or strategic purpose. Since not all units were required to provide a detailed breakdown of how funds in excess of the previous year's allocation would be used, there was little incentive to develop and track such breakdowns. Moreover, even with such details, there was not always an explicit statement of how the new initiatives would further the goals of the department or the university as a whole.
2. Base-budget requests often were not revised based on the previous year's spending patterns or on anticipated changes in the next year's spending patterns. For many units, the annual process of developing a budget simply involved taking the previous year's budget and adding to it the inflation amount allowed by the university's budget committee. Even in areas of a given budget where the current allocation would clearly not be fully utilized given current spending patterns, allocations were often increased by the fixed inflation percentage.
3. Those charged with reviewing and approving budgets did not follow a standardized process for scrutinizing proposals. After initial budgets were submitted, the quality of the review process varied significantly from area to area. In some areas, the reviewers were required to provide detailed breakdowns justifying increases, while in others, they were subject to significantly less rigor. Moreover, some reviewers made substantial efforts to reduce requests for new allocations by shifting funding from an existing project to one of higher priority.
4. The method of SAP data input obscured how allocations related to the projects or initiatives being pursued by the unit. Like any budgeting system, American University in Cairo required that budget allocations be associated with a particular category of spending, such as hospitality, travel, office supplies, and others. While this arrangement is useful for detecting sudden increases or decreases in these categories from year to year, it does not allow for easy viewing of the cost of funding specific programs or initiatives, as the cost of any given initiative is distributed over several types of spending categories. These totals represent the cost of that spending category across several initiatives, with no ability to disaggregate category totals.
5. There was a lack of transparency in decision-making on proposed budgets. For many, the only feedback they received after proposing

a budget was upon viewing SAP to see the revised, approved budget after the meeting of the Board of Trustees. Although total adjustments were clear, their rationale and underlying funding priorities were not. Moreover, it was not explicit how the budget of a particular unit fit into the overall budgeting strategy of the university.

6. Individual departments did not engage in long-term budgeting. The yearly allocations process encouraged a short-term view of the budgetary implications of new initiatives and strategies. Few units gave substantial thought to their long-term budgetary needs or to how endorsing a new initiative would affect the unit's budget over the long term.
7. New initiatives were informally documented and tracked across the university. Except for very large initiatives, such as launching a new department or academic program, the progress and ultimate success of individual initiatives across the university were not closely tracked or monitored. There was no central inventory of these initiatives, their costs or assessment mechanisms.
8. Requests for new personnel were not justified in a consistent manner, and revisions could be made at any point throughout the process. Many of those who submitted requests for new personnel were required to provide extensive information on the proposed position, while others received approval for new positions without providing such information. Moreover, because personnel requests were constantly being revised, it was often difficult to get a concrete sense of the current status of all requests.

Certainly, it would be impossible to resolve all eight problematic areas in the first year of implementation. The goal of the new process would be to set the stage for gradual improvement across these areas over a long period of time. For both cultural and institutional reasons, changing workflows was a complicated endeavor. Any new plans would need to be gradual, inclusive and reflective of the needs of those administrators who would ultimately execute any revised planning and budgeting process.

An additional complication was a pervading sense among budget administrators at the university that strategic planning was a transient event whose outcomes would have little direct impact on the budgets of individual cost centers. Thus, for individuals with this mentality to take the process seriously, there would need to be a strong sense of continuity from year to year and a clear link between strategic plans and the financial realities of individual units.

Key Players

The former process of yearly budgeting primarily involved the Budget Office and Human Resources. The role of the Budget Office was to distribute technical guidelines and facilitate the entry of budget data into SAP. Human Resources also played a critical role by administering requests for new positions and salary adjustments.

The Vice President for Planning and Administration and the Vice President for Finance oversee Human Resources and the Budget Office respectively. As such, these two individuals were the leaders of the yearly planning and budgeting process. The Vice President for Planning and Administration is supported by the Office of Institutional Research, which includes staff in both planning and assessment.

Separately, because the most substantial variable in the university's budget is tuition income, the Associate Vice President for Enrollment Management, under the Vice President for Student Affairs, plays an important role in projecting student enrollment.

The Proposed Solution

In a broad sense, Americn University in Cairo's goal was to integrate planning and budgeting, while resolving, to the greatest extent possible, the eight problematic practices previously outlined.

Knowing that several previous attempts had been made to synchronize budgeting and planning, a philosophy of incremental but enduring change was adopted. The goal of the first year in the process was to adopt a set of broad structures that would shift the mindset in the university at all levels towards three- year goals and the budgetary strategies required to achieve them. The thinking was that the first year of transition should be relatively easy for administrators to adopt, but would represent a substantial departure from business-as-usual.

The primary strategy for achieving a favorable outcome was to centralize the planning and budgeting process, thus paving the way for university-wide standardization and increased sophistication. To weigh against the drawbacks of decreased flexibility, increased workload, and relatively higher risk, the centralized process would offer a general framework for area heads to build upon and provide additional structure, as they saw appropriate, for their area.

The centralized approach would involve all documentation flowing into a single Planning Office charged with monitoring, maintaining data quality and providing reports. This Planning Office would report to the Vice President for Planning and Administration. As the central hub for all activities related to planning and budgeting, it would provide communications and support throughout the process, in addition to communicating best practices to various university administrators.

In addition to consolidating a Planning Office, the Vice President for Planning and Administration created a Long-Range Integrated Planning and Budgeting (LRIPB) Committee to monitor the revised planning process, provide support to those preparing budgets, and address issues as they arose throughout the year. The LRIPB Committee was critical to the success of the project, as it was composed of individuals from different areas of the university who had been historically central to the yearly budget allocations process.

The membership of the LRIPB Committee included:

- Vice President for Planning and Administration (Chair, Area Five)
- Associate Vice President for Finance (Area Two)
- Associate Vice President of Enrollment Management (Area Three)
- Executive Director for Institutional Research (Area Five)
- Executive Director of Human Resources (Area Five)
- Director of the Provost's Office (Area Four)
- Director of Assessment (Area Five)
- Director of the Budget Office (Area Two)
- Director of Staff Relations, Human Resources (Area Five)
- Associate Director, Budget & Financial Planning Office (Area Two)
- Associate Director for Staff Relations and Budgeting, Human Resources (Area Five)
- Finance Officer, Office of the Provost (Area Two)
- Special Projects Officer, Office of the Vice President for Planning and Administration (Area Five)
- Presidential Intern, Office of the Vice President for Planning and Administration (Area Five)

It was understood from the outset that adopting a centralized approach to integrated planning and budgeting would require the ability to manage significant amounts of data submitted by more than 200 units across the university. Because of the diverse representation on the LRIPB Committee, it was determined that this would be feasible given that the key players traditionally involved with the process would be able to closely monitor progress and work together through any problems.

The Planning Office would work closely with all members of the committee, maintain the database of information, and ensure that all requirements of committee members were met through the streamlined process. In as many cases as possible, previous processes were maintained and merely centralized in order to minimize the introduction of unfamiliar workflows.

CASE DESCRIPTION

At the core of the transformation was a "planning matrix" that integrated long-range planning and short-term budgeting into a single document, by asking cost centers how new allocations would be used, the objectives they would achieve, how those objectives would be assessed, their three-year budgetary implications, and how each furthered American University in Cairo's strategic goals. The data submitted in these matrices was entered into a database and filtered through a four-level approvals process, mirroring the versions of the budget in SAP. Detailed changes were made at each level, ensuring that appropriate attention was paid to both local and macro-level needs. Approvals, rejections and comments were tracked and changes centrally managed.

The old process of simply stating the desired budget, using inconsistent methodologies for documenting such requests, had been in place for many years at American University in Cairo. The planning matrix was viewed as an initial step in encouraging units to document how their budget requests fit into the university's strategic goals.

The planning matrix had three main features that were considered critical to its initial implementation. First, because the project's primary goal was to synchronize strategic planning and budgeting, the document asked submitters to group each of their budget requests by the objective it would achieve. Objectives could include anything from "increase the number of department majors" to "improve reliability of American University in Cairo's computer network." Furthermore, the submission identified which of American University in Cairo's six strategic goals the objective would further, and how. Objectives were composed of one or more initiatives, each of which provided details on the budgetary actions required to achieve the objective. This format differed dramatically from the former budgeting system, which grouped costs according to expense type. Grouping by objective and initiative allowed both the submitter and the reviewer to assess the cost, on its own, of taking on a given project, as opposed to seeing only in aggregate how new initiatives affect a budget by expense type.

Second, the planning matrix required cost information not just for the coming fiscal year, but for two additional years. This three-year outlook encouraged both submitters and reviewers to consider the long-term implications of endorsing a given set of initiatives. Furthermore, especially prudent units could identify funding requests that did not start in the coming fiscal year but would start in subsequent years, thus justifying additional preparatory planning and budgetary considerations. This kind of planning work was further encouraged by the fact that initiatives approved in the first year would continue to be funded at their requested level without the need to seek re-approval.

Finally, the planning matrix reframed the purpose of the yearly budgeting cycle, from one focused on developing a new budget to one focused on synchronizing departmental aspirations with short- and medium-term budgetary requirements. It did this by asking units for their mission statement, the status of their assessment plan and how they would measure the success of the initiatives proposed. This arrangement worked to debunk the idea that strategic planning was an occasional process resulting in volumes of one-time-use documentation. While having an existing

Figure 2. American University in Cairo's planning matrix

PLANNING MATRIX

New Initiatives for 2011 – 2013

Unit/Department:

Mission Statement:

Does your unit/department have an approved assessment plan on file with IR?

Yes Date Submitted:

No Reason

Submitted by:

Title:

Date:

PROPOSED OBJECTIVES AND INITIATIVES FURTHERING THE UNIVERSITY'S GOALS

List below only proposed new initiatives that have operating, capital, personnel or other costs. These should be grouped by the resulting measurable objective which furthers one of the university's six strategic goals.

1st Desired Objective:

Which of the university's six strategic goals does this objective further, and how?

How will you assess or benchmark the success of this objective?

Budgetary initiatives required to achieve this objective	FY 11 Budget				FY 12 Budget				FY 13 Budget			
	Operating	Capital	Personnel	Other	Operating	Capital	Personnel	Other	Operating	Capital	Personnel	Other
1.1												
1.2												
1.3												

2nd Desired Objective:

Which of the university's six strategic goals does this objective further, and how?

How will you assess or benchmark the success of this objective?

Budgetary initiatives required to achieve this objective	FY 11 Budget				FY 12 Budget				FY 13 Budget			
	Operating	Capital	Personnel	Other	Operating	Capital	Personnel	Other	Operating	Capital	Personnel	Other
2.1												
2.2												
2.3												

3rd Desired Objective:

Which of the university's six strategic goals does this objective further, and how?

How will you assess or benchmark the success of this objective?

Budgetary initiatives required to achieve this objective	FY 11 Budget				FY 12 Budget				FY 13 Budget			
	Operating	Capital	Personnel	Other	Operating	Capital	Personnel	Other	Operating	Capital	Personnel	Other
3.1												
3.2												

assessment plan was not deemed a prerequisite for receiving approval for new initiatives during the first year of this new process, it was strongly encouraged, and the Planning Office indicated that the assessment plan would be necessary in following years.

Although considerable thought was put into the initial development of the planning matrix, revisions made mid-stream created some confusion. Specifically, the original design did not envision planning units submitting detailed budget information such as SAP codes, equipment listings, and other precise information that would later be required to add approved funds to a given budget. A mandatory supplementary form was created to request this information, but many saw it as of secondary importance and did not provide complete or accurate information. The task of later tracking down these details was laborious.

A second flaw encountered early on in the process was that the envisioned size of a new initiative was not clearly defined. The original idea was that each unit would have no more than three objectives to be achieved by a handful of initiatives. In fact, more than one thousand initiatives were submitted, some as small as purchasing a new printer and others as large as launching new academic programs. The poorly defined scope of the initiative became problematic, as it created a burdensome load of data entry, made grouping of information difficult because levels of detail were not used consistently, and perpetuated a feeling that the university was funding hundreds of new initiatives.

Communicating the Strategy

An essential component to launching the revised planning and budgeting process involved outreach to the administrators who would ultimately be designing the strategies and budgets. More than a dozen information sessions were held with administrators across the university to answer questions and concerns about the changes being adopted. These were valuable not only for the attendees, but also for the committee, because issues raised included oversights that required action.

In addition to the information sessions, a number of points of contact were established. An e-mail address, planning@aucegypt.edu, was created to receive all queries related to the new process. A team of planners was made available to meet with administrators individually or as a department to answer concerns. Additionally, a website, "Planning and Budgeting Central", was created as a central repository of all documents shared with the community, and was updated frequently as deadlines approached. A newsletter was distributed close to critical deadlines, with updated information on the requirements. Finally, a blog, "FutureTalk", was created to promote transparency and encourage the community to share sincere, anonymous commentary on the university's strategic goals.

A key element of the communication strategy was the requirement that all documents be submitted to a single location, planning@aucegypt.edu. This centralization avoided confusion related to submitting multiple sets of forms to Human Resources, the Budget Office, and others. Since each was represented on the LRIPB Committee, e-mails received were routed to the appropriate individuals by the Planning Office and a central repository of received information was maintained. The use of a single point of contact was critical to projecting to the community that the planning and budgeting process was well synchronized and that the new requirements did not create a confusing bureaucracy of forms.

A final critical aspect to the communications strategy was the scheduling of one-on-one meetings between the Planning Office and individual units. Dozens of these, requested by units, were central to allowing administrators to voice their concerns, seek clarifications unique to their office, establish a point of contact for the process, and affirm that the new system was supported by knowledgeable administrators serious about deploying a revised process.

These communications strategies were generally successful and well received. In particular, the information sessions proved pertinent, because expert attendees familiar with budgeting noted unclear requirements and resolved disputes over incorrect information. Although these instances should have been avoided by beginning preparations earlier in the year, the committee spoke with a single voice after major issues were clarified. The ability to convene the committee quickly to resolve an issue was essential to deploying the new, integrated process.

That said, even with the support of the diverse membership of the committee, the confusion around technical issues, such as whether capital listings had to be submitted, which fields were mandatory, the circumstances in which a planning matrix was required, and so on, were a significant early setback to the deployment of the process.

The web presence, including the blog, was only valuable in the peak times of deadlines. In a community more accustomed to face-to-face interaction and telephone confirmation, voicing concerns by e-mail and listing requirements on a website is of reduced value. While the mere availability of an outlet for voicing feedback and finding consolidated information was a major step forward, it was not one from which the process benefited greatly.

Synchronizing New and Old Requirements

The diverse composition of the LRIPB Committee was critical to determining early on the specific requirements for centralizing the annual budgeting process. In the area of Human Resources, annual budgeting was associated with requesting new positions and salary adjustments. The revamped planning and budgeting process needed to incorporate these types of requests. Additionally, the university's Budget Office needed detailed coding information that was not originally required in the planning matrix. Without this coding information, initiatives approved on the matrix would not be translated properly into budget increases.

To address these issues, it was decided that both the information required by Human Resources and by the Budget Office would be received in a single planning and budgeting submission. New positions and salary adjustments would be documented as new initiatives on a planning matrix, and supporting forms specific to the Office of Human Resources would be forwarded to Human Resources. In the case of detailed budgeting codes, submission would also take place at the same time and forwarded to the Budget Office.

As previously mentioned, this coding information was introduced into the process in a secondary way that later created data quality problems. Moreover, because both this and human resources-related requests were not considered during the initial development of the planning matrix, the issue of maintaining synchronicity with data available to the Budget Office and to Human Resources was one that recurred and was slow in resolution. Although this issue was internal to the committee, the cost of additional labor for continuously checking data was high. The midstream resolution in the case of Human Resources was that a single numeric code would be used to uniquely relate requests for new positions and reclassifications on file with Human Resources with initiatives submitted through planning matrices. Although this numeric code did not circumvent the fact that synchronizing planning and human resource data was a manual process, it greatly eased the data synchronization troubles and emerged as a technique to replicate in the coming year.

Defining New Initiatives

Although all units should have ideally documented their three-year budgetary strategies on a planning matrix, the interim goal during this transition period was to simply ensure that increases to the previous year's base budget were appropriately documented. Because all base budgets were entitled to specific increases due to inflation, it was assumed that units who did not want to request funds in excess of this increase would not have to submit a planning matrix. Thus, questions were raised as to what the cutoff point was for a unit being required to complete a planning matrix. This was a major concern that emerged early on in the process and would necessitate establishing clear criteria for deciding whether a given unit was required to submit a planning matrix.

The question was important because some units would determine that their existing budget was adequate for serving their strategic goals. Indeed, those kinds of determinations should be encouraged. By the same token, however, certain unavoidable costs, such as interest payments or utility bills, were well beyond the previous year's allocation, but did not represent the pursuit of a new university initiative and seemed at odds with the concept of a planning matrix. Because there was no technical way to allow units to only create budgets inside last year's allocation plus inflation, it was critical that a clear rule be established for when a planning matrix was appropriate.

The determination was made that any increase to the previous year's budget in excess of inflation – regardless of the reason – was to be documented on a planning matrix. As such, budget submissions in SAP had to be very closely monitored, and area heads were asked to encourage violating units to reduce their SAP budget and submit a planning matrix.

This bright-line rule was not without significant drawbacks. Some felt that simply exceeding their previous year's budget allocation did not necessarily justify the completion of a planning matrix to document new theoretical initiatives that were being pursued. In some cases, the previous year's budget was just barely below the department's needs, thus mandating a planning matrix. Some viewed the requirement as superfluous and bureaucratic.

Ultimately, requiring that every cost in excess of last year's allocation plus inflation be documented was easy to understand and gave American University in Cairo the ability to attribute *every* incremental cost from last year's operation to a university objective. Although certain categories of costs did not, at first, seem appropriate on planning matrices, complete information on incremental costs in the university's budget fully documented the financial realities of operating the university.

A final definitional issue that became important was how to handle cases in which new initiatives were pursued using the reallocation of a unit's existing budget. The rule established for submitting a planning matrix excluded units who used this technique to pursue their objectives. In some cases, planning matrices were submitted to fund only a portion of an objective whose remainder was being funded through the reallocation of the existing budget. Because it was certainly a desirable outcome for units to reallocate existing funds toward higher-priority initiatives, it was affirmed that such cases did not need to be documented in the first rollout of the enhanced process.

Preparing the Database

The outcome of the introduction of a planning matrix was that a massive amount of data that would have previously been entered directly into SAP (namely, all budget requests in excess of last year's allocation plus inflation) would be submitted by more than 200 administrative and academic units as a Word document to an e-mail address.

To receive such an enormous amount of data, a Microsoft Access database was created with a parallel representation of the data requested in

Figure 3. Sample representation of database embedded table structure

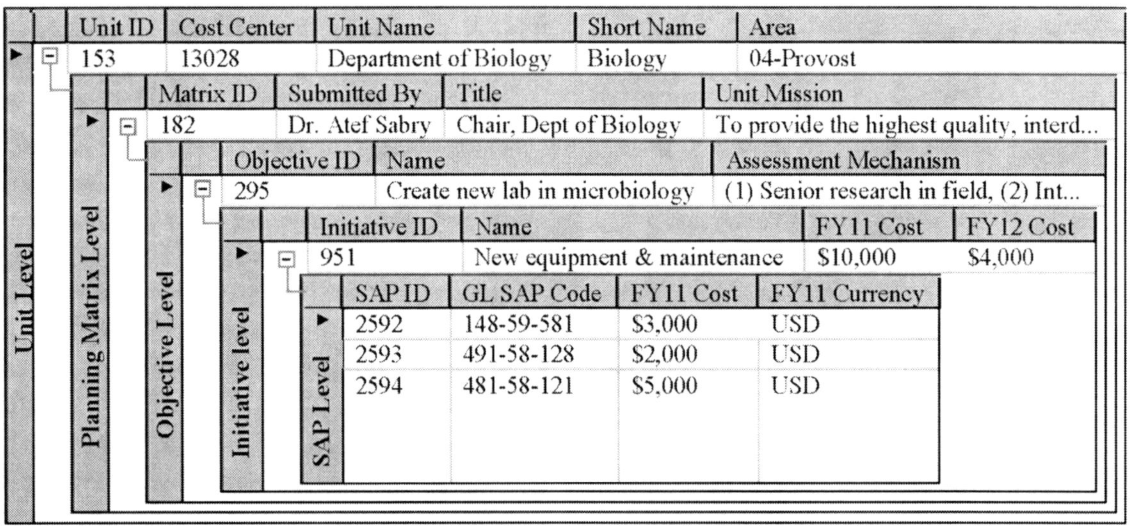

the planning matrix. An embedded table structure allowed for logical grouping of data.

As the format of the planning matrix was a Word document with no automated data validation, the quality of the data received contrasted significantly with what would later be required for entry of approved initiatives into SAP. As such, the Access database was critical to ensuring that submissions followed appropriate conventions, such as currency of the request, cost categories of requested funds, number of cost center, listing of capital equipment requests, and so on. The Access database would later serve as the source of all budgeting data for initiatives approved by the budget committee. Hence, it was critical that data quality be maintained.

The database was also the system for tracking which initiatives had been approved, rejected or revised. This served to produce reports on the volume of proposed initiatives and their costs; forms to condense the initiatives that area heads and the budget committee could approve or reject; summaries of investment by strategic goal and theme; and other non-budgetary documents. These diverse reporting requirements meant the database had to be structured in a manner that would allow for viewing data in many different ways and at many different levels of detail.

It was both to the advantage and disadvantage of the process that the database and its supporting scripts were developed as the new process was being executed. On the one hand, because the requirements had not been fully defined early in the process, database relationships were defined as needed. Reports from the database previewed to the committee or senior administrators could easily be changed even if they required restructuring or reprogramming. This was critical when the

Figure 4. Database relationships

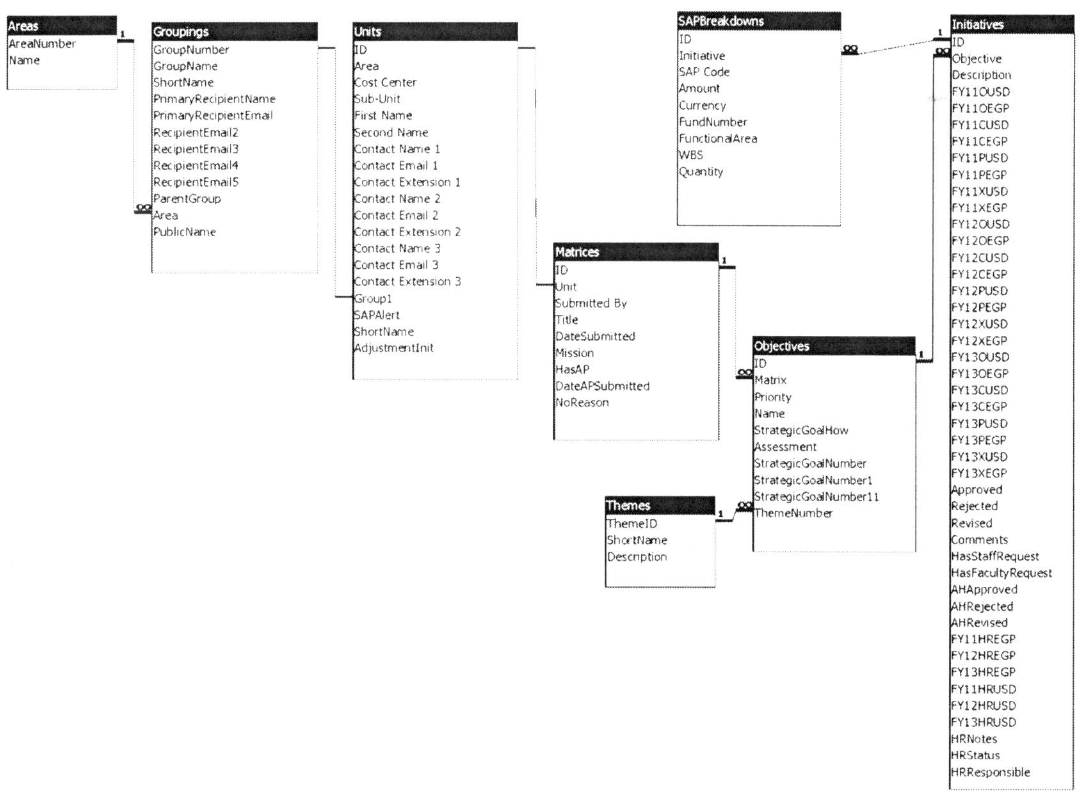

problem of varying levels of specificity emerged, since it was relatively easy to create new summary levels of information that grouped together minor initiatives in ways palatable to administrators. Naturally, the drawback of such an approach was poor technical documentation, a single expert on how to use the database, unreliable code, and reliance upon untested data. Although these never came to cause significant data problems, reports occasionally contained incorrect data, some information was lost, too many fields were created, unnecessary relationships abounded, and the codebase lacked formality.

Receiving the First Round of Data

The first deadline for submissions from the more than 200 administrative and academic units was in mid-October. By this date, all units were to submit completed planning matrices, requests for new personnel or salary adjustments, capital equipment proposals and detailed budgeting codes. More than 150 submissions were received and required entry into the Microsoft Access database.

Although this step in the process was extremely laborious, it was a moment of critical follow-up with submitters for a number of reasons. First, the quality of data, as expected, varied significantly. Every case of unspecified currencies, missing mission statements, unclear requests, incomplete or inconsistent information and others had to be documented and resolved with the submitting unit. Second, closely reviewing the submitted information and following up individually with submitters established a point of contact between the Planning Office and those who submitted matrices. This was important, demonstrating that the revised process would be taken seriously and was not simply a fruitless exercise.

Inevitably, incorrect and incomplete data was still entered into the system, and some submitters did not respond to requests for clarification. It was assumed that these issues would be corrected and resolved by the next administrative level that would review the submissions. Those charged with approving budgets were ultimately responsible for scrutinizing data quality and requesting follow-up information, where necessary.

At this point in the process, the data was in transition from the Word documents submitted by the originators to a streamlined format in Microsoft Access. This meant that any changes to be made to a planning matrix had to be documented in the Access database. An extremely careful process was established to produce PDF versions of submitted planning matrices after every change and to verify them with the originator of the matrix in order to guarantee accuracy. Maintaining synchronicity of versions was often difficult, because a number of administrators did not fully understand that the information was held centrally and that Word planning matrices were invalid after they were submitted. Changes were occasionally made to unit matrices without informing the Planning Office, creating parallel versions of documents. Furthermore, because only a single user could make changes to the planning database at a time, there were sometimes multiple versions, corrupted data, and erroneous updates within the database itself.

Once all data was entered into the database and appropriately cleansed, the next step was to prepare submissions for review and approval by associate vice presidents and deans. A streamlined presentation format was prepared to simplify the approval, revision or rejection of the planning matrices submitted by reporting units. In particular, PDF documents were created with checkboxes that could be filled electronically, indicating whether each initiative was approved, revised or rejected and allowing for any comments.

Associate vice presidents and school deans were encouraged to carefully review the submissions received and meet with submitters to compare the requested allocations to other budget and performance data. The Planning Office and LRIPB Committee were not closely involved in this substantive step in the process.

There was significant variance from office to office as to how this task was executed. As previously mentioned, some offices took this responsibility seriously and understood that the planning framework was designed to allow administrators to add requirements, supporting documentation, previous performance data and other details relevant to making an informed determination as to how to act on proposed initiatives. On the other hand, many simply rejected those initiatives that were obviously lacking proper support and endorsed the vast majority of proposals.

Once all data was reviewed and revised by associate vice presidents and deans, the database was updated accordingly and a new report format was produced for the area head. The new reports included consolidated information and summarized the nature of requested allocations. A similar review period followed. Again, the thoroughness of the review process varied substantially from area to area, with some using complete historical budgeting information to trim, modify and seek alternate funding for requested funds, and others focusing more on encouraging submitters to volunteer adjustments.

Approvals, revisions and rejections by area heads were entered into the Access database in a similar fashion. At this point, the data was ready to be sent to the budget committee, which would require another set of reports in a new format.

About the Initiatives Proposed

In the original round of proposals, Version Five, 1,363 initiatives were proposed by more than 200 administrative units for a total value of $9 million in additional operating costs, $24 million in additional capital costs and $2.8 million in additional personnel costs. Before this data went to the budget committee, the number of initiatives was reduced to 907 with a total value of $7.5 million in operating costs, $18.6 million in capital costs and $2.3 million in personnel costs.

The level of budgetary detail varied significantly from one planning matrix to another. The result was that what some considered an "initiative" encompassed a different scope than the definition used by others. As such, initiatives included minor items, such as office supplies for less than $100, and major items, such as an increase of more than $1 million in utility expenses.

The tremendous volume and cost of the proposed initiatives created significant work for the budget committee, since American University in Cairo would only be able to fund a fraction of the proposed initiatives. Because there was no limit to the number of initiatives that could be proposed and no maximum total cost, individual units had unrealistic expectations as to what was feasible. It later became exceedingly difficult to significantly reduce the number of endorsed initiatives, because only a small number was rejected before going to the budget committee.

To facilitate a simplified understanding of the initiatives being proposed, the Planning Office grouped initiatives at several levels of detail depending on the interests of the audience. Some were only interested in a single project being pursued by each school, whereas others wanted a complete listing of all major projects. Considerable time was spent working with the received proposals to group them appropriately.

Additionally, it was critical to ensure that all supplementary forms for new position requests and salary adjustments had been received. This required close coordination with Human Resources, which assigned median salaries to each new position requested based on information provided by the requestor. The use of initiative identification numbers that uniquely identified each request facilitated this process.

Presenting Data for the Budget Committee's First Round of Meetings

Remaining proposals included in planning matrices were then presented to the budget committee in a consolidated format. Meetings were held between the committee and each area head as well as with each dean to discuss in detail the initiatives proposed.

The budget committee reviewed every proposed initiative that the area heads and deans had approved. It had access to, and used, the highest level of submitted detail, which included initiatives of varying size and scope. Although this was certainly a drawback, and a minimum initiative size should have been established, it introduced the new process clearly to the committee.

As previously discussed, the volume of initiatives the committee had to review was disproportionate to the volume that would ultimately be approved. There were several causes of this problem. First, administrators at lower levels did not always significantly reduce the number of proposals they received. Second, no limit was set as to how many initiatives could be proposed or their maximum cost. Finally, there were no incentives that encouraged units to reallocate existing funds to new initiatives.

After the committee meetings, many adjustments were made to the initiatives, and the planning database was updated accordingly. At this stage in the process, the initiatives that had made it this far into the process were moved into the university's budgeting system for complete analysis in the context of the university's base budget and for consideration of further reductions and adjustments.

Moving Remaining Initiatives into SAP

In order to facilitate the transition of data into SAP, another set of reports was produced from the Access database, with the most detailed data available on the coding that was required to move initiatives into SAP.

Budgeting administrators in the office of each area head were charged with transitioning the remaining initiatives into SAP. They played a crucial role in providing a final review of all the data received. Moreover, a new task emerged, namely, that of keeping the data in SAP in sync with the data in the Access database. That is, it was important to guarantee that any further adjustments to or rejections of initiatives would be updated both in SAP and in the Access database of planning matrices. As there were only six areas, maintaining this synchronicity was initially straightforward and was facilitated by the Long-Range Integrated Planning and Budgeting Committee.

Once all data was entered into SAP, the budget committee reconvened in order to view the updated budget model produced by the budget office directly from SAP. Many adjustments to the included initiatives were made at this stage. Each required both an update in SAP and in the Access database. Unfortunately, because of the huge volume of updates in the academic area, synchronicity between SAP and the Access database was lost in the very last set of adjustments. In particular, changes were made to initiatives that had been transitioned to SAP without separately documenting the planning matrices and initiatives to which those changes corresponded.

The solution to this serious setback was to use information on the known total budgetary adjustment for each academic cost center to add bulk adjustments to each planning matrix that did not necessarily correspond with a particular set of initiatives but that did correspond to individual cost centers. The proposed medium-term solution to this problem was to communicate with the affected departments, asking them to update their planning matrices with details on the initiatives they intend to pursue in the context of the reduced budget.

The loss of synchronization between SAP and the planning database was considered a major setback to the process, particularly since it occurred in the final stages. What this meant was that unit budgets were being directly revised in SAP without knowing which initiative budgets were being changed. A five percent decrease in the biology department's office supplies budget, for example, could not be attributed to the relevant initiative(s) or base budget. Thus, data on the total cost of initiatives being pursued and the potential reallocations from initiative to initiative that would have been made by those units was unknown.

The longer-term solution to this problem turned out to have additional benefits. Since it was decided that units would be asked to update their planning matrices by specifying and detailing the initiatives they would pursue in light of the budget costs, the accuracy of the data could be confirmed. That is, more than six months after the original matrices were submitted, it could be affirmed which of the proposed initiatives would, in fact, be pursued. As a major flaw of the previous budgeting system was the lack of feedback after the Board of Trustees had approved the university's budget, this closure of the feedback loop was a substantial gain.

Summarizing the Approvals

Once a final set of initiatives was endorsed, it was possible to broadly characterize them. Given the nature of the data collected, initiatives could be viewed by university goal, area, nature of expense, and longevity of expense. This data offered the needed specificity for providing details on the university's strategic plan.

At the broadest level, one could quantify the investment in each strategic goal and quickly itemize the detailed costs associated with the initiatives that were intended to pursue that goal. It should be noted that these summaries were limited by the section of inaccurate data caused by the lost synchronization between actual budget and the planning database. That said, because of the interim solution to ensure that all totals were accurate, the distribution summary was still valuable as a broad representation of the university's intentions.

BENEFITS TO CENTRALIZATIN

On balance, American University in Cairo's first year in using a centralized planning and budgeting process achieved its initial goals. The downsides of centralization, such as its labor intensiveness and data quality issues, must be weighed against the benefits of a more controlled and informed process. As American University in Cairo looks to refine future planning and budgeting processes, it must select a strategy that further increases the effectiveness of the integrated planning and budgeting cycle.

Broadly speaking, the original expectation of the project was to integrate planning and long-term budgeting. American University in Cairo sought to encourage individual units to think about their strategic plans and how these fit in with the goals of the university. The catalyst for this shift in thinking was the budget allocation process, which encouraged these units to connect planning and budgeting.

Centrally managing proposals for new initiatives was extremely beneficial, because it allowed senior administrators to holistically view ideas for new projects in the context of the university's goals. Rather than informally pursuing a set of projects that were understood to connect to the university's three-year plan, the centralized database allowed for a detailed articulation of how more than 200 administrative and academic units were working together towards achieving the goals of American University in Cairo.

Moreover, given the university's ambitious goals in the context of relocating to its new campus, the revised planning and budgeting process encouraged units to think radically about how to take substantial steps toward those goals. The planning matrix offered them a "blank slate" to broadly outline what initiatives they could pursue to further the objectives of their departments. In contrast to the yearly mechanical process of simply increasing budgets by a fixed percentage, which encouraged maintenance of the status quo, the new system challenged assumptions on current operations and was a departure from a work-as-usual mentality.

With the documentation of the units' proposed initiatives came substantially increased accountability through the ability to track and assess those initiatives. Formerly, the only structured mechanism for documenting the objectives that units pursued was through the strategic planning process, which occurred irregularly and was not explicitly connected to year-to-year budgets. The revised planning process required units to both explicitly state what new work they would be pursuing and how they intended to assess the success of that work.

A further benefit of the revised process was the opportunity for those charged with endorsing budgets to make well-informed decisions. Throughout the process, units who provided detailed planning matrices that were positioned in a well-documented strategic plan were rewarded with financial support. Those who were less prepared were brought to the forefront and scrutinized. Moreover, the additional level of detail allowed administrators to share insights on possible improvements and identify opportunities for collaboration with other departments and areas.

A less tangible benefit o American University in Cairo lay in the investment in working as a team to affect incremental change. The LRIPB Committee brought together individuals with strong institutional memory but drastically different opinions on how planning and budgeting should be approached. Though often in disagreement, these individuals were charged with managing this process on a yearly basis, and their value came from the diverse constituencies they represented.

CURRENT CHALLENGES FACING THE ORGANIZATION

Policy Issues

As in any project, there were difficulties. Foremost among these difficulties was that the nature of the process encouraged submitters of planning matrices to propose initiatives without significant regard to their budgetary feasibility. Moreover, there was no way to distinguish initiatives that would generate income (such as starting a new academic program) from those that would not. Considerations such as the ability to self-fund a project, use outside sources or displace costs with generated income were not documented on the planning matrix and obscured the merit of such proposals.

The unfortunate outcome of this problem was a volume and cost of proposed initiatives that was significantly out of line with what would be feasible for the university to pursue in a single year. Although the poor definition of the word 'initiative' contributed partially to this issue, by counting very small allocation requests as initiative proposals, the problem remained that most units proposed funding new projects whose budget would represent a substantial increase to their current budget.

The cause of this was an issue of incentives. Ideally, units would first seek ways to reallocate existing funds to pursue new initiatives. In the process that was developed, however, units could both keep their existing funding and request additional allocations, while saving the work of determining what current expenditures were unnecessary. Although it was of great benefit for individual units to think strategically about their future plans, the element of practicality was missing.

The problem of volume further manifested itself in the number of proposals that reached the budget committee. As Figure 5 shows, most initiatives were rejected by the budget committee, while lower levels rejected a very small volume

Figure 5. Distribution and FY11 cost of proposed initiatives by approval phase

	Budget Committee (Version 2)				Area Heads (Version 3)				Deans, AVPs, Exec. Dirs (Version 4)				Department Heads (Version 5)			
Unit	#	Operating	Capital	Personnel	#	Operating	Capital	Personnel	#	Operating	Capital	Personnel	#	Operating	Capital	Personnel
Academic Area, School A	22	$14,501	$70,712		21	$9,679	$70,714	$99,554	32	$14,501	$683,730	$99,554	32	$14,501	$683,730	$99,554
Area Alpha	12	$78,554	$10,286	$54,593	14	$103,554	$11,982	$71,708	15	$103,554	$11,982	$76,474	15	$103,554	$11,982	$76,474
Academic Area, School B	56	$234,776	$180,967	$65,454	63	$268,169	$179,090	$261,146	98	$383,830	$184,702	$280,365	109	$391,325	$1,460,274	$280,365
Academic Area, School C	15	$282,979	$26,205	$23,222	10	$95,714	$26,518		15	$282,979	$26,205	$23,222	15	$282,979	$26,205	$23,222
Academic Area, School D	119	$71,522	$113,450	$46,872	148	$113,511	$248,895	$114,457	200	$185,615	$280,290	$133,199	214	$220,615	$308,861	$133,199
Area Beta	51	$442,588	$1,020,494	$205,962	55	$722,588	$1,030,405	$194,333	61	$722,588	$1,030,405	$257,308	61	$722,588	$1,030,405	$257,308
Academic Area, School E	44	$345,942	$186,011	$60,557	65	$420,848	$248,717	$126.775	77	$522,655	$261,144	$126.775	85	$522,655	$261,144	$126,775
Area Gamma	128	$2.380.901	$14.093.560	$206,505	194	$3,038,151	$15,500,263	$454,188	302	$3,189,365	$18,987,030	$611,878	324	$3,204,401	$19,563,262	$611,878
Area Delta	37	$287,773	$57,721	$64,000	41	$517,773	$223,793	$64,000	48	$1.097,773	$232,721	$75,225	48	$1,097,773	$232,721	$75,225
Area Epsilon	43	$510,655	$13,098	$46,600	39	$584,386	$8,455	$46,600	55	$681,064	$20,661	$48,207	55	$681,064	$20,661	$48,207
Academic Area, School F	68	$782,934	$17,947	$174,837	65	$1,075,871	$39,911	$199,536	78	$1.049,065	$21,518	$199,536	99	$1,079,851	$50,125	$199,536
Academic Area, School G	39	$87,473	$8,125	$20,146	30	$75,725	$9,018	$288,873	45	$87,473	$8,125	$288,873	45	$87,473	$8,125	$288,873
Academic Area, School H	126	$152,196	$440,265	$124,136	130	$153,089	$846,005	$279,073	152	$195,232	$442,408	$291,423	172	$205,232	$522,521	$345,691
Area Zeta	28	$379,600	$15,671	$85,555	32	$379,600	$155,671	$102,671	88	$529,750	$283,750	$235,508	89	$529,750	$283,750	$235,508
TOTAL	788	$6,052,394	$16,254,512	$1,178,440	907	$7,558,657	$18,599,437	$2,302,913	1266	$9,045,443	$22,474,670	$2,747,546	1363	$9,143,759	$24,463,765	$2,801,814

of the initiatives received. Under this arrangement, the committee had to do most of the heavy lifting in determining what projects should be pursued. Guidelines, training, incentives and strict limits would encourage lower levels to filter the volume of initiative proposals in a more useful and informed way.

An extension of this problem was that when associate vice presidents, deans and area heads were reviewing planning matrices, the level of scrutiny given to submitted matrices varied significantly. As mentioned, some put great effort into reducing requests on planning matrices, by reallocating funds from other projects, reducing the requirements of initiatives, and so forth; while others did not follow such a rigorous process and, accordingly, requests of low quality were approved that likely deserved further scrutiny.

Technical Issues

The primary technical issue faced throughout the process was the difficulty of updating planning matrices. Many administrators expressed frustration with not being able to directly make changes to submitted information through a web-based interface. Although great care was taken to ensure the consistency of all changes made, this would have been greatly simplified by giving submitters direct access to their matrices. Moreover, a publicly available interface would have saved significant labor in manually entering the hundreds of received initiatives into the database.

Due to the off-the-cuff administration of the Access database, it lacked the organization and reliability appropriate for a database of its size. The first issue facing database administration was the lack of automation. Because planning matrices were received in Word format, all data received had to be manually transferred into Access. Additionally, new fields were added to the database mid-stream through the process, resulting in lack of clarity as to what information was mandatory.

Database administration was also cumbersome, because it could not be done by more than one person simultaneously. All changes, no matter how small, had to be made from a single computer holding the Access database. Administrators wishing to make such changes were frustrated by having to e-mail a person in order to receive an updated planning matrix.

The final major drawback in database administration was the difficulty in keeping both the Access database and SAP synchronized at the later stages in the process. Essentially, after planning matrix data was transitioned into SAP,

Figure 6. Overview data on distribution of new initiatives by strategic goal and area

				FY 12 Budget			FY 13 Budget		
Goal	Operating	Capital	Personnel	Operating	Capital	Personnel	Operating	Capital	Personnel
Educational Excellence	$1,124k	$68k	$80k	$1,072k	$318k	$840k	$1,161k	$381k	$950k
Research Impact	$974k	$1,019k	$185k	$1,010k	$1,317k	$1,771k	$959k	$1,119k	$2,393k
Global Experience	$293k	$386k	$160k	$325k	$326k	$368k	$356k	$308k	$368k
Community Service	$705k	$505k	$156k	$707k	$1,479k	$320k	$751k	$98k	$330k
Institutional Quality	$2,957k	$14,277k	$597k	$2,848k	$11,021k	$1,050k	$2,823k	$5,357k	$1,116k
Total investment	**$6,052k**	**$16,255k**	**$1,178k**	**$5,962k**	**$14,462k**	**$4,349k**	**$6,051k**	**$7,263k**	**$5,157k**

	FY 11 Budget			FY 12 Budget			FY 13 Budget		
Unit	Operating	Capital	Personnel	Operating	Capital	Personnel	Operating	Capital	Personnel
Academic Area, School F	**$783k**	**$18k**	**$175k**	**$861k**	**$20k**	**$404k**	**$869k**	**$17k**	**$604k**
School F Global Adjustment	$-118k	$-22k		$-118k			$-118k		
Support new academic programs	$180k		$12k	$210k	$7k	$242k	$210k	$4k	$442k
Support new non-degree programming	$368k	$35k	$146k	$332k	$5k	$146k	$334k	$5k	$146k
Support operations and training	$353k	$5k	$16k	$437k	$8k	$16k	$443k	$8k	$16k
Academic Area, School G	**$87k**	**$8k**	**$20k**	**$48k**	**$804k**	**$58k**	**$19k**	**$42k**	**$58k**
Expand services and programs	$76k	$9k	$20k	$36k	$804k	$58k	$8k	$42k	$58k
School G Global Adjustment	$12k	$-1k		$12k			$12k		
Academic Area, School A	**$15k**	**$71k**		**$5k**	**$21k**		**$5k**	**$21k**	
School A Global Adjustment	$5k	$k		$5k			$5k		
Expand sustainable development efforts	$10k	$71k			$21k			$21k	
Area Alpha	**$79k**	**$10k**	**$55k**	**$80k**	**$4k**	**$72k**	**$82k**		**$72k**
Improve operations with new staff and capital	$1k	$10k	$55k	$1k	$4k	$72k	$1k		$72k
Meet interest and outsourcing expenses	$78k			$80k			$81k		
Academic Area, School B	**$235k**	**$181k**	**$65k**	**$152k**		**$495k**	**$221k**		**$495k**
Expand Exec. Training	$21k	$110k	$10k	$16k		$10k	$16k		$10k
School B Global Adjustment	$8k	$2k		$8k			$8k		
Support operational success	$206k	$69k	$55k	$128k		$485k	$197k		$485k
Academic Area, School C	**$283k**	**$26k**	**$23k**	**$230k**		**$23k**	**$230k**		**$23k**
Expand services and increase capacity	$96k	$27k	$23k	$43k		$23k	$43k		$23k
School C Global Adjustment	$187k	$k		$187k			$187k		
Academic Area, School D	**$72k**	**$113k**	**$47k**	**$118k**	**$141k**	**$1,105k**	**$183k**	**$96k**	**$1,388k**
School D Global Adjustment	$-1k	$9k		$-1k			$-1k		
Support operational success	$73k	$104k	$47k	$119k	$141k	$1,105k	$184k	$96k	$1,388k
Area Beta	**$443k**	**$1,020k**	**$206k**	**$376k**	**$7k**	**$384k**	**$226k**	**$4k**	**$411k**
Bolster outreach programming	$47k	$3k	$65k	$49k	$3k	$76k	$49k		$76k
Inc. publicity through coverage and center	$29k	$6k	$72k		$2k	$90k		$4k	$117k
Strengthen programming	$366k	$1,012k	$69k	$326k	$2k	$218k	$176k		$218k
Academic Area, School E	**$346k**	**$186k**	**$61k**	**$346k**	**$300k**	**$177k**	**$346k**	**$319k**	**$177k**
Expand resources	$254k	$83k	$48k	$254k	$190k	$65k	$254k	$200k	$65k
School E Global Adjustment	$82k	$-3k		$82k			$82k		
Support for academic programs	$10k	$105k	$12k	$10k	$110k	$112k	$10k	$118k	$112k
Area Gamma	**$2,381k**	**$14,094k**	**$207k**	**$2,484k**	**$11,772k**	**$298k**	**$2,555k**	**$5,503k**	**$337k**
Improve capacity through capital and staff		$300k			$300k			$300k	
Increase core investment	$1,769k	$12,155k	$10k	$1,921k	$9,339k	$10k	$1,978k	$5,148k	$10k
Increase staffing	$328k	$77k	$118k	$320k	$4k	$210k	$315k	$4k	$249k
Technology investment to ensure business continuity	$284k	$1,561k	$78k	$243k	$2,129k	$78k	$262k	$51k	$78k
Area Delta	**$288k**	**$58k**	**$64k**	**$171k**	**$83k**	**$260k**	**$170k**	**$69k**	**$260k**
Improve capacity through capital and staff	$5k	$9k		$5k		$4k	$5k		$4k
Provide technical and logistical support	$202k	$9k	$64k	$153k	$6k	$148k	$154k	$8k	$148k
Upgrade security	$80k	$40k		$13k	$77k	$107k	$10k	$61k	$107k
Area Epsilon	**$511k**	**$13k**	**$47k**	**$310k**	**$1k**	**$47k**	**$354k**	**$1k**	**$47k**
Area Epsilon Global Adjustment	$-27k	$4k		$-27k			$-27k		
Support for grants and financial aid	$246k			$286k			$324k		
Support operational success	$291k	$9k	$47k	$51k	$1k	$47k	$57k	$1k	$47k
Academic Area, School H	**$152k**	**$440k**	**$124k**	**$370k**	**$1,291k**	**$926k**	**$343k**	**$1,192k**	**$1,186k**
Enhance equipment	$27k	$528k	$20k	$57k	$607k	$237k	$57k	$437k	$317k
School H Global Adjustment	$-1k	$-404k		$-1k			$-1k		
Support and develop new programs	$31k	$238k	$33k	$158k	$496k	$376k	$188k	$514k	$466k
Support operational success	$95k	$78k	$71k	$157k	$188k	$314k	$99k	$240k	$404k
Area Zeta	**$380k**	**$16k**	**$86k**	**$411k**	**$18k**	**$99k**	**$449k**		**$99k**
Improve technological capacity and security	$21k	$8k		$18k	$18k	$14k	$18k		$14k
Increase financial support	$349k			$383k			$421k		
Support existing and recruit additional staff	$10k	$7k	$86k	$10k		$86k	$10k		$86k
Total investment	**$6,052k**	**$16,255k**	**$1,178k**	**$5,962k**	**$14,462k**	**$4,349k**	**$6,051k**	**$7,263k**	**$5,157k**

all future changes required double entry: once into SAP and another time into Microsoft Access. This also was error-prone, and because SAP was the ultimate source of budgeting information, it removed the incentive for keeping planning matrices up-to-date. This became especially problematic in the last phase, when synchronicity was lost between many changes made directly in SAP and the initiatives to which those correlated in planning matrices. Cuts made under pressure directly in SAP would later require submitters of planning matrices to provide updated information on the initiatives they would pursue based on the funding that was made available. This additional administration and lack of communication was clearly sub-optimal.

CONCLUSION

American University in Ciro's first year in restructuring its process of planning and budgeting was a step forward in using centralization to move a university with long-established processes toward rigorous and industry-standard practices of creating yearly budgets designed to achieve specific long-term objectives. The introduction of a planning matrix required by most cost centers was a gradual yet assumption-challenging step that captured the energy and ambition associated with relocation to a new campus. The outcome was engagement at a grassroots level with a high administrative cost in terms of the review of hundreds of proposed initiatives, the development of infrastructure to support centralization and the emergence of significant inconsistencies in budget review procedures. From the outset, American University in Cairo knew this would be an incremental process with inevitable missteps, but ultimately one that was aimed at gradually changing the institution's approach to integrated planning and budgeting.

Database technology played a significant role in advancing the ambitions of integrated planning and budgeting. Although the Access database had drawbacks related to the volume of data entry, data validity, and synchronization with the university's budgeting system, it created a meaningful structure for managing ambitious proposals to further both departmental goals and the university's strategic goals. It allowed individual units to submit detailed budgeting information, while producing high-level reports that categorized American University in Cairo's incremental investment by strategic goal.

Ultimately, centralization of planning and budgeting at American University in Cairo rested on the intersection of process development and database technology. Properly leveraging these elements put the university on a track toward gradual yet deliberate integration of planning and budgeting.

REFERENCES

Kaplan, R. K., & Norton, D. P. (2001). *The strategy focused organization: How balanced scorecard companies thrive in the new business environment.* Boston, MA: Harvard Business School Press.

Chapter 6
Premium International for Credit Services: Application of Value-Based Management

Eskandar Tooma
American University in Cairo (AUC), Egypt

Aliaa Bassiouny
American University in Cairo (AUC), Egypt

Nourhan El Mogui
American University n Cairo (AUC), Egypt

EXECUTIVE SUMMARY

Despite its success in creating a strong market for its product and growing its customer base, PICS is going through a restructuring phase to overcome a variety of operational and financial challenges. This case study examines the concept of value-based management (VBM) and how applying it to the company's restructuring process would help PICS'S management track its performance and make sound strategic decisions for the company. The protagonist is PICS CEO Mr. Paul Antaki, who is being presented with a proposal from 'Val-U' consultants on how VBM would create value for all PICS stakeholders.

The case follows through the history of PICS, presenting the business model and the market for its products. It then moves on to outline the financial position of PICS over the period 2002-2005,which shows that, despite double-digit growth in revenue, the company has suffered from poor bottom lines that have put the company in severe financial distress.

DOI: 10.4018/978-1-60960-583-4.ch006

ORGANIZATIONAL BACKGROUND: THE HISTORY BEHIND PICS

On an early Sunday morning in his elegant office in Dokki, Zafer Paul Antaki, CEO of Premium International for Credit Services (PICS), was sitting at his desk, looking through some of the company's latest financials. Taking a sip of his morning coffee, he began flipping through a report from 'Val-U' Consultation. The report included several corporate success stories on the application of value-based management (VBM) and a full-fledged proposal on how the application of VBM could help PICS create value for all its stakeholders.

The first spark for PICS came to Antaki back in 2000, when he was Managing Director of Consolidated Casuals Ltd, a market leader in the fashion retail business in Egypt and a licensee of well-known European brands, including NafNaf, Mexx and Daniel Hechter. Antaki introduced a loyalty program using a card, called Premium Card, that provided a payment plan for purchases made through the company's different outlets. Within a year, the demand for the Premium Card by both clients and merchants increased significantly. The success of the program captured Antaki's attention. He began thinking of how the company could capitalize and expand on the program in an emerging and growing market of credit card users. The involvement of new retail stores would better serve current customers, as well as attract potential customers.

After three years of study, the company formed a consortium with new business partners to establish PICS in 1997, with a 61percent ownership for the Antaki family. The vision of the new shareholding company, which was managed by Paul Antaki as CEO, was to be the world's leading interest-free credit card provider and the leading role model for banks, end-users and merchants within the consumer credit card industry throughout Egypt and internationally, starting with the MENA region.

To fulfill this ambitious vision, PICS management put together a mission statement to guide their decisions:

- To develop Premium International's logistics and infrastructure for international deployment
- To offer the Premium Card through all major banks
- To be the preferred credit card amongst consumers by offering them excellent services, a strong marketing and retailing environment such as department stores, and online and catalogue shopping
- To be recognized by a large merchant network as the highest generator of customer purchases with continuous growth

PICS™ became the first private sector credit card provider in the MENA region. The actual operation started in February 2002 after the official establishment of the first interest-free credit card, Premium Card, in Egypt. Through this step, PICS had validated a business model featuring an interest-free credit card designed to benefit consumers by improving their buying power rather than to maximize fees and interest charges.

PICS's uniqueness in the market of credit cards lies in being the only consumer credit card service provider offering 10 months interest-free payment plans for consumers. This feature distinguished its main product, Premium Card, from all other credit cards on the Egyptian market, giving PICS an edge and turning it into a market leader within a period of five years. The interest-free installment payment plans appealed to Egyptian society, especially the Muslim majority, since it did not entail any form of usury. Moreover, PICS'S extended network of merchant and bank alliances encouraged consumers to make use of the facilitated payment scheme. The number of subscribers had reached 70,000 customers by the

Figure 1. Board of Directors' profile and organizational structure

Board of Directors Profile

Board Members		
Dr. Ibrahim Kamel ***Chairman***	Kato Investments Group S.A.E Giza for Seeds & Herbs Co.	10%
Zafer Paul Antaki ***CEO***	Founder of Premium International Consolidated Casuals LTD	38%
Rami E. Antaki ***Board Member***	Co-founder of Premium International Managest International	23%
Nasser Chourbagy ***Board Member***	Consolidated Casuals Ltd	14%
Ahmed El Gibaly ***Board Member***	Co-founder of Premium International On Line Media S.A.E Xclusive Card	10%
Ayman Hamed Hamdy ***Board Member***	Kato Investments Group S.A.E	5%

Organizational Structure

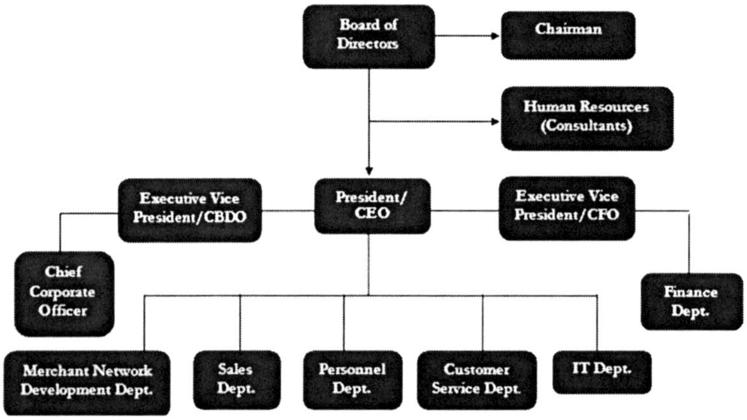

end of 2006, despite the absence of above-the-line marketing activities.

The Local Market

Egypt is considered one of the most populous countries in the Middle East and the second most populous in the African continent. Egypt's population is approximately 80 million as of 2007, with 58 percent and 48 percent of the population living in rural and urban areas respectively, and a Muslim majority.

Egypt macroeconomic performance has improved since the 1990s. Through sound fiscal and monetary policies, the government of Egypt (GOE) has improved the inflation rate and budget deficits, and built up foreign reserves. Egypt has been moving towards a more market-oriented economy through government reform programs focusing on privatization and the enactment of new business legislation. Since the appointment of Prime Minister Ahmed Nazif's cabinet in 2004, Egypt has made substantial progress in developing its legal, tax and investment structure. More reforms are expected to follow.

Egypt is mainly a "cash-based" society, where only 30 percent of its money supply is in the form of bank deposits. The habit of holding cash is deeply rooted in the society. A study by the National Bank of Egypt conducted in March 2006 shows that the total number of credit cards issued in Egypt reached 2,738,555 in 2005. In contrast, in Saudi Arabia, more than 2 million cards are held by a population of nearly 24 million people, while in Kuwait, a population of just 2 million people holds more than 1 million cards.

Figure 2. PICS progress

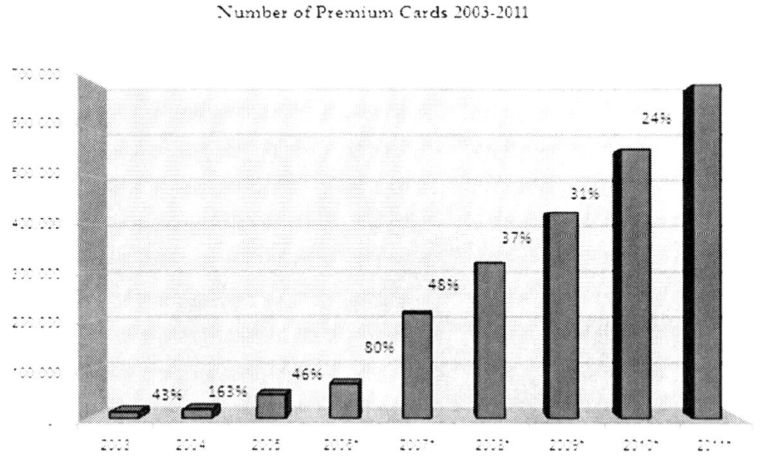

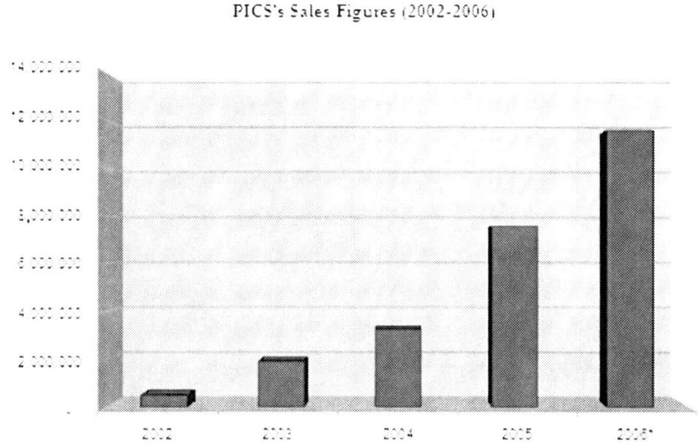

The low penetration of credit cards in Egypt can be seen as strong potential for the growth of this business. An analysis of the credit card market in Egypt by market structure and competition reveals the following:

- **Market Structure:** Credit card providers in Egypt are dominated by the public-sector bank, the National Bank of Egypt (NBE). It is worth mentioning that 36 percent of the total number of credit cards in Egypt are issued by NBE, with which Premium International has formed a strategic alliance.
- **Competition:** Being a market-led company, Premium International focuses on delivering innovative products at exceptional service levels. Since the latest of its pioneer products, Premium Card, has become well recognized in the market, three main competitors have developed similar financial products. Tamima Company has developed "Tamima Viza MasterCard", Shams Company has produced "Shams Ahli Master Card", and National Bank of Egypt has introduced "Ahli Takseet Visa Card". Premium Card, however, has maintained its leadership position, being the only 10-month interest-free credit card.

Figure 3. Breakdown of credit card providers

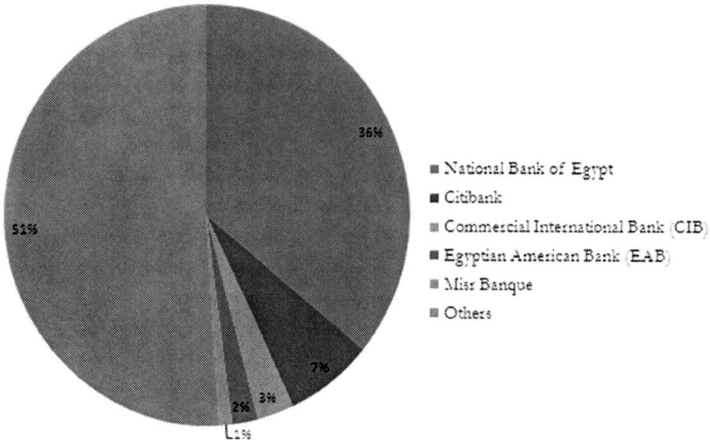

Figure 4. Comparison with competition

	Ahli Takseet	Tamima	Shams Ahli	Premium Card
Issuance Fees	100 (25 as an extra credit card)	Free	100	100
Renewal Fees	50 (25 as an extra credit card)	50	50	100
Max. Limit/card	150,000	50,000	50,000	50,000
Min. Limit/card	1000	1000	1000	1000
Min. Refund	10%	5%	5%	Equal Installments
Grace Period	25 days	25 days	25 days	25 days
APR	18%	18%	18%	18%
Advantages	Purchases from 65 outlets. Only 6 months interest free installments	Only 6 months interest free installments	Only 6 months interest free installments	450 different outlets. 10 equal free interest installments.

SETTING THE STAGE: THE PICS BUSINESS MODEL

PICS takes pride in its innovative and unique product and its intact business model. Core to Premium Card's successful penetration is both the facilitation of payment and the card's usability in a wide range of retail outlets.

The business model is built on creating alliances with major banks and corporations to identify potential cardholders. PICS uses the banks' databases to identify, assess and select potential clients it wants to market the card to. PICS'S network of bank alliances helped the company attain a base of over 70,000 customers without incurring marketing expenditures.

Selecting potential customers, contacting them and successfully issuing a Premium Card is only one aspect of the process. Four parties

Figure 5. The PICS business model

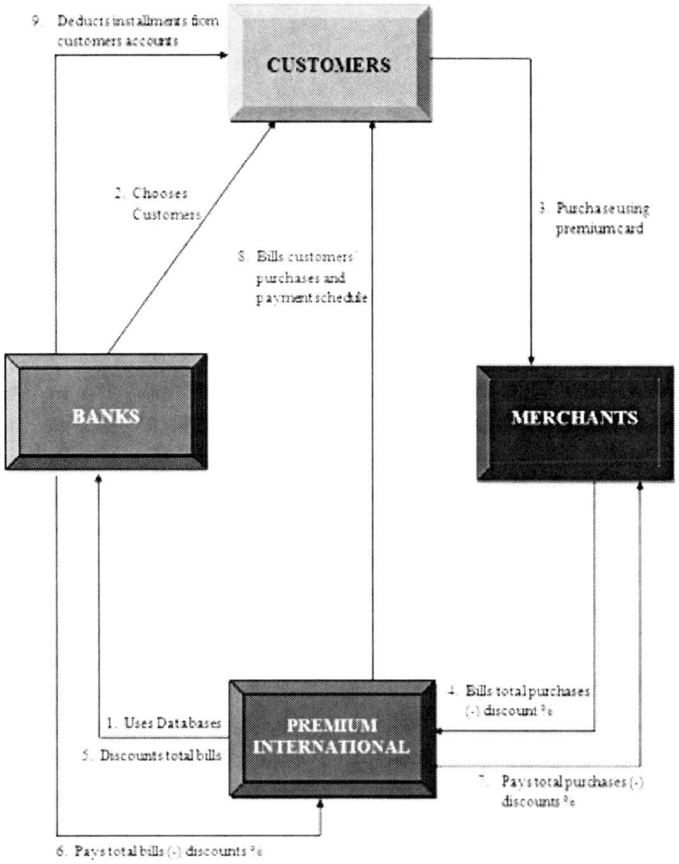

are involved in the issuance of the card: *PICS, the partner-bank, the merchant and the customer.*

The money flow through this model is as follows:

- Monthly reports are sent to allied banks showing the value of issued cards, all purchase transactions during that month as well as installments due.
- The bank then pays Premium International the total amount after deducting the agreed-upon commission.
- The bank is responsible for collecting the installments from the clients' accounts.
- Premium International pays back the merchant after deducting the agreed-upon commission.
- Premium International also deducts the balance of customer installments in the system.

Key Players: The Customer

To illustrate how the model works, let us take the following example of Mrs. Bassiouny:

"Mrs. Bassiouny, who has just been issued a Premium Card with her bank, the National Bank of Egypt (NBE), and paid a fixed annual fee of LE 100, is shopping around at City Stars. She finds a LE 200 bag she likes in a shop that is a member of the PICS merchant network. Mrs. Bassiouny decides to use her Premium Card for the purchase. As soon as the purchase is made and her Premium Card is credited for the LE 200, PICS informs

NBE of Bassiouny's purchase. Over the next 10 months, Bassiouny's account with NBE will be debited LE 20 a month."

The benefits of Premium Card are obvious to Mrs. Bassiouny. The card allows her to enjoy the privilege of buying on credit from 450 different renowned outlets in the domestic market and paying over a period of 10 months with no interest charge. For most customers like Bassiouny, the card has a minimum credit limit of LE 2,000, and is renewable annually for a fixed fee. The credit limit, which could be considered low, is actually quite adequate for most of Premium's target customers, who are mainly middle-class consumers.

To expand on this successful and innovative concept, PICS continuously develops new products and services for its clients. Some of the recent additions to PICS'S offerings include:

- **Premium Super Stores:** An established department store that combines several well-known brands under one roof. Premium Super Store is a sister company of PICS, founded to promote Premium Card. The first outlet was opened in City Stars Shopping Mall, among the largest malls in the Middle East, with expectations of more outlets in the future[1].
- **Individuals:** Instead of reaching customers through bank alliances, PICS has modified its business model to issue Premium Cards directly to individuals. This is usually done through corporate alliances. These types of alliances are formed through the development of direct relations with reputable organizations through which PICS targets employees as potential clients. The idea of targeting customers within certain organizations reduces the credit risk, since the credit value is guaranteed through the employee's salary.

  Individual clients can also be reached through direct agreements with individuals who have bank accounts or credit cards with banks that Premium International does not have alliances with. In this case, the company guarantees its credit by requiring customers to sign a check for an amount representing 110 percent of the Premium Card credit limit, in the presence of sales or customer service staff, renewable upon the card's renewal.
- **VIP Cards:** PICS is studying the possibility of introducing a new set of cards, targeted at "A" class customers. These cards are proposed to have higher credit limits than the Classic Premium Card, and to be categorized by gender: "Silver and Gold Cards" for men who differentiate themselves by elegance, and "Ruby and Emerald Cards" for trendy, fashion-conscience women.

Key Players: The Banks

Most of PICS customers are acquired through banking alliances. Bank alliances are formed by either cross selling or bundling:

- **Cross Selling:** This involves an exchange of client databases between PICS and the bank. Through the bank's database, PICS is able to identify potential customers, get to know their credit history and contact them easily. PICS has formed such alliances with the National Bank of Egypt (NBE), Banque Misr and Housing and Development Bank. A large number of current Premium Card holders are originally NBE clients, mainly of the "B" and "C+" classes. The company is still studying the formation of new alliances, given that the average usage per card has not reached full potential. Allies under consideration include BNP-Paribas, Arab African International Bank (AAIB) and Citibank.
- **Bundling:** This involves the creation of joint packages between PICS and the bank for a new customer who is not an existing

client of either party. It involves joining two related products and selling them as a single unit. PICS has successfully applied bundling with NBE by offering NBE Visa or Master Card with Premium Card.

Each card purchase entails a payment to PICS by the bank. However, in return for providing PICS with their databases and banking services, the bank will usually deduct a commission fee from the amount of each Premium Card purchase. The fee is negotiated between the two parties and varies from one bank to another. In the past, PICS used to pay an average commission fee of 7.5 percent to banks. This high fee was the main reason for PICS losses from 2002 until 2005.

To illustrate the dynamics of the relationship between banks and PICS, let us go back to our example. To get paid for Bassiouny's purchases, the bank will debit her monthly installments from her account and will pay PICS the total purchase amount less the commission fee. So, instead of paying LE 200 to PICS (which the bank takes through monthly installments), it will only pay PICS LE 200 - LE 15= LE 185.

Starting 2007, PICS has managed to extend its bank alliances. While most of its cards are issued by the National Bank of Egypt (El Ahly), PICS has also formed alliances with Bank Misr, Egyptian American Bank and Citibank.

Key Players: The Merchants

PICS's merchant network is central to the success of Premium Cards and the growth in the number of issuances. PICS currently has a network of 450 stores.

The expansion of the merchant network is very critical to PICS, since the greater the variety of merchants and retail outlets that give consumers the chance to use their Premium Cards, the greater the appeal and demand for the card. Because of the promotion of their outlets through PICS, the merchants give PICS a 10 percent discount on purchases made with the card. In the example of Mrs. Bassiouny, the loop is closed when PICS pays the merchant directly for Bassiouny's purchase. However, PICS will only pay the merchant LE 180, having deducted the10% discount.

Key Players: The Company

PICS'S revenue stream in the above business model comes from two main sources, a fixed one and a variable one:

- **Fixed Revenue:** Card Issuances. Each time Premium issues a customer a Premium Card, they charge a fixed annual fee of LE 100 for bank customers and LE 200 for individual customers. For card issuances by banks, the bank usually takes a sales commission on every new card issued.
- **Variable Revenue**: Spread between Merchant Discount and Bank Commission.

In the previous example, PICS'S revenue from Bassiouny's purchase is LE 5, which is the difference between how much the bank paid PICS and how much PICS paid the merchant (LE185-LE180).

These two main sources of revenue are used by PICS to pay for all of its direct and indirect costs. The main costs to PICS are:

- Outgoing calls to potential customers to promote the Premium Card
- Incentives paid to sales personnel responsible for issuing new cards
- Direct costs of new card issuances (including customer application forms, card printing, envelopes, newsletters, merchant lists, mobile SMS, etc.)
- Direct costs of card renewals

PICS is continuously improving its service offerings, to ensure a continuous growth in their

Table 1. Key indicators

Average purchase amount/active card	LE 822/month
Average card limit	LE 2,500
Average used limit per active card	LE 710/month
% of cards with bad debts (PICS)	1.1%
% of cards with bad debts (Banks)	2.7%
Number of new cards acquired monthly	3400
Number of complaints	10/month
Attrition Rate	300 cards/month

*Figures are simple monthly averages over the past 6 months

revenue stream. Some of their newly developed customer-oriented strategies include:

- **Information Technology (IT):** Like all banking and credit service providers, IT is the backbone of the company. PICS is committed to surpassing other providers in its service level, and to consistently delivering quality services to both its clients and allies. Using its own in-house technologies, the company has designed and developed a fully operational card infrastructure, including merchant acquisition systems, card production, point of sales, a complete cardmember reporting system and merchant system. Systems within the company are all coordinated using Premium's software, and are constantly being developed and upgraded to ensure high security levels and efficient flow of transactions.
- **Call Center:** A fully equipped call centre has been set up to respond to all consumer needs. PICS is driven by the belief that the most important thing for consumers is to use the service smoothly, get quick answers to their inquiries and be offered convenient solutions to any striking problem. The company strives to meet these needs by all possible means.
- **Customer Service:** PICS perceives customer satisfaction as one of its key success factors. Accordingly, the company ensures that customer-service employees are rigorously trained to work with customers, satisfying all their needs and providing all the assistance necessary. All complaints are carefully registered in the company's system and reports are distributed to various departments in order to identify and solve the problems customers face. PICS'S customer service department consists of more than 55 employees.

CASE DESCRIPTION: PICS'S FINANCIAL POSITION

Over the period 2002-2005, PICS was able to firmly establish a unique image, expand its client database, and achieve an increasing revenue growth rate. This success, however, was not reflected in the bottom line, as PICS suffered losses over the first four years of operation, amounting to a total of LE 5,356,488 in 2005. Although the company barely managed to break even in 2006, this was mainly due to large capital injections within this period that saved the company from bankruptcy and improved its ratio figures drastically.

PICS losses reflected ineffective operational management. PICS had suffered internally from the mismanagement of its commission system, paying bank commissions on purchases more than was discounted from merchants. Banks received not only a sales commission, but also an agreed-upon commission for every new issuance and card renewal. Indirect costs were also a major challenge, given the required quality standards for operations. As a result, costs exceeded revenues in two consecutive years: 2002 and 2003. In other words, despite the growing revenues and the success of the product, the rate of increase of costs was proportional to that of revenue, which made profits unlikely.

Figure 6. Historical financial statements for PICS

	2005	2004	2003	2002
Sales Revenue	**7,561,716**	**3,266,616**	**1,923,190**	**487,940**
COSS	(2,764,091)	(1,324,555)	(2,708,994)	(1,018,057)
Gross Profit	**4,797,625**	**1,942,061**	**(785,804)**	**(530,117)**
Less: Operating Expenses	(4,261,160)	(2,342,322)	-	(2,402,634)
Other Income	16,986	493	-	-
Operating Income/Loss	**553,451**	**(399,768)**	**(785,804)**	**(2,932,751)**
Less: Depreciation	(615,495)	(406,778)	(391,168)	(358,706)
EBIT	**(62,044)**	**(806,546)**	**(1,176,972)**	**(3,291,457)**
Interest Income			250	
Less: Interest Expense				56
Less: Taxes	-	-	-	-
Net P/L after tax	**(62,044)**	**(806,546)**	**(1,176,722)**	**(3,291,401)**
Unusual Items				
FX			1,417	9,419
Capital Loss				(30,610)
Net Profit/Loss	**(62,044)**	**(806,546)**	**(1,175,305)**	**(3,312,592)**

From an equity perspective, the ROE had improved from -3300% in 2002 to -39% towards the end of this time period. The main stimulus behind this, however, was the injection of capital that saved PICS from bankruptcy. A sum of LE1.95 million in 2004, followed by a further LE 4.95 million in 2005, helped the company acquire some financial stability before reaching breakeven in 2006.

PICS was committed to delivering outstanding service and innovative products. However, given the figures, expansion was impossible. A logical step was to hire a consultant to pump fresh ideas into the company and help implement an effective model that would increase profitability and control costs. VBM Models, such as those suggested by 'Val-U,' provide a holistic approach whereby the company can determine the key value drivers that contribute to its profits and returns and assess them against the various costs involved in the business. The outcome of this value-driven approach is a set of strategies that can help the company continue its revenue growth, and reflect this growth in the bottom line through various cost control strategies.

CURRENT CHALLENGE FACING THE ORGANIZATION

Discussions during several top management meetings have exposed the various pitfalls PICS has faced since its inception. The journey along the road ahead depends on how these challenges will be tackled. Despite the company's increasing revenues and reputable image, PICS incurred continuous losses in its first years, leading to financial problems. Shareholders managed to save the company through capital injections in 2004, 2005, and 2007 of LE 1,950,000, LE 4,950,000 and LE 5,000,000 consecutively. This gave rise to many questions, such as: Did the company over focus its efforts on obtaining alliances, while disregarding how to increase the current usage per present client? Why did the company have a nega-

Figure 7. Historical financial statements for PICS

	2005	2004	2003	2002
Assets				
Current Assets				
Cash	4,257,888	445,777	496,366	153,570
Accounts Receivables	11,915,982	4,260,310	4,228,957	2,163,361
Receivables	5,932,989	3,064,912	3,117,882	1,975,341
Debtors	3,162,595	1,118,803	1,111,076	188,020
Receivables from affliated companies	2,820,398	76,595		
Total Current Assets	**16,173,870**	**4,706,087**	**4,725,323**	**2,316,931**
Long term Assets				
Machinery			512,662	549,164
Equipment			73,914	63,051
Computers			88,408	44,693
Cars			88,888	102,923
Fixed Assets	1,131,978	765,153	763,873	759,831
Projects under implementation	421,796	562,395	834,999	1,107,603
Investment	220,000			
Total Long term Assets	**1,773,774**	**1,327,548**	**1,598,872**	**1,867,434**
Total Assets	**17,947,644**	**6,033,635**	**6,324,195**	**4,184,365**
Current Liabilities				
Short-term debt (merchants)	3,374,337	1,608,469	1,906,020	2,192,419
Account Payable	10,308,104	1,798,377	1,751,222	2,101,098
Creditors	2,621,692	5,871,235	7,054,853	3,103,442
Total Current Liabilities	**16,304,133**	**9,278,081**	**10,712,095**	**7,396,959**
Shareholders Equity				
Common Stocks (10 par, 1,000,000 shares authorized)	7,000,000	2,050,000	100,000	100,000
Accumulated Losses	(5,356,489)	(5,294,445)	(4,487,899)	(3,312,594)
Total Sharesholders' Equity	**1,643,511**	**(3,244,445)**	**(4,387,899)**	**(3,212,594)**
Total Liab.& Shareholders' Eq.	**17,947,644**	**6,033,636**	**6,324,196**	**4,184,365**

tive factoring commission in 2002 / 2003? What would be the ideal value of bank commissions and merchant discounts? Other major questions revolved around the size of customers served, the targeted segments, and a more profitable approach to reach the end-user. A closer analysis of the aspect of 'who we serve and how' gave rise to questions like: Why did the company end up with a large database of clients, yet negative profits? What would be the appropriate mix of client categories – bank alliance / individuals - that would optimize profits? How would the increase in the number of merchants PICS deals with, as well as bank alliances, benefit the business relative to other alternatives?

RECOMMENDED APPROACH: THE CONSULTANT

Antaki had invited 'VAL-U' to deliver a presentation on VBM during the next board meeting. He wanted the board and top management to become acquainted with the new idea, and gauge, through

Figure 8. Historical financial statements for PICS

	2005	2004
Cash Flow from Operating Activities		
Net Loss	(62,044)	(806,546)
Loss in Sales Fixed assets	(1,563)	-
Depreciation	615,496	406,778
Change in Working Capital		
Increase in A P	7,026,052	47,155
Decrease in A P		(600,482)
Decrease in A R		47,578
Increase in A R	(7,655,672)	(959,619)
Cash Provided by Operating Activities	**(77,731)**	**(1,865,136)**
Cash Flow from Investment Activities		
Increase in long term Invest	(220,000)	
Increase in Fixed Assets	(905,659)	
Decrease in Fixed Assets	65,500	
Cash Provided by Investment Activities	**(1,060,159)**	**(135,454)**
Cash Flow from Financing Activities		
Changes in Stockholders Equity	4,950,000	
Cash Provided by Financing Activities	**4,950,000**	**1,950,000**
Increase Cash	**3,812,110**	**(50,590)**
Beg Cash	445,777	496,366
Net Increase in Cash	**4,257,887**	**445,776**

their discussions, to what extent the integration of VBM would become a success. Antaki also thought it would be a good idea to share some reports that introduced VBM before the meeting with 'VAL-U', to make sure the discussion would be fruitful. The following is a summary of the key points that appeared in the reports.

- **VBM Concept:** VBM is a management approach that unites company units towards a single goal, that of creating value. It suggests that all the different strategies, plans and performance targets within each function must be aligned with this ultimate goal. What creating value normally means is maximizing shareholder value. This consistent focus on value can be attained within a company through:

1. Creating value (ways to increase or generate maximum future value = strategy),
2. Managing for value (governance, change management, organizational culture, communication, leadership) and,
3. Measuring value (valuation)" (Value-Based Management, n.d.)

There are two concepts that VBM stems from. The first is that a company's value is determined by its discounted future cash flows. Second, that value is created only when companies invest capital at returns that exceed the cost of that capital. VBM extends these concepts by focusing on how companies use them to make both major strategic and everyday operating decisions.

The proper execution of VBM entails an alignment of the company's overall objectives, analytical techniques and management processes. Accordingly, it centers the attention of management decision making on the key drivers of value. It is like restructuring towards certain focal points - key drivers of value - to achieve maximum value on a continuous basis. Its impact is often seen in improved economic performance.

Key Value Drivers

A company cannot directly affect value, but has to act on things it can influence, such as customer satisfaction, cost, capital expenditures, and so on. A key value driver is any variable that affects the company value. It is through these drivers of value that senior management learns to understand the rest of the organization and to create a dialogue about what it expects to be accomplished.

8:55am, Sunday, June 24th: The Meeting

'Val-U' executive team is setting up their presentation in one of PICS's meeting rooms. All of the top management team is present. Paul Antaki sits quietly at one end of the table, observing the attendees. The excitement of Val-U's team members is visible. "Can VBM be the miracle answer to getting PICS back on track and setting our strategies for the future?" he wonders thoughtfully. He looks forward to the presentation with interest.

REFERENCES

Management, V. B. (n.d.). *Business dictionary/ management dictionary*. Retrieved from http://www.12manage.com/methods_value_based_management.html

ENDNOTE

1 There are currently three outlets open.

Chapter 7
The Alexandria Mineral Oils Company (AMOC): A Strategic Assessment of AMOC'S IPO

Eskandar Tooma
American University in Cairo (AUC), Egypt

EXECUTIVE SUMMARY

This case deals with a critical question about the underlying motives for Initial Public Offerings (IPOs), using the events surrounding the IPO of the Alexandria Mineral and Oils Company (AMOC) in Egypt. AMOC, a government-owned company that was seeking partial privatization, was offered to the public at LE 45per share, and in no more than one week of trading, the share price skyrocketed to LE 85, almost doubling the company's price/earnings (P/E) ratio. This was a matter of major concern to the company's management, since the high P/E ratio detracted from AMOC's attractiveness to a strategic investor. The case gives an overview of AMOC's main business activities and of the local and international petroleum industry and highlights the process of an initial public offering as well as the parties involved.

INDUSTRY AND ORGANIZATIONAL BACKGROUND

Introduction

Those who acquired a stake, those who missed out on their piece of the cake, even those who have no real idea what is going on, are all talking about the rising star of the Cairo and Alexandria Stock Exchange (CASE). Among the flock, one person should be the happiest, for it is his star that rises up in the sky. Standing on the 21st floor of the elegant AMOC tower in Alexandria, Mohamed Magdy, AMOC Chief Financial Officer (CFO), stares through his office window at the big cloud swimming directly towards him across the dilated blue sky. Then he turns his back to the window and sits at his desk, reaching for the drawer, gently pulling out one of his fine Cuban cigars. As he lights it, he slowly leans back and stares at the door, thinking...

September 2005 witnessed the Initial Public Offering (IPO) of Alexandria Mineral Oil Company (AMOC), considered by many one of

DOI: 10.4018/978-1-60960-583-4.ch007

the most rewarding ventures for investors in the history of CASE. After only a mere one week of trading following the IPO, the price of AMOC stock rose from LE 45 to close at LE 85 later that week. This fact amused the traders and encouraged the uneducated public to look up to the stock exchange market as a strong prospect for making easy money by venturing into IPOs.

AMOC, the mineral-oil producing company, was partially offered to the public as part of the privatization process being applied to government-owned enterprises. Key players involved in the process were the National Bank of Egypt (NBE) and the Commercial International Brokerage Company (CIBC), as underwriter and book runner, respectively. After extensive research and valuation, AMOC was offered to the public at LE 45 with a P/E ratio of 7.5. Within one week this ratio reached 14.

"What could possibly have gone wrong?" thought Magdy. "We contracted an expert underwriter and conducted the planned road shows. But we offered our stock before acquiring a strategic investor. Now that our stock is soaring, the P/E is no longer attractive. Will we be able to complete the privatization process and acquire a strategic stakeholder?"

Struggling with his thoughts, Magdy pulled out the big blue file labeled "AMOC IPO", flipped to the company's accounting reports and started reading.

AMOC Profile

AMOC is an Egyptian company specialized in refining a wide range of mineral oils. It was established in May 1997 as a joint stock company operating under investment law number 8/1997, with an authorized capital of LE 2 billion, issued capital of LE 420 million and investment cost of LE 1,900 million. AMOC's purpose of establishment is to satisfy local needs for petroleum products and to export excess production to international markets.

Located in the Salina area, AMOC has a total production facility area of 500,000 m^2. The post capital increase in the company's current paid-in capital stands at LE 861 million. Operating under the investment law of 1997, AMOC enjoys a five-year tax holiday that expires in June 2007, after which the company will be subject to a 20 percent tax. The company is a major shareholder of Alexandria for Waxy Products (AWPC), with a 40 percent ownership share, equivalent to LE 0.4 million. AWPC is mainly involved in the marketing and selling of AMOC's different wax products.

AMOC houses two processing complexes in its production facility, the "*Lube and Special Oils Complex*" and the "*Gas Oil Complex*", which together have a total production capacity of 257k tons per annum. The company's products include base oils, transformer oils, automatic transmission fluids, and paraffin waxes, in addition to two by-products, namely soft /slack waxes and aromatic extracts.

AMOC is currently undergoing some minor expansions whereby a new treatment unit will be added to the Gas Oil complex to enhance sulfur production, at a total investment cost of LE 71 million. The company is also increasing its storage capacity for its heavy residue and fuel oil blend, at a total cost of LE 15 million, to relieve current storage bottlenecks.

AMOC's issued capital is LE 861 million, distributed over 86.1 million shares with a par value of LE 10 per share. This is a result of the board of directors' approval of a LE 41 million capital increase in 2005 via the issuance of 410,000 shares, and a 10:1 stock split that was approved in an executive general meeting dated June 20 of the same year.

AMOC's managers and employees are carefully selected. The company's senior managers are veterans from the Egyptian petroleum sector. The chairman, Eng. Abdel Razek El Kalabshawy, has been seconded from the Egyptian General Petroleum Corporation (EGPC) and has 30 years of experience in the petroleum sector. AMOC's

Figure 1. AMOC senior management

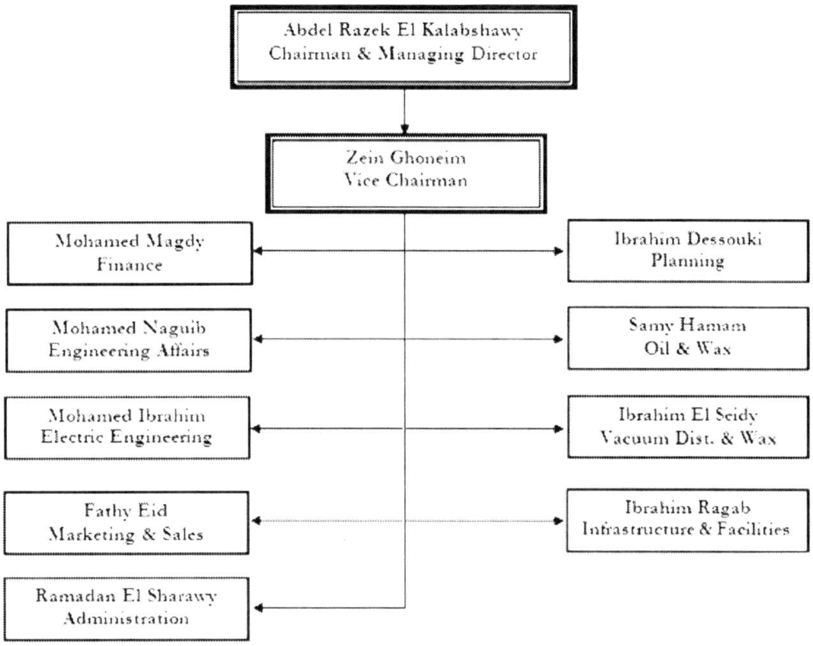

workforce is made up of 1,042 workers, of which the majority are highly qualified technicians and former employees of EGPC and its subsidiaries. The average age of the company's labor is 30 to 40 years.

Petroleum Industry Profile

Domestic Market Overview

The Egyptian oil market supply has exhibited a declining trend over the past ten years. Oil reserves have witnessed an average annual decline of 0.8 percent and oil production has dropped 4 percent over the same period. Production of refined petroleum, on the other hand, has been growing over the past few years, to reach 633,056 barrels per day in 2004, equivalent to 31.5 million tons. Imports have satisfied the growth in production, making up for the shortage resulting from the declining oil production and inability of refineries to produce the required light products from heavy/medium crude oil.

The Government of Egypt (GOE) exerts control over all refineries in Egypt. Currently, 9 refineries operate in Egypt, providing a full range of refined products. The Egyptian General Petroleum Corporation (EGPC) owns 8 of the refineries wholly, and owns 30 percent of AMOC indirectly, through its subsidiaries. Comparing local refining capacities to those in the African region, Egypt ranks second after South Africa, with a 23 percent share of total capacity.

The refinery market is heavily driven by a number of supply and demand forces. The main supply driving forces are: the declining oil supply, the addition of new refinery capacities, expansions of existing capacity, and the increase in crude oil prices. The main demand drivers, on the other hand, lie in gross domestic product (GDP) growth rates, natural gas substitution, and rising government subsidies on energy-related products.

According to market forecasts, new capacities are expected to come on stream over the next three years. Also, over the coming five years, consumption of petroleum products are expected to grow

Figure 2. Forecasted demand for petroleum products till 2010

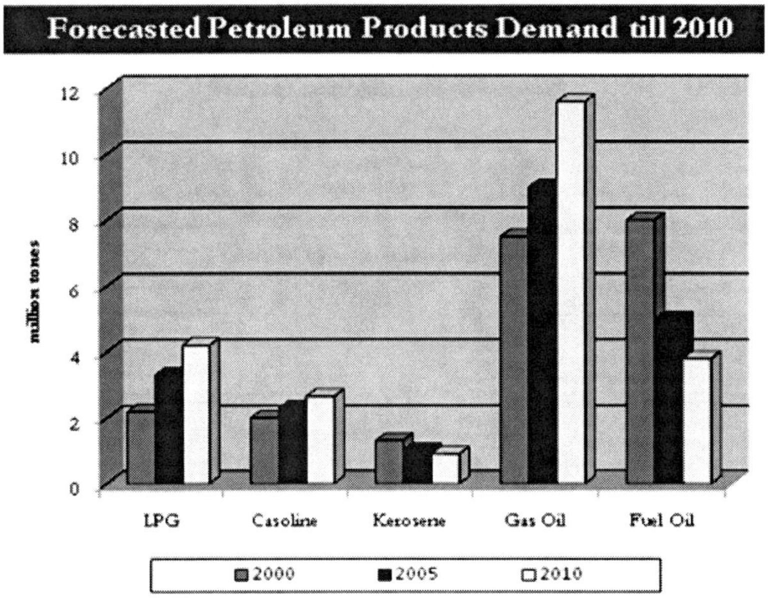

7 percent on average, driven mainly by the rising demand for liquid petroleum gas (LPG) and gas oil. Forecasts for gas oil and gasoline have a direct relation with GDP growth, which is expected to follow a positive development curve. As for demand for fuel oil, this is forecasted to continue to decline as it is further replaced by natural gas, leaving more room for exports.

International Market Overview

Oil is the most popular source of energy on a global level. Consumption of oil as primary energy in 2004 was at around 37 percent.

In 2004, global refinery capacity grew around 1 percent over 2003. The highest growth rates were witnessed by the developing regions, particularly by the Asia/Pacific region with its high demand potential. Demand and production capacity structures and their development patterns play a significant role in setting refinery margins. The higher the supply and demand gap (oversupply), the lower the prices of petroleum products; the lower the gap, the higher the prices.

The upbeat performance of the oil market over the past two years, coupled with the expected sustained growth in the performance of the global economy, indicate a potential growth in oil demand by an annual 2 percent on average until 2015. Driven by the anticipated growth in demand for petroleum products, the refining industry will require significant capital expenditures, mostly drawn from the upgrade and expansion of existing facilities in the short to medium terms.

SETTING THE STAGE

The Need to Go Public

Since the start of the privatization process in Egypt, the GOE has been searching for the best way to sell the most profitable publicly owned companies in a way that represents their fair market value. In the case of AMOC, the best way was to offer the company publicly on the stock exchange to investors, thereby increasing the company's market appeal while testing the success of the

Figure 3. Different petroleum products and their utilization

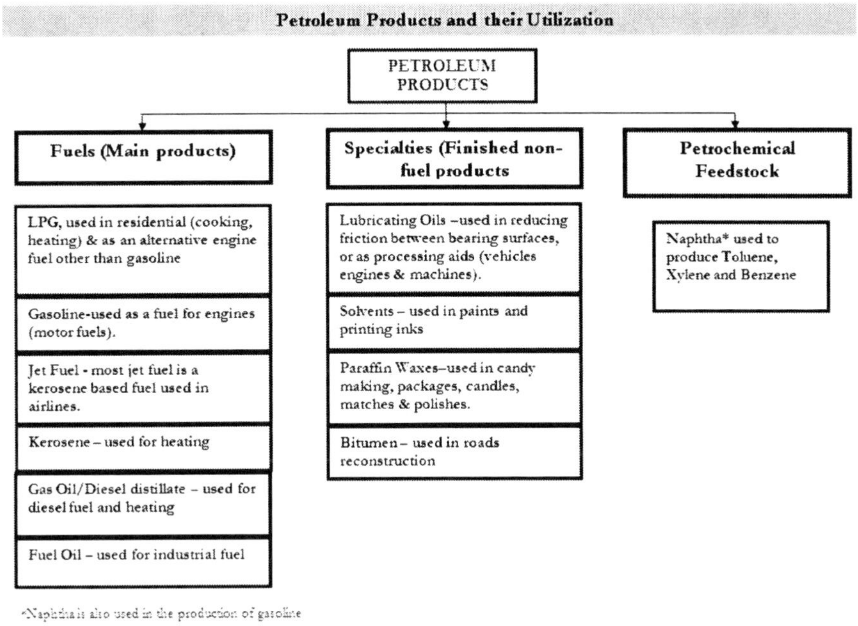

Figure 4. Supply and demand forces

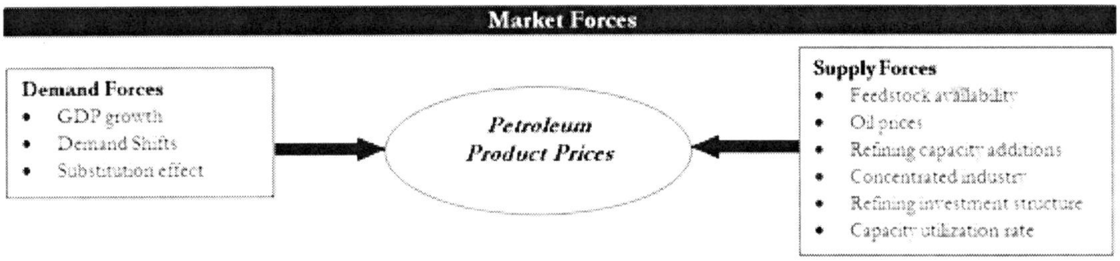

going-public process in order to replicate it with other profitable publicly owned companies.

CASE DESCRIPTION

Selecting the Underwriters

The first thing the GOE did to pursue this objective was to select the underwriter who would be responsible for the Initial Public Offering (IPO) process. An underwriter is an intermediary between the issuer of the security and the investing public, a role that is usually filled by an investment bank. In the case of AMOC, there was an agreement among underwriters to split responsibilities as follows:

The lead manager, also called lead underwriter, would be the National Bank of Egypt. NBE would have primary responsibility for organizing AMOC's stock issuance. The bank was to find other organizations to create a syndicate of underwriters, negotiate terms with the GOE and

Figure 5. Refinery margins vs. gap between supply and demand (2005-2015)

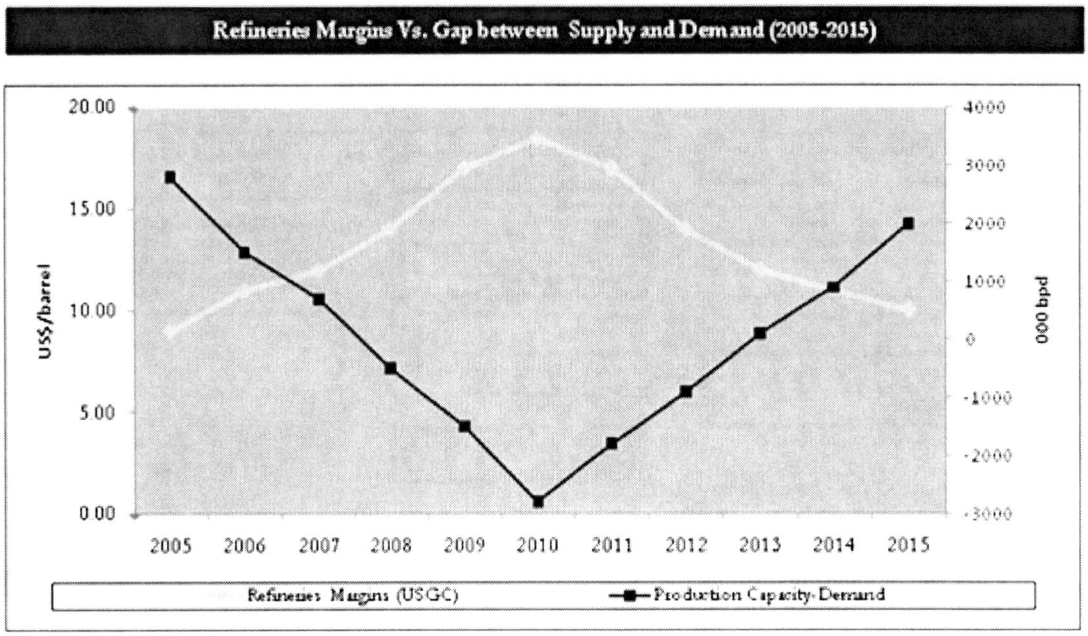

assess market conditions to determine the best time and place/market to promote the stocks.

The co-lead manager would be Commercial International Brokerage Company. CIBC would take on the role of valuating AMOC in order to recommend a fair stock price when making the public offering. CIBC would also be the book runner for AMOC, responsible for keeping records of interested investors who would come up during the next phase, namely the road show. This book-building process would keep track of two main factors: the number of shares requested by each potential investor who asked to be registered in the private placement and the proposed stock price offered by that same investor. This process would help the underwriter satisfy the needs of the highest bidder first and then the next in line and so forth.

Offering Details

AMOC was the second Egyptian state-owned petroleum company to be floated on the stock market in 2005; the first was Sidi Kreir Petrochemicals Company (SIDPEC). An offering of 17.22 million shares, representing a 20 percent stake of AMOC capital, was set to hit the market by September 23rd. The offering was executed on two levels:

First Level

- 8.61million shares to be offered for public subscription
- Offering price: LE 45/share
- Minimum subscription: 10 shares/subscriber
- Maximum subscription: 1,000 shares/subscriber

Second Level

- 8.61million shares to be offered on auction to qualified institutional buyers via a bidding process
- Offering price: A floor price of LE 45/share
- Minimum subscription: 50,000 shares/subscriber
- Maximum subscription: 350,000 shares/subscriber

Table 1. Shareholders' ownership structure

	Pre Offering		Post Offering	
	Shares	**% of Ownership**	**Shares**	**% of Ownership**
National Bank of Egypt	22,680,000	26.34%	16,200,000	18.82%
Misr Bank	17,220,000	20.00%	12,300,000	14.29%
Alexandria Petroleum Company	17,220,000	20.00%	17,220,000	20.00%
Misr Insurance Company	8,610,000	10.00%	6,150,000	7.14%
Petroleum Cooperative Society	4,305,000	5.00%	3,075,000	3.57%
Misr Petroleum Company	4,305,000	5.00%	3,075,000	3.57%
Insurance Fund for Gov. Sector Employees	4,305,000	5.00%	4,305,000	5.00%
Insurance Fund for Public Enterprise Employees	4,305,000	5.00%	4,305,000	5.00%
Chark Insurance Company	3,150,000	3.66%	2,250,000	2.61%
Free Float	0	0.00%	17,220,000	20.00%
Total	**86,1000,000**	**100.00%**	**86,1000,000**	**100.00%**

Valuation of AMOC

As a result of the exercise conducted by CIBC, AMOC's stock was projected to be LE 71.21 as fair value. Nonetheless, this fair price was not the official number released to the public. The official stock prices announced for the public subscription were LE 45 per share for the public offering and LE 56 for the private offering.

Public Offering

LE 45per share meant that AMOC was released to the public at 63 percent below its fair price. No reasons were given for this and the motives remain suspicious to this day. An acceptable explanation would be that the government wanted to launch AMOC at a competitive P/E ratio.

Private Placement

By convention, road shows are an integral part of the private placement process. Such was the case with AMOC. Road shows were conducted in Dubai, Abu Dhabi, Bahrain, Jeddah, Riyadh, Kuwait and London, to attract bigger investors than those sought through the public offering. During the road shows, offers from investors were collected as part of the book-building process.

The road show was conducted by NBE as the lead underwriter and CIBC as the co-lead underwriter and book runner, with the attendance of top management. During the road show, targeted investors were approached in an effort to seek competitive prices for major investments.

A generally accepted practice to determine the stock price for the private placement would have been to conduct a Dutch auction to maximize the benefit for the shareholders (in AMOC's case, the government). To everybody's dismay, a very unusual thing happened: after CIBC collected the prices offered by the investors, a weighted average price was set for all investors.

The investors' shares in the stock depended on the original number of shares they had requested as compared to the coverage ratio - meaning that each investor received a number of shares equal to the coverage ratio multiplied by the original number of shares requested by him.

Accordingly, AMOC's stock was set at LE 56 in the private offering – a figure that was way below its fair value.

Table 2. P/E ratio industry comparison

Company	Country	P/E 2004	P/BV 2004
Valero Energy Corp.	USA	10.8x	2.6x
Repsol YPF	Spain	14.5x	2.0x
Giant Industries Inc.	USA	14.0x	2.0x
Marathon Oil Corp.	USA	12.5x	2.2x
Whiting Petroleum Corp.	USA	10.9x	1.9x
Petro-Canada	Canada	18.5x	2.7x
Shell Refining Co.	Malaysia	4.7x	2.0x
S-Oil Corp	Korea	6.9x	2.6x
Cosmo Oil Co.	Japan	26.8x	2.0x
Jordan Petroleum Refinery	Jordan	46.2x	3.7x
Saudi Arabia Refineries Co.	Saudi Arabia	41.7x	1.2x
Industry Average		18.9x	2.3x
AMOC	Egypt	7.5x	3.5x

The Need for a Strategic Partner

Companies going public usually have a strategic reason for such a decision. The company might be in need of extra funding to take it to the next level; going public might be an exit strategy for the current company's owner; or, as in the case of AMOC, it could be part of the privatization process promoted by Egypt's cabinet, under Prime Minister Ahmed Nazif. Whatever the reason, such a decision needs to be carefully considered to determine the best possible new company structure that would maximize the value of the company.

A partnership with a strategic investor can add value to the company, providing it with a competitive advantage by achieving synergy, streamlining operations or moving the company up the value chain. A strategic investor may add new technologies to the company's business, accomplish vertical integration, or secure new businesses. In AMOC's case, the company might have considered a multinational oil upstream company that could secure the supply of oil and gas feedstock to its refineries, or it might have considered an international company that had new technologies, know-how and experience in operating refineries, or a partner that would help the company gain more access to the export market and increase its attractiveness in new markets.

THE CHALLENGE: STRATEGIC INVESTOR DILEMMA

Sitting in his office and staring fixedly at his laptop screen, Mr. Mohamed Magdy sees the current price of AMOC's stock on the CASE website standing at over LE 85, more than double its IPO offered price. With a simple calculation of the P/E ratio, he thinks how attractive the company was at its IPO price, when the IPO P/E ratio was 7.5 times. Currently, the ratio has doubled, coming close to the P/E average market ratio.

"I would have been sitting back at my desk, picking out a strategic investor from the long line of investors awaiting our approval," thinks Mr. Magdy ruefully. He decides to focus on the current situation and determine whether AMOC, given the current stock price, could still attract and secure the strategic investor that they are looking for, and if so, what kind of measures and strategies need to be pursued to attract and secure such an investor.

RECOMMENDATIONS

"Given our over-utilized facilities and the growing need for expansion to meet the strong market demand, finding a strategic investor has become an urgent matter," Mr. Magdy ponders. Turning away from his laptop, he notices the CIBC initiation of coverage report lying on the edge of his desk. He skims through the report and the following phrase catches his eye: "We believe that expansion would be a priority on a strategic investor's agenda, whereby volume will emerge as a growth driver alongside price." Now he feels an even greater sense of urgency to react to the situation, and with a mixture of panic and excitement at this uphill task, he starts quickly thinking again of possible strategies. "Will preparing a business plan for an expansion process that takes into account the added value of a strategic investor be enough to attract investors? Or is there a way to manipulate the P/E ratio temporarily on the stock market to make it more appealing to investors? Or maybe we should wait a while, in the hopes that oil prices will continue to increase and make AMOC an attractive catch?" Mr. Magdy is used to acting under stress and invariably lives up to the situation.

REFERENCES

Afif, A., Aziz, H., & Mohsen, M. (2010). *Class discussion and project.*

Commercial International Brokerage Company. (n.d.). *IPO valuation report.*

The Egyptian Exchange. (n.d.). *Homepage.* Retrieved from http://www.egyptse.com

Section 3
Management

Organizations operating worldwide adopt different strategies and marketing techniques in various geographic areas, depending on the cultural perception of the country in which they are active. There are diverse reasons for implementing different management strategies, even under the same organizational umbrella. Responsiveness to customers, market adaptability, and competitiveness with other organizations operating in the same sector are some of the most important. The first case, "Innovative Managerial Approaches in MENA Countries," examines the management strategies of a leading furniture company that started off as a small business and rapidly expanded globally. The case highlights the company's flexibility in adapting its organizational structures to the nature of the market in different countries, and its reliance on a cross-cultural management approach to marketing in order to increase product acceptance by consumers across the world. In today's hyper-competitive environment, understanding factors that contribute to effective management of change, and achieving strategic competitive standing is critical. The second case, "Facing Organizational Change and Stress Management," explores the implementation of two electronic banking delivery systems, namely ATMs and Internet banking, in a leading bank in Egypt. The case identifies and describes the bank's approach to managing change through Information Technology with regards to leadership actions, overcoming resistance to change, personal and organizational attributes, strategies, structures, business processes, culture, as well as organizational commitment.

Chapter 8
Path to Success:
Innovative Managerial Approach

Ahu Genis-Gruber
TOBB University of Economics and Technology, Turkey

Ramazan Aktas
TOBB University of Economics and Technology, Turkey

EXECUTIVE SUMMARY

Organizations operating worldwide adopt different strategies and marketing techniques in various geographic areas, depending on the cultural perception of the country in which they are active. There are diverse reasons for implementing different management strategies, even under the same organizational umbrella. Responsiveness to customers, market adaptability, and competitiveness with other organizations operating in the same sector are some of the most important.

The current case examines the management strategies of a leading furniture company that started off as a small business and rapidly expanded globally. The success the company has achieved through its innovative marketing strategies and use of international management techniques is presented. The case highlights the company's flexibility in adapting its organizational structures to the nature of the market in different countries, and its reliance on a cross-cultural management approach to marketing in order to increase product acceptance by consumers across the world.

ORGANIZATIONAL BACKGROUND

History of the Company

Founded in 1995 in the Inegöl district in the Marmara region of Turkey, Çilek is generally acknowledged as Turkey's leading company in the children's furniture industry and the design of children's rooms. Çilek was established with the aim of developing furniture products and accessories for children. It is the first brand to create products in the furniture sector specially designed for a particular age group. The company caters to the newly born all the way up to youth aged 24.

Çilek's mission is to offer the most functional, most secure and most economical furniture and to set the standard at all times and in all places for the sector in which it operates. The company's

DOI: 10.4018/978-1-60960-583-4.ch008

vision is to be a unique and unrivalled Turkish brand in its field.

Çilek, which has its own production lines, is the first brand in the children's furniture design and production sector to operate at a global level. The company launched its first exports in Switzerland in 1996. Having become a well-known brand, Çilek went on to open its very first retail store in Malta in 2001. That same year, the company's logo, brand and products were registered in 70 countries in the world.

Çilek's expansion policy is based on a franchise system. The company has a total of 150 concept stores in Turkey. It also operates in 68 countries - including countries in the Middle East and North Africa (MENA) - with a total of 135 concept stores. In addition, Çilek has institutional clients like Alghanim Ind in Kuwait, Kika Leiner in Austria, Möbel Pfister in Switzerland, Moniflor in Portugal, Elburg in Russia and Sweet Dreams in the United Kingdom (UK).

Çilek has clear requirements for specific age groups. The furniture should be practical, of high quality, original, different and durable. Since Çilek produces furniture for children, the most essential quality criteria are the use of anti-carcinogenic, anti-allergenic and anti-bacterial materials in production, a five-year guarantee period and a Geprüfte Sicherheit (GS) Quality Certificate. Hundreds of Çilek products are constantly subjected to tests in laboratories to ensure reliability. Çilek has received the GS Quality Certificate by certifying its products to GS standards one piece at a time.

In 2005, the high quality of Çilek's products earned the company the Superbrands International award in the furniture industry. Superbrands are determined by Turkey's Superbrands Selection Board, which is made up of professionally respected and qualified individuals. The board members assess all brands operating in Turkey, both domestic and international, against Superbrands International criteria.

Çilek has also been accepted into the Turquality Support Program. The program selects leading companies in their field to support Turkish brands in their work processes, offer vocational training to companies working in the same sector to help them gain competitive advantage in the global market, offer companies coaching services, and support companies financially on their path to becoming a global brand. Çilek was the first to get accepted into this program as a leader in the furniture sector.

Today, with 444 sales points, 2,200 employees, a sales area of 60,000 m^2 and a retail turnover of 110 million Euros, Çilek, which started off as a small, family-owned business, is on its way to becoming the leading international company in the furniture sector.

The history of the company is presented in Figure 1.

Çilek Companies

Çilek has different companies in various countries. These include:

- Çilek Mobilya A.Ş.:→ Founded in 1995. The general management and headquarters, sales & marketing departments are located in Istanbul and the factory and product support departments are located in Inegöl-Bursa.
- Çilek Germany GmbH:→ Founded in 2005
- Çilek USA Inc:→ Founded in 2007
- Çilek Bosnia Doo:→ Founded in 2009
- Çilek Japan Corp:→ Founded in 2009

Factory

Çilek's factory, which extends over 33,000 m^2, is located in the Inegöl region. The factory employs 900 workers to produce 150,000 bedroom furniture sets annually. Despite the global economic crisis, Çilek has decided to expand its facilities to cover an area of 45,000 m^2 in response to the growing demand.

Figure 1.

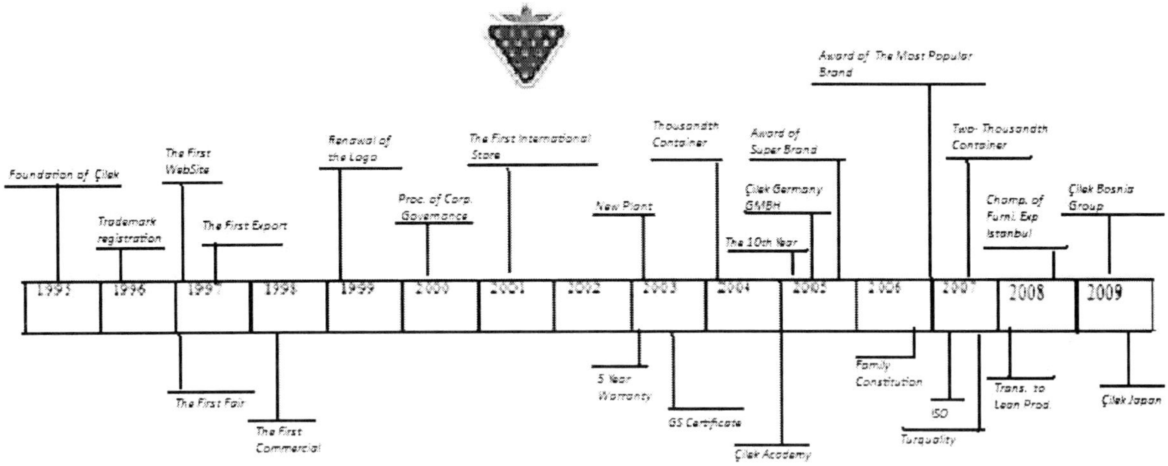

Child Safety

Through the use of advanced technologies, the company produces child-safe furniture that meets, and even exceeds, the standards set forth by the European Union. Çilek products are produced using the highest quality raw materials that consist of anti-carcinogenic, anti-allergenic and anti-bacterial melamine-coated chipboards. Specially tempered glass is also used. This way, the risk of accidental breakage that would normally result in sharp and jagged pieces that may cause harm to children is reduced. The fabrics used in Çilek products are not only fire retardant but also easy to clean. A costly process in production has allowed for the successful reduction of E1 formaldehyde levels to the point that its use in materials has become harmless.

Market and Competition

Çilek's aim is to become a worldwide brand in the niche market for unique furniture designs for infants, children and youth up to the age of 24. The company defines its customers as educated families from big cities who belong to the middle-to-high income bracket.

Çilek has created a new concept-store[1] perspective for entrepreneurs in the world and has opted to be an alternative brand. The company aims to increase brand awareness and expand its market share in all target markets using the same concept-store strategy.

Brand Values

i. *Conscious:* Çilek is determined to focus on the niche of furniture for the 0-24 age group and has succeeded in becoming the world leader in this sector.
ii. *Determined:* Çilek is a corporation that knows what it wants, provides the most functional, safest, and most economic furniture and tries to set the standard in all places and at all times.
iii. *Innovative:* Çilek is the first furniture brand in the world to focus on a specific age group and implement unique designs and products for this group.
iv. *Expert:* Çilek has introduced the term "young rooms" to Turkey. Çilek has identified its target age groups as infants, kids and youth, and is an expert in this niche.

v. *Leader:* Çilek is the first and only leader of the young-rooms concept-store chain in the world.
vi. *Passionate:* Backed by a hardworking and innovative team, Çilek is passionate about doing its best.
vii. *Visionary:* Çilek is an international brand that exports to 68 countries. It has 135 foreign subsidiaries and 110 franchised stores in Turkey. Çilek products are in more that 2 million children's rooms in various parts of the world.

Despite the major market challenges facing SMEs in Europe in general and Turkey in particular, and the host of management challenges facing small and large business as they expand their operations internationally, Çilek has been able to successfully expand its market to 68 countries in 9 main geographic areas in a relatively short time. Countries in which its products are sold include Algeria, Australia, Denmark, Egypt, Indonesia, Japan, Kuwait, Mexico, Panama, Russia, South Africa, and the USA, to name a few. In order to expand and increase its market penetration, the company is adopting a more aggressive marketing strategy in existing markets by opening new subsidiaries, not only in Turkey but also in different geographic areas around the world.

With its focus on the niche of furniture for a specific age group, its product diversification and emphasis on quality, Çilek has a competitive advantage over local and global competitors. The main challenge Çilek faces is low-quality imitation of its products. Other companies globally produce furniture for children using cheaper materials, imitating Çilek's concepts and designs.

SETTING THE STAGE

Overview of SMEs in Europe and Turkey

A strong and vibrant private sector is acknowledged as vital to educe economic dynamism, improve productivity and reduce poverty in developing and emerging economies. Accordingly, various strategies are being implemented to develop the private sector and promote SMEs that trigger the economy. SMEs create employment, maintain social stability and favor both entrepreneurial spirit and innovation. (Alkin & Okay, 2008)

In the European Union, SMEs are defined as companies that employ less than 250 people, whose annual turnover does not exceed 50 million Euros and/or whose annual balance sheet total does not exceed 43 million Euros. Under this definition, 23 million SMEs represent 99% of all companies in the EU and provide around 75 million jobs. (Alkin & Okay, 2008)

Turkey boasts a strong entrepreneurial culture. Indeed, SMEs constitute the backbone of the Turkish private sector, making up 99.5% of the total number of enterprises and 61.1% of total employment, and contributing about 36% of GNP (TUIK, 2003).

SMEs have been a key element in the social and economic structures of their countries in terms of industrialization, urbanization, efficient and equitable distribution of resources, elimination of interregional gaps in development, creation of employment and development of trade. Thus, they play an effective role in the processes of policy-making and strategy formulation in their respective countries. Unlike large enterprises, since they do not depend on high-cost investments, SMEs can adapt more easily and rapidly to technological developments, administrative and process changes, and market preferences. This characteristic of SMEs enables them to be more flexible during

Table 1. Definition of an SME

	Number of Employees	Annual Turnover	or	Balance-Sheet Size	Independence
Micro Enterprise	Less than 10	Up to 2 million Euros		Up to 2 million Euros	Shareholding by another firm not to exceed 25%
Small Enterprise	Less than 50	Up to 10 million Euros		Up to 10 million Euros	
Medium-Sized Enterprise	Less than 250	Up to 50 million Euros		Up to 43 million Euros	

Source: REX/264 EU-Turkey Joint Consultative Committee Access to financing for SMEs in the EU and Turkey, 25th meeting of the EU-Turkey Joint Consultative Committee Paris, France 18-19 November, 2008, pp.4

economic fluctuations, to rapidly adapt to demand and to control costs (Keskin, 2008).

Various market failures work against European SMEs, notably lack of infrastructure, limited access to financial resources and to innovation, shortage of skilled labor, the costs of market research, lack of bargaining power, and legislative impediments, including national and EU regulations concerning intellectual property rights, labor, and taxation. These market failures often generate costs that are difficult for individual SMEs to bear. (Alkin & Okay, 2008)

In terms of financial resources, alternative sources of financing, including capital market instruments, have not been created for SMEs. Macroeconomic factors are another important cause of the financing problems of SMEs. In an environment of increased financial vulnerability and instability, increases in exchange rate and interest rate have an adverse effect on the financial condition and profitability of these firms. (Alkin & Okay, 2008)

In the developing economies, the overall education level in SMEs is low and entrepreneurs with an engineering background are limited. A partnership culture is also not common; thus, the whole capital is provided by the entrepreneur himself. (Alkin & Okay, 2008)

A survey covering 40,000 SMEs in Turkey conducted by the Small and Medium Industry Development Organization (SMIDO) in 2005 revealed that 56% of the SMEs do not or cannot export their products. In addition, although 46% suffer from lack of funds and 63% need additional financing, 70% do not take any loans. It also revealed that 56% of SMEs have no registered trademark, utility model or patent, while 60% do not benefit from statistical quality control, 72% from performance management, and 76% from computer-supported production and sales planning (Alkin & Okay, 2008).

The SME sector in Turkey is characterized by great geographical imbalances. SMEs are very unevenly spread across the country. The Marmara region (which includes Istanbul) and Izmir together account for about 65% of the SMEs in the country. The Eastern regions, on the other hand, harbor less than 20% of all SMEs. But whereas those concentrated in the less developed regions represent the majority of smaller enterprises, the Marmara region attracts most of the medium-sized enterprises (Alkin & Okay, 2008).

Due to their capital structures, SMEs in Turkey have certain disadvantages in terms of self-financing. Since they have low capital intensity and operate mainly in labor-intensive sectors, the amount of depreciation set aside on fixed assets is low. As a result, they are able to set aside fewer funds in this way and cannot benefit from the capacity extension effect of depreciation (Alkin & Okay, 2008).

An exploration of the biggest challenge facing Turkish SMEs points to institutionalization. The general form of SMEs in Turkey is family-owned businesses, while the chances that the next generation will take over the business are limited to 5%. According to the literature, the main reason that micro enterprises go bankrupt is their conservative attitude towards production and new product lines; their resistance to innovation causes them to decline. An analysis of small enterprises, on the other hand, shows that their tendency to cover their expenses with their own resources results in limited investment. As for medium-sized enterprises, institutionalization appears to be the biggest challenge. Institutionalization requires knowledge at the management level. The lack of management know-how results in dependency on one person, mainly the enterprise owner. (Alkin & Okay, 2008) Production and production lines are learnt throughout the production process, though without an in-depth analysis of managerial requirements. Most of the time, the board of directors consists of family members, and financial and accounting functions are carried out by these members.

Going International

Globalization, the process of increased integration among countries, continues at an accelerated pace. Daily, more companies are going global and trying to increase their share in the global economy through international trade. As evidenced by the statistics, international trade and investments have been increasing over the past decades. An increasing percentage of total revenue comes from overseas markets.

Internet technologies have played a key role in globalization. They have changed the way organizations operate, making it easier for them to keep up-to-date and to communicate with each other. They have also changed the structure of the competitive environment, facilitating access of all organizations to information and raw materials and allowing them to provide goods and services worldwide.

Surviving in international markets is a challenge for small companies and multinational corporations alike. The challenges of going international include the need to adapt management strategies to the economic systems of different countries and regions; the strategy at headquarters may not achieve the same results in another country. Thus, international management - the process of applying management techniques and concepts in a multinational environment - has become crucial (Luthans & Doh, 2009).

Foremost among the issues to be considered in international management is the structure of the business. In the global world, there is no magic organizational formula that can be implemented anywhere and everywhere and guarantee success. As a result, new organizational theories are constantly being analyzed and implemented. Strict matrix organizational structures have given way to more flexible hybrid structures, and more flexible marketing strategies that are adapted to the cultural perceptions of the society in which the organization is active have come into being.

The literature on international management also presents various approaches to marketing. Levitt (1983) stated that the worldwide success of a growing list of products that have become household names is evidence that customers, despite cultural differences, are becoming homogenized. As a result, a multinational corporation's strategy of tailoring its products to the needs of multiple markets may put it at a severe disadvantage vis-à-vis competitors who apply marketing imagination to the task of developing advanced, functional, reliable standardized products, at the right price, on a global scale.

Levitt's argument was based on the assumption that consumer behavior is rational (De Mooij, 2003). Assumptions of consumer rationality are, however, a matter of debate and ignore cultural aspects (McCracken, 1989; Suerdem, 1993; Antonides; 1998). De Mooij stated that despite the converging economic and demographic systems, consumer behavior is diverging in Europe; both convergence and divergence take place at macro level depending on the various regions. Thus, if products converge across countries, convergence is weakest in economically heterogeneous regions and strongest in economically homogeneous regions. De Mooij noted that consumption differences between countries can be explained by culture.

Donnelly (1970) analyzed the impact of cultural differences on international advertising, showing the significance of such differences and indicating that these differences should weigh heavily in a firm's international advertising decisions. Donnelly's study results revealed that the importance advertising managers give to cultural variables is significantly related to their approach to international advertising in two specific areas: 1. The degree of autonomy given to local branch officials in making major advertising planning decisions for the local area. 2. The approach used in the preparation and placement of non-domestic advertisements. The study indicates that the approach taken by an international advertising manager to plan and place a foreign ad is affected by the manager's assumptions about the importance of cultural variables. If this is the case, then it is vital that the assumptions a manager makes about the role of culture be valid ones.

CASE DESCRIPTION

In this section, we analyze the management strategies of Çilek, which started off as a small family-owned business in Turkey and quickly expanded to become one of the leading companies in the sector at the global level. In particular, we examine how the company has positioned itself in international markets as a high-quality furniture manufacturer for infants, kids and youth using international management techniques and a cross-cultural marketing approach.

Organization and Management

Management Team

Çilek was founded by three brothers: Mr. Mustafa Çilek, an engineer who is responsible for the production process, Mr. Muzaffer Çilek, who has in-depth experience in the retail sector and is responsible for the company's work processes, and Mr. Muharrem Çilek, a specialist in international marketing who is responsible for developing the company's expansion strategies. All three brothers have equal shares in the company.

In terms of management, Çilek has not shown the typical features of SMEs in Turkey. Despite being a family-founded and family-owned business, the management of the business is carried out professionally. The brothers have shared responsibility for running the company, each in accordance with his experience and educational background. The rest of the management team is chosen from among a qualified pool of candidate managers.

Organization and Management at Headquarters

Çilek's organizational structure at headquarters is presented in Figure 2. The structure is typical of a functional structure, that is, one in which similar activities are grouped together from the bottom to the top of the organization. With a functional structure, all knowledge and skills related to specific activities are consolidated, providing valuable depth of knowledge for the organization.

A functional structure is most effective when in-depth expertise is crucial to meeting organizational goals, when the organization needs to be controlled and coordinated through a vertical hierarchy, and when efficiency is important. Such a structure can be quite effective when there is little need for horizontal coordination (Daft, 2007). With a functional structure, economies of scale can be achieved. Employees working in similar activities are gathered in one specific area, and can thus share facilities, resulting in cost savings. Working closely together also allows employees to learn from one another, and working on one specific function enables employees to gain more knowledge about the function and related subjects and to develop their respective skills. In this intense

Figure 2.

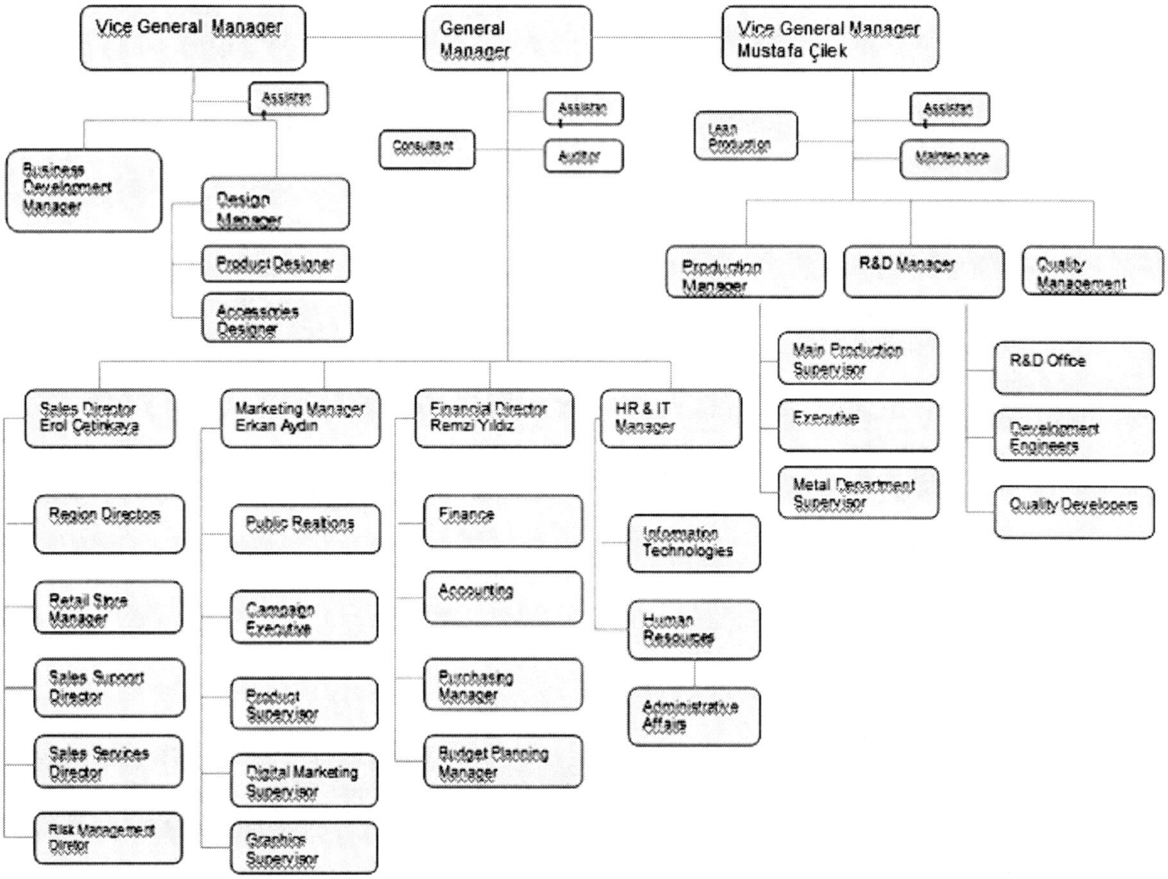

working environment, the in-depth knowledge of employees increases. Thus, the functional structure works well with one or a few production lines.

In this regard, the functional structure is the right choice for Çilek. Since the company's business focuses on the production of children's furniture, in-depth expertise is required. The existing structure allows the employees to respond to market needs with a limited number of production lines.

It can be observed that Çilek consists of functional units that allow for teamwork in a vertical manner. Each department is associated with the function, and lines of reporting work horizontally upward to the responsible functional manager. Strategic decisions and organizational goals, however, are determined by top management.

An in-depth analysis of Çilek's organizational structure shows that:

- Management levels are set horizontally in the organizational structure.
- Management areas are set vertically at the top management level.
- Communication channels flow from top to bottom along the pre-determined functional line.
- Span of control is set at most effective.

Çilek's management is made up of five levels:

General Manager: The most influential person in the organization. He is the only authority who plans, organizes, coordinates and controls activities in the big picture.

Department Managers: The most influential persons in their own departments. They are responsible for planning, organizing, leading, coordinating and controlling activities in their own departments. They report to the General Manager.

Vice Managers: They perform their duties within a predefined framework. They report directly to the Department Managers and hold responsibility in second degree.

Executives: They perform their set activities in accordance with their authority level. They hold responsibility in third degree for the activities undertaken by their department.

Employees: They perform their activities within the framework of the authority given them.

Organization and Management of Foreign Subsidiaries

Çilek's foreign subsidiaries show different organizational features depending on system needs specific to the area. These needs may include location, turnover and number of stores in the area. The structure can be made up of:

Stores executive, warehouse executive, store executive, sales adviser, maintenance employees

Or;

Store manager, sales adviser, maintenance employees

In this regard, the organizational structure in international markets shows diversification depending on the needs of the market. A geographical structure is also applied in various markets. In sum, a hybrid structure can be identified.

During the process of setting up a new foreign subsidiary, an advisor manager from headquarters is assigned to establish and implement the system. Teams are formed to adjust the organizational structure at the subsidiary. The store manager and warehouse manager employed by the foreign subsidiary are trained in Turkey and work for a period of time in one of Çilek's stores in the country. The advisor manager also gives on-the-job training to the subsidiary's team. The coverage and duration of the on-the-job training and orientation programs are planned by Çilek's human resources manager and department manager. On-the-job training is provided throughout the production process and, with each new product or implementation, allied training is given at the subsidiary where the store is performing.

Regional managers forward decisions made at headquarters, project information and all issues requiring communication to the related subsidiaries. Likewise, each month, Çilek's foreign subsidiaries send their warehouse and store inventory lists, product sales and order reports, employee-based turnover reports and financial reports to headquarters. The department manager visits the subsidiaries periodically and evaluates the reports with the store managers on the spot. The reports are consolidated at headquarters and form the basis for performance evaluation.

Corporate Business Strategy

Çilek's strategy is to be a unique Turkish brand, get the biggest share in the market through successful implementation of its unique designs in its field of expertise and become the most profitable corporation in the furniture sector. To this end, Çilek works to:

- Analyze its competitors' strategies;
- Evaluate sales channels;
- Identify target markets in the global area;
- Increase brand awareness;
- Set a good example by generating its own retail channels;
- Expand by contracting the best retailers in their own countries;
- Become a profitable brand for investors; and

- Understand the needs and expectations of individuals and provide products beyond those needs and expectations.

Çilek's five-year strategic plan is prepared with the participation of the management board and top managers. The plan, which is updated annually, covers the following issues:

- Promotion of the company
- Target markets
- Customer, product, distribution channels and competitor analysis
- Market-entry strategies
- Brand strategy
- Sales, marketing and operational plans
- Financial projections

Marketing Strategy

Çilek's marketing strategy is "to open more foreign subsidiaries and sell more Çilek products to more people". For Çilek, this poses the following question: "In today's democratic market where entrepreneurs and consumers have the choice, what can we do to be the chosen brand?" In response to the question, the company has determined the main features of its marketing strategy to be the following:

- Çilek should be present in markets where the potential is high (in malls, in zones where there is a concentration of children furniture shops, in the children's section of corporate clients, in e-commerce, and in catalogue sales)
- Çilek stores should be in the best locations
- Çilek stores should be of the highest quality, decorated with enthusiasm and always tidy
- Çilek store windows should be decorated attractively in accordance with the season
- Çilek sales team should provide entrepreneurs and customers with the best quality service
- Çilek stores should be highly profitable for investors
- Çilek products and accessories should be on the agenda of the target group
- Çilek should always ask existing and potential customers about their needs and expectations regarding the company's products, and design its products accordingly.

Brand Strategy

Çilek's brand strategy is to focus on a niche market and be an expert brand in this sector. Çilek differentiates itself from its competitors by producing a variety of furniture and furniture accessories for the 0–24 age group.

Requirements of the Brand Strategy:

What can be done?

- Communication among girl-boy or age classification
- Development of Social Responsibility projects and sponsorships
- Joint promotion with well-known children and youth brands
- Participation in design-focused fairs; sponsorship of such fairs
- Use of the smell and taste of strawberry ("strawberry" in Turkish is "Çilek")
- Opening of new stores in big cities in the world

What cannot be done?

- Cannot produce or sell any rooms other than for infants, kids and youth
- Cannot focus on luxurious and upper-class products and consumer segments

Table 2.

Business Strategy
Çilek's strategy is to be a unique Turkish brand. Through the successful implementation of innovative designs in its field of expertise, Çilek aims to get the biggest market share and become the most profitable company in its sector. Achieving this entails analyzing the strategies of competitors, evaluating sales channels, determining the right markets in a particular global area, increasing brand awareness, setting a good example by generating the company's own retail channels, expanding by contracting the best retailers in their own countries, being a profitable brand for investors, understanding the needs and expectations of individuals and providing products beyond these needs and expectations. After all, Çilek aims to expand globally.

Brand Strategy
Focusing on the niche of furniture for the 0-24 age group and being an expert brand in the sector.

Çilek rooms are the furnished environment of infants, kids and youth, responding to all expectations of the age group through a combination of furniture and accessories.

Brand Awareness
"Furniture and accessories for infants, kids and youth"

Brand Promise
"We provide them with the room of their dreams; thus, they prepare themselves for life with joy."

- Cannot focus on cheap products and lower-income consumer segments
- Cannot renounce its furniture or accessories product-line
- Cannot produce below European Union standards
- Cannot engage in custom manufacturing

Market-Entry Strategy

Çilek's market-entry strategy is implemented by comparing the entry policies of local and global competitors. In this regard, under the framework of the customer segment analysis data set, Çilek has analyzed its positioning strategies in relation to those of two other local competitors. The analysis is presented in Figure 3.

As can be seen in the graph, Çilek has created an important difference by implementing its concept-store and furniture & accessories combination model. Çilek plans to execute this strategy in its upcoming market entries.

Product Development

Çilek has gained a close understanding of the market for children's furniture in different parts of the world. Designers work jointly with psychologists to produce unique designs that are adjusted to the

Figure 3.

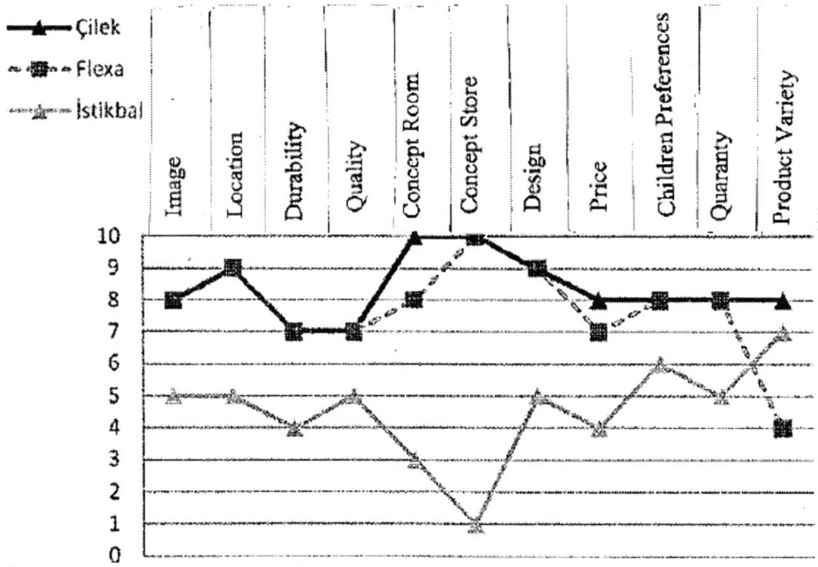

needs of children in different geographic areas. Ultimately, Çilek aims to create a dream world for infants, children and youth through common design features that make up "*Çilek Fashion*".

Basic Product Specifications that Result in Sales

- *Five-Year Guarantee:* All Çilek products have a five-year guarantee against deterioration, breakages and discoloration.
- *Quality:* Çilek produces furniture in conformity with European Union standards, and the specially produced melamine-coated chipboards Çilek uses in its raw materials are anti-carcinogenic, anti-bacterial and anti-allergenic. Because of this, Çilek is the first brand in its sector in Turkey to have received Geprüfte Sicherheit (GS) certification. The GS Quality Certificate is granted by Landesgewerbeanstalt Bayern (LGA) in Germany for high-quality and high-security products.
- *Security:* Çilek uses specially tempered glass to reduce the risk of accidental breakage that would normally result in sharp and jagged pieces that may cause harm to children. The fabrics used on Çilek products are not only fire retardant but also easy to clean.
- *Concept Unity and Design Focus:* Each Çilek room has a different character and mood. The designs are ergonomic and functional and rely on a combination of color and theme models. All products are designed jointly with psychologists and designers to produce unique designs that appeal to those aged 0-24.
- *Segmentation:* The 0-24 age category is segmented into infants, children and youth. Çilek products are designed differently for girls and boys, with a different concept for each.
- *After Sales Services:* The Çilek Service Support Center has been set up to facilitate communication with customers who have bought Çilek products.

Promotional Strategy

All Çilek advertising and communication activities are carried out in Turkey. Through original ads that distinguish the company from its competitors in the sector, Çilek seeks to increase brand awareness, strengthen the positioning of the company and reach its target markets. The ads, which target all customers in a particular global area, are designed to associate the brand in the minds of the target group with dream rooms for infants, kids and youth up to the age of 24.

Like other leading world brands, Çilek uses a universal language for kids. In all its advertising campaigns, the company uses a positive tone that respects the intelligence of children. Children from different geographic areas are casted in the ads, as a part of the company's cross-cultural management approach. However, the children all sing the same song and send the same message, creating a strong feeling of belonging to the Çilek brand.

In the promotions it carries out globally, Çilek is attentive to regional differences. The company takes into account local traditions, culture and values during the preparation of campaigns in a specific region. Consumer behavior tendencies and preferences in the region are also analyzed and the ads adjusted accordingly.

In Europe, for example, where consumers rank high on reading habits, Çilek's efforts to increase brand awareness focus on ads in newspapers as well as ads and special interviews in sector-specific magazines. Çilek also engages in sponsorships and celebrates special days of the region.

In Saudi Arabia, Çilek's promotional activities focus on ads in newspapers, since Saudi Arabian consumers tend to read newspapers more than they watch TV. Çilek ads targeting Saudi Arabian customers are designed to create an image of colorful, funny, high-quality furniture, in keeping with cultural preferences. Since Saudi consumers tend to change the furniture in their homes during the month of Ramadan, Çilek's marketing efforts in the country accelerate before and during Ramadan.

In Japan, standards are high and the Japanese consumer gives great importance to the quality and packaging of the product, rather than to price. A market analysis shows that Japanese female consumers tend to choose products that are promoted on the Internet and in magazines. Once they use a product, they will often share their experience about it on their personal websites and blogs. Consequently, in addition to placing ads in newspapers, Çilek's promotional efforts in Japan focus on the Internet and magazines. The emphasis is on presenting the company's high-quality products in as attractive a package as possible.

Pricing Strategy

Çilek products are priced individually and sold by the piece. The products are in the middle-to-high price range. As the leader in the furniture industry for the 0-24 age category, Çilek sets the prices in the sector. The company, however, has not adopted an international pricing strategy, so its high-quality products are sold at a price that is considered reasonable outside Turkey.

Financial Strategy

An analysis of Çilek's financial status, including annual company sales, expenses and profit, shows that the company enjoys very high liquidity. Çilek operates with its own equity capital. As a result, the company was not affected by fluctuations in the market during the economic crisis. Since Çilek has a high percentage of equity capital, its debt payback capacity, especially short-term liability is high. Inventory and credit turnover rate, as well as active turnover rate, are high. The conservative approach the company has adopted, however, is a survival strategy that leads to a liquidity reserve rather than a high profit margin over a short period. While Çilek has become a well-known brand, its active profit margin and equity capital profit margin are below what would be expected. In order to reach the desired profit level, Çilek's preferred strategy is to increase its asset turnover rate by focusing on exports.

Çilek operates with a JIT (Just-in-Time) system that does not allow for great amounts of inventory. Under normal circumstances, when the inventory turnover rate is low, the company faces late delivery problems that might lead customers to choose another brand. Çilek, however, has not experienced such a scenario. Customers have trust in Çilek products and tend to show brand loyalty.

CURRENT CHALLENGES FACING THE ORGANIZATION

Economies play an incremental role in shaping an organization's future. Fluctuations in an economy affect strategic and investment plans, while global economic crises change the path of organizations, affecting them in a number of ways, including their investment, human resource and expansion plans and their marketing and promotion strategies. Sector-specific challenges also play an important role in the growth and development of an organization. As a Turkish company that started off as a small enterprise, Çilek had to cope with many of the market failures and challenges facing SMEs in Turkey. As a company that is quickly expanding globally, the main challenges it faces today are organizational, management, marketing and financial ones.

1. *Organizational Challenges:* According to Peter Drucker (2006), to create and keep a customer, a company must be wedded to the ideal of innovation. A global company should shape the vectors of technology and globalization into its strategic richness. Organizational theory points to the fact that innovation in SMEs depends on the decision of the manager himself. Due to lack of institutionalization, an innovative approach is generally lacking. Teamwork is not seen often; rather, small working groups and individuals that report directly to the manager are appreciated, giving the manager direct control. Motivation techniques are not used much. The work process is labor-intensive. (Alkin & Okay, 2008)
   This is not the case with Çilek, which consists of functional units that allow for and encourage teamwork. But while the company has adopted a functional structure at headquarters - the most efficient structure to respond to fewer production lines – adjustments to the organizational structure of subsidiaries sometimes need to be made, depending on the requirements of the geographic area in which Çilek is operating. In some cases, the need for a more flexible and horizontal structure has led the company to develop a hybrid structure for foreign subsidiaries. For multinationals or transnational companies, the search for an appropriate organizational structure might last a while, which makes for a costly period. In the case of an expanding organization, the organizational structure at headquarters can sometimes not respond in a timely way to the expansion of production lines and to local adjustments. For Çilek, choosing the right organizational structure may be considered the main organizational challenge facing the company and has an impact on its marketing and human resource activities abroad.
2. *Management Challenges:* During the assignment of regional managers, a polycentric approach is implemented and local managers are employed based on their knowledge of the area and the environment. Prior to startup, on-the-job training is offered to local managers in Turkey in order to introduce them to Çilek's production lines, and these managers work in a Turkish store for a certain period of time.
   In the global era, the necessity of employing the right manager locally might present a challenge and a polycentric approach could shift to a geocentric approach. However, acceptance of the new manager by local staff might pose new challenges.

3. *Marketing Challenges:* In terms of marketing, Çilek implements a cross-cultural marketing strategy. Local requirements are taken into account and local people are hired for the ads. In this regard, searching for new strategies, finding adequate means of promotion, and developing culturally appropriate advertising and promotional campaigns are costly processes. Moreover, the need to develop new sales channels, such as e-commerce, is accelerating. Means of transportation, delivery and payment also need to be developed and adjusted to new sales lines, posing additional challenges.
   In terms of market competition, the greatest challenge Çilek faces is niche imitation using low-quality products. Other companies globally produce furniture for children using cheaper materials, imitating Çilek concept designs. In some cases, customer segmentation differs and price awareness also takes over.
4. *Financial Challenges:* Çilek enjoys very high liquidity and operates with its own equity capital. As a result, the company remained unaffected by fluctuations in the market during the economic crisis. The challenge is that the company's gross profit margin is low while its operational costs are high. The company's high marketing budget, promotional efforts, and the use of high-quality raw materials for production, coupled with administrative costs, push operational costs up. The highly competitive environment leads to a decrease in profit margins, as the market is shared with many companies operating in the same sector. The company's financial leverage is low compared to other companies operating in the same sector, which causes a growth deficit. Loans would help improve the ratio of net profit to equity.

CONCLUSION

Çilek started off as an SME in Turkey in 1995. The company differentiated itself in the furniture sector by focusing on the niche of furniture for the 0-24 age bracket. Çilek's high-quality products, costly production processes, right customer segmentation and international awards and certificates have reinforced the company's positioning in the market. Today, with its unique designs and themes, Çilek is the leading brand in Turkey in the sector.

Çilek's expansion strategy through foreign subsidiaries has opened up new markets for the company in 68 countries. By taking advantage of being the first in a niche market, adopting innovative and flexible management styles and organizational structures, and developing appropriate marketing strategies that rely on cross-cultural management techniques, the company has succeeded in positioning itself in international markets as a high-quality furniture manufacturer for children between the ages of 0 to 24. Çilek's successful positioning has relied on a rational analysis of the sector, a market-entry analysis that focuses not only on the competition but also on cultural features that would increase the rate of acceptance of Çilek products by the target group in the foreign market, and adequate financial strategies. Despite the challenges facing SMEs in general, Çilek has become a big brand company that enjoys tremendous popularity, both locally and internationally.

REFERENCES

Alkin, K., & Okay, E. (2008). *The process of alignment with Basel II by SMEs in Turkey and recommendations* (pp.68, 74). (Istanbul Chamber of Trade, Publication No: 2008-4).

Antonides, G. (1998). *An attempt at integration of economic and psychological theories of consumption. European Perspectives on Consumer Behavior*. Prentice Hall, Europe.

Daft, R. (2007). *Understanding the theory and design of organizations*. Thomson South-Western.

De Mooij, M. (2003). Convergence and divergence in consumer behavior: Implications for global advertising. *International Journal of Advertising*, *22*(2), 183–202.

Donnelly, J. H. (1970). Marketing notes and communications: Attitudes toward culture and approach to international advertising. *Journal of Marketing*, 60–63.

Drucker, P. (2006). *Classic Drucker*. Harvard Business School Publishing Corporation.

Keskin, E. (2008). *Access to financing for SME's in the EU and Turkey*. REX/264 EU-Turkey Joint Consultative Committee, 25th meeting of the EU-Turkey Joint Consultative Committee Paris, France, 18-19 November, 2008.

Levitt, T. (1983). The globalization of markets. *Harvard Business Review*, 92–102.

Luthans, F., & Doh, J. P. (2009). *International management, culture, strategy, and behavior*. McGraw Hill.

McCracken, G. (1989). Culture and consumer behavior: An anthropological perspective. *Journal of the Market Research Society. Market Research Society*, *32*(1), 56–73.

Suerdem, A. (1993). Social de(re)construction of mass culture: Making (non) sense of consumer behavior. *International Journal of Research in Marketing*, *11*, 423–443.

TUIK- Turkish Statistical Institute. (2003). *General census of industry and establishments*. Retrieved from https://www.tuik.gov.tr

ENDNOTE

1 In the late 1990s, some European retail traders developed the idea of tailoring a shop towards a lifestyle theme, in the form of "concept stores" that specialized in cross-selling without using separate departments.

Chapter 9
Facing Organizational Change and Stress Management: The Case of First Commercial Bank[1]

Elham Metwally
Misr International University & American University in Cairo (AUC), Egypt

EXECUTIVE SUMMARY

In today's hyper-competitive environment, understanding factors that contribute to effective management of change and achieving strategic competitiveness are critical. Based on management theories and best practices, this case study provides a detailed exploration, description, and explanation of the implementation of two electronic banking delivery systems, namely ATMs and Internet Banking, in a leading bank in Egypt. The case identifies and describes the bank's approach to managing change through Information Technology, with regards to leadership actions, overcoming resistance to change, personal and organizational attributes, strategies, structures, business processes, culture, as well as organizational commitment. The arrangement of the case followed a question-and-answer format rather than the traditional narrative. A series of questions and answers based on the semi-structured face-to-face interviews assessed the research topic. The researcher treated both products side-by-side throughout the case, as action planning was the same for each product. Outcomes revealed great commonalities, which meant tremendous overlap and repetition, had a separate case study been presented for each product.

ORGANIZATION BACKGROUND

It was mid-day on March 6, 2002 when Mokbel Hazim, chairman and managing director of First Commercial Bank met with the board of directors and senior executives in the bank's headquarters overlooking the scenic view of the Giza Pyramids. He reached for another famous Mexican cigar from his shirt's pocket, lit it and allowed the smoke flow out onto the air. "IT is one of the key sectors that facilitated shaping the model of globalization," he breathed. "It eliminated all hurdles and frontiers, and unsurprisingly this technological development significantly affected the financial industry, with the world's leading banking institutions compelled to implement the

DOI: 10.4018/978-1-60960-583-4.ch009

newest and most advanced technologies in order to prevent delays or failures in servicing their customers, improve work performance and the banking sector's efficiency." He suddenly rolled his eyes. "Without automation of all banking operations, we cannot move ahead with consumer banking services." He was holding the Mexican cigar was tightly between his teeth as he started to walk towards his office's panoramic window overlooking the Pyramids and his eyes swept the horizon with great excitement as he envisioned what he and his team will do.

First Commercial Bank is one of the largest banks in Egypt regarding assets, deposits, and loans. It is also one of the most profitable banks, always revealing strong financial results. However, Hazim's pressing worry was how he could possible make a successful deployment of IT-related delivery systems in the bank's everyday business functions. Though confident of the bank's capabilities to managing such a change, Hazim had to think about several issues, like ways to overcome resistance to change, personal and organizational attributes, strategies, structures, business processes, and culture, that are conducive to effective management of organizational change and stress in First Commercial Bank.

Structure of the Egyptian Banking Sector

The banking system in Egypt comprises the Central Bank of Egypt (CBE), 28 commercial banks (four of which are state-owned), 24 private and joint venture banks, 31 business and investment banks, and three specialized banks (two of which are state-owned banks) (see Appendix 1). Commercial banks are the most significant sub-sector as it represents about 81% of the total banking industry assets (The Economist Intelligence Unit). The four public sector banks, which are owned by the government, namely the National Bank of Egypt, Bank of Alexandria, Banque du Caire, and Banque Misr, lead the sector with 60% of total deposits, 55% of total assets, 70% of loan portfolio, and about 75% of all banking transactions (Bank Rankings 2004). They finance major public sector projects, such as the Aswan High Dam, state companies, as well as certain industries like textiles, steel, tourism, and so forth. In efforts to increase the effectiveness of their operations and achieve competitiveness, state-owned banks underwent several changes such as restructuring their activities and improving their operational processes (Bank Rankings 2004).

Despite the fact that state-owned banks dominate the sector, non-state-owned banks, or private banks, are greatly accountable for the development of retail banking, a field previously untapped by the public sector banks (The Economist Intelligence Unit). Joint venture commercial banks, most of which adopt western banking standards in their daily operations and are the most profitable in the Egyptian banking industry, were established since 1974 to promote foreign direct investments in Egypt (Abu-Musa, 2003: 46-48). They account for 25% of total market share and are mostly involved with financing trade with the service sector, thereby generating foreign currencies needed to finance imports activities (Bank Rankings 2004).

Investment banks account for a marginal share of 13.4% of the total banking system, and comprise private, joint venture, and off-shore banks or foreign banks that were permitted since 1993 to deal in the local currency provided; they keep a minimum requirement of $15 million worth of capital assets (Abu-Musa, 2003: 46-48). Examples of foreign banks operating as joint ventures with local partners are National Societe Generale Bank, and HSBC Bank Egypt (Bank Rankings 2004). Specialized banks comprise about 5.9% of the total banking sector in Egypt and are accountable for promoting the Egyptian industrial, agricultural, and construction projects by providing long-term loans (Abu-Musa, 2003: 46-48).

The most notable characteristic of the banking system in Egypt is that the industry is greatly fragmented. For example, the 48 smallest banks in the sector hold 39% of total assets, 29% of total deposits, and 43% of total loans; whereas, the ninth largest bank account for only 2% of total assets (Bank Rankings 2004).

Literature Review

Pursuing particular managers, as well as organizational characteristics, has become a necessity, in general, and especially nowadays with the enhancing invasion of information technology (IT) into everyday's operations. In the banking industry, in specific, IT have changed how banks compete (Abou Musa, 2003; American Chamber of Commerce, 2005; Cox, 1986; Curry & Penman, 2004; Liao & Cheung, 2003; Rao et al., 2003; Rayport & Jaworski, 2004; Swierczek, Pritam, & Bechter, 2005), and there is, accordingly, an increasing quest for certain personal and organizational attributes, as well as governance practices. Taking full advantage of the available resources and continuously capitalizing on opportunities became crucial as one of management's techniques (Bob, & Malcolm, 1989). Accordingly, issues of meeting challenges to change and change resistance have become at the center of attention and interest of several researchers like Anderson & Anderson, 2003; Burnes, 1992; Collins & Porras, 1989; Dooley, 1998; French, Bell, & Zawachi, 2000; Hamel & Prahalad, 1994; Hamel & Valikangas, 2003; Kitchen, 1997, 2002; Kotter, 1995, 1996, 1998; Nickols, 2004; Teare & Monk, 2002; and Tichy & Sherman, 1993.

A mounting literature highlighted the role of IT executives in effectively leading IT projects, facing different challenges to change, and in finding mindsets that can effectively manage change, develop effective IT capabilities, synchronize strategy and IT resources, think about information technologies' strategic impact as a change agent, and in general, make things happen (Anol & Rudy, 1997; Barnes, Mieczkowska, & Hinton, 2003; Johnson, Fidler, & Rogerson, 1998; La Porte, Demchak, & Friis 2001; Matsui, 2002; Picket, 2004; Prahalad & Krishnan, 2002; Proctor & Doukakis, 2003). And, in order to survive, organizations are bound not only to change but also to effectively manage such change. Accordingly, in an increasingly unstable and fast changing business environment, more pressure is placed on organizational leaders. They should be more alert to changes in the external environment to identify different forces, such as breakthroughs in IT that might alter competition and provoke planned change (Branch, 2005).

Little research though was conducted on best practices in managing IT and in effect, setting standards for IT governance were modest. Additionally, best practices for IT governance vary greatly among organizations and IT strategies change continuously according to a number of factors among which are a firm's industry, competitive pressures, financial status, sweeping changes in information technologies, IT expertise in managing IT risk and dealing with competitive forces, and accordingly, board members need to develop IT policies that strategically fit their firms' positions (Nolan & McFarlan, 2005).

Capitalizing on IT systems to earn strategic competitiveness is challenged by the extent to which organizations deal with a "change-management" condition, and by developing proper strategies for both short-term and long-term challenges. In explaining organizational strategic competitiveness, previous researchers' focus was mainly on organization's internal resources, capabilities and core competence, organizational innovativeness, learning organizations, the impact of cultural values and cultural competency on management systems and organizational practices, impact of nations, governments and industries, factors conditions and industry competition, as well as productivity levels (Amit & Shoemaker 1993; Hatem, 2003; Hitt, Ireland, & Hoskisson, 2001; Hofstede, 1984, 1991; Penrose, 1959; Porter, 1985, 1990, and 1998; Rogers, 1983; Schumpeter 1934; Senge 1994; and Wah 2002).

Some literature on mediating factors influencing the relationship between investments in IT resources and strategic competitiveness included issues on effective management of IT resources. In studying competitiveness, others like Ross, Beath, and Goodhue (1996), included issues on effective management of IT resources and recommended that in a business environment with a fast-evolving nature and technology-based operations, the major challenge is on how to effectively address changes in organizational roles, structures, and processes on adopting a new IT, which eventually enhances organizations' competitiveness. As such, development of a matching strategic agenda to help executives effectively deal with change and achieve a competitive advantage is always required (Liao & Cheung, 2003), and an information strategy and an appropriate corporate structure that ensure the optimum use of internal and external resources is also needed (Bob, & Malcolm, 1989). IT governance, appropriate infrastructures, committed and skilled labor, and concerns over security matters, mistrust among stakeholders, protecting personal privacy, preventing patents violations, etc., are some other determinants of effective management of IT.

Best-performing enterprises carefully plan to achieve superior financial result, and good corporate governance is associated with the achievement of an organization's desired profitability, productivity, and other related measures. Effective governance of IT resources was found to increase competitiveness through its impact on efficiency of quality service (Swierczek, Pritam, & Bechter, 2005). Successful IT governance involves incorporating many of the distinctiveness of the "transformational" leader. Capitalizing on recent technological advances requires active and supportive-to-change management skills to carry on transforming organizational structures, institutions, cultures, and strategies. Hence, according to previous studies, there is a connection between the existence of effective change leaders and organizational change and development (Kotter, 1995, 1998; Hamel & Prahalad, 1994; Hamel & Valikangas, 2003; Levasseur, 2001). Moreover, managers who motivated change, created vision, developed political support, and effective knowledge of change processes and change management skills, such as interpersonal skills, teaming skills, communication and persuasion skills, and creative and innovative thinking, sustaining the momentum, and so forth, were perceived as effective in managing organizational change through their influence on organizational culture and commitment (Brynjolfsson, & Yang, 1997; Brewster, et al, 2000: 221-222). As Hitt, Ireland, & Hoskisson (2001: 489-490) note: "A firm's ability to achieve strategic competitiveness and earn above-average returns is compromised when strategic leaders fail to respond appropriately and quickly to changes in the complex global competitive environment", and "strategies cannot be formulated and implemented to achieve above-average returns without effective strategic leaders." Therefore, technology could be a threat to banks if, for example, they are not updating their operations with new innovations, markets, competitors' actions, or if new technologies are unmet by demand and consumer acceptance (Liao & Cheung, 2003). Also, declining productivity gains of IT investments was attributed to the reality that changes in technology-outpaced changes in the more intangible human-side factors related to change (McNish, 2002).

This research therefore, aims at understanding the effect of managing change through information technology. In particular, the case study investigates the role of top management, through different leadership actions and personal and organizational attributes, in determining the direction and performance of the organization with regards to implementation of new IT-based delivery systems, and its influence on achieving strategic competitiveness. My approach in this study relies on sources of strategic competitiveness drawn from inside the organization; namely resource-based drivers of strategic competitiveness, and assumes that First Commercial bank can achieve strategic competitiveness through effectively managing change through information technologies. Given the same kinds of IT enabled-systems, different levels of strategic competitiveness are achieved depending on different leadership actions (Hitt, Ireland, & Hoskisson, 2001: 112, 390). Therefore, this study aims to answer one major question: what is the role of effective management of change through IT in achieving strategic competitiveness? To answer this question, the researcher draws on Egyptian banking sector data to further understand the link between competitiveness, IT-based applications, and effective management of change, and explore ways in which using IT, namely ATMs and Internet Banking, contributes to strategic competitiveness for a bank that have made it to the top. These managers' actions of influence on strategic competitiveness include, but are not limited to successfully creating readiness for change, managing resistance to change, empowering others to work on the vision, anchoring new approaches to the bank's systems, structure and culture. Expected deliverables include lessons learned and key issues, for further transferability of such practices to other low performing banks. As such, the researcher chose to study First Commercial Bank of Egypt as it seemed to be the most illustrative for the research topic, as it provides more insights about ways of strengthening the capacity of banking organizations and helping them lure more customers and investors, and accordingly, strengthen the Egyptian economy in general.

SETTING THE STAGE

First Commercial Bank was established in the early eighties as a joint venture bank to perform all commercial and investment banking, as well as investment banking activities in Egypt. The bank first started to function as a wholesale corporate bank, but then rapidly developed relationships with individuals and SMEs. Its customer base focuses on private sector corporations, multinationals, and export-oriented companies. First Commercial Bank launched its retail banking activity to provide an extensive variety of products and services, seeking to diversify its income mix and capitalize on the bank's powerful corporate foundation. The bank's advanced IT systems and infrastructure provide operational efficiency and better customer service, and through several external projects that increased delivery channels, and increased customers' satisfaction. At the crux of retail banking is gathering stable funds and providing an increasing number of products and services, as well as credit and debit cards. First Commercial Bank has no physical existence outside Egypt; it deals with a big network of correspondent banks globally.

First Commercial Bank focuses on human resources acquisition and development. The recruitment activities within the bank are set towards satisfying the bank's manpower supplies with the most excellent available quality of experienced employees and young graduates to guarantee the delivery of its business plan.

At the center of First Commercial Bank's attention is corporate culture and to incorporate its core competences and strategies across its different banking operations as a leading financial institution offering leading quality services to its customers, and at the same time maximizing shareholders' value.

CASE DESCRIPTION

Products and Services

First Commercial Bank provides its customers with a variety of personal and corporate banking services, that range from current and savings accounts to time deposits, credit cards, and loans, as well as a diverse payment services. This case illustrates the implementation of two of the First

Commercial Bank's products, to be precise ATMs and Internet Banking.

First Commercial Bank adopts state-of-art technologies to guarantee constant customers' access to its financial system.

Implementation Phases of Electronic Delivery Systems

Planning: Implementation of ATMs in First Commercial Bank went through the normal steps of implementing any new technology. It started with gathering of all branch managers and key persons who will be involved in the development of the product for brainstorming and making decisions. Goals were defined and surveys were conducted to know the needs and zones of customers to be accessed and traffic in target market. Key executives took decisions with regards to infrastructure. They determined brands to be acquired and selected the models to be used (for example, lobby machine, multitask night safe machine with deposits and foreign exchange, wall machine, or only deposits machine), and checked availability with vendors. Other action plans included deployment issues such as human resources, security issues, administrative regulations and procedures, logistics, images, frames, and outlay designs. Implementation of ATMs started with First Commercial Bank branches then expanded with offsite machines. The new product manager also coordinated among IT department and branches, as well as other departments concerned, such as the new Card Center to issue cards and organized stages of implementation, some of which went in parallel.

The bank followed the same procedures in planning for implementation for Internet Banking and making decisions with regards to work on webpage for customers according to their different categories (individual or corporate accounts), choosing and installed the right software (database, communication software) and modules to link website (internet server) with the mainframe (customer database).

To effectively implement the new system, the bank conducted training sessions for staff, especially those working in customer services. Sessions embraced training on implementation of hardware, software components, software use, maintenance and traffic management, and ATM machine replenishment. Training manuals and presentations clarified how to put the new system into operation.

In conducting training sessions on Internet Banking, First Commercial Bank further handled security issues such as deciding upon and installing the right "Fire wall" tool to protect customers' accounts.

First Commercial Bank incorporated the ATM system into the bank's financial transactions with customers and internal financial reporting and documentation. The bank's IT department conducted software runs to start the implementation phase and used a special module to operate the new systems simultaneously with the old system. Throughout conversion, staff interacted with peers and received technical support from the IT department, as well as the product development team.

Acceptance testing started with issuing cards to all staff of the bank as pilot launch to find out if there were any problems with the new product. After the product was tested on staff, approval of the retail banking senior manager was obtained before the product was then released to the bank's clients.

Internet banking service was launched and tested first on staff members before it was released to customers. The bank announced availability of the service through flyers delivered with account statements and on receipts of ATM transactions.

First Commercial Bank predetermines cut-off times and value dates for all its clients' transactions. Instructions received from clients within the cut-off times will be executed the same day and given a value date according to the bank's preset value dates indicated. For example, there is no cut-off time for transfers' applications to accounts held with the bank; accordingly the transaction is processed immediately. For telegraphic transfers' applications, the cut-off time is 12:00hrs at noon for the transaction to be processed on the same day. In the case where the client submits his/her application after 12:00, his/her instructions will be carried out the following day. To apply for a telegraphic transfer to Egypt or overseas and settle credit cards for different customers through Internet Banking, clients have to be subscribers of the "Digital Signature" service that First Commercial Bank provides through its webpage. Cash deposits in the local currency or in foreign currencies that are received on the counter or from an ATM channel are put on a one day and two days hold, respectively to be credited to the beneficiary's account. Clients can make online cash deposits into their accounts though through the bank's Instant Deposit' machines that are scattered in specified areas of Egypt. Requests for Demand Drafts and Cashier's Orders are processed and dispatched the same day if received before 14:00hrs; whereas, updating personal details is processed within one working day if instructions are received before 14:00hrs.

Target Market

New systems target all clients who keep personal or corporate accounts in the bank. Mostly, they are the educated people, the corporate market segment, and/or new generations of youth who are more computer-oriented and seeking new technology. "ATMs are used with great success with all people. Many organizations, including ministries are now resorting to ATMs in payroll payments," asserted Senior Manager, ATM Unit Banking.

ATMs are used with great success with all people. Many organizations, including ministries, are now resorting to ATMs in payroll payments. No problems are encountered since there is an Arabic language version. But ATMs are used with great success by educated clients who are technology oriented. Internet Banking, on the other hand, is only used with success among those who are educated and who are computer oriented, have computer skills, and who own or have easy access to computers.

Market segments that could be appealing in the future include children, youth, and school/university students, or new sectors like small and medium who might be interested in special features provided by the new systems, and find it easy to deal with their technical issues.

CURRENT CHALLENGES FACING THE ORGANIZATION

In general, all employees who were involved in implementation, either who were from the bank or who were recruited from outside the bank, participated willingly. However, in implementation of the new systems, the bank faced some challenges among which were convincing people of different qualifications and mentalities to use the new systems, assisting customers who are less computer-oriented, and reducing resistance among some staff who were not comfortable with the new work load introduced during implementation, training sessions, and simulation. Other challenges included technical challenges such as adding more features or calculations to the system, and administrative challenges such as finding the right and suitable resources especially for jobs which were interrelated. "Some of the staff was not comfortable with new work load introduced during implementation, training sessions, and simulation," declared the manager of one of the branches.

To overcome resistance to change, executives communicated the bank's vision in words both verbally through "walk and talk" approach and through memos. People were allowed to work overtime and were compensated for late hours they stayed at work to finish projects in hand on time. People failing to emit the desired behaviors were moved to other less customer-oriented departments.

SOLLUTIONS AND RECOMMENDATIONS

Leadership Actions in Managing Change

In managing change triggered by the implementation of the new delivery systems, management established a sense of urgency by making surveys examining the market and knowing the needs and zones of customers to be accessed and traffic in target market. Management then started planning its priorities and convincing the managers involved in implementation with the urgency of change through meetings and e-mails.

Management created a vision to manage the change effort. The conception was that the bank should work toward being the best innovative and best quality financial service provider by explaining the importance of the new product to the bank's clients, employees and developing strategies for achieving that vision.

A team was formed from employees with shared commitments who maintained enough skills and experience to carry out the implementation phases. The team studied the needs of the retail department, IT department, as well as other departments whose functions were delivered by the new systems such as credit, letters of guarantee, and foreign exchange departments. In communicating the vision, strategies for achieving it, and the time frame set for departments involved, management used brochures, meetings, and training sessions.

Management encouraged training and simulation sessions for some selected employees who were involved in executing the plan. Sessions were done by rotation for employees and the group that was trained then trains another group, and so on.

Though management developed a progress report to the team head in recognition of employees' contributions, in general they considered implementation of a new system a reward itself to the bank's employees. "Our bank is doing us a favor by involving us in this change," said the manager of one of the branches.

In consolidating improvements and producing more change, First Commercial Bank tested the new systems on employees first to detect whereabouts of changing systems, structures, and policies.

First Commercial Bank institutionalized new shared values consistent with new changes and articulated through meetings and e-mails the connection between these values and improvements in customer services after implementation of the new systems, and how these new systems contribute to these improvements.

Throughout the implementation process, management's role was vital to creating a team spirit which helped in increasing commitment, producing a good product development, and achieving strategic competitiveness.

Personal and Organizational Attributes

Finding a common base: First Commercial Bank conducted a one-day information session to all employees to introduce them to the new systems to be implemented. The sessions gave participants an overview of the product with regards to several issues such as its uses, advantages, services it provides to customers, prospective locations, planned implementation time, date of launching the product, and so forth. These sessions allowed some input, a common base, and sharing of experiences which resulted in high achievement, deliverables, and productivity.

Organization of implementation activities among staff: Prior to implementation, First Commercial Bank announced several internal job vacancies requiring staff to support a new product development. People were allowed to move from other departments and were trained accordingly. Each department involved made requests to the IT department with the required features to be incorporated into the new systems. Departments also produced a manual of procedures. The IT department handled the technical part of implementation, whereas the project management determined the resources needed from those departments whose functions were incorporated into the systems. These resources were then reserved and dedicated during testing period.

Adjustments to work assigned to people: The bank established job descriptions at all levels involved in implementation of the two products and reviewed job titles to better reveal functional responsibilities that were needed to accommodate for the growth of the bank within the rapidly changing banking industry, new competitors, and internal reorganization of the a variety of business lines.

With implementation of new systems, new management lines were opened to cope with increasing systems' requirements. Adjustments were either a "new job assignment" for staff moving within same branch or a "totally new job" for staff moving from the ATM Center, for example. Resources were dedicated for the new products/ systems until tests were completed.

Implication of new technologies implemented on the nature of work and job content:

New systems reduced the number of clients who showed up to the bank's counter, the vouchers/paper work carried out for transactions, work load and inquiries on employees, thus contributing to improving services provided to customers. New departments were created and new managers and staff members were recruited to introduce new systems, and with new systems, employees now have more powerful tools that they can use in providing services to bank customers in very creative and faster ways.

New delivery systems triggered new responsibilities in First Commercial Bank. In implementing the ATM system in First Commercial Bank, several units were involved, including the Customer Services Department, the ATM Center, the IT Department, and the Risk Department. The Customer Services Department was responsible for the product development part in the change process, preparing the system guide, procedures, and documentation of transactions, in addition to testing the new system. The bank's ATM Center was responsible for the issuing of ATM cards, handling complaints, detecting payment problems through journals, etc. The IT department chose the system the bank used and connected it with the bank's system and customers' database. It was also responsible for the ATMs' technical problems and maintenance of the system. The Risk Department monitored the system in general to make sure that ATMs were working properly.

In implementing Internet Banking, several departments were involved too. These comprised the Customer Services Department, the IVR Center, the IT Department, and the Risk Department. The Customer Services Department was responsible for the product development part in the change process. The IVR Center was responsible for opening/executing Internet Banking accounts, handling complaints, detecting payment problems, etc. The IT Department was responsible for choosing the system the bank used and connected it with the bank's system and customers' database. It was also accountable for maintenance/upgrading of the Internet Banking website and handling technical problems. Examples of some tasks performed by the IT department could be imaging, making studies on features, adding new features, and so forth. The Risk Department was responsible for monitoring the entire system to guarantee that it was fully functioning properly 24/7.

New skill requirements involved: During implementation, First Commercial Bank utilized the normal bank's skills requirements, such as high experience in banking to be able to deal with customers, high experience in tasks performed by each department having an input in new systems, leadership skills, interpersonal skills, good communication skills with vendor and departments, and fast decision making talents.

Training and on-the-job learning activities/ programs: In general, First Commercial Bank provides its staff at all levels with quality training through its Training & Development Division, as well as through other local and overseas training institutions. For example, in 2006, the bank conducted around 300 training events with about 60,000 training hours in-house, locally in training institutions and overseas. Training sessions were provided to employees based on the assessment of their needs. Teaching materials covered issues starting from introductory banking stage up to the uppermost technical and specialized ranks in all banking and management fields (Website of First Commercial Bank; First Commercial Bank's Annual Reports 2002-2006).

Employees participated in a one-day training session for each new product implemented. Trainers were then consulted throughout the period of hands-on application of the new systems. Training sessions handled both the technical and the customer services dimensions of introducing a new product. Training programs on technical aspects focused on on-the-job training, which began with the inauguration of the project/new system. Additional training was also conducted for new comers, for those who were not involved, or who joined the bank after implementation process. Training sessions also handled issues on how to deal with customers and acquaint them with the new systems.

Stakeholders involved in the implementation process: First Commercial Bank took into consideration comments, suggestions, and complaints of customers with regards to the new systems. The number of customers' transactions was further monitored and the bank increased the number of ATM machines in areas/outlets with high number of transactions.

First Commercial Bank had to obtain the approval of the Central Bank of Egypt, and be licensed to carry out IT-based delivery systems in Egypt.

Approaches and Strategies in Managing Organizational Change

Specific strategies in managing change: In implementation of the new systems, the bank followed its usual ambitious plans and procedures in carrying out the change. First Commercial Bank followed a strategy of copying its successful and market-leading position in corporate banking and diversifying its income by expanding its medium-sized businesses and retail banking in parallel with the expansion of its branch network. The bank's goal was to be a fully-fledged financial institution providing a complete variety of high quality financial services among all its branches to increase its market share and return on investments. The bank aimed at covering payment schemes and payroll services, in addition to increasing debit and credit cards. Its objective was to have an area monopoly of about 500,000 persons by 2008. Therefore, further investments in technology included a new retail banking system to maintain more innovation of products and services, as well as to achieve a full conversion to a networked bank in 2003. A better risk-management system has also been implemented. First Commercial Bank's eventual target was also to accommodate the Basle II by-laws. The bank invested too in developing and maintaining the high integrity of its staff. And though the bank promoted management from within, the development of new services through joint-venture companies entailed some outside recruitment. The bank's goal was to change its culture from being product-oriented to being customer oriented.

Strategies used to transform First Commercial Bank to the new systems: the bank used a mixture of the four strategies, Empirical-Rational Strategies, Normative/Re-educative Strategies of Change, Power-Coercive Techniques to Effective Change, and Environmental-Adaptive Methods to Change, thereby indicating sufficient expertise in managing change. Management also conducted a meeting with employees to allow brainstorming and sharing of ideas once every week. In 55% of the cases Environmental-Adaptive methods to change were used, in 30% Empirical-Rational Strategies were used, in 10% Normative-Re-educative Strategies of Change were used, and in 5% Power-coercive techniques to effective change were used. For example, management assumed people were rational and would help with new changes through their educational background, which according to Nickols (2004: 10-11) indicates the bank is experiencing weak resistance to change. Using different strategies also was dependent on employees' characteristics and dedication to change. Management used power-coercive techniques to effect change, as suggested by short-term change plans of implementing IT-based delivery systems (Nickols, 2004: 10-11).

Impact of IT on Organizational Structure

Changes in structure: First Commercial Bank created new departments and units such as application support, technical support, operations, and monitoring units; recruited new managers, staff, and transferred others from other departments to accommodate implementation of new systems. The bank recruited new, young managers who motivated employees and encouraged creativity.

The impact of implementing new systems on specialization: Retail banking individuals worked separately and specialized in one clearly defined task. In the IT unit though, individuals worked together and coordinated their actions to find the best way of performing the task.

The impact of implementing new systems on Integrating Mechanisms: During implementation, integrating mechanisms depended sometimes on a hierarchy of authority when new tasks were assigned to employees; while at other times they relied on task forces and teams in carrying out these tasks. Communication was usually done by e-mails. Only in cases of big issues, such as customer services or competition matters, meetings were conducted.

The impact of implementing new systems on Lines of Responsibility: Three new lines were involved throughout implementation including a manager, a unit head, and several employees. A hierarchical system of management was structured whereby authority and responsibility are passed downwards.

The impact of implementing new systems on authority to control tasks: Throughout implementation of the new systems, the authority to control tasks in First Commercial Bank was decentralized to a certain extent, depending on the problem. A problem could be solved at low levels, while another needed higher levels' interventions. Several units were responsible for implementation for both ATMs and Internet Banking. For each unit there was a unit head and several employees. An issue could be resolved at low levels, while another one needed higher levels' interventions.

In implementing the ATM system, the Customer Services Department, the ATM Center, the IT Department, and the Risk Department were all delegated the authority to control tasks, each in its own area of expertise and functionality. For example, the Customer Services Department was responsible for the product development, preparing the system guide, procedures, and documentation of transactions, in addition to testing the new system. The bank's ATM Center was responsible for issuing of ATM cards, handling complaints, detecting payment problems through journals, etc. The IT department chose the system the bank used and connected it with the bank's system and customers' database. It was also responsible for ATMs technical problems and maintenance of the system. The Risk Department monitored the system in general to make sure that ATMs were working properly.

In implementing Internet Banking, several departments were involved, including the Customer Services Department, the IVR Center, the IT Department, and the Risk Department. The

Customer Services Department was responsible for the product development; whereas, the IVR Center was responsible for opening/executing Internet Banking accounts, handling complaints, detecting payment problems through, etc., and the IT Department was responsible for maintenance/upgrading of Internet Banking website and handled technical problems.

The impact of implementing new systems on coordination of tasks and work process: First Commercial Bank is going by standardized rules and procedures in coordination of tasks and work processes that are applied throughout the bank and its branches.

The Impact of IT on Organizational Culture

Employees' involvement in the change process: Employees were allowed to participate by making complaints and/or suggestions on new systems. However, not everything was heard or put into consideration especially if it was after the bank had already committed itself and made investments in soft-wares, hard-wares, etc. Usually, final decisions were made at higher management levels. Still, some recommended worthy changes could be done after years.

Empowerment: "Employees' actions are controlled by bank's rules, policies, procedures, regulations," stated Senior Manager, ATM Unit Banking. Though employees' actions were controlled by the bank's set rules, policies, and procedures, to the extent that minimum creativity was left, employees were encouraged to emit creative, courageous, and risk taking behaviors, and develop cultural values that foster integration and coordination. To achieve employee empowerment, First Commercial Bank developed a new management structure to align the employees' performance and actions with the bank's goals and objectives, as well as promoting a culture that opened new routes of communication between staff and management. In general, about 50% of everyday work is done according to the leadership style of command and control; whereas, the rest depends on empowering employees, listening to them towards more flexible actions. Minimum creativity is left for employees.

Values, norms, and behaviors of the organization's members: In First Commercial Bank, a "Best Bank in Egypt" culture existed where all individuals believe themselves and their bank to be superior to other banks with regards to its quality performance. First Commercial Bank's culture throughout implementation of new systems contributed to the bank's continued success as it triggered employees to seek more customers, become more sales-oriented, and highly dedicated to work.

Dominating cultural pattern: During implementation of the new systems, the dominating cultural pattern was a mixture of a constructive culture and a defensive one since new transactions involved were regarded as critical and needed care in execution and monitoring.

Dominating cultural style: First Commercial Bank gives great attention to acquisition and retention of human capital of high caliber, maintains a core corporate culture and values, and uses its core competences to build on a sustainable competitive advantage as Egypt's leading financial service business providing foremost quality to its customers whilst maximizing shareholders' value. Therefore, 80% of the time, the dominating cultural style emphasized achievement, self actualization, encouragement, and affiliation; whereas, in 20% it was characterized by approval, conventional, dependence, and avoidance patterns.

Nature of employees' beliefs and orientations: In First Commercial Bank, people interacted with others and performed tasks that both assisted them in meeting their top-priority satisfaction needs and would not endanger their own safety.

Impact of New IT-Enabled Systems on Business Processes

New services entailed additional activities and steps in the business process. Examples include choosing machines' locations, imaging, studying needed features, adding new features required, planning new tasks and activities, monitoring achieved tasks, entry of clients' data to make clients profiles, sending clients' files to ATM center or IVR division to investigate and solve clients' complaints and/or suggestions, ATMs' replenishment, and Internet Banking monitoring for availability of service around the clock. Staff orientation to the new products, training, implementation steps, and actual sale of the products were also some of the activities involved. Newly added customer products and services also involved new experiences, support through on-the-job training or online training. Thus, new features added and increased number of clients entailed new activities among employees.

New work system's inputs include the bank's resources, customers' database, whereas outputs include its success rate, availability of services, customer satisfaction, shown in reports issued on a daily, weekly, monthly, and yearly basis.

New systems minimized effort and the time customers spend to conduct a transaction and made their accounts data available to them 24/7. Therefore, new systems increased customer satisfaction as they increased bank's working hours and reduced the number of times a customer needs to go to the bank. Also, new systems changed the type of customers to a one which is more demanding for technology and new products. For employees, too, the new systems facilitated work and reduced workload as fewer clients approached the bank counter, which reduces work load and cues. Shareholders were happy with new systems as they increased profits through commissions paid by customers and through cost reductions made in conducting transactions away from the counter. For example, the bank charges an ATM service fee of L.E. 35 (US$6.10) to issue or renew a new ATM card. Lead time and errors were reduced too due to the absence of human factor in transactions.

Communication with clients: New delivery systems increased communication with clients as they increased transactions' traffic. They reduced face-to-face interaction with clients though, thus reducing crowds and hassles which allowed better communication. Clients' complaints switched to problems with regards to offline periods, and their queries revolved around how to manage problems like when an ATM machines withdraws the client's card once he/she forgets to take it out of the machine after a transaction or how to navigate through the bank's webpage. First Commercial Bank encouraged customers to convey their suggestions and/or complaints via its call center.

Impact on track of transactions: Track of transactions were done manually before implementation of systems. After implementation, the process was done mechanically, which helped reduce costs. The human factor was not involved, except in some cases like ATMs replenishment or if there was a problem. New systems improved tracking of transactions. Logging on all transactions and mechanically tracking transactions reduced complaints' volume among clients.

Impact on motivating employees: New delivery systems motivated employees as they increased profitability and as long as the system was operating well. But it de-motivated them when problems emerged or when the system was offline. New delivery systems' development motivated employees also as they improved working environment since they facilitated and reduced work load on employees.

Some challenges that faced First Commercial Bank after installing new delivery systems included technical problems of the end-of-day run, carried out around 3:00 – 4:00 am, that caused problems in launching the system the following day. Also, the system sometimes went down which made customers turn to bank's counters to carry on their transactions, thereby adding extra work load on tellers, as well as on other employees in the bank. Usually problems faced were technical and were related to telephone lines' disorders or network connections. There were no problems encountered from employees in launching the systems.

Prevailing Commitment Profile

Extent of organizational commitment to change: In First Commercial Bank, employees are to a great extent committed to change and the evidence is the successful implementation and performance of both ATMs and Internet Banking products.

Prevailing commitment profile: In First Commercial Bank, the established commitment profile, attitude, and decision to stay in the organization reflect a mixture of an affective and continuance profile. The bank's environment is also protected with no hire and fire employment policy and the bank's expansions permitted recruiting a large number of young people, who were approximately at the same age. Reducing the age of managers thus produced a general understanding between them and new young employees and consequently reduced the breach that could have existed between two different generations.

Impact of New IT-Based Systems on the Bank's Customers

A. Response to Customers

After implementation of new systems, most products of the First Commercial Bank became available to customers all the time. Through its ATMs and Internet Banking services, First Commercial Bank's services are now delivered to customers 24/7 instead of only 27.5 hours per week. Additionally, the number of ATMs increased from 30 in 2000 to 350 machines in 2006. "Service Level Agreement" guarantees a speedy service by measuring rate of service response to customers. For example, cash deposits in the local currency or in foreign currencies that are received on the counter or from an ATM channel are put on a one day and two days hold respectively to be credited to the beneficiary's account. Requests for Demand Drafts and Cashier's Orders are processed and dispatched the same day if received before 14:00hrs.

For Internet Banking services, service quality control is guaranteed to customers through a default cut-off time set for Internet Banking transactions. For instance, the cut-off time for a telegraphic transfer application is 12:00hrs at noon for a transaction to be processed on the same day. In the case where the client submits his/her application after 12:00, his/her instructions will be carried out the following day.

First Commercial Bank's call center works around the clock to answer clients' investigations, their comments, and/or complaints. First Commercial Bank records telephone calls made to its Call Centre for business deal confirmation and quality management purposes. First Commercial Bank encourages its customers to consistently and cautiously provide their feedback on the service by verifying their bank account statements when they receive them and reporting to the bank immediately through the bank's call center, electronic mails, or by visiting any of its branches in case they find an error in any business deal or an illegal operation. Customers are also encouraged to contact the bank if they have any concerns or complaints about the service. Normally, the bank resolves its clients' queries immediately.

B. Customers Working Online

It was very difficult to decide upon the number of clients who work online because some clients just click on the site while others log on into their accounts to just check their balances. Still, some others go into the site and perform transactions. "Can't decide because sometimes customers log on into their accounts to just check their balances, and they might log off without doing any transaction," declared Senior Manager, ATM Unit Banking. So there is no direct relationship between the number of hits and actually using the site.

In general the traffic on ATMs increases tremendously during salary payment periods, in which about 60,000-70,000 transactions are conducted. An additional evidence for an increasing traffic on ATMs could be the growing number of ATM cards issued which increased by 70% from 2004 to 2006, reaching about 350,000 ATM cards in 2006.

C. Rate of Customer to Employee

There is no direct relationship between the number of customers and employees in the bank since both depend on branch location and services provided. But in general, the rate of customer to employee is going down as a result of new bank services channels (ATMs and IB) that are being opened.

D. Waiting Time to be Served

The waiting time a client waits to be served is incomparable after implementation of the new systems. There is a large difference between performing a transaction on an ATM machine or online through Internet Banking, compared to doing it through the bank's counter. The first usually takes about 1-2 minutes; whereas, the transaction performed at the counter could take about 15 minutes at minimum.

Looking Forward

Mokbel Hazim had only been in his post a few months, but he believed that to meet rapid change organizations must develop a more focused, comprehensive, and consistent approach to change. But what would the appropriate approach be? And what does the change function entail? And what are some differing issues that should we be tackling to achieve strategic competitiveness? Hazim questioned. They need to develop a human resource strategy, and address several dimensions: organization's structure, reporting lines, and job tasks; organizational culture including people's attitude, principles, and management approach; people's skills, staff capacity, and management qualifications; and human resources schemes which include four key activities of acquiring, developing, motivating, and retaining human resources. Hazim was too strong-minded, and his decision to go for implementation would have a significant impact on the bank's ability to achieve strategic competitiveness.

REFERENCES

Abou-Musa, A. A. E. (2003). Egyptian banking industry: Its history and future. *Journal of American Academy of Business, 3*.

American Chamber of Commerce in Egypt. (2004). *Bank rankings*. Egypt: American Chamber of Commerce, Business Studies and Analysis Center.

Amit, R., & Shoemaker, P. J. H. (1993). Strategic assets and organizational rent. *Strategic Management Journal*, *14*(1), 33–46.

Anderson, L. A., & Anderson, D. (2003). *Ten questions that catalyze great change leadership. Results from change*. Retrieved on July 22, 2004, from www.beingfirst.com/resultsfromchange/pastissues/200301.php

Anol, B., & Rudy, H. (1997). IT and organizational change: Lessons from client/server technology implementation. *Journal of General Management, 2*, 31. Retrieved August 28, 2004, from http://www.aucegypt.edu/library/libdata/subject.cfm?classid=2

Barnes, D., Mieczkowska, S., & Hinton, M. (2003). Integrating operations and information strategy in e-business. *European Management Journal, 21*(5), 626.

Bob, N., & Malcolm, P. (1989). Information: The key to effective management. [from http://www.umi.com.lib.aucegypt.edu]. *Library Management, 10*(23), 1. Retrieved September 19, 2005.

Branch, K. M. (2005). *Change management*. Retrieved from http://www.science.doe.gov

Brewster, C., Carey, L., Dowling, P., Grobler, P., Holland, P., & Warnich, S. (2000). *Contemporary issues in human resources management: Gaining a competitive advantage*. South Africa: Oxford University Press.

Brynjolfsson, E., & Yang, S. (1997). *The intangible costs and benefits of investments: Evidence from financial markets*. Paper presented in ICIS.

Burnes, B. (1992). *Managing change* (2nd ed.). London, UK: Pitman Publishing.

Collins, J. C., & Porras, J. I. (1989). Making impossible dreams come true. *Stanford Business School Magazine, 57*, 12–19.

Cox, E. B. (1986). *The bank director's handbook*. Dover, MA: Auburn House Publishing Company.

Curry, A., & Penman, S. (2004). The relative importance of technology in enhancing customer relationships in banking – a Scottish perspective. *Managing Service Quality, 14*(4).

Dooley, J. (1998). *A whole-person/systematic approach to organization change management*. Retrieved on July 22, 2004, from www.well.com/user/dooley/change.pdf

French, W. L., Bell, C. H., & Zawacki, R. A. (Eds.). (2000). *Organization development and transformation*. New York, NY: Irwin McGraw-Hill.

Hamel, G., & Prahalad, C. K. (1994). Competing for the future. *Harvard Business Review*, (July-August).

Hamel, G., & Valikangas, L. (2003). The quest for resilience. *Harvard Business Review*, (September).

Hatem, T. (2003). Understanding cultural differences between Americans and Arabs: The Egyptian case. In the *Proceedings of the tenth American University in Cairo Research Conference, Globalization Revisited: Challenges and Opportunities*, April 6-7, (pp. 249-271). The American University in Cairo (AUC), Egypt.

Hitt, M. A., Ireland, R. D., & Hoskisson, R. E. (2001). *Strategic management: Competitiveness and globalization*. United States: South-Western College Publishing.

Hofstede, G. (1984). *Culture's consequences: International differences in work-related values*, abridged ed. Beverly Hills, CA: Sage.

Hofstede, G. (1991). *Cultures and organizations: Software of mind*. London, UK: McGraw Hill.

Johnson, P., Fidler, C. S., & Rogerson, S. (1998). Management communication: A technological revolution? *Management Decision, 36*(3), 160.

Kitchen, P. (1997). *Public relations: Principle and practice* (1st ed.). London, UK: Thomson Business Press.

Kitchen, P. J., & Daly, F. (2002). Internal communication during change management. *Corporate Communications, 7*(1), 46–53.

Kotter, J. P. (1995). Leading change: Why transformation efforts fail. *Harvard Business Review*, (March-April).

Kotter, J. P. (1996). *Leading change*. Cambridge, MA: Harvard Business School Press.

Kotter, J. P. (1998). Winning at change. *Leader to Leader, 10*(Fall). Retrieved on July 25, 2004, from www.pfdf.org/leaderbooks/121/fall98/kotter.html

La Porte, T. M., Demchak, C., & Friis, C. (2001). Webbing governance: Global trends across national-level public agencies. *Communications of the ACM, 44*(1), 63. Retrieved on August 28, 2004, from http://www.aucegypt.edu/library/libdata/subject.cfm?classid=2

Levasseur, R. E. (2001). People skills: Change management tools- Lewin's change model. *Interfaces*, *31*(4), 71–73.

Liao, Z., & Cheung, M. (2003). Challenges to internet e-banking. *Communications of the ACM*, *46*(12).

Matsui, Y. (2002). Contribution of manufacturing departments to technology development: An empirical analysis for machinery, electrical and electronics, and automobile plants in Japan. *International Journal of Production Economics*, *80*(2), 185.

McNish, M. (2002). Guidelines for managing change: A study of their effects on the implementation of new information technology projects in organizations. *Journal of Change Management*, *2*, 3.

Nickols, F. (2004). *Change management: A primer*. Retrieved on July 21, 2004, from www.themanager.org/knowledgebase/management/change.htm

Nolan, R., & McFarlan, F. W. (2005, October 5). Information technology and the board of directors. *Harvard Business Review*, (October).

Penrose, E. T. (1959). *The theory of growth of the firm*. London, UK: Basil Blackwell.

Pickett, L. (2004). Focus on technology misses the mark. *Industrial and Commercial Training, 36*(6/7), 247. Retrieved on August 28, 2005, from http://www.aucegypt.edu/library/libdata/subject.cfm? Classid=2

Porter, M. E. (1985). *Competitive advantage* (pp. 11–15). New York, NY: The Free Press.

Porter, M. E. (1990). The competitive advantage of nations. *Harvard Business Review*, (March-April): 73–91.

Porter, M. E. (1998). *Competitive advantage: Creating and sustaining superior performance*. New York, NY: The Free Press.

Prahalad, C. K., & Krishnan, M. S. (2002). The dynamic synchronization of strategy and information technology. *MIT Sloan Management Review*, *43*(4), 23–34.

Proctor, T., & Doukakis, I. (2003). Change management: The role of internal communication and employee development. *Corporate Communication, 8*(4), 268. Retrieved on 28 August, 2003, from http://www.aucegypt.edu/library/libdata/subject.cfm?classid=2

Rao, S. G. M., & Monge, C. (2003). Electronic commerce development in small and medium sized enterprises. *Business Process Management Journal*, *9*(1), 11–32.

Rayport, J. F., & Jaworski, B. J. (2004). Best face forward. *Harvard Business Review*, December.

Rogers, E. M. (1983). *Diffusion of innovations*. New York, NY: The Free Press.

Schumpeter, J. A. (1934). *The theory of economic development: An inquiry into profits, capital, credit, interest, and business cycle*. Cambridge, MA: Harvard University Press.

Senge, P. (1994). *The fifth discipline field book: Strategies and tools for building a learning organization*. New York, NY: Doubleday.

Swierczek, F. W., Pritam, K. S., & Bechter, C. (2005). Information technology, productivity and pofitability in Asia-Pacific banks. *Journal of Global Information Technology Management*, *8*(1).

Teare, R., & Monk, S. (2002). Learning from change. *International Journal of Contemporary Hospitality Management, 14*(7), 334–341.

The Economist Intelligence Unit. (2005). *Egypt country profile*. Retrieved on February 15, 2005, from www.eiu.com/schedule

The Economist Intelligence Unit. (2005a). *The 2005 e-readiness rankings*. Retrieved on June 25, 2005, from http://www.ebusinessforum.com/index.asp

Tichy, N. M., & Sherman, S. (1993). *Control your destiny or someone else will*. New York, NY: Doubleday.

Wah, S. S. (2002). *Behavioral attributes of the transformational Chinese leader*. Unpublished doctoral dissertation. Maastricht School of Management, the Netherlands.

KEY TERMS AND DEFINITIONS

Banking: Financial institutions for individuals/groups financial needs.

Competitive Strategy: A strategy that states how a company or a business unit will compete in an industry.

Electronic-Based Delivery Systems: The use of electronic data processing systems to conduct business transactions.

Management of Change: Is a structured approach to moving/transforming individuals, groups, and organizations from a current state to a desired future state.

Organizational Behavior: Is the study and application of knowledge about how people, individuals, and groups act in organizations.

Organizational Development: Is a planned organization-wide effort to increase an organization's effectiveness and viability.

Organizational Structure: The formal setup of a business corporation's value chain components in terms of work flow, communicational, channels, and hierarchy.

Strategic Factors: External and internal factors that determine the future of a corporation.

Strategic Management: A set of managerial decisions and actions that determine the long-run performance of a corporation.

Strategy Implementation: The process by which strategies and policies are put into action through the development of programs, budgets and procedures.

Value Chain: The linked set of value-creating activities that begins with basic raw materials coming from suppliers and ends with distributors getting the final goods into the hands of the ultimate consumer.

ENDNOTE

1 *Copyright© 2009, El Khazindar Business Research and Case Center (KCC), The American University in Cairo (AUC), All rights reserved.* This case was prepared by Elham Metwally (Assistant Professor of Management at Misr International University) to stimulate class discussion and analysis in business education settings. The case is not intended to serve as endorsements, sources of primary data, or illustrations of effective or ineffective management. The circumstances and material incorporated in this case have been made available through the cooperation of the individuals and the bank involved. Names and situations have been disguised.

APPENDIX

Figure 1. Structure of the Egyptian banking sector

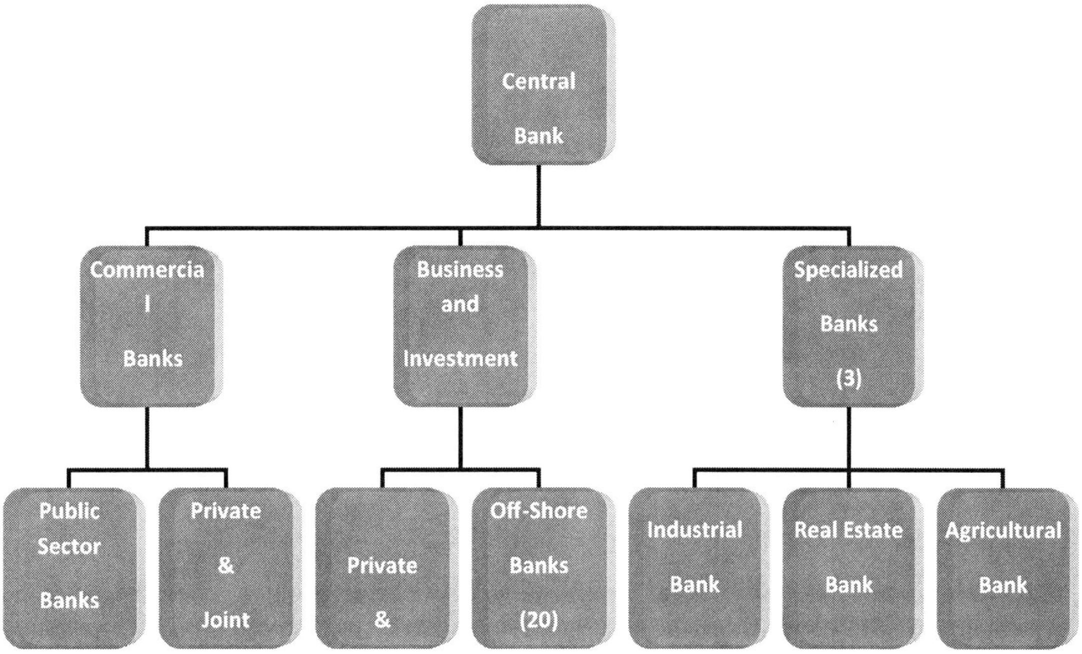

Section 4
Management Information Systems

To compete successfully in today's retail business arena, senior management are often demanding fast and responsive Information Systems that enable the company not only to manage its operations, but to provide on-the-fly performance measurement through a variety of tools including ERP systems, data warehousing, and Business Intelligence (BI) applications. The focus of the first case, "Strategic Role for Management Information Systems in a Multinational Company," is on the strategic role that Information Technology (IT) plays in two subsidiaries of an international company, one located in Egypt and the other in Sweden. The case explores the importance of balancing business, information, and organizational strategy in a manner conducive to business-IT strategy alignment. The second case, "Business Intelligence Systems in the Dynamic Sales Environment of Beverage Distribution," deals with the application of ERP system as the backbone for BI tools designed to provide sales and marketing units in a transnational company subsidiary in Egypt to effectively respond to the demands for agile information services. The third case, "Ghabbour Group -- GB Auto," has gone through two ERP successive implementations. The driver for the most recent implementation was to secure all the necessary platforms and management tools for enabling growth and improving efficiency and effectiveness of the company's business operation and resources. Following its public offering and registration in the CASE and CMA, GB Auto was legally required to provide annual and quarterly audit reports of its varied LOBs performance. The trajectory of implementation of integrated Enterprise Information Systems at the group is reviewed to assess its effectiveness and appropriateness in response to CASE and CMA audit reports.

Chapter 10
Strategic Role of Information Technology in a Multinational Company:
The Case of an Organization with Subsidiaries in Egypt and Sweden

Lazar Rusu
Stockholm University, Sweden

Mohamed El Mekawy
Stockholm University, Sweden

EXECUTIVE SUMMARY

The purpose of this case study research is to study the strategic role that information technology (IT) plays in two subsidiaries - located in Egypt and Sweden - of a multinational company with a federal organizational structure. Using a well-established evaluation framework and a widely accepted model, we examine two important aspects of the strategic role of IT: i) how IT supports business and organizational strategy; and ii) the maturity of business and IT strategy alignment. The case study discusses the importance of having a balanced relationship among business strategy, information strategy, organizational strategy, and the way in which business and IT managers should act to improve business-IT alignment, also referred to as strategic alignment. Based on the results of the comparative analysis of the two companies, the research presents concrete recommendations that IT decision-makers from the two subsidiaries of the multinational company should consider to improve IT performance.

1. INTRODUCTION

Information technology has become more important to business strategy than it was in the past. Today, IT is integrated into almost every part of the business process (Luftman, Bullen, Liao, Nash & Neumann, 2004). According to Tang and Walters (2006: p.2), as organizations evolve, so do their strategies. As a result, "IT and IT-enabled systems are now indispensable in supporting business

DOI: 10.4018/978-1-60960-583-4.ch010

strategies". In fact, about 36 years ago, McFarlan, McKenney & Pyburn (1983) introduced the strategic grid in order to help managers understand the strategic impact of information systems and of an application development portfolio in their companies. The importance of the use of information for strategic purposes was later addressed by many researchers (Porter & Millar, 1985; Earl, 1989). Further on, King and Grover (1991: p.293) analyzed the "organizational factors that facilitate or inhibit strategic use of information resources and the processes leading up to their adoption". Moreover, Bergeron and Raymond (1995: p.167) found that high performance is achieved by companies that combine a "strategic orientation with a strategically oriented IT management".

As we now see, the current business environment is a dynamic, fast-changing and highly competitive one. This can be explained, at least partially, by the tremendous leaps that IT has taken in the last 30 years, especially the last 10-15 years of the Internet era. As a result, IT has become an important factor in all organizations as an enabler of business and organizational change or a driver for transformation (Turban, Leidner, McLean & Wetherbe, 2006). In such an environment, it is essential that business managers understand the potential use and critical role of IT in promoting the success of companies (Huff, Maher & Munro, 2006). But in the study of the strategic role of IT, we could not ignore the concept of business-IT alignment, or strategic alignment (Chan, Huff, Barclay & Copeland, 1997), still considered by many company executives to be very important (Luftman & Kempaiah, 2008; Luftman, Kempaiah & Rigoni, 2009; Luftman & Ben-Zvi, 2010).

In the last few years, several researchers like Burn and Szeto (2000), Avison, Jones, Powell & Wilson (2004), Weiss and Anderson (2004) and Hu and Huang (2006) have contributed to the research on the assessment of strategic alignment. In the opinion of Chan (2002), organizations in which business and IT are strategically aligned improve their IT performance. Moreover, according to Kearns and Sabherwal (2007), in achieving greater strategic alignment (which can enhance the effects of IT on business performance), managers should also give due consideration to shared domain knowledge and planning behaviors as well as to the planning and implementation of IT projects. On the other hand, according to McKeen and Smith (2009), strategic alignment is only one of the problems facing IT managers in developing an IT strategy and, in the authors' opinion, IT is more important today in the development and delivery of a business strategy. In this context, the goal of our chapter has been to study both IT strategy in correlation with business strategy and organizational strategy, and strategic alignment through a case study research approach in two subsidiaries of a multinational company, one located in Egypt and the other in Sweden.

2. RESEARCH BACKGROUND

2.1 Frameworks and Models to Evaluate the Strategic Role of IT

In the introduction, we reviewed some of the research work concerning the strategic role of IT. The research literature holds many frameworks and models. In studying the strategic role of IT, researchers such as Rusu and El Mekawy (2009) have considered only those that are widely accepted, have a higher impact among practitioners and were well recognized by the management of the companies that were studied. In this research, we used the same approach with regard to the strategic role of IT in a multinational company, using the Information Systems Strategy Triangle (Pearlson & Saunders, 2009) and Strategic Alignment Maturity Model (Luftman, 2000). According to Pearlson and Saunders (2009), balancing the three corners of the Information Systems Strategy Triangle formed by business, organizational and information systems (IS) strategies is very important in every successful company. In fact, in successful companies, these three strategies are carefully balanced and organizational and information systems strategies are designed to complement the business strategy. In the opinion of Pearlson and Saunders (2009: p.23), "to perpetuate the balance needed for successful operation, changes in the IS strategy must be accompanied by changes in the organizational strategy and must accommodate the overall business strategy". Accordingly, "the business, IS and organizational strategies must constantly be adjusted".

Many strategic alignment models are presented in the research literature. Among the most well known are those of Henderson and Venkatraman (1993), Luftman (2000) and Reich and Benbasat (2000). Our selection of Luftman's Strategic Alignment Maturity (SAM) Model (2000) for assessing strategic alignment was based on a comprehensive comparative analysis (El Mekawy, Rusu & Haseeb, 2009) of various strategic alignment models. The reason for this choice is that SAM shows a bottom-up comprehensive approach for assessing strategic alignment maturity, starting from alignment components at the operational level to business and IT domains at the executive levels (Hu & Huang, 2006). In addition, SAM focuses on different areas by the modularity of its six criteria and offers an understanding of business-IT alignment at the operational, tactical and strategic levels. The SAM model helps not only to measure the strategic alignment of an organization, but also to examine the actual implementation and mutual effect of both business and IT strategy on the business operations of an organization.

2.2 Information Systems Strategy Triangle

The Information Systems Strategy Triangle (Pearlson & Saunders, 2009) is a framework that relates business strategy to information system strategy and organizational strategy. It is a simple framework used for understanding the impact of IS on organizations. It represents the three different strategies as corners of a triangle, with the aim of studying the relationships among the three strategies and the impact they have on one another.

Before we delve into our analysis of the two companies using the Information Systems Strategy Triangle, a short explanation of business strategy, organizational strategy and information strategy and the models used in the research literature to analyze each, is presented below.

Business strategy in every booming organization is the driver for both information strategy and organizational strategy. Business strategy is a well-expressed vision that illustrates where business aims to reach and how to get there (Peppard & Ward, 2004). The research literature offers different models, such as Porter's generic strategies (Porter, 1980) and D'Aveni's hyper competition (D'Aveni, 1995), that could be used for analyzing the different dimensions of business strategy in order to help top managers understand and define their business strategy.

Organizational strategy is a roadmap that reveals the way in which an organization designs, plans, performs and controls its functions in order to implement its business strategies and achieve its goals (Silva, Figueroa & Reinhart, 2007). Different models, such as Business Diamond (Hammer & Champy, 1994) and Managerial Levers (Cash, Eccles, Nohria & Nolan, 1994), have been developed to identify the important components of an organization's design, planning and control processes. In fact, these models help top managers to review the actual situation of their organization in order to identify problems and available opportunities.

Information Systems Strategy is defined as a roadmap for the use of information technology and information services to achieve business goals. The research literature offers different models for this purpose, such as the IS strategy matrix (Pearlson & Saunders, 2009), IT components' classification frameworks (Turban et al., 2006) and STROIS (Strategic Orientation of IS), an instrument to measure the realized IS strategy (Chan, Huff & Copeland, 1998)). Through the use of these tools, managers will have a high-level view of IT resources and usage in the organization and the way they contribute to achieving business goals.

2.3 Luftman's Strategic Alignment Maturity Model

Luftman's Strategic Alignment Maturity Model (2000) is a well-known one and can be used for the assessment of business-IT alignment, or strategic alignment. In fact, Luftman refers to the alignment as a mature relationship where IT and other business functions adapt their strategies to each other. In other words, strategic alignment can be defined as "applying information technologies in an appropriate and timely way, in harmony with business strategies' goals and needs" (Luftman, 2000: p.3). The Luftman Strategic Alignment Maturity Model is one that is often used by practitioners and makes it possible to rank organizations into the following five conceptual levels of strategic alignment maturity:

Level 1: Initial/Ad Hoc Process is the lowest level of strategic alignment maturity. Organizations at this level are characterized by unleveraged investments in IT and a separation between IT and business strategies. IT at this level is perceived as a cost for business.

Level 2: Committed Process indicates that an organization that stands at this level commits to beginning the process of aligning business and IT. Organizations at this level are characterized by local or functional planning of business and IT activities.

Level 3: Established Focused Process is the first level of real alignment. However, alignment is only oriented towards specific business objectives that are identified as highest priority for business needs. Organizations at this level see their governance, processes and communications tools as assets and business process enablers.

Level 4: Improved/Managed Process refers to effective governance and IT services throughout the organization. Organizations at this level view their IT as a means for business processes to obtain sustainable competitive advantages and as a driver for innovation and success.

Level 5: Optimized Process is the optimal level of alignment maturity, where all levels of an organization's governance facilitate the integration of IT and business processes. IT assets at level 5 are seen as a value centre on an enterprise-wide basis to be extended to the supply chains of suppliers and customers, marking their success.

Based on the input from both business and IT management, six different criteria for business-IT alignment are evaluated, namely communications, competency/value measurements, governance, partnership, scope and architecture, and skills. To facilitate the evaluation process, each criterion is defined by a number of attributes, as presented below:

Communications refers to the clear understanding between the business and IT communities, with an effective exchange and awareness of each other's ideas, processes and needs. Luftman (2000) assigns the following attributes to the *Communications* criterion:

- Understanding of business by IT
- Understanding of IT by business
- Inter/intra-organizational learning
- Protocol rigidity
- Knowledge sharing
- Liaison(s) breadth /effectiveness

Competency/Value Measurements is concerned with demonstrating IT values in figures that are compatible with the business community's understanding. Often, business and IT metric values are different. Luftman (2000) defines the *Competency/Value Measurements* criterion by the following attributes:

- IT metrics
- Business metrics
- Balanced metrics
- Service-level agreements
- Benchmarking
- Formal assessments/reviews
- Continuous improvement

Governance ensures that business and IT communities, formally and periodically, discuss and review their plans. It is important that priorities for allocating the required IT resources be clearly defined. Luftman (2000) associates the following attributes with the *Governance* criterion:

- Business strategic planning
- IT strategic planning
- Reporting/organization structure
- Budgetary control
- IT investment management
- Steering committee(s)
- Prioritization process

Partnership refers to the relationship between business and IT in terms of having a shared vision of the organization's processes in order to facilitate IT as an enabler or driver for transformation in the business's processes and strategies. Luftman (2000) describes the *Partnership* criterion as having the following attributes:

- Business perception of IT value
- Role of IT in strategic business planning
- Shared goals, risks, rewards/penalties
- IT program management
- Relationship/trust style
- Business sponsor/champion

Scope & Architecture illustrates the involvement of IT in all organizational processes. It defines the role of IT in supporting flexible and transparent organizational infrastructure. This facilitates the effective application of technologies and the provision of customized solutions in response to customer needs. The attributes of the *Scope & Architecture* criterion, according to Luftman (2000), are:

- Traditional, enabler/driver, external
- Standards articulation
- Architectural integration:
    - Functional organization
    - Enterprise
    - Inter-enterprise
- Architectural transparency, flexibility

Skills refers to all human resource considerations of an organization. Luftman (2000) assigns the following attributes to the *Skills* criterion:

- Innovation, entrepreneurship
- Locus of power
- Management style
- Change readiness
- Career crossover
- Education, cross-training
- Social, political, trusting environment

3. RESEARCH METHODOLOGY

The purpose of this research is to study the strategic role that IT plays in a multinational company's subsidiaries in different countries. Two subsidiaries were selected for the case studies, one in Egypt and the other in Sweden.

A case, according to Yin (2003), is usually unique, gives details by allowing deep understanding of a single subject or of a small group of subjects, and focuses on 'thick description' information in particular contexts. The multinational company selected for our case studies is IT-related, with a focus on software development, telecommunications, application development and customized services. Each of the two subsidiaries has 500 to 1,000 employees and both have similar general business and IT strategies that are mandatory but are implemented in accordance with local conditions. Because of issues of confidentiality (claimed by the subsidiaries of the multinational company) we will refer to these subsidiaries as Company A (for the Egyptian subsidiary) and Company B (for the Swedish subsidiary).

The case studies were conducted through semi-structured interviews with business and IT decision-makers from both organizations. All interviews were oriented towards finding the answer to the main research question of our chapter: How should IT be strategically involved in improving the company's IT performance? In order to answer this question, a top-down approach was adopted whereby high-level aspects were first studied, followed by an in-depth study of detailed aspects. At the high level, we applied the Information Systems Strategy Triangle (Pearlson & Saunders, 2009) in the two subsidiaries to study how IT supports business and organizational strategy. In-depth aspects, on the other hand, were examined by using the Strategic Alignment Maturity Model (Luftman, 2000) to analyze how IT strategy and business strategy are aligned. For data collection and analysis, the following activities were performed:

- First-round interviews with five respondents at the strategic and tactical levels of each company from both the business and IT domains (from November 2008 to March 2009). In these interviews, we asked specific questions about the relationship of business and IT, and their related effects. The semi-structured interviews had pre-determined questions, but the order could be modified depending on the interviewer's perception of what seemed most appropriate. We tried to repeat the same questions in different ways throughout the same session, in order to get better answers and a consensus of responses. Based upon the respondents' answers and their opinions, which were graded on a scale of 1 to 5 in the questionnaire, we quantified the company's strategic alignment maturity.
- Desktop analysis (from March 2009 to June 2009) for general findings and definitions of different strategies (business, IT and organizational). In this phase, we identified business, IT, and organizational strategies in both companies using the Information Systems Strategic Triangle (Pearlson & Saunders, 2009). This analysis enabled us to understand how the two companies formulate different business, IT and organizational strategies, and the way in which they perpetuate the required balance for the successful operations of their business. In addition, the analysis helped us to understand the impact of the triangle's three pillars as a reciprocal relationship. Consequently, we needed to conduct a more precise examination of business choices and information systems modifications, so the need for further questions became apparent.
- Second-round interviews with another 5 respondents at the tactical and operational levels of each company from both the business and IT domains (from June 2009 to October 2009). We first presented our preliminary findings and perceptions to the interviewees. We received their feedback and discussed the problem areas we had highlighted. We then asked more detailed questions about the relationship of business and IT and their related effects. Here again, we tried to repeat the same questions in different ways throughout the same session, as well as to different people in other sessions, in order to get better responses and a consensus of answers. To help us in measuring the alignments, we also asked all respondents to quantify their answers/opinions on a scale of 1 to 5.
- In-depth analysis (from October 2009 to January 2010). The focus, in this phase, was on analyzing the relationship between business and IT strategies by revising our preliminary findings and analysis based

on the detailed data collected from our interviews. The results were complemented with an assessment of the strategic alignment maturity of both companies using Luftman's Strategic Alignment Maturity Model (2000).

4. DATA ANALYSIS AND RESULTS

4.1 Company Profiles

Our multinational company is headquartered in the United States and has subsidiaries in different countries around the world. In this research, we have analyzed the strategic role of IT in only two subsidiaries, one in Egypt and the other in Sweden, identified in this study as companies A and B. The multinational company in the United States is responsible for decisions regarding the company's main business and IT strategies. Business and IT agendas for fulfilling the strategic goals of the company at the local level are left to each subsidiary. This type of IT organization is, according to Luftman et al. (2004: p.226), one of the most common forms of decentralized IT organizations and, in his opinion, is "a variation that combines the pros of both centralized and decentralized organizations while eliminating many of the criticisms". Furthermore, Luftman (2004: p. 232) mentions that "a major benefit of the federal model is that it can typically best achieve strategic alignment' and 'provides IT with the ability to effectively communicate which each aspect of the business".

For a better understanding of our analysis, some information about the business profile of each of Company A and Company B and the role of IT in each is provided below.

Company A

Company A is concerned about its position in the marketplace. Accordingly, its IT budget constitutes more than 75% of the organization's total budget. Since the core business of Company A is IT-related, most of the employees are aware of the technology potentials. However, there is no IT representation on the Business Executive Board. This limits the technology awareness of staff working in the business domain. On the other hand, Company A considers IT to be a single, separate unit. This allows it to deal more easily with business units as well as with customers. Last but not the least, a priority part of the business strategy of Company A is looking for better ways to manage their projects, services and customers.

Company B

In Company B, the management has seen future prospects in e-business that could be supported by the strong IT infrastructure in Sweden. Accordingly, the company has invested heavily in IT. Since the company promotes e-sales, most of the employees possess the requisite IT and business skills for their functions and roles. They can easily find the link between the goals and requirements of each of the business and IT domains in their work. Company B has separated its traditional IT (that is used internally) from customer-service related IT. In this way, the company has found an easier way of classifying relations and the effects of IT on business strategy and organizational structure. The IT department is headed by the Chief Information Officer (CIO), who is a member of the management team. In addition, there is a Business Consultant Department headed by a manager who acts as a link between both the business and IT domains, manages external contacts and leads business orientations. Being a technology-related company supported by a well-established physical and non-physical infrastructure, Company B does not hesitate to adopt the latest technologies to meet evolving customer needs. As a result, the company modifies its IT strategies frequently.

4.2 Role of Information Technology in Business and Organizational Strategy

Company A

Business Strategy. In talking about Company A's business strategy, the company's CEO noted that: '*now it is only about growing and growing, so we can expand our business and change our way of delivering services and solutions, not only in the Egyptian marketplace but also in the North Africa and Middle East regions*'. Clearly, the main business goal of Company A is to grow and expand its markets, while the secondary goal is related to scaling in the number of customers. This business strategy is supported by the company's trend to increase the number of private - as well as governmental - partnerships and to expand its services to other countries in the region.

In fact, Company A uses a differentiation strategy, focusing on offering slightly different services to its customers by providing smart, customized solutions. Looking more closely, we note that Company A uses two differentiation strategies: a growth strategy, since it seeks to maintain its competitive advantage through acquisitions; and an innovation strategy, as it aims to take the lead in providing new services. The company's main business strategies can be summed up as follows:

- Providing its customers with as complete and satisfactory a service as possible. Usually, one happy customer will bring more customers to the service. The company attaches great importance to high stakeholder satisfaction. The aim is not simply to increase the number of users, but rather, to scale up in a sustainable manner. This suggests that the number of users should increase through greater satisfaction of existing customers with the quality of the service. The company listens carefully to its customers and other stakeholders in order to understand their diverse needs and to create new and better solutions based on what is learnt from this interactive process.
- Continuously seeking to invest in new products, or new applications of existing products, to meet customer needs. This provides the company with opportunities for seeking out new knowledge that can be used for predicting and creating new windows of success.
- Believing that there is always a better way of doing things. This is a driving force for the company to lead in its industry. Company A has recently developed an innovative concept called Daily Direct Deliveries (DDD) that allows it to offer an outstanding delivery service by eliminating local inventories, focusing instead on lean and flexible production and faster access for all customers to the company's full range of products, accessories and even technical support services within 24 hours.

IT Role in Business. Company A relies on IT to achieve its business strategy of providing the best products and being innovative in addressing the needs of customers and other stakeholders. Through the use of IT applications, the company is able to get feedback from its customers on what they need and how to improve its products. By developing the desired products, the company can add value to its business. While Company A uses IT intensively in support of customer interactions, suppliers interested in cooperation are asked to contact the company directly to evaluate issues related to quality, delivery and price. Special IT applications are used to evaluate the company's business performance and to manage its resources.

Organizational Strategy. Company A has a clear vertical organizational structure. One of the main reasons for this is the domination of business orientations and growth trends. The company has six distinct departments: Sales, Solution and Service Development (SSD), Technical,

Administration, Training and Marketing. The business management team consists of the CEO and the head of each of these departments. The SSD and Technical departments are considered to be the company's two IT divisions. While the SSD Department is responsible for developing different applications and solutions, the Technical Department is responsible for solving all kinds of problems, from pre-installations to technical support services. The two departments are led by two different managers but cooperate closely.

Although IT is perceived to be of great significance to the company, the decision-making process is conducted by the top business managers. Accordingly, the company is an example of centralized decision-making. Future directions in the company are decided by the management team in meetings that take place every three months. In such an environment, IT is seen as an enabler or support tool rather than a strategic partner. IT is facilitated in every department according to needs and requirements. However, integrations and knowledge sharing through different departments are limited.

Company B

Business Strategy. The company's main business strategy is differentiation, both at the external and internal levels. At the external level, the company is oriented towards innovations, as evidenced by the continuous modernization and repackaging of its services. At the internal level, a Business Consultant Department was installed in 2008 to increase collaboration and teamwork between the IT and business domains in the provision of services. The company's differentiation strategy is complemented with the following features:

- A trend to position the company to allow for fast response to technical support needs and new opportunities. This is mainly achieved by a concept called 'sprint', which allocates a three-week period to every project. Moreover, a benchmark is set to reorient the project, if needed, and also to link goals with customer needs and market trends. Usually, a new release is ready at the end of this three-week period, when all goals and sub-goals are achieved.
- A well-developed infrastructure that facilitates strong networking throughout the supply chain, linking the company with suppliers and customers. This has enabled the company to lead in e-business as well as e-technical support. Through online forums, the company shares information, knowledge and experiences that are potentials for future targets.
- Openness to the European marketplace, whereby the company is keen to participate in yearly conferences in Europe and the United States. These meetings bring new ideas, services and opportunities for cooperation with other subsidiaries and with partners.

IT Role in Business. IT plays a major role in the formulation of Company B's business strategies.

Through the development of technology and different types of infrastructure, IT provides smart solutions to customers and keeps the company accessible. Company B has come to rely on multiple enterprise solutions and applications, rather than single solutions, to achieve market penetration, a new trend that not only provides the company with customer-oriented enterprise solutions but has also helped to improve its internal integration processes. IT has been centralized in one unit to allow for better control, to support innovation and to speed up company response to market changes. Accordingly, IT is considered a good partner for business, as well as a driver for company transformation.

Organizational Strategy. Like most Swedish organizations, Company B has a predominantly horizontal organizational structure. In line with human rights legislation, organizations in Sweden tend to ensure a good working environment. The company has five distinct departments: Sales, Technical, Administration, Training and Marketing. Information flows both vertically and horizontally among departments and to and from top management. Owing to the horizontal system, power is equally distributed among employees. Top managers have different roles and responsibilities, but have less control over workers.

As the company has a flat organization, decision-making is decentralized at the top management level. All decisions are taken by the divisions and the decision-making group, which includes managers from every department, so that an IT manager is a member of every management team in his/her business area. The business manager relies totally on IT personnel when it comes to IT structure, but decisions regarding IT applications and how to use and modify them are made in close collaboration with business staff. IT personnel have reasonably good business knowledge, whereas people from the business domain have an adequate level of IT knowledge.

4.3 Analysis of the Strategic Role of IT Using the Information Systems Strategic Triangle

The results of the comparative analysis of the strategic role of IT in companies A and B using the Information Systems Strategic Triangle (Pearlson & Saunders, 2009) are presented in Table 1.

The results of the comparative analysis of both subsidiaries show the following:

- Both companies invest in IT, but since the CIO in Company B sits on the Business Executive Board, the company does not hesitate to adopt the latest technologies in order to meet evolving customer needs. On the other hand, since there is no IT representative on the Business Executive Board of Company A to encourage the board members to take IT initiatives, the members are reluctant to adopt new technologies.
- Company B has separated its traditional internal IT function from its IT customer service. This IT system helps the company to identify easier ways to classify relations and to determine the effects of IT on business strategy and organizational structure. In Company A, on the other hand, IT is seen as a separate unit that deals with different businesses. This contributes to the separation of the IT strategy from the business and organizational strategies and, in turn, decreases the probability of integrating all three types of strategies, hence obstructing an overall view of the company's strategy.
- Although both companies understand the importance of a business-IT partnership, they have different business priorities. Company A prefers not to go after investments in technology. Instead, the company's priority is to be the leader for change. As a result, the IT strategy follows the business strategy and is seen as a tool for achieving the company's business goals. Company B, on the other hand, places clear emphasis on its IT strategy by making cru-

Table 1. Business, organizational and information strategies in Companies A and B

Type of Strategy	Company A	Company B
Business Strategy	IT representative does not sit on the Business Executive Board	IT representative sits on the Business Executive Board
Organizational Strategy	IT is a separate unit that deals with business units	Separate internal and external IT functions
Information Strategy	Company does not adopt new information technologies Business goals are driven by information technology	Top managers lay emphasis on IT strategy IT strategy is considered to be a driving force

cial decisions to change technologies to suit customers' needs. As the company's IT solutions develop and its IT strategy is modified, its business strategy changes in turn, and its organizational structure is modified accordingly.

4.4 Analysis of the Strategic Role of IT using Luftman's Strategic Alignment Maturity Model

The Strategic Alignment Maturity (SAM) Model provides a set of criteria for assessing the maturity of strategic alignment over a five-level scale (Luftman, 2000). Assessment of strategic alignment is based on six criteria, namely: communications maturity, competency/value measurement maturity, governance maturity, partnership maturity, scope and architecture maturity and skills maturity. The results of the assessment of the strategic alignment of Company A and Company B using the SAM model are detailed below:

Company A

Communications. In Company A, employees do not have a strong relationship with their colleagues from different hierarchical levels. Communication is formalized, especially at the cross-departmental level.

In the opinion of business executives, IT is seen in Company A as an important tool rather than a strong partner for success. Accordingly, all decisions regarding new IT technologies, solutions or resources are taken by the Business Executive Board, and discussions within the IT domain also occur at the board level. Consequently, within the company it can be noticed that business people's understanding of IT is higher than the understanding of business by IT people. Regular meetings between employees in the business and IT domains are limited and occur only at the strategic level. Thus, there is a lack of trust between people in the two domains, especially at the tactical and operational levels.

There is a noticeable trend in Company A to encourage group work and group cooperation in order to achieve synergic results. However, the overlapping responsibilities of the SSD and Technical departments, in addition to competition between them in getting internal projects, obstruct transparency in sharing IT-related knowledge. At the same time, the domination of the business domain discourages IT people from getting involved in the company's business and sharing ideas or knowledge. *Communications* maturity is, hence, negatively affected. Each department owns the information and outcomes of its projects. Even though all information can be requested by any department, the information is not available for re-use, and hence, the overall analysis and evaluation of the company's business are affected.

Competency/Value Measurements. Given the domination of the business domain in Company A, there is a clear separation between both the business and IT departments. In such an environment, the internal and external services of the IT unit are also separated. IT metrics in such a context provide concrete analyses of both inbound performance and outbound (customer and supplier-related) performance. Because the business domain dominates, there is only control over and review of business metrics, with no formal feedback on the efficiency of IT metrics or the IT services that are offered to business. Additionally, workers in Company A are not always subject to the same benchmarks and formal assessments, especially if they are working in different domains - IT or business. This negatively affects the company's *Competency/Value Measurements* maturity.

Governance. Strategic planning in both the business and IT domains of Company A usually covers a period of two to three years. The vertical organizational structure makes for more formal rather than close relationships among the different hierarchical levels within the organization. Control over performance is exercised through formal rules of reporting, clear investment processes, as well as steering committee meetings. However, the social orientation of Egyptian society, which is characterized by the development of informal relations, diminishes the negative impact of formalized processes on *Governance* maturity.

Partnership. As IT is not represented on the Executive Board in Company A, it mainly plays an enabling role in the transformation of structure and business processes. IT is seen as a cost for the company, and a support for helpdesk functions and network maintenance. Additionally, IT strategies and projects are not prioritized. Future directions and new business areas are explored by the managers only from the business side. Therefore, there is no shared risk between business and IT. Instead, the business domain takes full responsibility for driving the company's transformation and bears all associated risks. The IT domain, on the other hand, is responsible from start to finish for promoted IT projects. Clearly, this situation results in an insufficiently transparent environment, not only between the two domains, business and IT, but also within each domain. As a result, IT is perceived as a separate support unit rather than a partner for the business.

Scope & Architecture. Although IT does not hold a leadership position in Company A, it applies standards across the organization that are integrated into the organizational structure according to business needs. On the one hand, the company achieves sufficient flexibility in this way regarding their business plans and goals; on the other, the unstable economic and political conditions in the country do not allow the company a very flexible architecture, even though different scale changes are always required. Adoption of any change is a very difficult process; wisdom, forethought and thorough evaluation are required.

The company is involved in many governmental and military projects, clearly affecting the transparency of the architecture and leading to changes in procedures. Rigid conditions on architecture exist that deprive workers of the flexibility required in most of their tasks. With a clear vertical organizational structure, different changes and process integrations might be required depending on the project, the customer and the level of the organizational structure. ***Skills.*** At the departmental level, individuals are strongly encouraged to develop their skills and are rewarded for doing so by their bosses. Moreover, the increasing number of university graduates, unstable economic conditions and highly competitive working environment push individuals to develop their skills and seek out additional channels for development. Opportunities for learning, training and change are always there, and are provided by managers as required by the company's strong business orientation. Some individuals, however, are very eager to develop at a faster pace and to acquire knowledge in no time, given the uncertain environment and conditions. But while some employees find the company culture suited to their lifestyle, others find it difficult to change.

People in the company are highly skilled in their tasks. They are trained to work in a multicultural environment, since the company has different projects in surrounding countries, in both the Middle East and North Africa regions. The organization invests heavily in IT and its operations rely on the IT skills of its employees.

The values resulting from the assessment of the strategic alignment of Company A using Luftman's model (2000) are presented in Figure 1.

Company B

Communications. The stable economic and political conditions, as well as the well-established infrastructure in the country, lend stability to both the business and IT departments. People work in a fairly static environment that is free of job uncertainty. This helps the company in developing very clear strategies and applying feasible standards of knowledge sharing. The company's goals and objectives are clear to people in both the

Figure 1. Measured strategic alignment of Company A

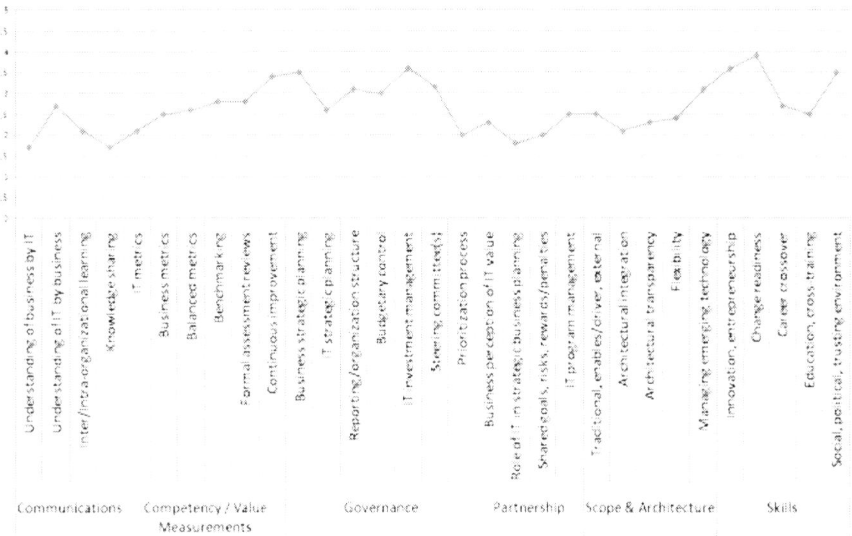

business and IT domains, reflecting a very good level of understanding of business by IT staff and of IT by employees in the business domain. As a result, the two units are able to work effectively in an inter/intra-cooperative context. This creates a supportive environment for learning from others without pressure. The lack of competition and easy communication between workers from both the business and IT domains promotes informal relationships between top managers and employees that facilitate knowledge sharing.

Throughout the interviews in the various study phases, we obtained the same answer, that group cooperation - rather than individual achievements - is highly encouraged at all working levels. Communication through internal seminars, project forums, and even through two daily coffee breaks, is encouraged and supported. However, the relaxed Swedish health system, small number of staff and allowance for long paternity leave affects both the amount of time spent on meetings among employees and follow-up processes. Communication between the business and IT domains at the strategic as well as tactical/middle management levels is organized and performed in a semi-structured way. As a result, different kinds of data can be obtained from different departments for analysis and evaluation.

Competency/Value Measurements. Company B uses IT and business metrics to evaluate the involvement of IT in the business. Different established IT metrics are used to evaluate the services provided in different business areas. The IT metrics go beyond the traditional services for facilitating the use of application tools, to evaluating issues related to customer satisfaction and effectiveness of application development. However, because business people do not understand the potential of IT, they do not consider these IT metrics useful to them. At the same time, no formal feedback mechanisms are in place through which they can react to the information coming from the use of IT metrics. Business metrics, on the other hand, are more widely used, to avoid uncertainty in jobs and future careers. People work on their individual tasks within their teams or projects, and as soon as a certain iteration or task is completed, it is made visible and communicated to the whole team for further action.

Governance. The multinational organization of which Company B is a part has allowed the company flexibility in defining its IT and business strategies. But while the strategic planning efforts of top executives in both the business and IT domains came across clearly during all interviews, the executives exhibited a clearer understanding of IT strategic planning than strategic planning for business. This is largely due, on the one hand, to the involvement on the Business Executive Board of the CIO, who constantly pushes for greater IT support and prioritization at the strategic level, and, on the other hand, to the fact that people in relaxed working conditions are generally more interested in fulfilling their tasks than in understanding business strategies. However, people in the IT domain rely totally on the business domain to drive the company.

As an IT-related organization, Company B has a well-developed physical and non-physical IT infrastructure. Moreover, the company has a clear flat organizational structure, and a high level of transparency is maintained that leads to accountability for the outcome of IT projects.

Partnership. The CIO of Company B has a seat on the Executive Board and plays an important role in driving the company's transformation in terms of structure and business processes. In addition, the CIO holds a leadership position in the company and shares responsibility with the business executives when it comes to risk taking. But while IT is seen as a partner rather than a support tool, IT strategies and IT projects are not given priority.

Future directions and new business areas, on the other hand, are explored only by business executives and the Business Consultant Department. Accordingly, business people take full responsibility for the associated risks, as they consider it their duty to keep the business going, especially given the current global economic crisis. This offers insufficient transparency for workers.

Scope & Architecture. Owing to the importance of ensuring stable and less uncertain working conditions, business people dominate the company's external relationships, including relationships with suppliers and customers. These relations are maintained and managed by the Business Consultant Department. Nevertheless, the IT unit applies standards across the organization, although these standards are not formally integrated into the organizational structure. This environment is conducive to the creation of a very stable and highly secure architectural system, and new technologies are only adopted after careful consideration. So, the need for sufficiently flexible, rather than highly flexible, IT infrastructure with sufficient integration within all business levels is clearly understood. Expressing his opinion on the matter, the Chief Information Officer said: '*We need to be more rational and efficient in using IT. We are in deep and need to manage our resources, people and organization.*' On the other hand, the uncompetitive environment supports the establishment of informal integrations of the functional processes, especially during important projects. Such informal integrations allow for the exchange of experiences, application of new technologies, improvement of business processes and provision of customized solutions.

Skills. The skills of people in Company B are highly mature, a clear effect of the well-established educational system in universities and of training courses at work. The pressure-free environment at work encourages workers to take initiative. Some employees, however, especially in the business domain, are negatively affected by the relaxed working conditions, exhibiting almost zero development. Additionally, and because of different specializations, the company does not support cross-training, which affects the affiliation of its people.

With a smaller number of qualified people outside the company and difficult hire-and-fire regulations in the Swedish system, managers encourage individuals to develop their skills. The facilitation of training programs, seminars, and lectures on a virtual campus encourages people to share knowledge and experiences. It is important to note that the society in general is characterized by a relaxed and low workload and a love of change. As a result, people tend to change their jobs frequently, reflecting a low level of affiliation to businesses.

The values resulting from the assessment of the strategic alignment of Company B using Luftman's model (2000) are presented in Figure 2.

4.5 Comparative Analysis of Company A and Company B Using Luftman's Strategic Alignment Maturity Model

The comparative analysis of companies A and B using Luftman's Strategic Alignment Maturity Model (2000) is presented below in accordance with the six SAM criteria.

Communications. In Company A, communication occurs in an unstructured way. Information is not available for re-use, affecting the overall analysis and evaluation of the company, which decreases *Communications* maturity. In contrast, communication in Company B occurs in a semi-structured way. Accordingly, data can be obtained from different parts of the company for analysis and evaluation.

Competency/Value Measurements. In Company A, data about customers, suppliers and different processes, etc., is available and stored in the company through IT systems. But since IT is seen as a single unit and is not integrated with business, data is not used for performance analysis and improvement of customer services. In Company B, on the other hand, IT metrics provide a concrete analysis, with some of the metrics used for inbound performance evaluation, and other metrics used to evaluate outbound (customer and supplier related) performance.

Governance. With regard to governance and organizational structure, Company A has adopted a vertical and centralized structure represented by separations among departments. This results in rigid business and IT strategies for facilitating different tasks and functions. A well-established reporting system, however, allows different resources to be shared in order to meet the needs of different projects. Company B, on the other hand, has a flat organizational structure that allows the company to have flexible strategies and to customize different strategies according to

Figure 2. Measured strategic alignment of Company B

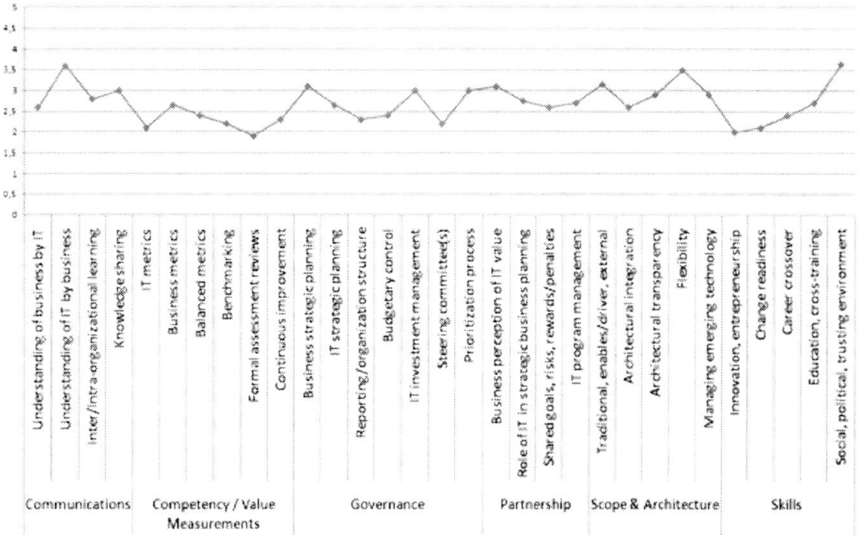

departmental conditions. This enables IT to be a strong partner in the company's investments and prioritization processes and, in turn, to participate more effectively in the company's development.

Partnership. In Company A, IT is seen as a separate unit. Business processes are the enablers for change and IT strategies and projects are not prioritized. Future directions and new business areas are explored by the managers only from the business side. As a result, IT is only considered a tool for supporting business changes. The situation is different in Company B, where IT is a driver for change. The partnership between business and IT reflects harmonized goals and services, where IT plays a crucial role in exploring new markets and new business areas, improving customer services and creating competitive advantages for the company.

Scope & Architecture. Although IT does not hold a leadership position in Company A, it plays an important role in setting standards across the organization. With the support of a vertical organizational structure, these standards enable the company to have a clear scope and architecture. However, because of the company's involvement in a large number of military and governmental projects, the architecture is not always transparent or integrated with other parts of the system. Through regular meetings, periodical conferences and common research and development activities between departments, the company can exchange experiences, acquire greater transparency, apply new technologies in different environments, improve its business processes and provide customized solutions. In Company B, the stable conditions of the Swedish business environment, especially the economic and political aspects, make it possible for the company to plan longer ahead and build more mature architectures with focused scope. The only problem facing the company is the limited flexibility when change is needed.

Skills. In Company A, the environment is more political, with no shared risk. There is a lack of trust, especially between business and IT employees. Outside top management, career crossover is not encouraged. In contrast, Company B's management offers its employees a flexible, comfortable, non-political and trusting environment where risk is shared and innovation is encouraged. Career path crossover, involving different departments and projects, is also encouraged with the aim of knowledge sharing and the promotion of greater company affiliation.

Training is encouraged in both companies. In Company A, training programs take place as a strategic choice of the company in order to improve its competence, while in Company B, training is a matter of individual choice.

The results of the comparative analysis of the strategic alignment maturity of Company A and Company B are shown in Figure 3.

Figure 3 reveals how companies A and B stand against the six strategic alignment maturity criteria. As can be seen from the figure, there is a gap between the two companies in terms of level of *Communications* maturity, as Company B (Level 3+) shows a better understanding of IT by business than Company A (Level 2+).

In terms of *Competency*, both companies come closer to each other. However, Company A has a higher competency level (Level 3-) than Company B (Level 2+) because of the big differences in the *Formal Assessment Reviews* and *Continuous Improvement* attributes.

With regard to *Governance*, both companies have a similar - middle/high - maturity level (Level 3+). This is clearly affected by the main business and IT strategies designed by headquarters. On the other hand, Company A scored high on the *Business Strategic Planning* attribute, since doing business in a difficult marketplace such as Egypt requires wise planning in order to mitigate risks. In Company B, however, *IT Investment Management* and *Prioritization Processes* are well established, as the company is moving to invest in IT - particularly as Sweden has a well-established information and communication technology (ICT) national infrastructure.

Table 2. Strategic alignment maturity results in Companies A and B

Criterion	Company A	Company B
Communications	• Understanding of IT by business is low • IT is more of a service provider	• Understanding of business by IT slightly dominates • Good awareness of business goals and needs
Competency/Value Measurements	• Business metrics are used for evaluation • Business metrics are used to assess the importance of services	• IT metrics are not controlled • No formal feedback and mechanisms to react to IT metrics used in the company
Governance	• Short-term strategic planning due to unstable conditions • Rigid hierarchical structure provides formal reporting systems and strong steering committees	• Good IT and business strategic planning • Prioritization of IT processes is clear
Partnership	• IT does not have a seat on the Business Executive Board • IT is an enabler for change in the company's structure and processes	• IT holds a leadership position • IT executives accept responsibility and risks.
Scope & Architecture	• IT provides more flexibility regarding business plans and goals • IT applies standards across the organization	• IT provides a flexible infrastructure for integration • IT provides sufficient integration at the business level
Skills	• Business and IT skills are balanced	• Employees are trained to work in a multicultural environment

In terms of *Partnership* and *Scope & Architecture*, Company B's maturity level is higher than Company A (3+ versus 3-). The environment is more ready in Company B for a *Partnership* relationship between the business and IT domains. This situation is supported by the CIO's seat on the Business Executive Board, which contributes to bringing the two domains together. In terms of *Scope & Architecture*, Company B shows greater flexibility in decision-making and a more relaxed working environment than Company A, resulting in a more flexible architecture than the rigid vertical one in Company A.

Finally, both companies have similar scores on most of the attributes related to *Skills*. However, employees in Company A scored higher on *Innovations* and *Readiness for Change,* since they give great attention to self-development

Figure 3. Comparison of the strategic alignment maturity of Companies A and B

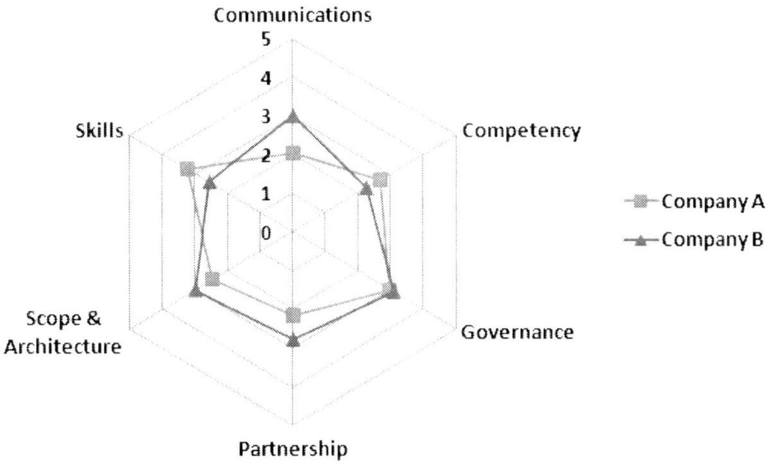

and career advancement. As a result, Company A scored higher (level 4+) on *Skills* maturity than Company B (level 3).

5. CONCLUSION AND RECOMMENDATIONS

Our findings from our interviews with business and IT managers from the two companies under study reveal that there are several similarities in their IT, business and organizational strategies. However, these similarities reflect how the general strategies of the multinational corporation are implemented in the local environment of each subsidiary. Clear differences, however, can be seen in the strategic alignment of the two subsidiaries and the way they are looking to gain a competitive advantage in their business marketplace.

Regarding the Information Systems Triangle, IT decision-makers from the two companies should consider the following recommendations to achieve a successful relationship among their business, information system and organizational strategies:

- IT should be integrated with business, because for a company to compete in the information era it cannot have a stand-alone business strategy.
- The IT manager/CIO should be more involved on the Business Executive Board, as is the case in Company B, in order to ensure a common strategic view of the company's business.
- Unlike Company A, IT should not be separate or seen as an isolated unit, because this leads to viewing IT strategy as a static tool that is only used in support of business operations.

Concerning strategic alignment, the following recommendations represent how IT decision-makers should consider the relationships between the business and IT domains:

- In both companies, business and IT should use a structured way of communicating and sharing information. This will make the information available for re-use and will also improve customer services and performance analysis.
- Both companies should develop their formal measurements and metrics, providing clear descriptions of each, especially in the IT domain. This will increase the link between IT functions and related business goals, rather than only measure IT individual performance.
- Although both companies have formal reporting structures, they need to encourage informal partnership structures between the business and IT domains, as both companies lack knowledge of the extent to which IT participates in their resources.
- Both companies have the IT architecture and scope to support business processes. However, the architecture's integration should extend to all strategic, tactical and operational levels, rather than only revolve around communications, as in the current situation.
- IT should assume the role of enabler or driver for change in business processes, as in Company B. Even though Company A does not adopt the latest information technologies, giving a leadership position to the IT domain will increase the involvement of IT in business achievements, and hence, increase *Partnership* maturity.
- As in Company B, an organization should provide a low-stress work environment and use their developers as a source of IT innovation. This will increase their affiliation to the company, which is one of the most important factors for business success.

In summary, through a comparative analysis of two subsidiaries of a multinational company, we have offered an approach for studying the strategic role of IT and provided recommendations that need to be taken into consideration by business and IT managers in both companies to improve their IT performance. The results of the current comparative analysis also provide useful information on how business and IT managers should use IT for strategic purposes. Evaluating how IT supports business and organizational strategies and assessing strategic alignment should be considered the two main priorities for every IT decision-maker.

REFERENCES

Avison, D., Jones, J., Powell, P., & Wilson, D. (2004). Using and validating the strategic alignment model. *The Journal of Strategic Information Systems*, *13*(3), 223–246.

Bergeron, F., & Raymond, L. (1995). The contribution of IT to the bottom line: A contingency perspective of strategic dimensions. *Proceedings of the 16th International Conference on Information Systems*, Amsterdam, 167-181.

Burn, J. M., & Szeto, C. (2000). A comparison of the views of business and IT management on success factors for strategic alignment. *Information & Management*, *37*(4), 197–216.

Cash, J. I., Eccles, R. G., Nohria, N., & Nolan, R. L. (1994). *Building the information-age organization: Structure, Control, and Information Technologies*. Boston, MA: Richard D. Irwin.

Chan, Y. E. (2002). Why haven't we mastered alignment? The importance of the informal organization structure. *MIS Quarterly Executive*, *1*(2), 97–112.

Chan, Y. E., Huff, S. L., Barclay, D. W., & Copeland, D. G. (1997). Business strategic orientation, information systems strategic orientation and strategic alignment. *Information Systems Research*, *8*(2), 125–150.

Chan, Y. E., Huff, S. L., & Copeland, D. G. (1998). Assessing realized information systems strategy. *The Journal of Strategic Information Systems*, *6*(4), 273–298.

D'Aveni, R. (1995). Coping with hypercompetition: Utilizing the new 7S's framework. *The Academy of Management Executive*, *9*(3), 45–57.

Earl, M. J. (1989). *Management strategies for Information Technology*. Upper Saddle River, NJ: Prentice Hall.

El Mekawy, M., Rusu, L., & Haseeb, N. A. (2009). Business-IT alignment: An evaluation of strategic alignment models. *Communications in Computer and Information Science, 49*, 447-455. Berlin / Heidelberg, Germany: Springer Verlag.

Hammer, M., & Champy, J. (1994). *Reengineering the corporation: A manifesto for business revolution*. USA: Harper Business Press.

Henderson, J. C., & Venkatraman, N. (1993). Strategic alignment: Leveraging Information Technology for transforming organizations. *IBM Systems Journal*, *32*(1), 4–16.

Hu, Q., & Huang, C. D. (2006). Using the Balanced Scorecard to achieve sustained IT-business alignment: A case study. *Communications of AIS*, *17*(8), 181–204.

Huff, S. L., Maher, P. M., & Munro, M. C. (2006). Information Technology and the board of directors: Is there an IT attention deficit? *MIS Quarterly Executive*, *5*(2), 55–68.

Kearns, G. S., & Sabherwal, R. (2007). Strategic alignment between business and Information Technology: A knowledge-based view of behaviours, outcome and consequences. *Journal of Management Information Systems*, *23*(3), 129–162.

King, W. R., & Grover, V. (1991). The strategic use of information resources: An exploratory study. *IEEE Transactions on Engineering Management*, *38*(4), 293–305.

Luftman, J. (2000). Assessing business-IT alignment maturity. *Communications of AIS*, *4*(14), 1–50.

Luftman, J., & Ben-Zvi, T. (2010). Key issues for IT executives 2009: Difficult economy's impact on IT. *MIS Quarterly Executive*, *9*(1), 49–59.

Luftman, J., & Kempaiah, R. (2008). Key issues for IT executives 2007. *MIS Quarterly Executive*, *7*(2), 99–112.

Luftman, J., Kempaiah, R., & Rigoni, E. H. (2009). Key issues for IT executives 2008. *MIS Quarterly Executive*, *8*(3), 151–159.

Luftman, J. N., Bullen, C. V., Liao, D., Nash, E., & Neumann, C. (2004). *Managing the Information Technology resource: Leadership in the information age*. Upper Saddle River, NJ: Pearson Education Inc.

McFarlan, F. W., McKenney, J. L., & Pyburn, P. (1983). The information archipelago - plotting a course. *Harvard Business Review*, (January-February): 145–156.

McKeen, J. D., & Smith, H. A. (2009). *IT strategy in action*. Upper Saddle River, NJ: Pearson Education Inc.

Pearlson, K. E., & Saunders, C. S. (2009). *Strategic management of Information Systems* (4th ed.). Asia: John Wiley & Sons.

Peppard, J., & Ward, J. (2004). Beyond strategic information systems: Towards an IS capability. *The Journal of Strategic Information Systems*, *13*(2), 167–194.

Porter, M. (1980). *Competitive strategy*. New York, NY: Free Press.

Porter, M. E., & Millar, V. E. (1985). How information gives you competitive advantage. *Harvard Business Review*, (July-August): 149–160.

Reich, B. H., & Benbasat, I. (2000). Factors that influence the social dimension of alignment between business and Information Technology objectives. *Management Information Systems Quarterly*, *24*(1), 84–113.

Rusu, L., & El Mekawy, M. (2009). The strategic role of IT: A case study in two Swedish retail companies. In D'Atri, A., & Saccà, D. (Eds.), *Information Systems: People, organizations, institutions, and technologies* (pp. 559–567). Berlin/Heidelberg, Germany: Springer-Verlag.

Silva, L., Figueroa, E., & Reinhart, J. G. (2007). Interpreting IS alignment: A multiple case study in professional organizations. *Information and Organization*, *17*(4), 232–265.

Tang, Z., & Walters, B. (2006). The interplay of strategic management and Information Technology. In Walters, B., & Tang, Z. (Eds.), *IT-enabled strategic management: Increasing returns for the organization* (pp. 1–15). Hershey, PA: Idea Group Publishing.

Turban, E., Leidner, D., McLean, E., & Wetherbe, J. (2006). *Information Technology for management. Transforming organizations in the digital economy* (5th ed.). USA: John Wiley & Sons.

Weiss, J. W., & Anderson, D. (2004). Aligning technology and business strategy: Issues & frameworks, a field study of 15 companies. *Proceedings of the 37th Annual Hawaii International Conference on System Sciences* (HICSS'04), January 5-8, 2004, Hilton Waikoloa Village, Island of Hawaii, USA, IEEE Computer Society Press, (pp. 1-10).

Yin, R. K. (2003). *Case study research: Design and methods* (3rd ed.). Thousand Oaks, CA: Sage Publications.

KEY TERMS AND DEFINITIONS

Business Strategy: A clear plan defining where a business seeks to go and how to get there.

Business-IT Alignment (also referred to as Strategic Alignment): The application of IT in a way that is timely and appropriate and in line with business needs, goals and strategies.

Communications: Refers to a clear understanding between the business and IT communities, with an effective exchange and awareness of each other's ideas, processes and needs.

Competency/Value Measurements: Concerned with demonstrating IT values in figures compatible with the business community's understanding.

Governance: Ensures that business and IT communities formally and periodically discuss and review their plans and also define their priorities for allocating the required IT resources.

IT/IS Strategy: A plan of how an organization provides information services.

Organizational Strategy: A plan for designing an organizational structure and different choices for developing work processes.

Partnership: Refers to the relationship between business and IT in having a shared vision of the organization's processes in order to facilitate IT as an enabler or driver for transformation in business processes and strategies.

Scope & Architecture: Illustrates the involvement of IT in all organizational processes. It defines the role of IT in supporting flexible and transparent organizational infrastructure.

Skills: Refers to all human resource considerations of an organization.

Chapter 11
Implementing Business Intelligence in the Dynamic Beverages Sales and Distribution Environment

Sami Akabawi
American University in Cairo (AUC), Egypt

Heba Hodeeb
American University in Cairo (AUC), Egypt

EXECUTIVE SUMMARY

To compete successfully in today's retail business arena, senior management are often demanding fast and responsive Information Systems that enable the company not only to manage its operations but to provide on-the-fly performance measurement through a variety of tools. Use of (ERP) systems have been slow in responding to these needs, despite the wealth of the internally generated business databases and reports as a consequence of functional integration. The specific nature and demands by those senior management staff require the congregation of many external data elements and use data mining techniques to provide fast discovery of performance slippages or changes in the business environment. Data Warehousing and Business Intelligence (BI) applications, evolved during the past few decades, have been implemented to respond to these needs. In this case write-up, we present how the ERP system was utilized as the backbone for use by BI tools and systems to provide Sales and Marketing units in a transnational company subsidiary in Egypt to actively respond to the demands for agile information services. The Egypt subsidiary is the HQ of the African region's operations of several franchises and distributers of the company products, in addition to operating a beverage concentrate manufacturing plant in Egypt, which services the entire region's beverage products needs.

DOI: 10.4018/978-1-60960-583-4.ch011

BACKGROUND

Company Overview

The case firm considered in this chapter is a transnational company subsidiary in Egypt, which is located in the Free Zone in Nasr City district, in the country's capital, Cairo. The company owns and operates a beverage concentrate plant within the domain of its facility for producing the concentrate syrup used in all its beverage products. These concentrates are then delivered to many bottling operators in African countries for the production of the final product mixing, bottling, packaging and trade fleet distribution in their respective territories. The concentrate plant is among the few plants of the transnational company world-wide, where the technical know-how formula of the company is produced, and the plant caters for the supply of concentrate syrup for the entire African, Middle East and Asian bottling territories.

The company is divided into a number of business units (BU). Egypt's subsidiary assumes the function of the head office to the African business unit which constitutes more than 25 franchises and distributers in many African countries. In this case-paper, we consider the analysis and evaluation of the information systems categories used in the head office of the company's subsidiary in Egypt for the Sales and Distribution management in the region. In particular, we detail how the backbone Enterprise Resources Planning (ERP) and business intelligence systems (BI) are integrated and used to leverage the need for agile management of the operations in the Sales and Distribution functions within the highly dynamic competitive beverage market.

Brief Economic Outlook of the Country Where the Case Company Operates

Forecasts put Egypt's food and drink exports growing by 59.4 percent between 2007 and 2012, which is not only a reflection of the free trade agreements ratified by the government of Egypt since late 90's, but also the country's improving food and drink processing industry. Regional trade agreements such as the Greater Arab Free Trade Area (GAFTA) have also given producers access to a far larger market. Having gone into effect in 2005, GAFTA has gradually lowered customs on locally produced food across a broad range of Middle Eastern countries. These agreements opened larger markets for Egyptian producers, given the similarity of diets and lack of language barrier. Meanwhile, Africa is also becoming another key export market, mainly for its proximity and lack of domestic production capacities in the African countries.

Sharply rising food prices have been the cause of growing unrest in Egypt over the past two years. Though the Egyptian government has taken a number of measures to deal with the mounting public discontent, inflation hit the 20 percent mark and food prices skyrocketed, and a dire situation has evolved in the country.

Egypt is a rather unique market for the region as it benefits from a very large population (over 80mn) and an unsaturated food and drink market. However, the food and drink trade balance is highly dependent on imports. In addition, inflation, in a country with national poverty rate of 22.9 percent according to the World Bank Development Data Group, (2002) and Earth Trend Country profile estimating 20 percent of the population below the poverty line, led to increased levels of political risk and unrest. Against a backdrop of worsening global financial market turmoil and rapidly accelerating inflation, particularly in emerging markets, Egypt has significantly more economic hardship clouds on the horizon. Nonetheless, Egypt receives a pretty high score in the region for its food and drink market due to its per capita food consumption growth. Egypt does not fare well for the country structure indicator, with low GDP per capita, although the size of its population and lack of market maturity help pull up its score.

SETTING THE STAGE

Companies in the beverage industry often operate as producers and distributors of canned and bottled soft drinks, concentrate and other juices and liquid beverage products. They experience rapid changes in the way they have to do business. For one thing, increased commoditization and diversification of beverage products has made it more difficult than ever for beverage manufacturers to differentiate their products and their brands against rivals and competing brands.

In addition, beverage consumers are demanding greater product variety, higher levels of service and more value for their money (Bingham, 1999). The increased global competition, escalating retailer demands and increasingly stringent government regulations have added to the pressure on those companies, making it harder for them to compete globally. With growing concerns with food safety issues, these companies are also finding it necessary to monitor and track every phase of operation – from raw ingredients through finished product, to packaging, storage and distribution – to ensure compliance with the higher safety standards.

Driven by these challenges, beverage producing and distribution companies are looking more and more to their manufacturing processes and supply chain in an effort to increase production efficiency, reduce operational costs and effect better overall management of the enterprise and its assets to sustain desired levels of profitability and growth.

Business Imperatives

Historically, there has been resistance to the introduction of technology in the beverage industry except perhaps to automate certain production processes (e.g. mixing, canning, bottling and packaging). In many large companies, use of information technology (IT) has been limited to off-the-shelf or custom-tailored systems implemented to assist employees with such discrete business processes as accounting, corporate finance, human resources and purchasing. However, in the past few decades, many firms have implemented Electronic Data Interchange (EDI) and host of functional separate systems, often in response to customer and vendors demands or management directives for adopting business-to-customer (B2C) and business-to-business (B2B) e-business functionalities. Despite all of the information flowing through these disparate systems across the enterprise, the information services to operational and top management more often than not lacked integration, timeliness and comprehensiveness.

The lack of timely financial information, integrated with order and production flow would hamper the ability of firms to know where they stand from day to day, both from financial and operations point of views. In most companies, by the time financial information becomes available in a report, it's historical and too late to change course to correct problems. In today's fast-paced global economy and rapidly changing marketplace, the lack of integrated, real-time information to provide business and market analysis, business intelligence and decision support tools negatively impact profitability, growth and ability to act quickly to external marketing forces. Moreover, efficient order entry, materials and inventory control and fast turnover dictate the need for agile and responsive information systems to minimize waste and delivering efficient customer service. In market-driven industries, once the product is made, time is not nearly so critical – but storage, transportation and distribution are.

On the beverage industry side, we see an astonishing level of diversification fragmenting this industry. Where once there were a finite number of carbonated and non-carbonated soft drinks occupying the competitive landscape, today there is an almost infinite explosion of choices – from pure juice and juice blends, to sodas of every kind, waters, and host of beverages. Sales in this area are market-driven, so producers tend to rely on special packaging, competitive pricing, event-driven promotions and other attention-getting techniques to differentiate themselves. For these firms, forecasting and timing of product-to-market are crucial. Market-driven companies thus need to be able to put a product out on the shelves, see how it sells, then turn to adjust production to match demand.

The preceding characteristics illustrate that each segment of the beverage industry has its own challenges to overcome whether it competes in local, national, regional or global markets. However, to retain customer loyalty and grow market share, all beverage manufacturers and distributors need greater flexibility to respond quickly – whether to changing customer expectations, government regulations, or fluctuations in the marketplace resulting from seasonal changes in drinking patterns. In short, beverage producer and distributer companies are finding they have to increase the speed or decrease the lag time between when their products are made and when they are out on the market. To coordinate their production capabilities, manufacturers also need to increase their ability to handle different materials and product lines simultaneously. If they are to improve procurement and inventory control, they must find a way to accurately track both raw materials and finished goods. And, to build their company and product brands among customers and consumers, they must be able to ensure consistency of quality across product lines.

On the business end, optimizing plant operations can be a tremendous source of savings. Companies attaining high visibility and close control of key production elements opt to simplify complexity and better manage cash flows. They need to be able to forecast more closely to customer demands – avoiding either overextending or under-producing – to improve their return on corporate assets. The use of enterprise resources planning (ERP) systems becomes the natural choice for fulfilling such needs (Davenport, 1998). ERP systems operate on enterprise-wide domain to ensure integration among all business functions and result in one large single view of the company's data resources. If those systems are well matched to the business and well implemented, many benefits can be accrued such as: decreased reaction times, better logistics flow, increased responsiveness to market and customer changes and improved supply chain management (SCM).

Information Systems Backbone Implementation in the Case Firm

By early 2000, the case company presented in this chapter planned to acquire an ERP system to replace its aging legacy systems. The company looked for a proven technology platform for its business applications with strong functionalities in areas such as financial applications, procurement, order entry and fulfillment, planning and scheduling, inventory management and optimization, product configuration, flexible product costing, manufacturing, EDI capabilities, and support of multiple plants and/or warehouses and complex distribution system. To that end, a blanket, multilayer deal with highly reputed ERP vendor was selected and configured to run several business application modules to cut costs and share data through multiple distributed systems located in multiple regional datacenters, with secured global access. These applications are built around ERP, customer relationship management (CRM) and SCM modules as well as set of integration middleware tools. The system aimed at helping improve the logistics of store deliveries, sales orders and the back office operations of the networked company's manufacturers, bottlers and distributors around the globe. This distributed approach targeted the improvement of market execution, better service to consumers, in addition to giving a more integrated system platform to serve the information needs at the store level and account level, and more effective management of the business on the street. The implemented distributed ERP systems provided the following application and service tiers:

1. The back office tier which included several modules. The African region implementation provided the following modules:
    a. Marketing Expenses Management
    b. Business Travel Management (BTM)
    c. Human Resources (HR)
    d. Financials and Sales
    e. Logistics
    f. Supply chain and Manufacturing
2. Data warehouse and decision support tier which included the following modules to serve the African business unit:
    a. Value chain modeling, the module manages everything that adds value to a product. Starting from raw material used to produce the product such as sugar, water, vitamins and caramel, to the time employees spend on various functions and the salaries of employees, to the trucks used to distribute the product and the gasoline needed for the trucks. It uses all those individual costs to know how much the product should sell.
    b. Forecasting module, the sales business intelligence module is responsible for everything related to sales. It manipulates three types of data: historical data, which include the actual weekly sales; the business plan data, which constitutes the forecasting for the sales of the year; finally, the rolling estimate data, which is a more accurate prediction of the sales based on the discrepancy between the actual sales and the business plan.
    c. Decision support System, this module helps sales function managers in making decisions based on sales by providing the following services:
        - Sales flash report issued on specific day of the week. Sales reports of the week are sent to employees on company-provided blackberries. The weekly sales updates are given versus business plan predictions or versus prior years. In addition, sales is always directly related and translated into market share. The company used push strategy to alert the employee that he/she has received an email.
        - Telecom reporting is used to control the escalating costs of telecommunications within the African business unit. Managers get periodic data from mobile service operators to determine how much their units pay for mobile services. This particular application used the EDI facility provided by the system through the middleware layer.
        - Margin minder report is used to track sales in every outlet, and provides small outlets with data on how to make more profit. For example if a small café is buying more of a certain Stock Keeping Unit (SKU) but the reports show that the café is not selling much of it, the system then recommends that the outlet buys less of this SKU and buys another one that seems to be selling good at the particular café. In addition, it does the 'Right Execution Daily' (RED) that manages the product display and the picture of success (pos), i.e., to make sure that company logo is put at the entrance of sites, that the tempera-

ture of the product is set at the prescribed temperature, that the company refrigerators given to sites have their products only.

d. Business Intelligence (BI) tools which perform activities such as collecting and transforming data from a variety of systems, consolidates and aggregate these data in readiness for reporting to assist in decision making. A visual reporting component was missing from this battery of tools for presentation of knowledge to assist with decision. At this stage of implementation, as such, this tier did not incorporate dashboard to provide visual summary of the operations key performance indicators (KPIs). This particular shortage is the subject of the additional development addressed in this chapter.

Additionally, there are some applications used in the African region Egypt HQ that the IT manager referred to as 'ko' which literally means 'knock-out', but what it actually meant is that it is site-specific, internally developed by the company, for the network of sites in the African business unit

A middleware tier was deployed by the company to achieve integration among these disparate enterprise applications through using several reporting and communications layer comprising:

- Mail: the mail system used by the company is 'lotus notes' platform. This platform provides a collaborative work environment as well as email service.
- Microsoft office: the end-user productivity tool for the client side hardware (PCs, laptops, PDAs, etc.)
- Share point portal service: used as the gateway/ portal through which authorized employees can gain access to the various service provided by the host of applications in site or globally.

The architecture of the technology service layers after the implementation of the ERP system in the datacenter accessed by Egypt subsidiary HQ is shown in Figure 1. Some of the modules were implemented in a "vanilla" standard mode while

Figure 1. Architecture of the IS layers used in the company before the new BI dashboard implementation

Figure 2. Sales reporting process before implementation of the IDB system

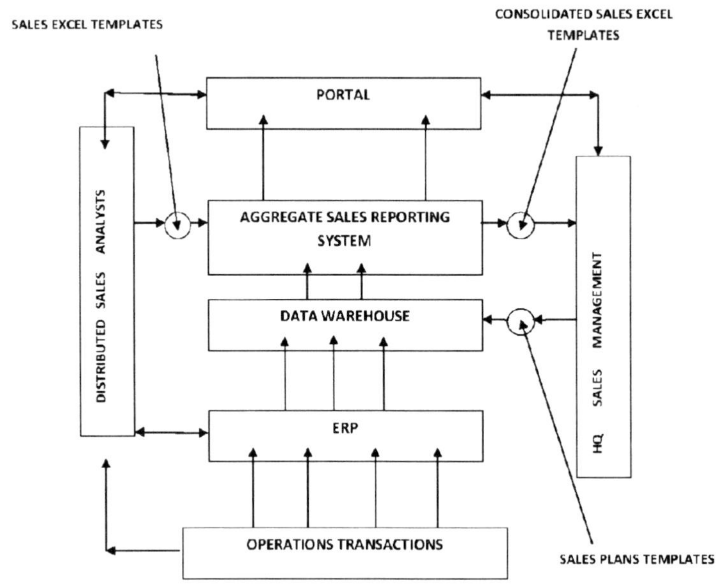

others were customized to adapt to the beverage industry-specific operations. The company gets, through a blanket contract, upgraded versions of the modules on a periodic basis (for the standard application modules only).

The network and communications infrastructure provided connectivity to the corporate datacenter for all sites in the African BU. Business transactions are entered on real-time basis into the respective ERP module. Each site must thus secure the health status of its internet/private connectivity and monitor its operational effectiveness and availability of its links.

The Sales Reporting System Prior Implementing the New Dashboard Facility

For each regional site, the specific reporting and operational needs (which included manufacturing supply chain, sales force management, marketing, inbound and outbound logistics), are accessible remotely from the regional datacenter of the company in Africa. Several functionalities were considered for the management of the African BU in Egypt's HQ site, which is concerned, among other business functions, with the consolidated sales within its domain. The process with which this objective was initially achieved is described in Figure 2. In this process, sales data exchanged between the franchises/bottlers and the HQ constituted:

- Actual sales figures**:** These are the actual sales volume reported by the bottlers. Actual sales were communicated on a daily basis through e-mails, via Excel templates, sent to every franchise analyst.
- Rolling estimates (RE) figures which reflect the adjusted sales on a monthly basis to adjust targets during the course of a year, thus reflecting changes in the market and used to predict sales volume for the balance of year. These figures are confirmed after communication between the franchise managers, the business planning manager and the HQ office. Once confirmed, the business planning manager sends the final confirmed version of the file which contains the actual sales so far and the balance

of year figures on a monthly basis for all sites in the domain countries

- Business Plan (BP) figures are set by the BU management at the beginning of the year. They do not change during the course of the year. The BP dictates target sales per brand per pack per month.

Sales Excel sheets Templates which are formatted by the sales analyst of each franchise/bottler liberally, are used by the company for sales reporting. These templates constitute the following reports:

1. **Daily Reports:** Bottlers of each country send daily sales reports that include the daily actual sales volume in both physical and unit case volumes to the franchise sales analyst. If they send it in physical cases, the franchise analyst converts it into unit cases using the unit case conversion factors. The reports include sales by brand and pack for every day of the week. The drawback of this reporting scheme is that there is no fixed template format for the daily reports sent by bottlers, who communicate the daily sales volume to the HQ.
2. **Weekly Reports:** The franchise Sales Analyst prepares and sends weekly reports after consolidating the daily sales sent by the bottlers to get total weekly figures. The reports also display the rolling estimates split weekly in addition to the weekly budget split and prior year weekly split. The Business Planning managers use the data communicated through those reports and consolidates data of all franchises to send consolidated weekly reports to HQ.
3. **Monthly Reports:** Every franchise analyst is requested to submit monthly reports as per deadlines dictated by a quarterly reporting calendar communicated by sales analyst. Those monthly reports include the following:
    - Best estimate for current month, draft of upcoming month RE and upcoming month weekly split. This data is usually communicated before the current month is closed.
    - RE volume by brand and pack. This report is submitted after the month is closed, it communicates the 'Actuals' of the closed month in addition to the RE figures of the balance of the year data. All 'Actuals' and RE figures are provided with a brand/pack split.

The HQ Sales Analyst then consolidates monthly brand/pack data sent from all franchisees to prepare brand/pack monthly RE updates.

As noted from this process, there are many countries involved in the reporting cycle of the sales results and many reports are communicated back and forth, using email and non-standardized Excel sheet templates between the country sales analysts and their corresponding managers in the HQ site. Many errors and inefficiencies continuously existed due to the use of those sales templates. The oft problems encountered included the following:

- Data inconsistencies due to inconsistency in product coding and Excel template variations led to lateness in reporting;
- Miscommunication due to network problems, variable semantics and other inconsistencies resulted in many duplicate data items (same data repeated in several reports);
- Consolidating non-uniform templates data and variable-semantics led to waste of time and efforts;
- Lack of analysis due to meager analytical competence of sales analysts;
- Lack of standardization led to too many data but no information;
- Redundant processes resulted in data chaos (too many templates causing confusion).

To that end, the focus of this case write up is to determine how the company utilized a new business intelligence dashboard tool, to provide the Sales and Marketing units with the necessary agile and fast decision making platform and to respond to the dynamic market and consumer changes over a wide geographic area; at the same time overcome the critical impediments illustrated in the process described earlier and schematically diagramed in Figure 2.

Literature Review

During the past two decades, many organizations adopted the ERP as their preferred backbone information system for data and information management, since then world ERP market poised to command a little under $65 billion by the end of 2009, according to AMR Research Market Analytix Report (2005). The use of ERP systems by those organizations targeting cost reduction, increase productivity, improve customer satisfaction and suppliers relations in the drive to improve competitiveness in the global networked market space (Davenport, 1998). The cost expended for the acquisition and implementation of ERPs exceed millions of dollars and affect the overall firms' earnings and revenues (Davenport, 1998) and their market values, (Chatterjee et al. 2002). With such huge capital investments, many firms are forced to assess carefully their return of investment (ROI) of such an infrastructure.

The impact of adopting ERP normally goes beyond the immediate control of the business resources, it sets the grounds for organizational changes and the way business processes are performed, (Kallinikos, 2004). As noted by Brazel and Dang (2008), the implementation and use of ERP systems represent a radical change from the operation of legacy systems. Many researchers have therefore studied ERP use and adoption from various perspectives. As a category of information system, several authors approached research on ERP from the perspective of information systems success model (DeLone and McLean, 1992, 2003; Gable, et al. 2001 and 2003; Seddon, 1997; Sedera, et al. 2004; Ifinedo, et al. 2006a and 2007; Robey, et al, 1999).

ERP implementation is a challenging endeavor for many organizations, spanning many functional areas (Yen, et al. 2002), demanding high level of coordination among all stakeholders and adjusting to changes and synergy in the procedural workflow by every business function. Use of such systems implies changes in the workflow of business processes (Kallinikos, 2004). To that end, success of the implementation projects and the critical factors influencing this success was studied by many researchers to investigate ERP implementation success factors, (Bancroft et al, 1996; O'Leary, 2002; Ptak, et al, 2000). Other studies aimed at identifying the critical factors impacting implementing ERP projects (Fryling, 2005). Factors such as those influencing successful implementation, from the operational (rather than technical) point of view were addressed by many researchers, for example, the business operations coverage of the package and the number of licensed users (Francalanci, 2001; Kumar, et al. 2001; Markus, et al. 1988; Parr and Schanks, 2000).

The impact of system configuration and/or setup revisions and enhancements was also studied by Fryling (2005), Nicolaou, et al. (2004 and 2007), Light (2001), Mensching, et al. (2004) and Nah, et al. (2001); impacts of organizational and national cultures (Krumbholtz et al. 2000; Soh, et al. 2000); the configuration and setup of the package's parameters tables and their overall impact on the architecture and flexibility of the ERP packages for rapid adaptation (Fan et al. 2000; Spott, 2000). Some articles also addressed the impact of ERP process standardization and the restructuring of organization tasks or business processes reengineering (Kumar and Van Hillgersberg, 2000). The ability of the system to provide quality and trusted information for operational and executive management decision making has been identified by many researchers (Xu, 2003; Madapusi, et al. 2007).

ERP integrates all functional areas of the organization, acting as the backbone of the information management platform of the organization (Chou, 2005). With its integrated database, ERP systems integrate other functional business components such as Customer Relationship Management (CRM) and SCM systems data resources to support informational needs for decision making. Since ERP system is internally looking, the need to accommodate access to data across the organization boundary is required for decision making at the strategic and organization-wide levels. It is not that ERP systems don't have wealth of information, they do; the challenges lie in the ways of mining them. ERP cannot facilitate real-time decision support function for several operational reasons. Since information is the foundation of every critical business decisions, Decision Support Systems (DSS) are vital for any organization (Drucker, 1998). Report writers can access data from multiple ERP modules and consolidate them with other data elements for decision support. Business Intelligence (BI) is about getting the right information, to the right decision makers, at the right time (Alter, 1980). It is an enterprise-wide platform that supports multi-dimensionality reporting, analytics and decision modeling leading to fact-based decision making and enabling to get a "single version of the truth" (Rasmussen et al., 2001). The common pain points that BI is used to solve are typical examples of what most organizations experience:

- Data everywhere, information no where
- Different users have different needs
- Excel versus PDF
- Pull versus push
- On demand – on schedule
- Your format – my format
- Takes too long – wasted resources/efforts
- Security
- Technical "mumbo jumbo" … Why I just can't get it to you when you want it.

By integrating business intelligence (BI) tools and ERP modules, data flows directly from the ERP database on real-time basis. However, some reliability, availability and scale efficiency may arise as a consequence – particularly due to the excessive access load that may hinder transactional operations. Separating the active ERP database from that of the BI resulted in embracing a second data storage tier, a data warehouse (McDonald et al., 2002). The ERP-BI, On-line Analytics Processing (OLAP) and DSS tools integration framework is based on congregating all needed data from the ERP system and other external data resources, load them into a Data Warehouse or a data Mart, then link to several BI tools, such as OLAP, data mining, analytics tool and reporting systems to create more consistent and knowledge-centric data reporting. BI tools provide such functionalities. More and more organizations extend their ERP beyond the level of back-office to improve sales, customer satisfaction, and decision making (Stedman, 2002).

Integration of the BI and ERP system contributes additional values to businesses (Chou, 2005). According to Holsapple and Whinston (1996), characterization of common DSS features, BI generates different views for available data systems, a scaled data mart or data warehouse providing rich, timely and well structured and cleansed information to the BI. Bolt-on BI systems are also used to view financial, marketing and sales queries by using different tools (CRM2day.com, 2004). Customer Experience Management (CEM) in retailing has also been researched within the framework of BI by score of researchers such as Ding, et al. (2006) and Kamaladevi, B. (2010). Issues of integration of SCM with customer experience management were dealt with by Chou (2005). Approaches to building and implementing BI systems were investigated by Celena Olszak, et al. (2007) being an important decision to many implementing organizations.

CASE DESCRIPTION

Technology Concerns and Needs

Within the context of the studied case, a new Sales Reporting process was developed to address the inefficiencies and pitfalls of the template based sales reporting system described earlier. Egypt's HQ IT department together with the Sales unit, embarked on the development of a new BI tool which was code-named the IDB (information dashboard). The new IDB tool was designed to provide enhanced method for uploading sales data, address the inconsistencies of the country sales figures and the cumbersome method of obtaining the consolidated reports at the HQ. Analysts were trained to upload data on the new IDB platform using a newly developed product coding system. They get the codes from commonly accessible codes database. The coding system is based on a code consisting of 10 digits. The first four digits represent the brand type and flavor. The last four digits represent the package size and type. The two digits in the middle represent the type of syrup whether liquid for normal packages or powder supplied to machines. This level of breakdown for any product provided an easy and efficient facility for tracking Stock Keeping Unit level since it embedded all the necessary information regarding the product whether in terms of brand type, flavor, package size, type, format……etc.

The implementation of the IDB tool availed single unified interface for users to upload the sales data from the respective country to provide aggregate reporting of sales for the HQ in Egypt. The tool allowed drill-down granularity for users. We will first analyze the structure of this implemented information dashboard tool (IDB) and then describe the new sales reporting process. The IDB acted as the single "database" view for all trade related information used by all franchisees and is used through applying several data mining techniques. It is a customized web based application built to access the warehouse database and allowed access from anywhere through the company's network. Furthermore, the IDB is used as the reporting vehicle to management - globally, retiring the use of once prevalent sales templates and the use of the email for posting these templates. Access to the IDB is achieved via web browser using specific URL or via the Company Portal (based on MS Share Point platform). Users log in through their IDs and passwords. After updating the system with the daily, weekly or quarterly sales, figures, respective users can log in and retrieve any report needed at any granularity level for any specific period.

The sales reporting process constituted several activities. Every franchisee analyst is to prepare the weekly sales data using the relevant codes and upload the data on the IDB. The upload is performed automatically through an Autoloader and scheduled on Mondays every week. The system decodes the uploaded codes and maintains the actual data on the system. Business plan figures and rolling estimates figures are also uploaded in the same format and manner. Whenever any discrepancy in the uploaded data on the IDB of a single country affect the accuracy of the data of the total business unit, control measures are promptly carried out to assure the integrity and accuracy of data on the system. After all franchisees upload their weekly figures on the IDB, the HQ Sales Analyst verifies the data on the system and adjusts/deletes any discrepancies found by detecting the countries responsible for the discrepancies and suggests methods for resolving these conflicts with the concerned analyst. The Sales Analyst can also report any variance detected on the IDB due to any error in the application engine through Business Applications Call Logging system, used by the IT department as the support tool for any encountered technical problems while using the IDB.

The HQ sales analyst is also responsible for planning and coordinating all IDB activities with all franchisee analysts in terms of training analysts, installing new IDB applications and communicating with IT to resolve encountered problems. The HQ sales analyst is also responsible for issuing new codes for newly launched packs that are not on the system by filling a request form. The HQ Analyst also monitors the status of expired codes and de-activates them.

Developing the IDB Dashboard Layer

The described new sales business process is depicted in Figure 3. Upon upload of the sales data on IDB, users can simply log into the system from anywhere and access the reports menu via the portal or the specially provided URL and pick the type of report required using drop down lists. These lists include all product parameters. The IDB system enabled users to get any type of information by selecting the specific criteria needed in the downloaded report with any degree of granularity. In other words, users can customize the reports retrieved from the system by choosing the appropriate parameters from the displayed scroll down lists. Drill down lists may include, but not limited to, parameters such as:

- Country
- Bottler
- Period (Year/Month/Week)
- Brand
- Flavor
- Package type
- Pack size
- Historical data
- Business plan data
- Rolling Estimate (RE) data
- Analysis of sales performance versus prior years, BP, RE.....etc.

Access to the facilities offered in the IDB system is granted though a robust and premeditated authorization scheme. IT unit provides authorized users with their respective personal user name and

Figure 3. Sales reporting process after implementation of the IDB system

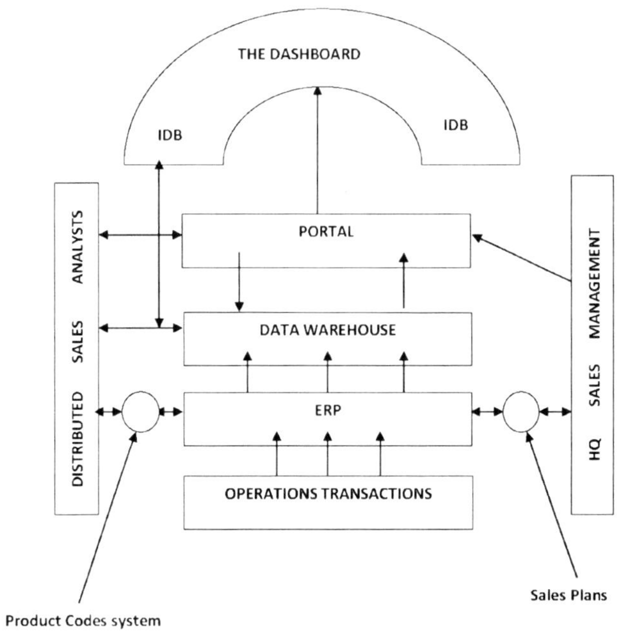

password for authentication, however accessing and retrieving information at various data-granularity levels are subject to authorization policies. This authorization scheme is set by the respective country management, and communicated to the IT department, to provide various access privileges for the various organizational hierarchical levels.

The Impact of the IDB System on the Effectiveness of the Sales Reporting Process

The use of the IDB facility as a component of the battery of BI tools of the Company's IS platform enhanced the Sales reporting cycle in many ways and had increased the overall efficiency of the Sales Reporting Process. The major areas of improvement IDB offered are:

- First of all, it has eliminated the redundant process of sending the former sales reports templates that were subject to various interpretations, wasting time and effort and causing inconsistencies and mistrust of data.
- Using IDB as an outer shell of the data warehouse provided a very useful tool as it integrates all types of information required whether historical data, brand information, package information, business plan figures…etc. Before using IDB, managers and analysts had to go through many Excel files and sheets to obtain information which is time consuming and some of the required data were lost or hidden. Besides, the same information was sometimes obtained with different values from different sources causing confusion.
- Provided multi-dimensionality reporting using "slice and dice" operations by the analysts.
- IDB acted as a timely and trustworthy reporting tool with a single source of sales data which is not subject to various interpretations. All analysts are bound by specific deadlines to upload their data, so the managers are confident to find the data on time and to retrieve it in a standard format to facilitate the data integration and the decision making process.
- IDB provided analysis facility. Reports retrieved facilitated comparisons and analytical measures that can be used to help managers in the decision making process.
- IDB helped in determining profitable trading partners through the use of multi-dimensionality data mining
- Augmented and replaced cumbersome previous spreadsheet-based system.
- Enabled driver-based planning to streamline and focus efforts around HR plans, manufacturing requirements, or sales resources.
- Enabled use of rolling forecasts to increase forward visibility.
- Reduced the need for consolidation, close and reporting cycles by days or weeks..
- Facilitated conducting what-if scenarios for different revenue projections or changes in business lines.
- Facilitated tracking key corporate performance indicators from desktop.

Beside these impacts on the performance of the Sales function, it enabled giving brand, marketing, and sales managers the knowledge they need to strongly impact the top line through the use of brand, sales, promotion/marketing and delivering a full range of sales management analyses. With the IDB tool, near-real time measures by account, channel/channel segment, promotion, and campaign - can be used to improve the effectiveness of other business cycles such as the full range of brand, portfolio, and product analyses along with the ability to ask random, ad hoc questions and alert when actual performance varies substantially from plan.

In a nutshell, the IDB tool enabled getting the right information, to the right decision makers, at the right time. It is an enterprise-wide platform that supported multi-dimensionality reporting, analytics and decision modeling leading to fact-based decision making and getting a "single version of the truth."

The integration of the marketing data warehouse with the IDB tool also resulted in many benefits such as:

1. Financial process management of annual marketing budgets. Through the marketing Business Warehouse the brand managers gained autonomy in managing this process themselves through accessing this option on the IDB, where they would directly input their budgets online and the embedded workflow would proceed to request granting the necessary approvals. Budget managers were also able to perform internal budget shifts if need be as well as raising new purchase orders where previously it was done manually.
2. Ensuring internal system adherence to corporate financial and procurement procedures, there was no need for manual issuance any more as the ERP system provided the necessary constraints through budget coding, online approval requirements through a hierarchy workflow.
3. Monitoring marketing spend per brand and ensuring correct allocation across the marketing mix. The IDB reports were very malleable in their structure - can be driven by specific periods, campaign types, seasonality, segmentation by below the line marketing activities, or above the line, even by media type which allowed brand managers and marketing managers a better ability to assess the direct impact of a campaign spend over sales in a particular moment in time.
4. Providing budget reporting across franchise functions. Again, this has been a dissolved manual role as the new system allowed for automatic retrieval as explained in the point above.
5. Reporting on brand contribution and profitability per brand, pack, flavor and concentrate. The integration with the company-wide planning system allowed further report segmentation by account, for example, how each cost contributed to the overall profitability of a brand by integrating other operating expenses (OPEX), capital expenses (CAPEX) reports- this type of reports are high level top-line data that were accessed by top managerial staff and also depended on the level of data-breakdown details that were fed in by accountants.

The final Information Systems infrastructure architecture of the company after the IDB implementation is depicted in Figure 4.

CURRENT CHALLENGES FACING THE CASE FIRM

The ERP system has been put in place in the company for many years. Employees did not have an option, they had to use it. Though the company managed to streamline and align some of its business processes and operations to the "best practice" processes embedded in the ERP, with minimum changes, to adapt to the specific nature of the beverage industry, customized bolt-in additional tools were inevitably used to cater for those specific characteristics. This was quite evident in the sales and marketing functions. As a result of the deployment of the new IDB system, several problems showed up.

The following obstacles and challenges were observed after installing the IDB

- User reluctance to abandon the use of old Excel templates increased resistance of

Figure 4. Architecture of the IS layers used in the company after IDB implementation

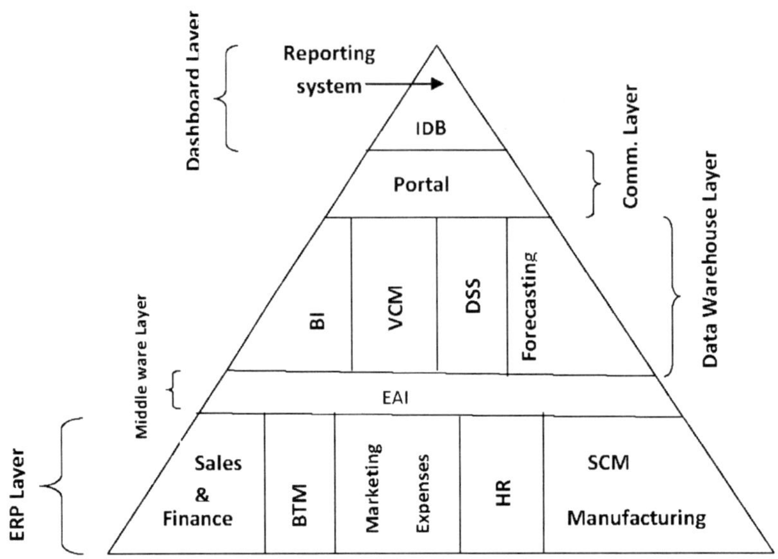

the use of the new developed data entry facility.

- Training analysts to use IDB was a challenging feat. The dispersed remote locations of analysts made it difficult and costly to provide them with the necessary skills for optimum use of the new tool. Though conference calls and video-conferencing were used to tackle this obstacle, the level of operational excellence in using the tool was less than satisfactory as postulated by the management. Incompetency of use of the facilities of the system was also observed due to the lack of analytical proficiency.
- Unrealistic expectations were anticipated in a relatively short period.
- Lack of in-house technical expertise (The IDB support team is remotely located).
- Real-Time data reporting was accessible once accounting inputs are uploaded into the system in due course. Errors in data entry may thus lead to wrong information and decisions. As one employee contends:

"The initial step when we switched from the legacy system to the new setup involved data migration. This was a very tedious task and involved many months of intricate detailed work where existing data had to be assigned codes similar to the coding on the ERP to allow smooth transition. The challenge was to transition with almost zero error and entailed at certain moment of time to halt transactions entry to ensure all real-time data is captured. There was a mechanism to double check on validity of data after transition."

- Employees were not receptive to adapt to change and resisted system implementation by initially rejecting the idea for months. Advanced training technology-based methods were adopted to allow for virtual help where global ERP Power Users were able to access local employees' screens to guide them through a step by step process. Adaptability took about one whole year as the users gained more confidence in system maneuver.

- Although the idea of the ERP is to eliminate a lot of paper work, the case was not so in Egypt in some areas as the embedded ERP workflow involved external as well as internal stakeholder's input in the system. For example, marketing assistants raising new purchase orders through the transaction modules were required to attach three different quotations from three different suppliers. The idea is that suppliers were to send those quotations through an interface mechanism that allowed automatic attach to the purchase order. Given that the business climate in Egypt is still underdeveloped in terms of technology maturity, many continued to send their quotations manually by courier messenger, or fax, rarely few at the time were used to the idea of sending through email. This created a bottle neck since the marketing assistant had to then scan those documents and upload them manually to process the purchase order – where a purchase order raising should have taken about an hour for completion ended up consuming a whole day while it has still not been sent to the brand manager for approval. In some situations this produced further time bottlenecks as some suppliers required down payments prior to activation of the required job on the system.
- Brand managers viewed their newly added task of managing the input-output process of budgets themselves and purchase order requisitions as a waste of time as they previously did not do so. They viewed it as a purely transactional administrative task that should be performed by the accounting department or rather assigned to a department secretary for coordination. In the beginning, they did try to perform the processing themselves, but later, decided that this administrative tasks have impeded their focus on managing the brand with consumers from a marketing perspective.
- An operational issue of ERP is currency variations. Although the system allowed for multiple currency input, the final marketing budget to be approved by division heads and headquarters had to be submitted and received in dollars. This created some issues where brand managers initially prepared their budget in Egyptian pounds per the various local quotations and pricing they received. This total amount however did not sometimes equate for the same amount assigned by global HQ on the ERP which was in dollars. The challenge for the finance was to constantly adjust rates according to fluctuations in exchange rates and other market factors such as inflation and so forth which also resulted in some chunks of the budget in Egyptian pounds being eaten away due to these adjustments. It continues to be an ordeal as concentrate pricing is also in US dollars while other transactions are in multiple currencies.
- The deployment of technology into everyday business is still not very mature within people's mindset in Egypt. For example, the lack of trust still persisted in the Egyptian ideology, where the deployment of online signatures through ERP protocol was still viewed with a suspicious eye. Middle managers especially in the accounting unit still requested a pen-written on paper signature-it made them feel secure. However this required that paper formats of ERP documents were printed and managers were requested put their pen signatures. This did not help in achieving a more lean and streamlined operation which the system was supposed to create.
- End-User Support and Maintenance

A few years ago, for an employee to report an IT problem they had to call the local help desk and technical staff will attend to the call to solve the problem for him or her. However, the company HQ has developed a new process that employees experiencing problems will have to make a call to call center, give their employee ID and describe the technical problem about the software or the hardware. The call center, remotely accessed, will give the employee a ticket number with the problem code and send them an email summarizing the problem. The problem could be simple enough to be solved over the phone (i.e., the center tells the employee on the phone what he or she could do to solve the problem). If it's not then the center directs the problem to the local help desk to solve it. Then the center sends the employee an email asking if the problem has been solved or not to close the ticket. Some employees found this process difficult and time consuming

Future Measures to Enhance the Reporting Cycle and Recommendations

The preceding analysis revealed that key success measures that may help the company to overcome the obstacles cited and leads to turning the IDB system into a success story include the following:

- Executive management involvement and support
- Clear project ownership by including sales analysts in the project management team
- Proper planning
- Hard working and focus by all member countries' analysts
- Clear communication between business and IT by setting meetings, discussing problems and analyzing issues and providing continuous feedback
- Clear role definition for both analysts and IT professionals
- Instituting efficient and effective change management process
- Proper and continuous staff and analysts training

To that end, the company is planning to install new version of the IDB system in the upcoming years. The new system will allow users to create their own queries with specific design and more advanced sales breakdown. Also, the company is planning to use more advanced analytical tools such as the "Instant Visual Analysis" tool which is a simple versatile tool that will make volume analysis and graphic representation faster, easier and more flexible. The Instant Visual Analysis tool uses pivot table reports to help analyze and graph numerical data, answering questions, exhibiting trends, etc. With a few mouse clicks users can see who sold the most where, which brands were the most successful, and which pack sold best.

REFERENCES

Alter, S. (1980). *Decision support systems: Current practice and continuing challenge*. Reading: MA Addison Wiley.

Bancroft, N. (1996). *Implementing SAP R/3*. Greenwich, CT: Manning Publication Co.

Bingham, D. (1999). *Food and beverage companies need to integrate information enterprise-wide*. Beverage Online.

Brazel, J. F., & Dang, L. (2008). The effect of ERP system implementations on the management of earnings and earnings release dates. *Journal of Information Systems*, *22*(2), 1–21. doi:10.2308/jis.2008.22.2.1

Chatterjee, D., Grewal, R., & Sambamurthy, V. (2002). Shaping up for e-commerce: Institution enablers of the organizational assimilation of Web technologies. *Management Information Systems Quarterly*, *26*(2), 65. doi:10.2307/4132321

Chou, D., Tripuramully, H., & Chou, A. (2005). BI and ERP integration. *Information Management & Computer Security*, *13*(5), 340–349. doi:10.1108/09685220510627241

CRM2day. (2004). *Business intelligence*. Retrieved from www.crm2day.com/bi

Data monitor. (2001). *Business intelligence from data to profit*. Retrieved from www.researchandmarkets.com

Davenport, T. (1998). Putting the enterprise into the enterprise system. *Harvard Business Review*, *76*(4), 121–131.

DeLone, W., & McLean, E. (1992). Information systems success: The quest for the dependable variable. *Information Systems Research*, *3*(1), 60–95. doi:10.1287/isre.3.1.60

DeLone, W., & McLean, E. (2003). The DeLone and McLean Model of Information Systems success: A ten-year update. *Journal of Management Information Systems*, *19*(4), 9–30.

Ding, D., & Chen, J. (2007). Supply chain coordination with contracts game between complementary suppliers. *International Journal of Information Technology & Decision Making*, *6*(1), 163–175. doi:10.1142/S0219622007002332

Drucker, P. (1998). The next information revolution. *Forbes*. Retrieved from www.forbes.com

Fan, M., Stallaert, J., & Whinston, A. (2000). The adoption and design methodologies of component-based enterprise systems. *European Journal of Information Systems*, *9*, 25–35. doi:10.1057/palgrave.ejis.3000343

Francalanci, C. (2001). Predicting the implementation effort of ERP projects: Empirical evidences on SAP R/3. *Journal of Information Technology*, *16*(1), 33–48. doi:10.1080/02683960010035943

Fryling, M. (2005). ERP implementation dynamics. *Information Science and Policy*. University at Albany. State University of New York, Oct. 2005.

Gable, G., Sedera, D., & Chan, T. (2003). Enterprise systems success: A measurement model. *Proceedings of the 24th ICIS*, (pp. 576-591). Seattle, Washington.

Gable, G., van Den Heever, R., Erlank, S., & Scott, J. (2001). Large packaged application software maintenance: A research framework. *Journal of Software Maintenance and Evolution: Research and Practice*, *13*(6), 351–371. doi:10.1002/smr.237

Holsapple, C., & Whinston, A. B. (1996). *Decision support systems: A knowledge based approach*. Minneapolis, MN: West Publishing.

Ifinedo, P. (2006a). Extending the Gable et al. enterprise systems success measurement model: A preliminary study. *Journal of Information Technology Management,17*(1), 14-33.

Ifinedo, P., & Nahar, N. (2007). ERP system success: An empirical analysis of how two organizational stakeholder groups prioritize and evaluate relevant measures. *Enterprise Information Systems*, *1*, 25–48. doi:10.1080/17517570601088539

Kallinikos, J. (2004). Deconstructing information packages: Organizational and behavioral implications of ERP systems. *Information Technology & People*, *17*, 8–30. doi:10.1108/09593840410522152

Kamaladevi, B. (2010). Customer experience management in retailing. *Business Intelligence Journal*, *3*(1), 37–54.

Krumbholz, M. (2000). Implementing enterprise resource planning packages in different corporate and national cultures. *Journal of Information Technology*, *15*(4), 267–280. doi:10.1080/02683960010008962

Kumar, K., & Van Hillegersberg, J. (2000). ERP: Experience and evolution. *Communications of the ACM*, *43*, 23–26.

Kumar, V., Maheshwari, B., & Kumar, U. (2001). An investigation of critical management issues in ERP implementation: Empirical evidences from Canadian organizations. *Technovation*, *23*(10).

Light, B. (2001). The maintenance implications of the customization of ERP software. *Journal of Software Maintenance and Evolution: Research and Practice*, *13*(6), 415–429. doi:10.1002/smr.240

Madapusi, A., & Kuo, C. (2007). Assessing data and information quality in ERP systems. *Proceedings of the Decision Sciences Institute Annual Meeting*, Arizona.

Madapusi, A., Kuo, C., & White, R. (2007). A critical factors approach to ERP information quality and decision quality. *Proceedings of the Decision Sciences Institute Annual Meeting,* Arizona.

Markus, M., & Robey, D. (1988). Information Technology and organizational change: Causal structure in theory and research. *Management Science*, *34*, 583–598. doi:10.1287/mnsc.34.5.583

McDonald, k., et al. (2002). *Mastering SAP business information warehouse*. Canada: Wiley Publishing.

Mensching, J., & Corbitt, G. (2004). EPR data archiving- a critical analysis. *Journal of Enterprise Information Management*, *17*(2), 131–141. doi:10.1108/17410390410518772

Nah, F. H., Faja, S., & Cata, T. (2001). Characteristics of ERP software maintenance: A multicause study. *Journal of Software Maintenance and Evolution: Research and Practice*, *13*(6), 339–414. doi:10.1002/smr.239

Nicolaou, A. (2004). *ERP system implementation drivers of post-implementation success*. Decision Support in an Uncertain and Complex World: The IFIP TC8/WG8.3 International Conference, 2004, (pp. 589-597).

Nicolaou, A., & Bhattacharya, S. (2007). Organizational performance effects of ERP systems usage: The impact of post-implementation changes. *International Journal of Accounting Information Systems*, *7*(1), 18–35. doi:10.1016/j.accinf.2005.12.002

O'Leary, D. (2002). *Enterprise resource planning systems: System lifecycle, electronic commerce, and risk*. Cambridge, UK: Cambridge University Press.

Olszak, C., & Ziemba, E. (2007). Approach to building and implementing business intelligence system. *Interdisciplinary Journal of Information, Knowledge, and Management*, *2*, 135–148.

Olszak, C., & Ziemba, E., (2006). Business intelligence systems in the holistic infrastructure development - supporting decision-making in organizations. *Interdisciplinary Journal of Information, Knowledge, and Management, 1*.

Parr, A., & Schanks, G. (2000). A model of ERP project implementation. *Journal of Information Technology*, *15*(4), 289–304. doi:10.1080/02683960010009051

Ptak, C., & Schragenheim, E. (2000). *ERP: Tools, techniques and applications for integrating the supply chain*. London, UK: Series on Resources Management, St Lucie Press/APICS.

Rasmussen, N., Goldy, P., & Solli, P. (2002). *Financial business intelligence: Trends, technology, software selection and implementation*. New York, NY: Wiley.

AMR Research (currently part of Gartner inc.). (2005). *Market Analytix Report: ERP 2004-2009*.

Robey, D., & Boudreau, M. (1999). Accounting for the contradictory organizational consequences of information technology. *Information Systems Research*, *10*, 167–185. doi:10.1287/isre.10.2.167

Seddon, P. B. (1997). A re-specification and extension of the DeLone and McLean model of IS success. *Information Systems Research, 18*(3), 240–253. doi:10.1287/isre.8.3.240

Sedera, D., Gable, G., & Chan, T. (2004). Measuring enterprise systems success: The importance of a multiple stakeholder perspective. *Proceedings of the 12th European Conference on Information Systems*, (pp. 1-13). Turku, Finland.

Soh, C., & Tay-Yap, J. (2000). Cultural fits and misfits: Is ERP a universal solution? *Communications of the ACM, 43*(4), 47–51. doi:10.1145/332051.332070

Spott, D. (2000). Componentizing the enterprise applications packages. *Communications of the ACM, 43*(4), 63–90. doi:10.1145/332051.332074

Stedman, C. (1999, November 1). Failed ERP gamble haunts Hershey. *Computerworld.* Retrieved April 16, 2006, from www.computerworld.com

Stedman, C. (2002). Maximizing the ERP investment. *Competitive Financial Operations: The CFO Project, 1*, 1–6.

Xu, H., Nord, J., Brown, N., & Nord, D. (2002). Data quality issues in implementing an ERP. *Industrial Management & Data Systems, 102*(1), 47–58. doi:10.1108/02635570210414668

Yen, D. C., Chou, D. C., & Chang, J. (2002). A synergic analysis for Web-based enterprise resource planning system. *Computer Standards & Interfaces, 24*(4), 337–346. doi:10.1016/S0920-5489(01)00105-2

KEY TERMS AND DEFINITIONS

Business Intelligence (BI): Refers to computer-based techniques used in analyzing business data, such as sales by products and/or departments or associated costs and incomes. In addition, BI technologies avail historical, current, and predictive views of business operations. Common functions of Business Intelligence technologies are reporting, online analytical processing, analytics, data mining, business performance management, benchmarking, text mining, and predictive analytics.

Dashboard: Is the application of visual iconic tools that indicate the status of a particular measurable quantity, event or value. Within the context of business performance measurement, the use of the dashboard may aide decision makers in quickly spotting the status of some KPIs of interest to them.

Data Mining: Is the process of extracting patterns from data. Data mining is becoming an increasingly important tool to transform the data into information. It is commonly used in a wide range of profiling practices, such as marketing, surveillance, fraud detection and scientific discovery. Data mining is often used to uncover patterns in data pertaining to functional or departmental data sets.

Data Warehouse: Is a repository (collection of resources that can be accessed to retrieve information) of an organization's electronically stored data, designed to facilitate reporting and analysis. Data warehousing arises when an organization need reliable, consolidated, unique and integrated analysis and reporting of its data resources, at different levels of aggregation.

Decision Support Systems (DSS): Constitute a class of computer-based information systems including knowledge-based systems that support decision-making activities. DSSs serve the management, operations, and planning levels of an organization and help to make decisions, which may be rapidly changing and not easily specified in advance.

Enterprise Resources Planning (ERP): Is an integrated computer-based software system used to manage organizational internal and external resources. It is an architecture which facilitates the flow of information between all business functions within the boundaries of the organization and manages the interfaces with outside stakeholders.

Key Performance Indicators (KPI): Measures commonly used to help organizations define and evaluate how successful their businesses are, typically in terms of making progress towards long-term organizational goals. KPIs can be specified by answering the question, "What is really important to different organizational stakeholders?"

Chapter 12
Ghabbour Group ERP Deployment:
Learning From Past Technology Failures

M. S. Akabawi
American University in Cairo (AUC), Egypt

EXECUTIVE SUMMARY

Ghabbour group "GB Auto," an Egyptian auto trading and manufacturing establishment, has gone through two ERP successive implementations within the past 12 years. The newer implementation has experienced several impediments. The executives and the Board of Directors at the group have thoroughly and aggressively examined the status of the IS services provided by this ERP system and assessed their impact on the quality of decision making at all levels of management. The driver for this was to secure all the necessary platforms and management tools for enabling growth and improving efficiency and effectiveness of the company's business operation and resources. The extent of lack of control and effective utilization of the use of resources in the group has been cited by the top management in many interviews. Following its public offering and registration in the CASE and CMA, GB Auto was legally demanded to provide annual and quarterly audit reports of its varied LOBs' performance. The existing information management infrastructure was not providing such agile services. The trajectory of implementations of integrated Enterprise Information Systems at the group was reviewed in this case study and was duly investigated to assess the effectiveness and appropriateness in servicing those purposes and increasing the company's competitive advantage.

DOI: 10.4018/978-1-60960-583-4.ch012

ORGANIZATION BACKGROUND

Ghabbour Group (GB) name has become closely linked to the automotive industry in the Egyptian market – from distribution and manufacturing to after sale services – spanning the full spectrum of the transportation arena. This led the group to adopt the motto "GB Auto - everything on wheels." By the 1990's, privately owned GB group became widely associated with Hyundai passenger cars as a distributor and car assembly manufacturing.

The group's role and history in the Egyptian economic field dates back to the 1940's. During this era, the two brothers, Kamal and Sadek Ghabbour established their private auto trading company. The firm was officially incorporated in 1956 as "Ghabbour Brothers." The business area of the firm included trading in automotive products, construction materials, home appliances and electronics.

During the 1960's, the Ghabbours' legacy was firmly maintained despite the economic constraints and hardships in this period, when Egypt embraced the Socialist economic doctrine. By the early 1970's and as a result of the Egyptian government's initiative to adopt the economic open door policy, the group's vision to become serious establishment in the automotive industry not only as a trader, but as a manufacturer, took shape. To that effect, the company started focusing on acquiring licenses and agencies for passenger cars, buses, trucks and automotive parts.

The first manufacturing operation of the group started in 1985 by assembling bus bodies under technical agreement with Scania AB. During this era, Egypt's sole automotive manufacturer was the state-owned El Nasr company for automotive which failed to establish the robust infrastructure for sustainable automotive manufacturing base [removed phrase]. The initial industrial base of GB group started near Cairo-Alexandria Agricultural Road in Qalyubia governorate, which was quite a convenient site due its proximity to major markets and easy access.

With the transfer of management to the younger Ghabbour generations in the early 1990's, the GB group witnessed phenomenal growth and expansion. Horizontal expansion was manifested by the addition of new lines of business (LOB) and diversification of product mixes. While vertical expansion was manifested by increasing the manufacturing base capacities, trade partners and brand names licensing. Hyundai car manufacturer of Korea granted GB group the exclusive agency for the distribution of its passenger cars in Egypt since 1992.

In 1995, GB group was also granted by Hyundai the technical license to assemble passenger cars - Completely Knocked-Down (CKD) units in addition to trading in the Completely Built Units (CBU). Since then, GB group acquired additional agencies for Mazda passenger cars, two and three wheelers products of Bajaj of India; assembly licenses for Mitsubishi trucks and buses; and Volvo trucks and buses. In 2006, GB group entered the transportation services area, for both passengers and cargo, by establishing the new subsidiary - Haram Company.

In 2003, Chairman of the GB Group, Dr. Raouf Ghabbour, established the Raouf Ghabbour Investment Company (RGI) as the holding company of the group's subsidiaries operating in varied LOB portfolio. A list of these subsidiaries is shown in Table 1 together with the business activities pertaining to each subsidiary. In Table 2, we list the various corporate business organizational units in the group and the associated business activities each performs. Those corporate business units provide services across the entire functional activities of the group's subsidiaries.

Before year 2006, RGI (S.A.E) operated as the holding company for GB group's affiliated companies which were wholly owned by RGI. However, one of the groups' affiliated companies – GB Capital was subsequently named as the holding company for the group and RGI became in effect a wholly owned subsidiary. In April 2007, GB capital name was changed to GB Auto.

Table 1. GB holding company and subsidiaries

Ser.	Company Name	Business Activities	Number of Employee
1	RG Investment S.A.E (RGI)	Holding Company for Consolidated Subsidiaries (prior 2006)	101
2	International Trade Agencies Marketing Corp. S.A.E (ITAMCO)	Sales & Dist. Of CBU & CKD PC unites. Spare Parts Dist. Operation of PC after Sales Service Network.	1444
3	Interland Motors S.A.E.	Sales & Dist. Of Volvo heavy range trucks.	33
4	Egyptian Vehicles Manufacturing Company (Ghab-bour Misr) S.A.E	Assembly of mini-bus and large coaches, operation of Commercial Vehicles after sales service network and spare parts. Distribution of Volvo Construction equipment	1779
5	Haram Transport Company S.A.E.	Operation of passenger and Cargo Transportation Service	904
6	Cairo Individual Transport Industry CITI S.A.E	Operation of motorcycle and scooter (2 & 3 wheelers) LOB.	64
7	Prima Engineering Industries S.A.E. (PRIMA)	Assembly of Hyundai CKD PC and Mitsubishi light Commercial vehicles, Manufacturing Semi-Trucks	45
8	Vehicles Components Industries S.A.E (VCI)	Manufacturing Semi-Trucks and super-structure, as well as PC Components	45
9	Ghabbour Continental Trading Company free Zones (Alex) S.A.E	Distribution of PCs, mini-buses, spare parts and tires from Alex FZ	17
10	Engineering Company for Marketing and Trading S.A.E	Distribution of tires	33
11	GB Buses, S.A.E (GE)	Manufacturing of bus and Coach bodies	134
12	GB Auto	Holding Company after 2006	1

Source: http://www.ghabbourauto.com

Table 2. Corporate cross-functional business unites in the group

Unit	Activities
Finance & Accounting	Manages & administer all the group's subsidiaries and the holding company's accounting and finance
Supply Chain	Control all the group warehouses, purchasing and logistics
Internal Auditing	Performs the audit function for all the group's activities in all subsidiaries
Legal Affaires	Administers all legal affairs for the group
Information Technology	Provides and Manages IT/IS Services to the groups' companies
Administrative Services & HR	Human Resources administration for the group

In July 2007, GB Auto made its Initial Public Offering (IPO) and applied to the Cairo and Alexandria Stock Exchange (CASE) and the Capital Market Authority (CMA) to become a share-holder company with the name of GB Auto (S.A.E). The Ghabbour family maintained ownership of majority of the shares (71 percent). However the offering attracted many foreign and local share holders. A board of directors was formed soon after, and Dr. Ghabbour assumed the position of the Chief Executive Officer of the group.

In September 2007, the group applied to the CMA and the Ministry of Investment for possible merge of its eleven subsidiaries into two major

Table 3. GB auto results for the full-year 2008

(LE million)	FY2008	FY2007
Passenger Cars Revenues	3,675.5	3,314.4
Commercial Vehicles Revenues	740.9	590.0
Motorcycles & Three-Wheelers	571.3	528.2
Other Revenues	204.7	197.5
Total Sales Revenue	5,192.4	4,630.1
Gross Profit	872.3	670.2
Gross Profit Margin	16.8	14.5
Selling & Administration	-277	-218.8
Others – Income / (Expenses)	32.2	18.3
Operating Profit	627.5	469.7
Net Provisions	19.0	112.4
EBIT	646.5	582.1
Foreign Exchange Gains (Losses)	-18.3	2.8
Net Finance Cost	-116.2	-98.4
Earnings Before Tax	512.0	486.5
Taxes	-94.1	-50.7
Net Profit Before Minority Interest	417.9	435.8
Minority Interest	-2.0	-2.3
Net Income	415.9	433.5
Net Profit Margin	8.0	9.4

subsidiaries keeping the smaller free zone companies out of this merge. This merge was legally effective by January 2008.

Business Growth Outlook for the GB Group during the Past 5 Years

The historical business growth trajectory and performance of the GB group before the public offering is one of the few business success stories by the Egyptian standards. The group's workforce has also witness substantial growth during the last four years. This growth is manifested by the nearly tripled human resources tally employed by the group in the period from 2004 to 2008. Table 3 exhibits GB Auto Corporate financial results for the year 2008, while Table 4 shows the increase trend of the employed workforce according to the various broad areas of business activities.

The revenues breakdown of the group from the various broad lines of business as identified above is shown in Figure 1 for FY07.

The last graph identified several lines of business which comprised the following products.

1. Passenger Cars (Hyundai-Built CKD and CBU).
2. Commercial vehicles including (Mitsubishi buses and trucks, Hyundai buses, Volvo trucks and other super structures).
3. Two and three-wheelers of Bajaj brand/ models.
4. Others, including material handling equipments for Linde brand of Germany, tires for Lassa brand of Turkey and Double Coin

Table 4. GB workforce growth within 2004 - 2007

Business Activity	2004	2005	2006	2007
Passenger Cars	1021	1702	1998	2321
Commercial Cars	624	887	1308	1518
Scooter & Motorcycle	22	33	57	61
Others	92	193	806	1096
Central / Corporate	615	697	1041	1144
Total	2392	3512	5210	6140
Annual % increase	—	46.82%	48.83%	19.3%

Source: http://www.ghabbourauto.com

Figure 1. Revenues breakdown by LOB (Source: http://www.ghabbourauto.com)

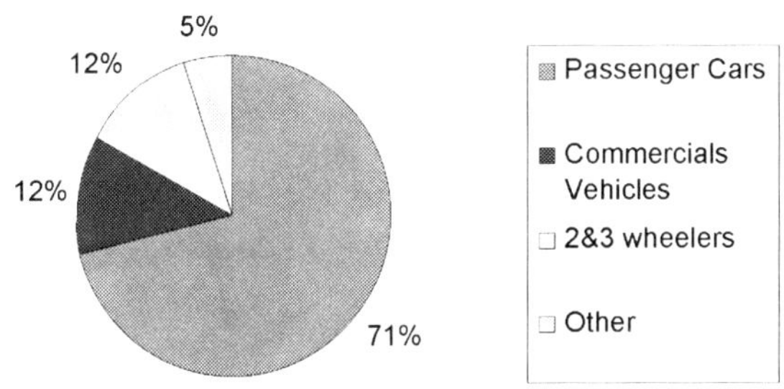

brand of China, Volvo brand construction equipment as well as Monroe brand shock absorbers.

Management Structure of the Case Firm

GB group's management structure has seen constant changes in response to the changes that occurred during its trajectory of business evolution. We will not indulge in presenting these evolutionary developments. Rather will highlight the major organizational and structural changes before and after the IPO milestone which represented major phase change in the GB group's business practices.

Prior the public offering, GB group has been managed through a hierarchical structure typical of a privately owned company. Dr. Ghabbour, the chairman, was the ultimate decision maker in any major group–wide decisions. The group was run by a number of senior administrators – reporting directly to the chairman. Senior administrators' organizations were identified according to the particular LOB in which their organizations operate. For example, passenger cars sales organization was led by a vice-president who has control over all the related activities of passenger cars, such as sales, marketing, after sale services and warehouses in addition to the company's showrooms.

Likewise, commercial vehicles which by nature spanned several products, was divided among several organizations; each concerned with a particular product line, for example bus sales, marketing and after sale services were headed by a sector director. While heavy trucks sector was assumed as a different organizational unit with a different sector head.

The functional sector divisions are provided with corporate services that cut across the whole group's functional units and subsidiaries. These services are provided by the following divisions:

- Finance and Accounting
- Information Technology
- Legal Affairs
- Logistics and Supply chain
- Human Resources and administration
- Internal Audit

Figure 2. GB auto organization chart in 2007

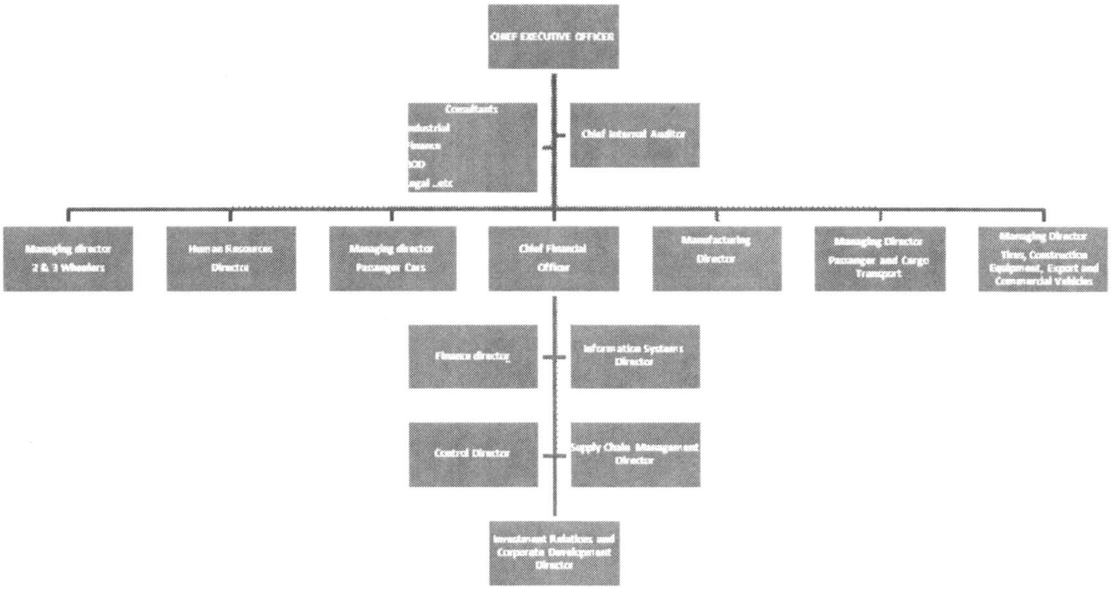

In addition, industrial and construction projects were treated as corporate projects under the direct administration of the group's chairman. Upon the incorporation of the group subsidiaries and the holding company as a joint stock company with the name GB Auto S.A.E, the group has witnessed major organizational restructuring. This resulted in promotions of division heads and the recruitment of key corporate positions such as a Chief Financial Officer (CFO) and investors relations corporate development director. Further Dr. Raouf Ghabbour was named the CEO of the incorporated company. A board of directors (BOD) was formed composed of share holders representatives and industry and finance experts. The GB Auto's organization chart by mid 2007 is exhibited in Figure 2. The management of such a wide range of activities performed by the group cannot be easily described according to the classical organizational theory. However one can postulate that the group is organized according to business sectors as well as product divisions with centralized support service sectors providing cross-functional services to other business sectors and product divisions.

SETTING THE STAGE

Research Method

In this case study, we examine the use of enterprise resources planning (ERP) system in a longitudinal case study to assess the factors impacting the success and failure of adopting those systems within the context of a developing country's business, legal and political environment. ERP systems are often regarded as an organizational "*administrative framework for planning, conducting and monitoring a large array of functionally segmented operations in a way that both accommodate, in real time, the intrinsic cross-functional interdependencies underlying these operations.*" This postulate implies that '- [ERP systems] *are packages particularly germane in influencing human agency at work*", Kallinikos, (2004, p9). The use of those systems will require making changes in the workflow of the business processes, either through redesigning the old ones to fit the ERP's embedded "best practice" or the re-alignment of the existing workflow. Moreover, ERP systems cut across all levels of management. They are used as the transaction processing workhorse, populating the ERP database with transactions initiated from various business units. The intent is to have one unified enterprise view of the organization's business operations. The prerequisite of such condition is to ensure the timeliness and integrity of the resulting database. To that end synergy among the operational units in organizations has to be provisioned to all stakeholders through a real-time procedural platform. Some members of the user community act as creators/initiators of data items, others as consumers, with each alternating role according to the business model ensued. Such a network of use role-playing will put the ERP operation at the center of the organization's information management model.

The information systems (IS) research on the use of ERP systems in organizations followed two approaches: variance- and process-based approaches (Mohr, 1982). The variance approach included two streams. The first focused on identifying the critical success factors (CSF) that facilitate implementation and "going live" of ERP systems (Bancroft et al, 1996; O'Leary, 2002; Ptak, et al, 2000). The other focuses on development of constructs that assess impacts of ERP systems on work practice (DeLone, et al, 2003; Seddon, 1997; Sedera, et al, 2004; Ifinedo, et al, 2007; Ross, et al, 1999). Conversely, a process based approach focuses on understanding the dynamics of change "how change emerges, develops, and diminishes over time" (Markus, et al, 1988).

We examine the dynamics and success of adoption of the ERP's "administrative framework" during the deployment of two successive implementations at GB Auto, the firm studied in this case. A longitudinal multi-year research project is thus conducted using variance research approach. The study was conducted in two phases, the first, taking almost three years, included the analysis of the dynamics of an operational ERP system, in production for nearly nine years. Phase two of the research began after the "go live" of the second implementation and took one year.

Longitudinal case study approaches are well established in social research. Qualitative panel or cohort studies are commonly used when measuring change over time, whether in attitudes, behaviors or experiences and when looking at causal links. Moreover, the dynamism of the techno-social world points to the need for dynamic methods of enquiry. People's perspectives on technology artifacts use are not fixed and are liable to change for a multitude of reasons. Consequently, research methods with potential to capture this fluidity may be more illuminating than other approaches. These circumstances create a unique role for longitudinal qualitative research which can provide rich information on people's perspectives and how and why these are perceived to have changed over time. The contemporary longitudinal study involves repeat follow-ups of a single sample, panel or cohort and is the approach followed in this research.

To that end, focus group forums from GB Auto, the case firm, were formed to gain understanding of the implemented ERP's operational dynamics during the post implementation period. This is not to be confused with "action research" methodology since no attempt was made by the researcher to make changes in the operation during the study. Those forums enabled direct observations of the working of the system and conducting interviews with all stakeholders. Thirty focus group sessions for different business units were conducted. Each session lasted three to four hours with average participation of 10 to15 persons comprising representatives from business unit management, system users and IT specialists. The researcher acted as session mediator with selected business area specialists as subject-matter process references. Session note-taking and minutes were administered by an MBA student who worked as an intern with the firm.

Theoretical Perspective

Many researchers examined the impacts of the success/failure factors on the accrued value of the ERP systems use to the adopting firms (e.g. Sedera et la (2002), Gable et al (2003), Sedera et al (2004), Ifinedo (2006a), (2007)), and the extent of success in adopting those systems at multiple organizational levels. In this research we pose the following question: "*how relevant those success factors are for the adoption of ERP services in the evolving business organizations within developing countries (DC) business culture"?* The work of Sedera and Ifinedo stands particularly relevant to this scope. To that end, this research is divergent from their works on two aspects: a) cultural context, and b) methodology and analysis tool. On the one hand, the work of Sedera (2002) focused on assessing ERP post-implementation success factors across the organizations' stakeholders (employment cohorts) within Australian Public sector Organizations, and used "*a dual survey approach*". The statistical sample used comprised of 27 Queensland Government agencies, running live SAP systems. While Ifinedo and Nahar (2007), on the other hand, addressed, more or less, the same research domain within the Baltic-Nordic region in Europe. Their sample survey focused on private sector organizations, again using survey measurement instrument which targeted around 500 firms in the Baltic-Nordic region. Conversely, this research is conducted within the Egyptian business domain and targeting the same research questions addressed previously, using longitudinal Case study approach, as opposed to survey methodology. Qualitative analysis was used for the study of the complex dynamics of the techno-social interaction during the ERP post-implementation phase. The use of longitudinal Case approach was chosen due to several reasons. First, comprehensive and precise information on the rate of penetration of the ERP use in the Egyptian business market proved hard to compile. Second, ERP vendors' statistics on their respective ERP product deployment in the Egyptian firms were extremely misleading. During our study, we noticed there was no differentiation between use of limited number of modules and the use of the full ERP suite modules. Such shortage of information defies the objectives of analyzing success factors for the category of Enterprise-wide IS. Third, the extremely low survey responses, the method that is commonly used for IS variance studies in more advanced and developed countries, discouraged conducting survey data collection within the less matured DCs environment. Instead, as contended earlier, the focus group approach in a longitudinal case setting was used involving all stakeholders in the Case study.

Review of Literature

The two successive ERP implementations in this case falls in the class of commercial off-the shelve software. Those configurable packages are perceived as embedding "best practice" of business processes and the ensued workflows. Often, the objectives of companies in adopting this strategy in managing their information processing needs are to seek cost reduction, increasing productivity, improve customer satisfaction and relations with their suppliers, and ultimately improve their competitiveness in the global networked market space (Davenport, 1988). Due to the far reaching impact of such implementations, many researchers have focused on the identification of the critical success factors (CSF) which facilitate successful implementation and "go live" of the system.

Further, successful adoption of ERP systems is often viewed from the perspective of IS success measurement model developed by Delone and McLean (1992, 2003). This model postulated six independent dimensions. Each dimension provided a measurement construct for the assessment of the extent of success of the IS use. Those six constructs were viewed from the perspective of IS use at large. Many researchers argued that, due to the specific nature of the ERP systems, D&M's model would have to be modified to encompass these peculiarities (Seddon, (1997), Sedera et la (2002), Gable et al (2003), Sedera et al (2004), Ifinedo (2006a), (2007)). For example, Gable, et al (2002), projecting those measurement constructs on ERP, argued for limiting the dimensions to four: a) Information Quality, b) System Quality, c) Individual Impact, and d) Organizational Impact; eliminating the User Satisfaction and Use dimensions in the original D&M model. Ifinedo (2007) then extended those four dimensions by adding the two constructs: Vendor/consultant Quality and Workgroup Impact. Fryling, (2005), in attempting to accommodate the special character of ERP project implementation, advocated "*user acceptance and IS success are highly influenced by the user community for which the ERP system is intended. The earlier a user is involved in the process the more likely they will ultimately be satisfied with the ERP and the more likely they will actually use the system*". This assertion considered the original D&M IS success model as relevant only during the implementation project execution. The novelty of the extensions made by those researchers for the ERP systems success lies in the recognition that ERP implementation and deployment is multi faceted encompassing technological, operational, managerial, strategic, and organizational related components. In particular, the inclusion of the workgroup factor by Ifinedo (2007) as an additional dimension is striking, since successful implementations in large firms depend largely on availing reliable communication infrastructure to empower collaborative work among the user community.

Other critical factors that were researched also in relation to ERP implementation and deployment are the information quality dimension and system configuration. For example, Xu et al (2002) and Madapusi et al (2007) alluded to factors such as top management support, training, communication, employee relations, project team, quality controls, and change management, being crucial in achieving high ERP information quality. The impact of ERP system configuration and/or setup revisions and enhancements of the ERP on the deployment success were also studied by Fryling (2005), Nicolaou (2007), Light (2001), Mensching (2004) and Nah (2001a). Those studies asserted that both the nature and timing of system changes are significant factors to be considered in this respect. As noted in the case, those factors have not received much attention. However, most ERP practitioners considered these factors having profound impacts in the post implementation phase. They assert the importance of the Vendor/Consultant quality factor postulated by Ifinedo (2007). As Fryling (2005) asserts and from our experience, ERP products are continuously subject to software maintenance in the form of patch fixes, version upgrades, add-ons and licensing policies changes by the ERP vendors. The likely disruptions in the operations in such mission-critical applications due to such incidents will undoubtedly send mixed signals to all stakeholders involved. Management will be forced to consider what measures should be taken to secure business continuity, for example through investing in operational redundancy to achieve 24x7x365 operation mode. End-users will have to be alerted and retrained because of the implications of the fixes and/or upgrades on the look and operational changes upon applying these upgrades. IT organizations will alternate between working in project operation mode that these upgrades require, constrained by money, people and time; and at the same time guarantee the "business as usual" systemic use mode of the ERP system by the organizations.

Moreover, it is observed that implementation and utilization of ERP systems in organizations represent a radical change from the operation of legacy systems as noted by Brazel and Dang (2008). ERP workflow crosses functional boundaries that exist in large organizations. The changes Ifinedo (2007) proposed to include the workgroup parameter to D and MIS success model are recalled here to manifest this. In the context of ERP adoptions, operational (rather than technical) factors were also addressed by many researchers. For example, factors such as: business operations coverage of the package and the number of licensed users (Francalanci, 2001; Kumar, et al., 2001; Markus, et al., 2000b; Parr and Schanks, 2000), the implementation process details (Sawyer and Southwick, 2002). The impacts of organizational and national cultures (Krumbholtz et al., 2000; Soh, et al. 2000), users and organizational learning (Fleck, 1994; Parr and Schanks, 2000), knowledge transfer from suppliers to the host organization (Lee and Lee, 2000), the configuration and setup of the package's parameter tables and their overall impact on the architecture and flexibility of the ERP packages for rapid adaptation (Fan et al., 2000; Spott, 2000). Some articles also addressed the impacts of ERP process standardization and the restructuring of organization tasks or business processes reengineering (Kumar and Van Hillgersberg, 2000). The entanglement of the ERP technology with other technological artifacts, such as networks, servers, workstations, etc., as well as commercial interests and external social practices have been addressed by Ciborra et al., (2000), Ciborra and Hanseth, (1998), Fleck, (1994), and how the interdependencies of those components impact the implementation and adaptation in organizations.

CASE DESCRIPTION

Information Systems Services and IT Deployment in GB Group

The deployment of IS/IT services in GB group has seen evolutionary developments since the early 1990's. This evolutionary process can, roughly speaking, be divided into three overlapping phases:

- **Phase 1:** Early adoption phase, which spans the period from year 1990 to1997.
- **Phase 2:** First ERP implementation period, covers the years 1997-2006.
- **Phase 3:** Second ERP deployment phase, which covers the period from 2004 to today.

It is worth noting here that documented records on the details and nature of the IS/IT utilization in phase 1 are missing. This is due to the disappearance of the technical staff for the support of these services and/or the non-existence of physical archives that one can reference to enable the analysis of the usage nature during this phase. In order to shed light on the nature of the use of IT/IS in the group during this era, we have turned our attention to collect data from IT service providers of the group. Also, we asked old timer employees in the finance, accounting and IT divisions to help in identifying the nature of use of IS/IT in the group during this period.

Based on those sources and the remnants of the old systems that were found in the various affiliated companies, the next section provides the foundation of the IT/IS service map in the group during phase 1.

Phase 1: Early IT/IS Deployment

We can assert here that the first serious IT/IS services deployment in Ghabbour group dates back to 1994. Two of its manufacturing subsidiaries, namely PRIMA and VCI companies contracted ORASCOM firm, an Egyptian technology firm, for the deployment of the MFG PRO package of USA-based QUAD Company. MFG PRO runs the following application modules in both factories:

- Inventory management;
- Purchasing;
- Manufacturing, which included
    - Bill of Materials (BOM)
    - Routing
    - WIP

    - Quality Control
- Financials, which included
    - General Ledger
    - Accounts Payable
    - Accounts Receivables
    - Fixed Assets
- Invoicing.

The package was in operation for the period from 1994 to 2003, running on HP 9000 server using HPUX, the HP UNIX variant operating system platform. In an interview with Engineer Albair Shafik, IT specialist in the Ghabbour group IT department, who prior working for the group, was the resident consultant of ORASCOM responsible for the implementation of the MFG PRO package. The following account on the implementation process of the package in the two targeted sites is given next:

"Soon after the contract between ORASCOM and GB group was signed, I was assigned the task of the lead implementation consultant in 1994. We started the first implementation with PRIMA site which lasted for 12 months. We followed this with the VCI site, which lasted for another 6 months. The two factories were new and there were no old IT systems to match. The team started a kind of "clean slate", applying the standard MFG PRO processes and procedures. This made our task much easier and controllable. We have to upload all the master data for the items, suppliers and customers from manual documents. We developed coding system for the master databases, which was arbitrarily coined without regard to any particular standard. There was even no coordination between the coding systems adopted by the other subsidiaries. The main feature in those two implementations is that we did not do any major customizations and when we needed such customizations, the task was wholly outsourced to the implementer, ORASCOM. Since the implementation and operation of those two factories, they operated satisfactorily until they were migrated to the BaaN system in December, 2003. In my view, this implementation was very successful because it fit properly the user requirements on the one hand. The user did not contest the new system operation and adopted the package's inherent "best practice" processes without much resistance".

In his opinion, this system survived for nearly nine years and gained acceptance and stability due to several factors, among these are:

- Extensive user training was carried out in the early stages of the implementation;
- GB group's MFG PRO implementation was among the first "customers" using the package in Egypt. This has prompted ORASCOM to fully support it in order to make a success story and identify it as its flag-ship in the course of marketing this package;
- The implementer has gone through a thorough and detailed business requirements analysis which helped in properly configuring the package to suit these requirements;
- The system support was totally outsourced after the "go live" for some period, and with the eagerness to make a success story, the vendor exerted every effort to operate the system efficiently and effectively.

Concurrent with the implementation of MFG PRO, ITAMCO and Ghabbour Egypt subsidiaries implemented a sales and distribution package called LEADER, which run on Windows server platform. A third package called El Mokhtar was also implemented for the notes receivables (NR) application for the finance and accounting department. These two implementations were run and operated by separate IT units in each beneficiary division.

This phase of IS/IT deployment can be truly characterized as initiation stage and the implementation of technologies can only be described as fragmented and as such, has caused a great deal of headache for the company when senior management decided at last to streamline all systems under one company-wide unit.

It is an interesting observation to note that even though there was a great deal of common data between the different subsidiaries, each division created their own master databases and respective coding system. This, of course, resulted in duplication of databases among the subsidiaries, thus creating inefficiency within the divisions and increased difficulties when the decision was made to integrate all systems. Also, a great deal of time and money was wasted on the company's behalf. If all relevant information had been shared from the beginning, it would have saved the GB Group a large sum of money and a great deal of time.

The separation of the master databases (customers, suppliers and items) led to the adoption of non-standard and non-coordinated code. The non-standardization of both data structures and processes was deeply rooted in the group's culture. This impeded the subsequent enterprise-wide IS/IT adoption and created mounting problems to the IT organization in trying to fulfill the integration among the group's subsidiaries.

The fledgling islands of computing in the group's companies have taken the IS/IT adoption curve to the second stage of Nolan's (1979) stage model, deepening the non-standardization ailment and strengthening the "silos" mentality in the group's IT management. This particular issue had the gravest impact on the implementation of the first ERP system across the entire group. It dictated an architectural design of this implementation that led to its failure and eventual abandonment as will be seen later.

The senior management of the group realized the imminent increased dependency on the use of IS/IT services all over the group's companies. A decision to centralize those services under one single group-wide unit was thus made. A large enough system to service not only the existing companies but any further expansions in the group's lines of business was to be acquired.

Phase 2: From Expansion to Control, the First ERP Implementation Era

By the year 1997, GB group top management invited prospective systems providers to bid for the procurement, installation and implementation of integrated information systems to serve the needs for the entire group's affiliated companies. Several proposals were presented. Afterwards, the group accepted an offer submitted by a Saudi company named Integrated Systems International (ISI). ISI, the sole agent for BaaN ERP in the Middle East, was chosen to provide the full spectrum of the BaaN application modules. These modules included: manufacturing for discrete and process industries, distribution, finance, service and maintenance, project, transportation, Business Organization Dynamics, Enterprise Modelling and Orgware.

A central IT unit was established as a corporate unit serving the entire group's affiliates. The unit was mandated to install the necessary infrastructure needed for the implementation and operation of the BaaN ERP system. The IT division subsequently contracted IBM branch in Egypt for the acquisition of the hardware, system software and database management system in preparation for the BaaN implementation. The initial configuration installed as the platform for the ERP system operation consisted of the following:

- Three RS/6000 IBM servers, one model H70 to be located in Kalyoubia site and two machines, H70 and H50 models to be located in ITAMCO company at Abo-Rawash site;
- AIX OS, IBM's Unix operating system variant was used for all servers;
- Initially, the T-Base database management system (DBMS) engine was installed,

which was replaced in 2001 by the DB2 DBMS

In 1998, BaaN release IV was successfully installed. A fascinating point of interest in this case is that even though BaaN release IV provided an option for group configuration, GB Auto decided to forgo that opportunity in favour of speeding up the implementation process.

The implementation project was executed in 3 stages; the first started with the trading companies and took three years to complete. Thus, in 2001, implementation had taken place in the following companies: RGI, Pre-custom Company, GCT (free zone), GIT (free zone), EMT, ITAMCO, and INTERLAND. Stage two took place during the period of 2001-2003, and resulted in five companies' implementation of BaaN: Ghabbour Egypt, GE Manufacturing, PRIMA, PRIMA Inventory, and VCI.

What is important to consider in those implementations is that from the start, integration was never deliberated. Each company was to be configured as a separate instance with all its master data- even though there was great amount of common data (customers, suppliers and items) among those instances. For example, the customer master database was separately compiled for each individual company regardless the repetition. Another issue that is evident in this case is that the analysis of requirements done prior to the implementation was never thoroughly documented. Also, there was a great deal of customizations taking place in the implementation process in order to fit in the non-standard business processes of each individual company. These customizations have provided nothing more than problems in the long run. In essence, they only encouraged non-integration between the subsidiaries and led to multiple fundamental operational difficulties. The vendor's support was greatly lacking and the group's relationship with them became strained. Due to these problems, as well as others, the IT division had to rely solely on in-house experts who were unable to keep up with the frequent errors due to their limited knowledge on this system.

These problems, as well as the difficulties inherent in the system usage practices led to a fundamental distrust in the system. Data manipulation became commonplace, bringing about the issue of data integrity and validity. This is how the "Excel" culture of Ghabbour Auto came about. As the program aged, costs rose and it became evident that the BaaN operation had come to a dismal conclusion. As Engineer Adel Nassem, the then newly appointed IT and Business Director in 2002 recalls:

"In 2002, when I took charge, the level of business relationship with the BaaN system vendor representative in Dubai was so strained that I had to call BaaN headquarters in Europe asking for help and their interference".

Help was indeed received, BaaN HQ diverted Mr. Nassem's support request to India subsidiary. As a result, GB group contracted two Indian specialists to be on board for fixing the problems of BaaN system which was falling in a vortex spin.

The situation gone from bad to worse by deepening the extent of customizations, forging the non-integration and prohibited scalability and/or upgradeability of the system. Basic functionalities such as consolidating financial reporting were never achieved. Period closing (quarters and/or yearly) was never achieved and data fixing was common practice without regard to audit rules and/or accounting best-practice. In short, what the group ended up with by 2004, a disparate database repository that is totally open for manipulation with no audit trails and no confidence in the validity of the data values.

By 2003, stage three of the implementation project started and the MFG PRO package's operation at both PRIMA and VCI manufacturing installations were stopped. Their databases were migrated to BaaN system, still as separate companies. What is intriguing is that no attempt was made, during this migration process, to perform any form of data cleansing, standardization of the coding systems and/or the processes. This has furthered the "silo" IT operation feature, albeit using the same BaaN "ERP" infrastructure.

As a result of this data chaos, the professional staff in the various functional areas (finance, accounting, logistics, manufacturing, etc) developed the "evil" habit of extracting the data from the BaaN database to their Excel sheets. They performed whatever manipulation they need on this data without regard to audit rules and/or validation and verification controls. To respond to the management demands for performance reporting and to enable fast reply to ad hoc queries whenever decisions are imminent, the "Excel" culture proliferated. Data from BaaN was continuously uploaded to individuals' PCs. This led to creating multiple pictures for the same fact violating issues of data integrity, security and increasing the risk of loss of resources. As engineer Nassem contends:

"The BaaN system has become totally open to the extent that any one from any department could make changes that may be reverted next day just to cover up some mistakes or fix some figures"

The operation of the BaaN, besides its functional flaws, has come to a disastrous and risky juncture when the cost of operating the hardware platform reached prohibitive limits. At the start of the BaaN operation, in order to secure safe and reliable operation of the system, service contracts were signed with IBM for the maintenance of the hardware, systems software and the DB2 DBMS. With the aging of the hardware, the support contract bill rose to extremely high values with no evident ROI. The IT division decided to sever this contract and opted for another hardware support contract other than IBM with the implications of lower performance. The same policy was also extended to the BaaN support contract with the risk of not having support at all for this package, this led to the division becoming under siege and dependent on the foreign (Indian) hired specialists

To worsen the situation even further, with no in-house know-how of database house-keeping, the database sizes for some instances (companies) reached critical levels (85percent to 90 percent limits) requiring major re-configuration process. A situation when referred to the BaaN vendor was unprofessionally exploited by the vendor to recover lost revenues.

Technology Concerns

At this point in time, Dr. Aram Youssef was recruited as the new Vice-Chairman of the group. Dr. Aram felt that it was time to seek the services of external consultants in order to establish where the group went wrong. As a result, a team from the American University in Cairo was consulted. The consultants were requested to evaluate the current IT/IS infrastructure effectiveness and the services provided by the applications. And to propose solutions and recommendations to help the group establish a responsive information systems services. The team met with the group's Chairman, Dr. Raouf Ghabbour; the Vice-chairman for support functions, Dr. Aram Youssef and the IT and Business development Director, Mr. Adel Nassem in February 2004 and were requested to investigate the current IT/IS infrastructure and applications problems and propose recommendations and solutions for the group to establish a robust and responsive information systems services. The team spent eight weeks in activities related to fact finding and data gathering, analysis of the existing IS utilization and other issues related to the operation of the BaaN system effectiveness. The team also surveyed the supporting IT infrastructure and the IT organization unit. At the end of this period, a report was presented to the group's senior management with a proposed action plan to establish a robust and responsive information systems infrastructure. The proposal called for the rejuvenation of the three building blocks of IS building blocks in the group: the systems platform (hardware and system software), the network and communications infrastructure and the business application software platform. The chairman of the group, Dr Raouf Ghabbour, approved the recommendations and the plan was carried out accordingly as will be discussed later.

The consulting team's diagnostic report made several observations explaining the reasons and factors that made the process of BaaN implementation reach a dead end and finally abandonment. These observations were in complete congruence with most of the classical failure factors of ERP implementations found in academic references, text books and research articles (Binji, P. et al.; 1999; Davenport, T., 1998; Lycett, M. et al. 1999; Schwalbe, L, et al., 2000; Akkerman, H. et al., 2002; Turban, E et al., 2006). Among those identified factors are:

i. Lack of Top Management Support

In almost all cases of major ERP implementations, the top management involvement and support is considered a tipping point between potential success and failure. At some point of the BaaN ERP implementation project at GB group, management was not fully involved as they should be. At first, the management looked to the project as externally provisioned services by the contracted firm. This has impeded making radical changes (re-engineering) of the business processes and standards within the group's business practice. Such re-engineering endeavors are the norm for successful ERP solution implementations. It was a surprise, for example, to see the requirements document defining separate non-standard business rules among the group's companies. This is by no means what the top management would have required had they been involved in the requirements definition phase of the implementation. This particular issue has led to the fragmentation of the project to a separate company implementation route, impeding any future integration between the instances within the ERP system. Enforcing the integration at the requirements definition phase would have needed the authority and clout of the top management.

ii. Lack of Project Team Competence

In reviewing the project team composition, it was striking to see that the implementer is a start-up firm with no or little prior experiences and/or showcases of similar size projects. Further, although the BaaN contract was signed with a regional software firm affiliated to BaaN, the number of implementations provisioned through this firm was also meager to guarantee the success of such a huge undertaking. The counterpart team of the GB group was relatively small and with little or no previous BaaN or integrated information systems experience. Their training was shortened in favor of early start of the implementation process.

The introduction of BaaN ERP system in the region was also so sparse, implicating the scarcity of experienced professionals in both project management and functional know-how using the BaaN ERP system. This explains why GB group ended up with one single qualified trained staff with no redundancy or back up personnel who can effectively operate and maintain the system. This kind of organizational deficiency placed the group in a liability situation impeded any efforts for professional development plans for the existing scarce professionals, who were denied the opportunity to leaving the operation for extended periods for training.

iii. Lack of Project Ownership

Like any project, if there is no champion of the project acting as the owner of it, the chances that the project would succeed are usually slim. The pre-requisite qualification of this owner in the group would be one who is not affiliated to one

Table 5. BaaN master database per each company

Company	Customers	Vendors	Items
GE	29,087	2,517	121,102
EMT	29,212	2,518	1,680
ITAMCO	12,857	3,069	50,278
PRIMA	12,317	4,421	17,736
VCI	41	4,385	5,144
Interland	2,808	4,421	48,283
Total BAAN	86,322	21,331	244,223
Oracle	21,366	2,154	41,451
Repeated	64,956	19,177	202,772

particular subsidiary – but has the group-wide responsibilities. There was no such candidate in the group with such credentials except the Chairman or the group's CFO (back in 1998); both candidates were not acting as the BaaN project champion. Instead, each company's top manager acted as the champion of his individual company's implementation project, furthering the "silo" approach which was reflected in the architecture the BaaN ended up with.

iv. Lack of Standardization

The lack of standardization on both levels of data structures and processes among the group's subsidiaries, as postulated earlier entrenched the fragmentation and increased the level of customization of the BaaN system. As Engineer Adel Nassim contends, highlighting the gravity of this customization;

"To show how the extent of customization impeded the success of BaaN, the Indian expert who was on board since 2002 was not able to upgrade the BaaN version from IV to V. The effort to do that would have amounted to man-days equivalent to a fresh BaaN implementation in order to incorporate the number of customizations put in version IV. He was barely able to upgrade the operating system AIX version from 4.1 to 4.3 which did not add much functionality to the system."

Engineer Nabil Naguib, the then database administrator for the currently operating Oracle system provides the following account on the magnitude of the inconsistencies in the databases as a result of the non-standardization of the group's data structures;

"The biggest task we encountered when we started the migration of the master databases from the BaaN. The amount of inconsistencies found in these disparate databases was humungous. The code duplications and the inconsistencies were of such a magnitude that it took us months to perform data cleansing. As you can see from Table 5, the repeated records in the source data were nearly triple the number of the actual unique codes for the customer data, nearly 9 times for the suppliers and 5 times for the items data. The effort we expended for the cleansing of this data is humongous. This by no means resulted in 100% clean master database, some items in the master files were still need to be cleansed and were left to be individually dealt with as we come across them in the current Oracle operation".

v. Vendor Support and Partnership

Although at the time of selecting BaaN as the application software for the information systems infrastructure for the group, this ERP package was considered one of the top 3 ERP systems world-wide. However, the selection criteria did not take into consideration other critical factors in the selection such as:

- Vendor support capabilities in the region;
- Availability of professional skilled staff in the local market;
- The size of the customer base of the vendor in the region;
- Proximity of the support location.

In this case implementation, it was clear that the above critical factors were not readily fulfilled in a satisfactory way to warrant embracing such a complex undertaking. Time has proved that those factors were detrimental to the success of the group's implementation project.

vi. Architecture Choice

The high level design for the BaaN implementation, in acknowledging the legal requirements for the separation of the group's companies, developed an architecture based on separate instances. This compromised the fact that these separate entities have common back office business processes. For example, the finance and accounting division operates within the framework of corporate resources allocation which proved impossible to implement in this separate instances architecture. This has led to dividing the finance and accounting function to logically disjoint units - each responsible for an instance (company) without regard to the integration nature of those companies. Had the implementation considered the alternate approach in using the BaaN "group" facility coupled with some re-engineering of the integration requirements to cater for the legal considerations, the project may have had a different fate.

Despite the good intentions of the implementation of the BaaN system during the period from 1998 to 2004, the objectives to gain better control over the disparate databases and their integrity were never accomplished. To the contrary, the openness of the BaaN system resulted in the proliferation of the "Excel" culture, fostering the non-integrity of the group's data resources. Based on the findings of the diagnostic study a recommendation document outlining the strategy for implementing new responsive and integrated information systems infrastructure was presented to the management. The strategy addressed the following six major actions:

i. Phasing out the current BaaN ERP system in favor of implementing a new one that avoids the pitfalls of the previous experiences.
ii. Development of a blue print for the communications and network infrastructure to serve the current and future connectivity needs for the operation of the integrated business information systems model. Such a blue print must satisfy the following operational requirements:
    - Redundancy;
    - Reliability;
    - Diversified providers;
    - Ample and extendible capacity;
    - Provides good and solid security and safe communications environment;
    - Use of tie lines, MPLS, WiFi and RF technologies for the connectivity of the geographically dispersed locations;
    - Use of the VPN technologies to facilitate virtual presence and mobile access in a secure manner.
iii. Establish modern, versatile and high availability datacenter with back up facilities. Acquire and install new server farm infrastructure that will enable serving both

the needs for the new information systems infrastructure and the network and communications infrastructure.

iv. Establish highly responsive IT team with in-house capacities for operating and maintaining the trilogy building blocks: the information systems, the network and the server farm;

v. Enforce centralized IT service delivery, centralized IT planning process and standardized data structures, databases and processes.

vi. Develop the Standard Operating Procedures and Policies (SOP&P) that govern and ensure adequate IT service level delivery to the group's divisions and units.

It has become apparent that there is a need for something more when it comes to the information system at GB group. On the issue of the appropriate selection of the new ERP system, the Oracle e-Business Suite (EBS) was selected. The rationale for this decision was based on several key factors, many of these mentioned previously in the case analysis as problems during the BaaN implementation. There is a local support base for Oracle in Egypt. There is evidence of sustainability and commitment of Oracle to the Egyptian Market. At the time, the business outlook of Oracle is clearly on the rise. EBS functionalities cover almost every line of the business that GB Group is or will be involved in. Also, there is an availability of knowledge workers trained on the full spectrum of the needed professional activities in support of this project.

Phase 3: Technology Components: The New Oracle ERP Implementation

By April, 2004, RGI – the then holding company of the GB group, signed a contract with Oracle Egypt for the licensing of its EBS software which included the following 18 modules:

- Finance which included the five modules – GL,AR, AP, FA and CM
- Distribution which included the three modules – OM, PO and INV
- Human Resources which included the modules – HR foundation and Payroll
- Systems utilities which included – Web Discoverer and Alert manager
- Manufacturing modules which included the six modules – BOM, QC, WIP, MRP, CRP and MPS

Concurrently, RGI invited prospective local Oracle implementation firms to bid for the implementation of the EBS in the group. Two finalists were identified by April, 2004. The implementation contract was finally awarded to the Egyptian implementer CITE company. Their presented technical solution acknowledged the architecture of one implementation instance and not separate instances for the group's companies. This particular concept was the tipping factor in the evaluation of the offered proposals and the selection process of the implementer. Such a solution was thought to guarantee the enforcement of standardization of data structures, database design and the business processes across the entire group's companies.

The implementation plan called for phasing the process into two stages. The first would include the finance, distribution, human resources and the utilities modules; while the second stage will complete the implementation of the manufacturing modules.

In deciding on the operating system platform, use of UNIX operating system as the system layer for the Oracle application was first recommended. This decision was in-line with the best-practice adopted by many organizations for operating Oracle system. However, this recommendation was contested by the management. Among the reasons for this, the not-very satisfactory experience with IBM's AIX support during the BaaN operation. It was subsequently agreed to adopt the

Figure 3. The IT organization chart for the GB group during the implementation phase

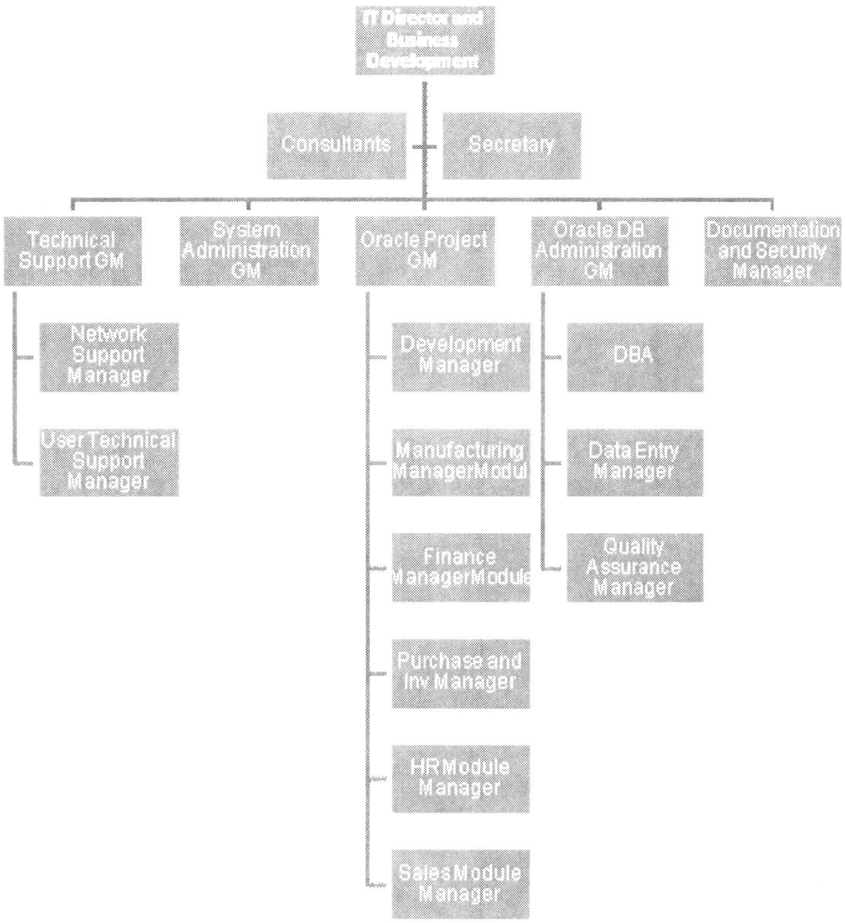

option of using Windows 2000 server operating system platform with the caveat of mitigating security vulnerabilities of the Windows platform by deploying adequate security infrastructure. At that time, the 64-bit Windows server architecture was not yet released by Microsoft. This particular issue will be shown to negatively impact the sustainability of the Oracle ERP operation using this platform.

On the organizational level, the consultant team, together with the senior management opted for recruiting an Oracle Project team. The proposed composition of this team is shown in Figure 3. Within few months of setting up the project, the project team positions were duly filled with appropriate professional staff, some were drawn from the existing IT organization, others hired from the market.

An Oracle Steering Committee (OSC) was also formed. The OSC was to meet on a regular basis to set the project execution strategies and policies, and review the progress presented by the Oracle PM and recommend the necessary actions to deal with any problems or delays in the project time line. The committee composition is as follows:

- The Vice-Chairman for support functions
- Chair of the OSC

- Representatives from the implementation firm CITE
- Representatives from Oracle Egypt
- The IT and Business Development director
- Oracle Project manager from GB
- Oracle DBA from GB
- An external IT Consultant (the author)

Management and Organizational Concerns

The original Oracle project implementation plan stipulated, with the consent of the project steering committee, the conclusion of stage-1 in nine months starting by May 1st, 2004. However, with the unfortunate event of fire breaking in one of the major buildings of the Prima manufacturing company in Abu-Rawash site in December 2004. This resulted in the relocation of the finance and accounting division from this site to the GE company site, some 40 kilometers away from the group's headquarters in Abu-Rawash. Besides the relocation, it was impossible to keep the senior management focused on the project schedules and commitment to the Oracle project in such disaster and damage-control period. The "Go Live" milestone date was subsequently moved to June 2005.

Meanwhile, the project team successfully configured the hardware and the system software infrastructure and readied the platform for the operation of the Oracle application in early 2005.

Soon after, the BaaN databases conversion activities stage started. In this stage, activities such as data cleansing and standardization of data structures, were completed and the databases were uploaded into the readied platform thereafter. Testing, end-user training and go-live for stage one of Oracle project started in early November 2005.

During the live operation of the EBS on the Windows platform, the project team encountered many difficulties and obstacles. The most serious of those was related to the in-adequacy of the WINTEL platform to withstand both the database size and the number of concurrent users using the Oracle application. Although the sizing of the platform was performed collaboratively by both Oracle and HP, the vendors for both the application and the hardware respectively, this glitch persisted. The issue was raised to the top severity level at Oracle's Technical Assistance Request group (TAR) who recommended many solutions and fixes with no avail. It was finally affirmed by both Oracle and Microsoft that the problems encountered were primarily due to the 32 bit addressing limitations inherent in the 32-bit Windows server operating system. The implications of this issue were debated in the project steering committee and a decision was reached to replace the HP/Windows 2000 platform by IBM/UNIX platform. As a consequence, two IBM 570 pSeries machines were procured running AIX operating system. The platform was operationally ready by October 2006. Subsequently, the EBS system was successfully migrated to the new platform and operated by October 2006.

Due to the impending IPO date, the BaaN operation was extended to the end of 2006 and Oracle was placed on the backburner until then. The "Go Live" date was set for December 3,1 2006. This of course had a negative impact on the process of institution and adoption of the new Oracle EBS system. It only meant that user training sessions would have to be repeated and online transaction data entry would cease in favour of BaaN entry.

The go live plan called for populating the balances in all data structures by the 31st of December, 2006. With concerted efforts between the various stakeholders, the system operation started as planned on January 1st, 2007, marking the real start of the third phase of IT/IS deployment trajectory for the GB group.

CURRENT CHALLENGES FACING THE ORGANIZATION

January 1st, 2007 brought about the date that the BaaN system operation was plugged off, and

Oracle EBS was put into gear. The IT division at RGI offices was overwhelmingly busy with maintaining smooth and painless transition from the old BaaN culture to the new environment. This was not at all their first encounter with the Oracle EBS live operation. As described before, for a short period of time during 2006, the system operation was in full force – which represented excellent rehearsal of what to be expected after the "Big Bang" of day one in the live of Oracle at GB group. During this period, the team tackled most of the technical glitches related to either the hardware, operating system or the application. It was not therefore a surprise to observe no panic or "fire fighting" reactions in the early weeks after the second EBS "go live" kick off. Nevertheless, change management procedures were noticed to be overly overseen. The after effects of the "cultural changes" started to pile up. The old "Excel" model began to slowly creep back into the company's business process operations. This was manifested by the overwhelming requests made by the users from the business area coordinators for the development of "Excel-like" discoverer reports (reports that are tailor made using the Discoverer tool of Oracle). By midyear 2007, there were over 400 discoverer reports, 90 percent of them mimicked the Excel tabulation. In their pursuit to appease and entice the end-user, the Oracle team submitted to these requests without questioning their effectiveness and /or use that may be accomplished through otherwise standard Oracle built-in reports.

As we mentioned in the beginning of this Case, year 2007 witnessed the start of the preparation for IPO offering under the group's holding company GB Auto. This has created a heavy load on the finance and accounting division, which demanded responsive and agile information system infrastructure. With the limited experienced professional staff in the IT division, handling of those excessive user requests was less than satisfactory from the user's point of view. Coupled with the natural resistance to use the new system in timely manner – the Oracle implementation was perceived by the user as yet another IT failure. At the transaction processing level (TPS), populating the database was in some business areas not performed in on-line, real-time mode. In other instances, entry to the TPS was in error and/or incomplete due to use of untrained employees. The result of such inaccuracies yielded database that does not reflect the real world and a user community without confidence in the Oracle system outputs.

On the management control level, with little or no training in using the Oracle standard reporting system; managers, whether in the middle or top levels, depended on their subordinates' reporting. Those subordinates were compelled to respond through the only way they seem familiar with, downloading data from Oracle and use "Excel" to formulate the required reports. This behavior has proliferated right from the first level management to the most senior level, fostering the perception of the inability of Oracle system to respond to their information needs.

The Oracle post-implementation review conducted by the author and the technical staff suggested that the newly introduced ERP system is passing through critical stage in its adoption path. From an IT planning and control perspectives, it appeared that all the technical ingredients necessary for successful delivery were in place – providing the illusion to the IT management and staff that they have a successful implementation. Blaming the business units/personnel and management of not being receptive to the needed changes. Claiming resisting control and fighting the cause of adopting Oracle within the fabric of the GB group information flow and decision making pattern. On the other hand, focus interviews and direct observations of the various levels of user groups, we found a general perception that the current provisioned Oracle services are not in-line with their needs, neither on the transactional nor on the management reporting levels.

SOLUTIONS AND RECOMMENDATIONS

Following the GB Auto IPO, the CEO together with the BOD members realized that the group's successful growth resulted in the expansion of the organization with a mixture of decentralized management functions at the Business Unit level, while other management functions remaining centralized. Furthermore, the current organization structure showed a relatively high level of vertical layers within each major function, with no clear and effective horizontal communications. This structure led to delays in decision making and impeded progress of work flow, as well as creating conflicts that require top management involvement.

An organizational review has been contemplated to address these issues. Several potential management consulting firms were solicited to bid for this task in early October 2007. The request for proposal objectives included:

1. Working with the GB group's management team to develop the most effective responsive (and lean while capable of continued growth) type of organizational structure, with clear definitions of:
   - Centralized functions versus functions at the Business Unit level
   - Structure of each major areas or function, including definitions on the scope of responsibilities and attributions for each key position
2. Optimization of the operational and administrative processes under the new organization, and incorporating the use of the IT systems to the extent possible.
3. An evaluation of the existing human talent, and a needs assessment in view of the current and future needs of management and professional talent

GB Group intended that the review will focus on those areas that will ensure the effective management of the group and its varied lines of businesses. In January 2008, GB contracted the selected management consulting firm from the three bidders and work on the project started soon after. Among the objectives of the consultant's tasks are the following:

i. Optimizing Processes Across the Organization

For a growing organization being able to scale processes and systems is essential to avoid constant reengineering. Also leveraging benefits of scale of similar activities across business units makes managing a growing business simpler. Comparison with standard processes and review of the current processes against a set of best practice industry standard processes will help assess where the biggest gaps are and the advantages of moving towards standardized processes and if needed redesign those non-standardized ones.

ii. Developing Effective Organization Structures and Role Accountabilities

All employees who work with a process should be clear on what their accountabilities and responsibilities are. By making this clear and structuring the organization effectively it is possible to reduce the conflicts and confusion between different parts of the organization.

Meanwhile, with the arrival of a newly appointed Chief Finance Officer (CFO) in the senior management level for the group in early 2008, he soon observed that the IT team from one side was accusing the user community of not being receptive to the change. On the other side, users grew more and more resistant to Oracle system adoption, perceiving that Oracle will have to work in the way they are accustomed to and finally consider the Oracle application as a failure since it cannot be customized to their liking.

With ample knowledge of the central role of ERP systems and the implications of its adoption in business organizations, the CFO established an independent task "Oracle Facilitation and Coordination" (OFC) division. The objectives and scope of work of this division were set as follows:

- Review the effectiveness and current use of the current Oracle processes, modules and reports, inform users of all that is available and assist on any alterations or additions needed to the existing Oracle set up in order to operate effectively
- Analyze the current business processes in the various business areas, assess their correctness, validity and appropriateness always keeping in mind operational controls and if needed, redesign those processes to be streamlined with the Oracle configuration
- Document and understand those reports required at the business units and not currently available in Oracle and arrange for them to be included in Oracle by the Oracle system maintainers
- Document reference policies and procedures (P&P) for all business processes in the business functions that have been analyzed as defined in the above points and then monitor the operation on an ongoing basis
- Assess for development any additional KPIs for all management levels in addition to those already existing as well as those in the Oracle DBI module. Coordinate with the IT division for any implementation of business intelligence tools to secure rational approach in managing the group's business resources and operations
- Participate in the implementation of new Oracle modules and assisting in communicating and training end-users
- Conduct on-going training on existing modules to all personnel involved in the use of the developed tools and redesigned operations
- Advise IT division on user requirements and security issues

The scope of work for the new task force would span the entire group's business activities. Work to be done includes:

- Analyze, design and /or redesign the business processes in all the group's line of business
- Analyze, document and evaluate the current configuration of business process operations within the Oracle system and establish gaps between the business needs and the services provided by the Oracle system
- Develop the necessary framework needed for the institution of the Oracle in all business units
- In collaboration with the IT teams and the business unit representatives, develop, institute and operate the business intelligence facilities, either within Oracle or otherwise to maximize the benefits from using the centralized, integrated databases. In collaboration with the group's management, establish the mostly needed KPIs to manage the vast resources of the group
- Provision of on-going monitoring mechanism, overseeing the utilization of, and adherence to Oracle's P&Ps
- Ensure smooth integration of the various activities of the group and institution of any new activities as a result of expansion in new line of business, within Oracle system operation

To that end, efforts of the OFC division team would be aligned with the organization-wide process reengineering initiative to be executed by the management consulting firm, in a concerted effort to pave the way for the institution of the Oracle EBS.

REFERENCES

Ackerman, H., & Van Heden, K. (2002). Vicious and virtuous cycles in ERP implementation: A case Study of interrelations between critical success factors. *European Journal of Information Systems*, *11*, 35–46. doi:10.1057/palgrave/ejis/3000418

Bingi, P. (1999). Critical issues affecting an ERP implementation. *Information Systems Management*, *16*, 7–14. doi:10.1201/1078/43197.16.3.19990601/31310.2

Brazel, J., & Dang, L. (2008). The effect of ERP system implementations on the management of earnings and earnings release dates. *Journal of Information Systems*, *22*(2), 1–21. doi:10.2308/jis.2008.22.2.1

Ciborra, C. (2000). *From control to drift*. Oxford, UK: Oxford University Press.

Ciborra, C., & Hanseth, O. (1998). From tool to Gestell. Agendas for managing information infrastructures. *Information Technology & People*, *11*(4), 305–327. doi:10.1108/09593849810246129

Davenport, T. (1998). Putting the enterprise into the enterprise system. *Harvard Business Review*, *76*(4), 121–131.

DeLone, W., & McLean, E. (1992). Information systems success: The quest for the dependent variable. *Information Systems Research*, *3*(1), 60–95. doi:10.1287/isre.3.1.60

DeLone, W., & McLean, E. (2003). The DeLone and McLean model of Information Systems success: A ten-year update. *Journal of Management Information Systems*, *19*(4), 9–30.

Fan, M. (2000). The adoption and design methodologies of component-based enterprise systems. *European Journal of Information Systems*, *9*, 25–35. doi:10.1057/palgrave.ejis.3000343

Fleck, J. (1994). Learning by trying: The implementation of configurational technology. *Research Policy*, *23*, 637–652. doi:10.1016/0048-7333(94)90014-0

Francalanci, C. (2001). Predicting the implementation effort of ERP projects: Empirical evidences on SAP R/3. *Journal of Information Technology*, *16*(1), 33–48. doi:10.1080/02683960010035943

Fryling, M. (2005). *ERP implementation dynamics*. Information Science and Policy University at Albany. State University of New York.

Gable, G., et al. (2002). Enterprise resources planning systems impacts: A Delphi study of Australian public sector. *Proceedings of the sixth Australasian Conference of Information Systems (PACIS 2002),* 2-4 September 2002, Tokyo, Japan.

Gable, G., et al. (2003, December). *Enterprise systems success: A measurement model*. Paper presented at twenty-fourth International Conference on Information Systems, 14-17, Seattle, USA.

Ifinedo, P. (2006a). Extending the Gable et al. enterprise systems success measurement model: A preliminary study. *Journal of Information Technology Management, 17*(1), 14-33.

Ifinedo, P. (2007). Investigating the relationships among ERP systems success dimensions: A structural equation model. *Issues in Information Systems*, *8*(2).

Ifinedo, P., & Nahar, N. (2007). ERP system success: An empirical analysis of how two organizational stakeholder groups prioritize and evaluate relevant measures. *Enterprise Information Systems*, *1*, 25–48. doi:10.1080/17517570601088539

Krumbholz, M. (2000). Implementing enterprise resource planning packages in different corporate and national cultures. *Journal of Information Technology*, *15*(4), 267–280. doi:10.1080/02683960010008962

Kumar, K., & Van Hillegersberg, J. (2000). ERP: Experience and evolution. *Communications of the ACM*, *43*, 23–26.

Kumar, V. (2001). An investigation of critical management issues in ERP implementation: Empirical evidences from Canadian organizations. *Technovation*, *23*(10).

Lee, Z., & Lee, J. (2000). An ERP implementation study for a knowledge transfer perspective. *Journal of Information Technology*, *15*(4), 281–288. doi:10.1080/02683960010009060

Light, B. (2001). The maintenance implications of the customization of ERP software. *Journal of Software Maintenance and Evolution: Research and Practice*, *13*(6), 415–429. doi:10.1002/smr.240

Lycett, M., & Paul, R. J. (1999). Information Systems development: A perspective on the challenge of evolutionary complexity. *European Journal of Information Systems*, *8*, 127–135. doi:10.1057/palgrave.ejis.3000315

Madapusi, A., & Kuo, C. (2007). Assessing data and information quality in ERP systems. *Proceedings of the Decision Sciences Institute Annual Meeting,* Arizona.

Markus, M., & Tanis, C. (2001b). The enterprise system experience – from adoption to success. In Zmud, R. (Ed.), *Framing the domains of IT management: Projecting the future through the past* (pp. 173–207). Cincinnati, OH: Pinnflex Educational Resources.

Mensching, J., & Corbitt, G. (2004). EPR data archiving- a critical analysis. *Journal of Enterprise Information Management*, *17*(2), 131–141. doi:10.1108/17410390410518772

Moon, Y. B. (2007). Enterprise Resource Planning (ERP): A review of the literature. *International Journal of Management and Enterprise Development*, *4*(3), 235–264. doi:10.1504/IJMED.2007.012679

Nah, F. H. (2001a). Characteristics of ERP software maintenance: A multi-cause study. *Journal of Software Maintenance and Evolution: Research and Practice*, *13*(6), 339–414. doi:10.1002/smr.239

Nicolaou, I., & Bhattacharya, S. (2007). Organizational performance effects of ERP systems usage: The impact of post-implementation changes. *International Journal of Accounting Information Systems*, *7*(1), 18–35. doi:10.1016/j.accinf.2005.12.002

Nolan, R. (1979). Managing the crisis in data processing. *Harvard Business Review*, *57*(2), 115–126.

Parr, A., & Schanks, G. (2000). A model of ERP project implementation. *Journal of Information Technology*, *15*(4), 289–304. doi:10.1080/02683960010009051

Sawyer, S., & Southwick, R. (2002). Temporal issues in information and communication technology enabled organizational change. *The Information Society*, *18*, 263–280. doi:10.1080/01972240290075110

Schwalbe, K. (2000). *Information Technology project management*. Cambridge, MA: Course Technology.

Seddon, P. B. (1997). A re-specification and extension of the DeLone and McLean model of IS success. *Information Systems Research*, *18*(3), 240–253. doi:10.1287/isre.8.3.240

Sedera, D., et al. (2002). Enterprise resource planning systems impacts: A Delphi study of Australian public sector organizations. In *Proceedings of the Pacific Asia Conference on Information Systems (PACIS)* (pp. 584-600). Tokyo, Japan.

Sedera, D., et al. (2004). Measuring enterprise systems success: the importance of a multiple stakeholder perspective. In *Proceedings of the 12th European Conference on Information Systems* (pp. 1-13). Turku, Finland.

Soh, C. (2000). Cultural fits and misfits: Is ERP a universal solution? *Communications of the ACM*, *43*(4), 47–51. doi:10.1145/332051.332070

Spott, D. (2000). Componentizing the enterprise applications packages. *Communications of the ACM*, *43*(4), 63–90. doi:10.1145/332051.332074

Turban, E. (2006). *Information Technology for management: Transforming organizations in the digital economy* (5th ed.). John Wiley & Sons Inc.

Willcocks, L., & Sykes, R. (2000). The role of the CIO and IT function in ERP. *Communications of the ACM*, *43*, 33–38. doi:10.1145/332051.332065

Xu, H. (2002). Data quality issues in implementing an ERP. *Industrial Management & Data Systems*, *102*(1), 47–58. doi:10.1108/02635570210414668

KEY TERMS AND DEFINITIONS

Action Research: Is a process of progressive problem solving led by individuals working with others in teams or as part of a "community of practice" to improve the way they address issues and solve problems. Action research can also be undertaken by larger organizations or institutions, assisted or guided by professional researchers, with the aim of improving their strategies, practices, and knowledge of the environments within which they practice.

Business Process Management: Is a management approach focusing on aligning all aspects of an organization with the wants and needs of the stakeholders. It is a holistic management approach that promotes business effectiveness and efficiency while striving for innovation, flexibility, and integration with technology. If business process management attempts to improve processes continuously, the approach is then described as continuous process improvement (CPI). While, if the approach attempts to revamp the process, then it is often called business process re-engineering (BPR).

Enterprise Resources Planning (ERP): Is an integrated computer-based software system used to manage organizational internal and external resources. It is an architecture which facilitates the flow of information between all business functions within the boundaries of the organization and manages the interfaces with outside stakeholders.

ERP Implementation: To implement ERP systems, companies often seek the help of an ERP vendor or of third-party consulting companies. These firms typically provide three areas of professional services: consulting; customization; and support. The client organization often employs a change program management, business process analysis, and deployment management specialists to align their business requirements with the embedded ERP business processes during implementation.

IS Critical Success Factors: Is the term for an element that is necessary for IS project to achieve its mission. They are the critical factors or activities required for ensuring the success of deploying and adopting the IS in the organization. They represent those managerial or enterprise area that must be given special and continual attention to bring about high performance of implemented IS.

IS Success Model: Is a framework and model for measuring the complex dependent variable in IS research. IS Success Model is attributed to DeLone and McLean who originally developed and published the model in 1993 with an update in 2003, which discussed the utility for measuring IS system success within the framework of e-commerce systems.

Longitudinal Case study: Is a research study methodology that involves repeated observations of the same items over long periods of time. Longitudinal studies are often used in social science research context. The reason for this is that unlike cross-sectional studies, longitudinal studies track the same people, and therefore the differences observed in those people are less likely to be the result of cultural differences across generations. Because of this benefit, longitudinal studies make observing changes more.

Nolan Stage Model: The stages-of-growth model is a theoretical model for the growth of information technology (IT) in a business organization. It was developed by Richard L. Nolan during the 1970s, and published by him in the *Harvard Business Review*.

WINTEL Platform: WINTEL is a portmanteau of Windows and Intel. It usually refers to a computer system or the related ecosystem based on an Intel compatible processor and running the Microsoft Windows operating system.

Section 5
Marketing

In a highly competitive and turbulent market environments, carefully formulated, orchestrated, and meticulously implemented marketing strategies are imperative for gaining and retaining market share and profitability. The first case, "Ariel in Egypt," examines the past and present challenges facing Ariel, a long-time market leader in the detergent sector in Egypt whose market share has started to slip. In particular, it examines the marketing strategies and performance of Ariel High Suds, which is witnessing a declining market share as well as a decline in the overall high-suds market due to fierce competition and the growing low-suds market in Egypt. The second case, "Social Marketing in Egypt," focuses on the application of social marketing by charity and development-focused Egyptian NGO called Nahdet El Mahrousa (NM). NM initiated a creative model, whereby individuals and institutions are encouraged to seek NM's support in the start-up of any developmental initiative in Egypt. One of the projects that NM is proud to support is the "Young Innovators Awards" (YIA) program. After several successful years, the managing team faced the challenge of finding alternative sources of support in a tight time frame to avoid halting stopping the program all together. The third case, "The International Commercial and Industrial Investment Company, S.A.E (ICII)," operates in the trading of high-end power products and construction equipments, with Honda power products taking up the majority of the company's portfolio. Since the introduction of Chinese products into the Egyptian markets, Honda sales have been increasing, however at a decreasing rate. ICII is facing a number of challenges commonly faced by companies that operate in a highly segmented markets targeted by a plethora of product assortments. The main question raised is: what marketing strategy should the company implement in order to ensure its success and sustainability?

Chapter 13
Ariel Egypt:
From Market Penetration to Fierce Competition

Ahmed Tolba
American University in Cairo (AUC), Egypt

EXECUTIVE SUMMARY

This case study examines the past and present challenges facing Ariel, a long-time market leader in the detergent sector in Egypt whose market share has started to slip. In particular, it examines the marketing strategies and performance of Ariel High Suds, which is witnessing a declining market share as well as a decline in the overall high-suds market due to fierce competition and the growing low-suds market in Egypt.

INTRODUCTION

"Ariel ranks number one top-of-mind brand in Egypt, ahead of even Coke and Pepsi! That's an incredible success story," said Hany Farouk, Ariel Egypt Brand Manager, beaming at Waleed Azmy, Account Manager of Saatchi & Saatchi, the promotional company of Procter & Gamble (P&G), and at Hamed Ibrahim, its General Manager. Ibrahim nodded in satisfaction, saying: "Ariel will always be the brand of the people that provides superior cleaning no matter what happens in the market, thanks to 13 years of road shows and events that have brought Ariel so close to the hearts and minds of Egyptian consumers." Smiling, Azmy added: "And don't forget that Ariel was the pioneer in introducing the reality concept in its campaigns, and competitors are just trying to replicate our ideas." Farouk took a deep breath and added: "But we need to save the position of Ariel Hand Wash in the market. We

DOI: 10.4018/978-1-60960-583-4.ch013

have lost significant market share to competitors and to Ariel Automatic Wash as well."

After Azmy and Ibrahim left, Farouk returned to his office. He glanced quickly through his Ariel High-Suds file, pausing for a minute as it opened on one of the office's most prized documents, a one-page memo addressed to the head of P&G's Board of Directors about Ariel Hand Wash (High Suds) Egypt. The memo was included in a book on P&G's success stories, honoring the brand as one of the major successes in P&G's history. Farouk had spent the last 8 years at P&G and had witnessed a great part of Ariel's success story. As he reflected on the evolution of Ariel in Egypt, he pondered its future. "Will Ariel be able to maintain its lead position, both in the market and in the minds of consumers?" he wondered. He believed that saving the brand from the various challenges in the market was a serious responsibility.

Taking the file with him, Farouk left his office to go to a very important meeting with Ahmed Samy, P&G Egypt General Manager. The meeting had been convened to discuss the future of Ariel High Suds in Egypt. Samy recognized the urgency of the problems facing the brand and wanted a detailed discussion and analysis of the situation in order to take quick action.

As Farouk made his way to the meeting, he mentally reviewed Ariel's history and Ariel High Sud's marketing strategies and performance.

ORGANIZATIONAL BACKGROUND

Procter & Gamble

P&G was established in 1837 by two Europeans who immigrated to the United States: William Procter, English candle maker, and James Gamble, Irish soap maker. Headquartered in Cincinnati-Ohio in the USA, P&G is considered the leading consumer goods company, with a mission to improve the lives of consumers wherever it operates. P&G is an internationally owned company with publicly traded shares, currently owned by over one million shareholders from around the globe.

Since 1980, P&G has quadrupled the number of consumers it serves with its brands, to now reach about 5 billion people around the world. P&G operates in more than 80 countries and markets more than 250 brands in 130 countries. The multinational company employs nearly 106,000 people worldwide.

One of the chief reasons for P&G's success is its emphasis on Research & Development (R&D). In the year 2000 alone, P&G invested $1.7 billion in R&D through 19 technical centers and about 100 universities around the world. Extensive market research has allowed P&G to understand what consumers want and need, and to invest massively in scientific and technological research to develop new products that satisfy such needs. Many of these world brands (Ariel, Tide, Pert Plus, Pantene Pro-V, Head & Shoulders, Pampers and Always) have become famous household names and can be found in almost every home. (See Tables 1 and 2 and Figure 1)

Procter & Gamble Egypt

P&G Egypt began its operations in 1986, producing Camay soap and Crest toothpaste in a plant located at 6th of October City, right outside Cairo. For the remainder of the decade, P&G continued expanding its manufacturing operations. Expansion activities included the construction of a synthetic detergent tower in 1990 to produce the Ariel brand. Since the turn of the century, P&G Egypt has continued to introduce new products in the market. Examples include Tide and Downy alongside Ariel automatic and Ariel hand wash in the detergents sector; baby care products such as Pampers; feminine products such as Always; shampoos such as Pantene, Pert Plus and Head & Shoulders; and - in addition to Camay - soap bars such as Zest.

P&G Egypt employs over 1000 highly trained people. Through capital investments of over LE

Table 1. P&G sales per global business unit (2002)

Global Business Unit	Key Brands	Sales ($ billion)	% Total Sales
Baby, Feminine & Family Care	Pampers, Charmin, Bounty, Always	11.9	30%
Fabric & Home Care	Tide, Ariel, Downy, Lenor, Bold, Swifer, Bounce, Fairy, Febreze	11.6	29%
Beauty Care	Pantene, Head & Shoulders, Olay, Pert Plus, Clairol Herbal Essences, Hugo Boss, Ivory, Camay, Zest, Old Spice, Physique	8.1	20%
Health Care	Crest, Vicks, Asacol, Actonel	5.0	12%
Food & Beverage	Pringles, Sunny Delight	3.8	9%

Table 2. P&G global financial summary (2002) (in million dollars)*

	2002	2001	2000	1999	1998
Net Sales	40,238	39,244	39,951	38,125	37,154
Operating Income	6,678	4,736	5,954	6,253	6,055
Net Earnings	4,352	2,922	3,542	3,765	3,780
Core Net Earnings **	5,058	4,615	4,442	4,338	3,947
Net Earnings Margin	10.8%	7.4%	8.9%	9.9%	10.2%
Core Net Earnings Margin	12.6%	11.7%	11.1%	11.4%	10.6%
Basic Net Earnings Per Common Share	3.26	2.15	2.61	2.75	2.74
Diluted Net Earnings Per Common Share	3.09	2.07	2.47	2.59	2.56
Diluted Core Earnings Per Common Share	3.59	3.27	3.10	2.98	2.68
Dividends Per Common Share	1.52	1.40	1.28	1.14	1.01
R&D Expenses	1,601	1,769	1,899	1,726	1,546
Advertising Expenses	3,773	3,612	3,793	3,639	3,801
Total Assets	40,776	34,387	34,366	32,192	31,042
Capital Expenditure	1,679	2,486	3,018	2,828	2,559
Long-term Debt	11,201	9,792	9,012	6,265	5,774
Shareholders' Equity	13,706	12,010	12,287	12,058	12,236

* Except for per share figures
** Core excludes restructuring costs

Figure 1. P&G sales per global business unit (2002)

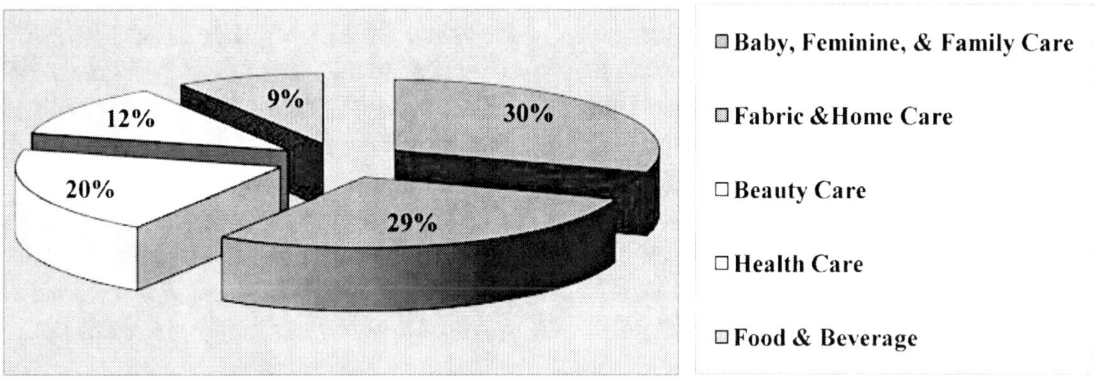

120 million (about $20 million), the company has confirmed its commitment to further growth in the Egyptian market by expanding its Ariel production facilities to create the largest detergent tower in the region, making P&G Egypt the regional production center for Ariel. Its total investments increased from LE 12 million in 1986 to LE 800 million in 2002.

The Detergent Market in Egypt

In 1989, the Egyptian market had hardly any detergent products. P&G took the lead in introducing the first detergent brand in the market: Ariel. This was quite a challenge, since it meant changing the old washing tradition of using laundry bars, to introduce consumers to a new way of washing that they were unaccustomed to. Ariel's positioning was "*a detergent with excellent cleaning performance, tough stain removal, and superior whiteness.*"

SETTING THE STAGE

Product Introduction

In developing countries like Egypt, a very high percentage of the population cannot afford to buy an automatic washing machine and so use hand wash detergents instead. Ariel was introduced in Egypt in 1986 as a washing machine detergent (Ariel Low Suds). By 1989, the laundry bar dominated the hand wash and non-automatic washing machine market, while the automatic washing machine market was still premature. In 1990, P&G decided to introduce Ariel High Suds for hand washing and for non-automatic washing machines to strengthen its operation and benefit from the potential target market. The challenge was to educate consumers to get them to shift from bar soap to a premium detergent like Ariel.

Consumer Behavior

In order to efficiently satisfy their target markets, businesses should focus on identifying market needs and/or wants and create a product that is "driven by that understanding" (Meredith, 2010). One of Procter & Gamble's secrets of success is its heavy reliance on marketing research. P&G likes to study potential markets extensively, even if this makes the company relatively slow to enter a new market. Investing in valuable research helps the company not only introduces successful products, but also sustains this success over a long period of time. Accordingly, P&G conducts extensive research in the Egyptian market through focus groups, ethnographic research and other qualitative research methods. Ethnographic research is especially beneficial because it shows how people behave in their homes and how they use the product. It also deepens marketers' understanding of consumer behavior, allowing them to reflect their observations on their marketable products (Anderson, 2009). P&G discovered that the cleaning process in Egypt was very long and that Ariel would provide consumers with a solution that both saved time and ensured superior cleaning.

Prior to the introduction of Ariel High Suds, consumers used to have a "*Washing Day*" that involved a whole process. *Soaking* was the first step in the process for most consumers. This activity, whose purpose was to ensure better cleaning and removal of stains, required more than 8 hours; so many of the consumers would soak their washing overnight. Most consumers used detergents in soaking, while a few used bleach. *Boiling* was the second step in the washing process and lasted about 30 to 40 minutes. The objective of boiling was to ensure proper cleaning, prevent infection, remove stains, and ensure whiteness. *Rubbing* was the last step in the washing process and was done to ensure cleaning and stain removal. In the long rubbing process, housewives used mainly bar soaps at first; then, gradually, they started shifting to powder detergents.

Educating Consumers: Changing the Rules of the Game

The idea of *superior performance using the power of built-in additives* was totally new to the market. Extensive efforts were needed to educate the consumer, so that they would, first, believe in this new technology, and second, decide to use it. One of the major challenges facing Ariel was how to change consumer habits. As a matter of fact, the first trial activities showed that consumers were resistant to the idea of using a detergent with additives. It was initially assumed that they would appreciate the time saved, but surprisingly, they did not. *Washing Day* was a social event where rural women would not only see each other and chat, but also compete for the best cleaning recipes! Cleaning for these women was like cooking; it showed how competent they were. Asking them to use one detergent that substituted all their efforts faced strong social resistance. The marketing team had to find a way to convince the consumers of the value offered and to change their social habits.

Trial Activities

P&G started educating consumers through trial activities, skimming through the market to reach consumers personally. Obviously, advertising was not the tool to use at this stage of market development. The company needed to show consumers what the product was capable of doing. In 1991, P&G launched one of the biggest *Door-to-Door* (DTD) activities in the region, covering 5.5 million homes in 6 months (almost 95% of the total urban population) and offering consumers the product at 20% of its price. A year later, another DTD activity was conducted in rural areas, covering 3.8 million homes. In parallel, the product was pushed to consumers through in-store promotions, and to customers through auxiliary sales forces to reinforce distribution and ensure product availability in the areas covered by the trial activities.

Despite the size of the campaign and the extensive efforts involved, the marketing team was not satisfied with the results achieved. Consumers were not yet convinced. Most of them used the product occasionally, while maintaining their traditional washing processes. People needed to be convinced through further face-to-face activities. Also, they needed to relate to the brand emotionally and link it to their daily lives. It looked like a tough challenge, but the P&G team was determined to overcome it. The question was: How?

The "Road Show" Concept: The Breakthrough

Again, P&G decided to rely on its strongest competency: research. The objective was to find a creative way to talk to consumers and convince them about the product. From here came the idea of meeting consumers in their gathering places. Research results pointed to two possible gathering events: 1) The "Utensils Washing Day", where women would get together by the lake in the morning to chat, joke and wash their utensils; and 2) The marketplace or "*souk*", where people flocked to buy a variety of household and other items and to see each other. From an execution standpoint, the first option was not feasible and option 2 seemed more doable. Extensive research was conducted on *souks* in Egypt. Existing *souks* in all 26 governorates were mapped and 824 *souks* all over the country were identified. Through them, the marketing team expected to target at least 90% of the women in the country – in addition to men, if they were the decision makers, especially in conservative areas like Upper Egypt.

The "Ariel Road Show" was the first broad-scale innovative sampling program in Egypt, and since then, has become a world-famous marketing tool that has been replicated in several countries. Road shows are one of the pillars of Ariel's success. The idea was to have a van or big truck with branding all over it, bringing joy to people in the villages. P&G would also paint the walls of the village buildings with Ariel logos, to increase awareness and popularity. The road show would start off as an entertainment event, to attract consumers and create awareness. In the earlier road shows, musicians stood in small trucks, playing music to attract consumers. Later, bigger trucks were used, well-equipped with huge TV screens, videos and advertisements, along with a big sound system and microphones that blared out the most popular songs of the time. It was a full day of entertainment for thousands of people. A clown would play with children, and raffles were held and prizes distributed. Afterwards, the P&G team would do some "demos" - take a piece of clothing, ask a woman from among the spectators to put some mud or dirt on it, and get her to wash it in front of everybody. Field challenges were also introduced to convince consumers that Ariel does it all. Ariel packs were initially sold at a very low price, then at a discounted price, then at full price.

Event marketers believe that in order to assess the success of road shows, objectives should be set prior to the event and then compared to the actual results generated after the event, a task most marketers neglect to perform. Following up with customers after the event and repeating the events frequently could yield more positive results (Barker, 2005). In the case of the Ariel road shows, the objective of the project was to cover the 824 *souks* using 12 teams working in parallel. When evaluating the impact of the road shows, some of the *souks* were found to be more effective than others, especially the ones that take place on a weekly basis. Currently, Ariel road shows cover about 400 *souks* that are believed to be the most significant.

CASE DESCRIPTION: PATH TO MARKET LEADERSHIP

Over a period of four years (1990-1993), Ariel managed to double the powder detergent market with a commanding 37% market share, by growing its sales volume 12-fold! In 2003, Ariel High Suds was still leading the detergents market, maintaining its dominating market share despite fierce competition and the economic downturn in the Egyptian market. Ariel was so successful in Egypt that P&G was and continues to be referred to as "*The Ariel Company*". Ariel's success model was applied in other countries, such as Russia, Morocco, and Yemen.

Market Analysis

Prior to the introduction of Ariel High Suds, the market was dominated by laundry bar soap (100% household usage). Detergents represented almost 30% of the market and consisted basically of a couple of low-quality local brands. The introduction of Ariel was a turning point in the market, to the extent that in 1996, the market share of detergents reached more than 70%, while bar soaps were used in only 30% of households despite the fact that Ariel was 60% more expensive on a per gram basis.

By 1996, the detergents market was divided between high-suds detergents, which are used only in hand washing and non-automatic washing machines, and low-suds detergents, used specifically in automatic washing machines. By that time, the high-suds detergent market was 2.5 times that of 1990. High suds were used by 80% of the population (C, D, E classes mainly in rural areas), while the remaining 20% (A, B, C+ classes living in urban areas) used low-suds detergents.

Competition

Prior to the introduction of Ariel, two local low-quality high-suds detergents were competing in the market (Savo and Rabso). Savo and Rabso were produced by companies owned by the public sector. The two brands were low-tier products – low-price brands targeting the C&D social classes. Ariel was the only brand in the high-tier market, targeting the upper social crust of the population

Table 3. High-suds market trends (1990-1996)

	1990	1992	1994	1996
Detergents	100	135	188	282
Laundry Bar Soaps	225	185	140	100
Detergents (% Market)	31%	42%	57%	71%
Bar Soap Usage (% Household)	100%	65%	40%	30%
Market Shares				
Ariel	0%	24%	28%	39%
Persil	—	—	10%	8%
Omo	—	—	4%	7%
Total High-Tier	0%	24%	42%	54%

that typically uses relatively high-priced products of better quality. Ariel remained the only brand in the high-tier market for 3 years, until Unilever introduced Omo and Henkel introduced Persil. By 1996, the high-tier market represented 54% of the detergents market (39% Ariel and 15% Persil & Omo combined). (See Table 3). There was a clear growth trend in the detergent market at the expense of laundry bar soaps. Similarly, there was a growth trend in the high-tier market at the expense of the low-tier market. Ariel had a commanding lead on the high-tier market, given its first-mover advantage. However, it was expected that Persil and Omo would try to acquire market share in this maturing market.

Marketing Strategy

Ariel was successful in Egypt because of its integrated marketing strategy, where each element in the marketing mix was consistent with the brand's overall strategy.

Brand Positioning

Ariel's global brand positioning is "*Detergent with excellent cleaning performance, tough stain removal, and superior whiteness*". Global brands usually seem attractive to businesses because they are cost effective and because they achieve efficiency from operating on a global scale. However, global brands need to relate to their customers by customizing their positioning, taking into consideration cultural differences amongst nations (Eisingerich, & Rubera, 2010). Ariel High Suds in Egypt was positioned consistently with its global equity, stressing on superior cleaning and stain removal. Consistent with its positioning, Ariel was introduced to the Egyptian market at a premium price that is fairly justified by the quality of washing it offers. The magic formula was positioned as a substitute for all the additives used in the long washing process. The P&G team always stressed Ariel's superior performance in cleaning and removing stains, and this image has remained in the minds of consumers through Ariel's 13-year lifetime.

Road shows had a direct impact on consumers, who associated Ariel with feasts, festivals, joy, music, and prizes. The road shows helped develop Ariel's brand character: "*brand of the people*". It is impossible to separate "superior performance" and "brand of the people" because together, they formulate Ariel's equity in the Egyptian market. Along with advertising excellent stain removal, Ariel engaged in social activities such as sponsoring TV programs like *El Sit Dih Ommi* and *Kalam Min Dahab*, which link the brand to people not just from a social responsibility dimension, but from a "brand fundamentals" perspective. The minute the marketing team forgot about the superior cleaning or link-to-the-people dimension, brand performance was immediately negatively affected.

Product Strategy: Continuous Innovation

Consistent with its brand equity, Ariel simply stands for "*Superior Performance*". Ariel has always been perceived as a premium product. The concept of "*power of built-in additives*" was very successful in the first six years when the market was being developed and consumers were switching from bar soaps and the traditional washing day system to Ariel's magical formula.

Product innovation is a crucial attribute that gives brands a competitive advantage and ensures the sustainability of the product's market share. In order to successfully "innovate", a company should have adequate knowledge of their target market and their competitors as well as an efficient R&D department (Durisin, Calabretta, & Parmeggiani, 2010). Innovation was a key ingredient in Ariel's strategy. Continuous offerings were essential to bring news to consumers and keep them updated on what Ariel would offer next. Upgrades every now and then were crucial to sustain Ariel's image and ensure consumer satisfaction. Market research was continuously conducted to ensure that the product was appealing to consumers. Through market research, new ideas were obtained to help in strategic and tactical planning.

Ariel was the first detergent to use enzymes and bleach. It was also the first detergent offered in "polybag" *packaging*, while all other detergents available in the market at that time were offered in cartons. Polybags have the advantage of being much cheaper than cartons, yet provide consumers with relevant moisture protection. Ariel was also the first detergent to introduce a "*single wash*" package size, leveraging from research on local habits. A 125gm sachet has been (and still is) the most successful size in the detergent market.

Pricing Strategy

As a brand offering superior performance, Ariel's pricing strategy was clear: to be at the high-end of the market, where the value offered to consumers justifies the premium price. When it was first introduced, the price of Ariel was at +60% compared to bar soaps on a per gram basis.

Distribution Strategy

One of Ariel's major strengths is its distribution system. The system follows its marketing activities, such as its DTD activities and road shows. The objective is to make the product available in the areas covered by awareness and trial activities. Ultimately, the aim is to reach all segments all over Egypt. Accordingly, the slogan "brand of the people" does not target a particular segment. By 2003, Ariel's distribution successfully covered 90+% of the market.

In 1990, when Ariel was still in its early stages, the market was totally fragmented, with 120,000 stores. The public sector played a major role in product distribution through its network of 2,500 outlets. Accordingly, P&G started its distribution drive by focusing on public sector outlets, which worked as wholesalers for the smaller retail and grocery stores. Alignment between marketing and sales drives was key to Ariel's success. Ariel was easily distributed in rural areas, where consumer pulls existed (given Ariel marketing activities such as its DTD activities and road shows). Later on, when the number of retail stores increased significantly, P&G recognized the need to have exclusive distributors to help the sales team cover as many outlets as possible through qualified sales people. To this end, a large number of sales people were hired and trained.

Visibility is a key element in the distribution strategy. Egyptians generally like big things. So Ariel offered its customers big flags and big posters through its successful road shows.

Advertising and Promotion Strategy: The "Reality" Concept

Here again, Ariel's strategy was consistent with the two fundamentals of its equity: superior cleaning and brand of the people. Ariel's promotion strategy was built on two major vehicles: targeted advertising and sponsorship of TV programs.

A. Advertising Campaigns: The Reality Concept

Through research, P&G's marketing team came up with another innovative idea for its advertising campaigns: using "*real-life people*" in the ads to illustrate a "*real slice of life*". The team realized that no one could speak to simple people in their language and relate to their lifestyle better than one of them. This approach gave more credibility to the ads, and tied in perfectly with the "brand of the people" concept. This strategy was replicated not only by competitors in the detergents market, but also by companies in other sectors, such as Vodafone, the mobile company! All Ariel campaigns aimed to convince consumers to switch from bar soaps and additives to Ariel detergent. The main objective was to *develop the market* where competition was almost non-existent.

A key success factor in Ariel's strategy was the *nation-wideness* of ads, which touched all kinds of people all over Egypt. The first four campaigns (1990-97) stressed the concept of "*power of built-in additives*". Real-life women, rather than celebrities, were used in the ads to ensure credibility. These women talked in a way that other Egyptian women could relate to.

Changes from one campaign to the other were limited to the campaign idea. No changes were made to the campaign vehicle or concept. The idea was to capture the attention of consumers and maintain their excitement about the product by continuously introducing something new that would reinforce the superiority and innovativeness of the brand.

In 1997-98, a celebrity called Karima Mokhtar led Ariel's campaigns. She was a public mother figure and enjoyed a high level of credibility. She was famous for her programs on health issues and family planning. Her role in the campaigns was to make people aware of the importance of Ariel in their lives, including its role in hygiene, such as killing germs and removing odors.

In 2000, Ariel's ads started to deviate from the core fundamental advantage of "superior cleaning" by portraying some side functional benefits, like rejuvenation and the all-in-one aspect. It was argued that the competition (mainly Persil) benefited from this deviation, taking the opportunity to stress heavily on superior cleaning and performance in their ads.

Currently, Ariel has recognized the importance of emphasizing the two major equity dimensions in its ads: "superior cleaning" and "brand of the people". The "reality" concept is also being further exploited. Research has shown that real-life people in ads should be inspirational, so that consumers can associate with them and aspire to be like them. Consumers also need to get away from their problems. Accordingly, Ariel started to rely on more cheerful people telling stories about their lives, and placing greater emphasis on execution to make the ads more effective. (See Table 4)

B. TV Programs

As a starting point, Ariel exclusively sponsored "*Kalam Min Dahab*" - or "Words of Gold" - the best-rated TV program in Egypt at that time. The idea of the program was to ask consumers some general knowledge questions; the winner received a gold Egyptian pound. At the end of the show, Ariel donated money or offered help to people in need. In addition, Ariel offered raffle prizes

Table 4. Ariel advertising campaigns

"Rural Women" (1990-92) The objective of this TV campaign was to bring about a change in habit and encourage consumers to switch from bar soaps to powder detergents. The key points differentiating Ariel from bar soaps were superior cleaning and nice smell. The campaign also stressed that there was no need for additives. The campaign slogan was: "*Not just cleaning, but cleaning that dazzles*". The team went nationwide trying to find real-life women who could be cast in the ads.
"Book of Ariel" (1993-95) By that time, the road shows were successfully convincing consumers that additives were not needed. The stories in the ads were very natural and used colloquial Arabic and jargon that people could relate to. These stories, which built on the successes of the road shows and stories of real-life people, were included in Ariel's special book, which was distributed at special events and road shows.
"Millions of Women" (1995/96) Again, the main objective of this campaign was to convince women that, with Ariel, they did not need additives to clean their clothes. The change was in the campaign idea, not the vehicle or the concept. Innovation was needed through either product or conceptual upgrades. First, the focus was on the power of built-in additives and the removal of tough stains; later, a green powder was introduced as a new addition to the formula that improved the product significantly.
"The Map of Egypt" & "Memories from the Heart" (1997) The objective of the ads was to show that Ariel had the power of super soap; it was an all-in-one product that provided the best cleaning. The ads also emphasized the emotional aspects related to the "brand of the people" equity.
"Pride of the Nation" (1998-99) This was a nationwide campaign that involved real-life women telling their stories. At times, the content was too candid, which led to censorship issues. The objective of the campaign was to communicate that Ariel is the brand of the people and an integral part of daily life, and that it makes one look good and helps one achieve more in life.
"Rejuvenation" (2000) This campaign did not focus on actual functional benefits. Rather, the idea was to make clothes look new. The campaign was not very successful at the time because it deviated from the fundamental benefit of superior cleaning.
"Demanding Professionals" (2001) The ads were back to real-life women, with improvement in execution, focusing on the professions and achievements of their husbands.
"Demanding Persons" (2003) The ads moved from successful professionals to demanding persons with high standards. Ariel helps them achieve success in their life in general, not just in their career or profession.

for people who proved loyal to the brand by, for example, collecting the largest number of bags in a specific period of time. This program strengthened the bond between Ariel and its consumers. Special songs and jingles were introduced in the show and ads to increase recall. The show was very successful, boosting Ariel's image as the brand of the people and giving it popularity and appeal among Egyptian consumers. The program lasted for a long period of time and consistently helped Ariel sustain its image in the market.

At a later stage, Ariel continued to use TV programs, such as "*El Sit Dih Ommi*" - or "This Woman is my Mother." This was another successful program that aimed to show the role a mother can play in the success of a person, usually a celebrity. It highlighted the emotional relationship between mother and son/daughter. Ariel, the sponsor, inserted its ads and prizes. The program helped Ariel maintain its rapport with consumers, as they continued to relate Ariel to their personal lives.

C. Social Responsibility & Public Relations

As the "brand of the people", Ariel claims a duty much bigger than normal social responsibility. Part of its equity is to run social activity programs in order to reinforce the bond with people. Through road shows, TV programs, raffles and prizes, Ariel has maintained a credible and reliable image in the

Table 5. Pricing comparison

	Ariel	Persil	Omo	Tide
Price vs. Ariel	100	100	95	85

Table 6. Market share trends

Brand	1999	2000	2001	2002
Ariel	51%	49%	43%	39%
Persil	14%	16%	18%	22%
Tide	4%	4%	5%	6%

minds of consumers, who await Ariel's surprises every year.

CURRENT CHALLENGES

Market Growth and Competitiveness

Market Analysis: From Developing the Market to Defending Market Share

Ariel has definitely enjoyed "first mover advantages" (FMA), a widely known marketing concept that refers to how companies that are pioneers in entering a market enjoy the lion's share of profits since they gain "a head start" over competitors (Frynas, Mellahi, & Pigman, 2006). However, starting 1997, two multinational companies, Unilever and Henkel, recognized the potential in the growing detergent market in Egypt and decided to follow P&G into the market. *Unilever* introduced "Omo" as a high-quality brand to compete with Ariel in both the high suds and low suds markets. Similarly, *Henkel* introduced "Persil" as a high-quality brand in both the high suds and low suds markets. The high suds market was divided as follows:

- **High-Tier Market:** Ariel (P&G), Persil (Henkel) and Omo (Unilever)
- **Mid-Tier Market:** Tide (P&G)
- **Low-Tier Market:** Rabso (local companies) and Savo (local companies)

Competition

Tables 5, 6 and Figure 2 show the pricing and market shares of Ariel and its competitors. It is clear that the high-tier market is declining in relation to the mid/low tier markets. Additionally, Ariel is suffering loss of market share to Persil. Ariel's major competitive challenge is basically to dominate the high-tier market and stop Persil's growth. At the same time, Ariel needs to convince loyal consumers to stick to Ariel, which offers superior value, instead of switching to lower-tier brands.

High-Tier Brand: Persil

Positioning: Persil was positioned as a premium detergent with superior cleaning performance. A lot of Persil's equity has been acquired from Ariel's positioning. However, Persil has not been able to acquire the concept of "brand of the people".

Product: Persil's product is comparable to Ariel in terms of cleaning performance. Persil has also improved its formula over time by introducing continuous product upgrades.

Pricing: Persil was initially priced at parity with Ariel. However, in 1996, the price of Persil

Figure 2. Market share trends

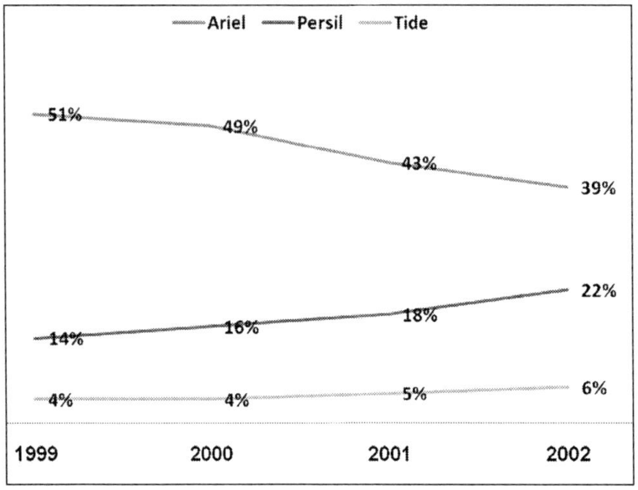

was reduced to a 15% discount compared to Ariel, in the hope of gaining market share. It had taken some time for Persil to establish itself in the market, but the discounted price was a successful trial tool. In 2001, Ariel also cut its price and since then, both brands have been priced at parity.

Distribution: One of Persil's weaknesses was its modest distribution, which represented an edge for Ariel in the 1990s. Through aggressive trade margins and promotions, Persil eventually improved its coverage significantly to reach almost 80% today (versus Ariel's 90+ %). It is clear that the distribution gap between the two brands is shrinking.

Promotions and Advertising: Persil has strived to find a strong position in the market by emphasizing superior cleaning, the "German" formula, the use of new technology, and its latest concept "*removing stains from the roots*". Persil used a very popular and credible celebrity called Abla Kamel whom people simply loved and who she was definitely the energizer of Persil campaigns. Persil's ads also replicated Ariel's idea of using real-life women. Abla Kamel would convince them to switch to Persil by "going inside the fabric and removing the stains from their roots". This campaign was very successful, especially at a time when Ariel was advertising side benefits like rejuvenation. Consequently, Persil used the campaign slogan "*All of Egypt is switching to Persil*", which had a powerful impact that was reflected in their share growth, especially as Ariel was suffering from boycott issues, being an American company.

Mid/Low-Tier Brand: Tide

Tide is P&G's brand in the mid-tier market, with a market share of almost 7%. The mid-tier market lies between the high and low tier markets; it offers good quality products at reasonable prices. Tide was positioned as a good cleaning brand that provides "*superior whiteness*". It is priced at a 15% discount compared with Ariel and Persil. Its major problem is poor distribution. Greater emphasis needs to be placed on advertising to create an adequate consumer pool that, in turn, will drive better distribution. The brand is growing because of adequate pricing and promotional efforts. However, the current level of spending on the brand is not enough to ensure further growth.

Table 7. High-suds market trends (1990-2002)

	1990	1992	1994	1996	1998	2000	2002
Index vs. 1990	100	135	188	282	260	240	230
Index vs. two years prior	100	135	139	150	92	92	96

Future of Ariel High Suds

Market Saturation and Trends

Despite the growing competition, the total high-suds market has started to shrink because of market saturation as well as the growth of the low-suds market. It has been predicted that this trend will continue as long as consumers' purchasing power for automatic washing machines continues to grow. Several factors have encouraged the shift from high-suds detergents to low-suds detergents. For instance, P&G conducted a campaign with IDEAL (a local manufacturer of home appliances) whereby any customer buying an IDEAL washing machine would get free Ariel (Automatic) detergents for 1 year. (See Table 7)

Ahmed Samy glanced through Ariel's latest Business Review and said to Farouk: "It seems we need to act fast; otherwise, we will lose more market share. Ariel High Suds has a history and we need to save its position in the market." Several questions ran through his mind: What could be done to defend Ariel's market share given the fact that the brand had become a cash cow, now that the high-suds market was approaching the decline stage? How could they defend Ariel's leadership and stop Persil's continuous growth? Was the declining high-suds market worth investment in the first place, or should they allocate more resources to the growing low-suds market led by Ariel? Samy decided to call an urgent Executive Leadership Committee meeting to discuss the issue from all dimensions. Time was of the essence and, if they waited, competitors would take action that might negatively affect Ariel High Suds sales.

REFERENCES

Anderson, K. (2009). Ethnographic research: A key to strategy. *Harvard Business Review*, *87*(3), 24.

Barker, J. (2005). Show time. *Sales & Marketing Management, 157*(26).

Durisin, B., Calabretta, G., & Parmeggiani, V. (2010). The intellectual structure of product innovation research: A bibliometric study of the journal of product innovation management, 1984-2004. *Journal of Product Innovation Management*, *27*(3), 437–451. doi:10.1111/j.1540-5885.2010.00726.x

Eisingerich, A., & Rubera, G. (2010). Drivers of brand commitment: A cross national investigation. *Journal of International Marketing*, *8*(2), 64–65. doi:10.1509/jimk.18.2.64

Frynas, J., Mellahi, K., & Pigman, G. (2006). First mover advantages in international business and firm-specific political resources. *Strategic Management Journal*, *27*(4), 324. doi:10.1002/smj.519

Meredith, B. H. (2010). Where does growth really come from? *NZ Business*, *24*(1), 63.

Chapter 14
Social Marketing in Egypt:
A Case Study on the Use of Marketing by "Nahdet El Mahrousa" NGO

Mohamed Ads
Danette, Egypt

Ahmed Tolba
American University in Cairo (AUC), Egypt

EXECUTIVE SUMMARY

The following case focuses on the concept of social marketing in Egypt and how it is applied at the charity and development-focused non-governmental organization (NGO) Nahdet El Mahrousa (NM). This is one of the recently established NGOs; it has initiated a creative model, whereby individuals and institutions are encouraged to seek their support in starting a local developmental initiative. One of the projects that NM is proud to support is the "Young Innovators Awards" (YIA) program, which was launched in 2004. It could be considered one of the success stories of social marketing. However, after several successful years, the program turned into a dilemma for its managing team, when its main source of funding was not available anymore. They were faced with the challenge of finding alternative sources of financial support in a limited amount of time to evade the drawbacks of stopping the program all together.

INTRODUCTION

On the 17th of September 2009, Chairman of the board of directors of Nahdet El Mahrousa (NM) NGO, Loay El Shawarby, was looking outside his office window in Downtown Cairo, as he was thinking deeply about the dilemma that got into his hands. He had just received a call from the Director of the Young Innovators Awards program (YIA), Mohamed El Zarkani, confirming the news that the program's main sponsor, who supports over eighty percent of the funds is withdrawing as of the 2009-2010 academic year. The YIA program aims at enhancing the culture of research and develop-

DOI: 10.4018/978-1-60960-583-4.ch014

ment amongst Egyptian scientists. El Shawarby, who was one of the founders of NM, and the one who started YIA, remembered the program's early days when it only existed at a single university and was funded by three individual donors.

Today, five years later, YIA has grown exponentially, covering all 22 universities in Egypt and has more than five hundred participants. The YIA program is one of the main projects of NM, and also one of its success stories. However, a large part of this exponential growth was based on the surge of funds coming from only one donor institution, which also contributed to his current issue, as the absence of this donor institution in the academic year of 2009 -2010 threatens to bring the program to a halt that year, which could undermine all the past success of YIA and adversely affect the credibility of NM.

As El Shawarby observed the afternoon rush hour, he was going over possible solutions before going into the meeting with NM's managing board and YIA's program director and coordinators. They had to decide on the next steps, which have to be determined before September 22, the starting date of the YIA, as agreed upon with the universities across Egypt. He knew that the continuity of this program now depended on their success in developing a new marketing strategy to raise the needed funds from other sources to cover its projected expenses, within a limited time to plan and act before the scheduled start date of the academic year.

BACKGROUND: NAHDET EL MAHROUSA

Established in 2003 by a group of young Egyptian professionals, NM sought out to promote a positive spirit amongst Egyptian youth, building their sense of ownership towards their country, to be able to positively impact Egypt's "Cultural, economic and Social development" on the long run (See Figure 1), according to their official website. The NGO's mission is "engaging and activating Egyptian young professionals in the development and public arenas and in shaping Egypt's future". Their vision is to create "a developed Egypt through the active participation and belonging of its young professionals." NM's Board of Directors is composed of seven members with the task of ensuring that NM's operations conform with all regulatory rules and requirements; building managerial, financial and human resources' capacity for the organization; offering support to new incubated projects; and managing NM's communication with all external entities. Furthermore, NM is operating with the collaboration of several strategic partners such as British Petroleum (BP), El Sewedy Cables, LINKdotNET, Mobinil and Procter & Gamble (P&G). In addition, members of NM can further assist the organization by paying for membership, becoming a staff member or by volunteering to its operations.

NM introduced the innovative model of the "Incubator," which acted as a flourishing spot for different development ideas, by pooling resources of various stakeholders who can contribute in the establishment of these ideas into sustainable social enterprise. An "Incubator" by definition is "an economic and social development process designed to advise potential start-up projects, and through a comprehensive capacity building and assistance program, help them establish and accelerate their growth and success". NM was the first in the world to create an incubator for Innovative Social Enterprises and is now trying to spread this concept throughout all of Egypt. All incubated ideas have to be innovative, with a clear plan and potential impact on society's development, and stemming from the areas of enrichment of youth, arts and culture, health services, preserving and protecting the environment, as well as bridging education to employment, and promoting scientific research and development culture.

The founders of NM believed in the importance of managing their young NGO as a growing

Figure 1. Growth rate of NGOs in Egypt during the past ten years. (According to Mr. Ihab Medhat, directing manager of the center of information and decision support of NGOs in Egypt)

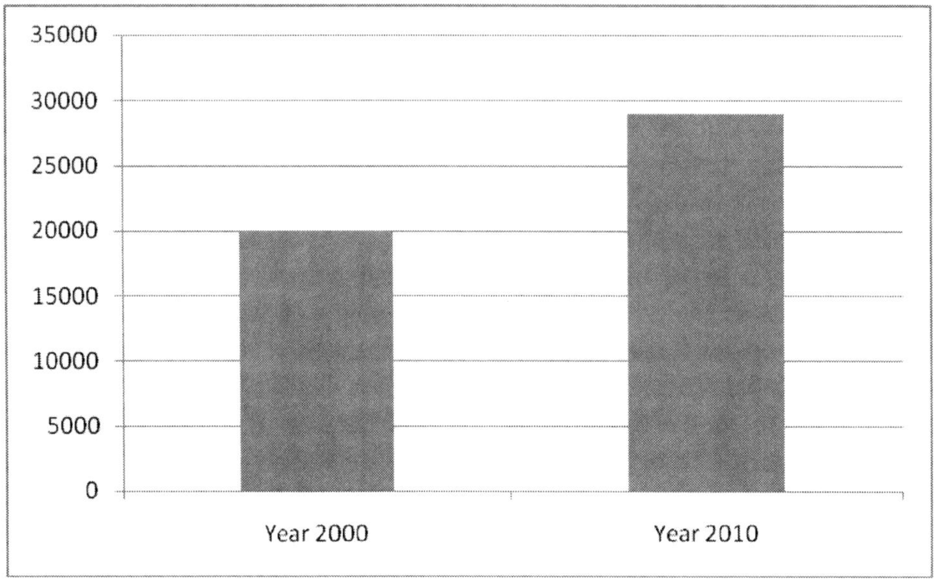

- 9000 New NGOs registered in the period from 2000 till 2010, at an average rate of 900 new NGOs per year.

brand, which needs to present a clear, consistent and focused message to external stakeholders to be able to achieve sustainable growth. Also, the founding members realized the value of building and maintaining credibility of the organization and its impact on NM's growth potential, thus they set out to foster the credibility of their organization through capitalizing on the credentials of the founding team. Then they focused on providing constant feedback to stakeholders on achievements to enhance and further nourish the credibility of the organization.

THE "YOUNG INNOVATORS AWARDS" (YIA) PROGRAM

Stimulated by a discussion with one of his Swiss friends in early 2003, El Shawarby, who was then a member of the board of directors at NM, realized the value that scientific research and patents can add to the economy of his home country. El Shawarby dreamt of starting a project that would instill the culture of research and development in Egypt, which would eventually result in increasing the Egyptian patents across different sectors. Through proposing a preliminary idea of his dream to NM, El Shawarby benefited from the incubator by having the whole team working on the idea to develop it into a working action plan. The project would be implemented as a contest that would target the senior students in science majors across Egypt, by giving a monetary award to the group who would propose and implement the best idea of research as part of their graduation project at the university.

The idea of focusing on university students came from the fact that they represent the future leaders and they needed to explore the arena of research and development before graduating to decide if they would like to take it as a career. The program is divided in two main steps, the first is a series of lectures to provide students with the needed information on proposal writing, and the role of intellectual property rights. They would then submit their proposals to be reviewed and screened. Finally, the judging committee decides on the winning teams, who receive a monetary prize to cover part or all of their research expenses.

MARKETING FOR NGOS, THE EVOLUTION OF SOCIAL MARKETING THEORY

The use of marketing by NGOs for non-commercial purposes and to benefit society in general started as early as the 1960's, when public awareness health campaigns to change the behavior of people regarding a number of issues, including immunization, family planning and nutrition in developing countries (Bellamy, Salit, & Bell, 1997). At that point, the concept of social marketing started to evolve, and its use spread across the world, in developing and developed nations alike (Bellamy et al, 1997). Prompted by the evolution and growth in the use of social marketing, many scholars and professionals attempted over the past forty years to develop a proper definition of the social marketing concept. This effort led to the generation of more than 45 definitions until this day (Dann, 2009).

Definition of Social Marketing

One of the most comprehensive and contemporary definitions for Social Marketing is *"the adaptation and adoption of commercial marketing activities, institutions and processes as a means to induce behavioral change in a targeted audience on a temporary or permanent basis to achieve a social goal"* (Dann, 2009, p.5). This definition stresses on the importance of taking commercial marketing as a reference for social marketing, for the concepts and tools are stemming from the same base yet with some differences in the application.

The major difference between conventional commercial marketing and social marketing is lies in how each is set out to "induce change of behavior" of the target audience, while it is for a individual, business or company in commercial marketing, it is for the benefit of the society at large in social marketing (Elliott, Unsworth, Gomel, Saunders & Mira, 1994). Even though social marketing started in the early years as basic social advertising, the elements of price, place, product and promotion should be incorporated to maximize the impact and achieve best results (Elliot et al, 1994). It is also worth noting that social marketing is not restricted to NGO's as it encompasses the activities of corporations as well, if they run campaigns that aim for general societal benefit (Elliot et al, 1994).

Target Audience

For most NGOs, the target audience of social marketing initiatives are split into two main categories, first is the customers, who represents the beneficiaries of the organization's efforts may it be a developmental effort, as an education campaign for poor people or a charity effort such as food distribution to the less privileged members of society. The second category is the stakeholders, who represent all the potential supporters of the NGO, who could actively help the organization in reaching its goals through funding, facilitating the different campaigns or even volunteering to help in goal achievement (Marketing Strategies used by NGOs). In the developed countries, the marketing dimension focused on stakeholders aims not only to secure funds and support, but also to ensure that this support comes from various streams to evade being over-dependant on one source of revenue or support that could decrease its independence and long term growth (Wells, 2001).

The Marketing Mix

Going to further detail, the 'product' element in Social marketing refers to "ideas and behaviors that are regarded as socially desirable" (Elliot et al, 1994). This mostly does not involve the sale of a tangible good, in contradiction to commercial marketing. The target for such organizations is to trigger long-term change of behavior, rather than short-term response to a commercial campaign.

The 'place' element refers to the point of interaction with the target audience, which is usually limited following the model of service marketing. For example, the place in the context of a developmental NGO would refer to the location where it runs its different programs. Thus, it would be focused not requiring high logistics of distribution as in the case of commercial goods.

On the other hand, the 'price' dimension represents the main difference vs. commercial marketing, where it usually refers to either the donations collected from supporters or the intangible cost of giving up a certain practice like smoking by customers (Elliot et al, 1994).

The 'promotion' element of social marketing holds the highest resemblance to commercial marketing in that all activities starting from personal selling to mass media can be used by NGOs to reach their objectives. Yet it is worth noting that personal selling has a high weight in Social marketing as it is closer to service marketing with the lack of a tangible good (Elliot et al, 1994).

EVOLUTION OF NGOS IN EGYPT AND THEIR USE OF SOCIAL MARKETING

Located at the heart of the Middle East, Egypt is the largest Arab country in terms of population, with latest estimates of population reaching 80 million people, 90 percent of whom are Muslims and the remaining 10 percent are mostly Coptic Christians. (CIA, the world fact book). In contrast to its neighboring GCC countries who have a high GDP per capita, Egypt has a GDP per capita estimated at $6,000 in 2009. With almost one-fifth of the population estimated to be below the poverty line (CIA, the world fact book), there has always been a high need for charity and development activities to be directed at the less privileged population.

When it comes to charity, Egyptians are already known to be active in the arena of giving to others, driven by the religious concepts of Zakah and Sadaqah, for Muslims and Ushr for Copts. Zakah is one of the five pillars of Islam and it is mandatory charity, every Muslim has to give out to the poor 2.5 percent of their annual income or 10 percent of their profit based on the profession. On the other hand, Sadaqah is voluntary charity, it is the practice of giving from one's wealth to the benefit of the poor people that is prompted by Islamic Faith. Ushr is the counterpart of Zakah for Coptic Christians, also known as Tithes, which is giving out the tenth of the total wealth to the poor (Atia, 2008). Also, besides the great need of charity and development organizations and the underlying culture of giving, Egypt enjoys a high rate of NGO establishment, growing from 20,000 NGOs in the year 2000 to reach 29,000 in the year 2010 (See Table 1), most of which focused on charity activities according to Managing Director of the Center of Information and Decision Support of NGOs in Egypt, Ihab Medhat.

In Egypt, there are two main form allowed for the establishment of NGOs in accordance to the law. The first is associations, or Gam'iyat, which need at least 10 founding members according to the law, while the second type is foundations, or mu'assassat, which only require three founders. In general, the legalities governing the work of foundations is much simpler than those imposed on associations. Nevertheless, to date associations have been the more widespread form of NGOs in Egypt with around 400 foundations in comparison to the 209,000 associations

Table 1. NM background information (As quoted from Official NM Site: http://www.nahdetmasr.org/node/113)

NM's Vision A developed Egypt through the active participation and belonging of its young professionals.
NM's Mission Engaging and activating Egyptian young professionals in the development and public arenas and in shaping Egypt's future.
NM Objectives • Activating and engaging young Egyptian professionals to become "social entrepreneurs" active in the development of their communities • Mobilizing young professionals & spreading the culture of contributing to local communities • Addressing Egypt's toughest development problems through innovative approaches • Creating a strong community of social entrepreneurs, non-profits, businesses, academia, government and international agencies and donors
NM's Values Diversity, Tolerance, Transparency, Accountability, Pro-active Social Responsibility.
NM Website Address: www.nahdetmasr.org

registered at the Ministry of Social Solidarity, which is the official body for NGOs (Atia, 2008). NGOs in Egypt represent the main constituent of 'Institutionalized Philanthropy,' which act as one of the main channels for Egyptians to deliver their charity money to the different beneficiaries (Atia, 2008).

When it comes to the use of social marketing by NGOs in Egypt it is considered to be significantly under developed as most NGOs applying very basic activities only to secure funds to sustain their existence and aid in short-term charity activities. Only a few number of NGOs have started o use more full-fledged social marketing tools and concepts in to secure funds and support their cause, and most of these NGOs are the ones having development orientation, requiring constant cash flow for operation. The use of social marketing to reach and influence the beneficiaries by NGOs is even more minimal as the majority of activities are focused more on charity that is delivered to the door-step of the needy people. According to Ehab Abdou, one of the founding members of NM, there are also some NGOs who started to apply the concept of social enterprise, whereby the NGO manages the process to produce, market and sell products so that the profits of the process can be used to finance the other activities of this NGO.

MODELS OF SOCIAL MARKETING IN EGYPT BASED ON SIZE OF ORGANIZATIONS

A Small-Scale NGO Model: An Organization

During the last 10 years, several NGOs have emerged in Egypt, each having a different size and focus, and each have chosen to apply specific tools of social marketing to its benefit. Better World (BW), which is a young NGO focused on development of under-privileged youth through training, chose a below the line technique in reaching both customers and supporters. According to Hany Amin, one of the founding members of BW, their strategy was to use networking as the tool to reach their beneficiaries to inform them about the training courses they were organizing. Using word of mouth, they have spread the information about the first group of trainees, which were successful. This strategy was used in building credibility with the external stakeholders who had the most effective impact in attracting their clients. As for attracting support, they again resorted to networking in their first years to invite trainers to come and administer training sessions for free to the beneficiaries. By time, the success of the first round also enabled them to collect donations as donors could see a credible organization with concrete activities. However due to their size, they still did not venture into above the line tools such as television advertising in attracting either supporters or beneficiaries, and resort more to focused awareness campaigns including seminars and trips.

A Large-Scale NGO Model: An Organization

On the other hand, Resala NGO has tried applying all the tools possible of marketing to achieve their goals of attracting support or reaching beneficiaries. Resala, which started as a university charity club in 2000, mainly focused on orphanages in their first year of operation. According to Al-Moataz Bellah Mohamed, the head of marketing and advertising at Resala, their experience with marketing could be defined as a learning curve. Taking their first premises in Giza as a base, the team handling Resala marketing at the time capitalized on the general tendency of Egyptians to donate in support of orphans, to collect funds through basic marketing tools such as flyer distribution in the neighboring area. Adding other activities as food distribution to poor families gave Resala a further advantage as they could attract a wider set of youth volunteers besides adding to their track record. In that time, they resorted heavily on networking through emails and positive word of mouth, besides expanding the geographical coverage of their flyer distribution. The team handling the marketing at Resala had decided to benchmark their activities against commercial marketing done by corporations, as there were not many examples of NGOs practicing social marketing to be taken as a reference. During that time they started adding awareness tools to their portfolio starting with newspaper inserts, radio ads and television, which made them evolve into one of the most prominent and successful models of NGOs in Egypt.

They key success factors were their stress on gaining and maintaining credibility through constant communication of achievements, maintaining a database of supporters for ongoing commitment and testing new initiatives continuously while applying KPI measures. Despite the tendency of Egyptians to donate for short-term focused activities, Resala received a high level of support for their development operations, as they consistently approached the public with a portfolio of long and short term oriented projects that ensured constant support. Also, Resala benefited from having a wide portfolio of supporters, by attracting donations from individuals and from corporations which aimed at implementing corporate social responsibility (CSR) activities, where these corporations assign part of their budgets to be used in serving the society where it operates by developmental and charity initiatives.

A Large-Scale NGO Model: An Institution

While Resala as a large organization still depended to a large degree on volunteers, Misr El Khair, which is one of the largest development-focused NGOs in Egypt decided to build a long-term model by hiring professional staff in all key positions, including brand managers with multinational company experience to handle all marketing activities. Misr El Khair, having had a trustee such as Shiekh Aly Gomaa, Egypt's Grand Muftlty, one of the highest Muslim religious posts in Egypt, capitalized on his presence in their advertisements to act as celebrity endorsement. According to Sherif Salem, Senior Brand manager at Misr El Khair, the institution, which organizes and manages its own development projects as well as provide financial support for other smaller NGOs working in the field of charity and development, resorted to using high impact advertising focused during the month of Ramadan to attract donations from the public. Ramadan is the month where Muslims are used to focus their benevolent activities, thus focusing the advertising in that period promised to attain the maximum impact possible. This television advertising reached the Egyptian public when they were ready the most to react to the development message, and provided them with a credible venue to direct their donations for the aid of the less privileged population. Also, having a unified bank account number at many banks across Egypt was a key factor in facilitating the collection of funds from donors in all areas of the country. However, despite this success in attracting large funds, the marketing team identified several opportunities to improve their future campaigns, through having a more focused positioning in their ads about their areas of activity. Also, injecting a positive spirit in their advertising since the older versions raised a degree of negative PR and was criticized for being too focused on the calamities of the poor people of Egypt.

NM The Birth of a Different Model of Development

NM's incubator model allowed for the co-existence of a portfolio of projects as mentioned above, which widened the scope of the organization and provided various venues for participation from volunteers (See Table 2). Building on this, NM started to actively build and maintain a database of all people who got in contact with the organization, and established a mechanism of ongoing connection with them through the cost efficient means of electronic media. This initiative lead to the organic growth of NM as more people got to join the network through word of mouth, and also was a great tool for NM to collect feedback on any initiative from their network to apply continuous improvement. Also, the incubator model allowed for engaging stakeholders through the utilization of the available resource, as the team had realized that one of the barriers to participating in long-term development projects is the fear of over commitment by people. The incubator model gave the interested and motivated supporters of NM a chance to engage in development activities, even of by little donation of time, money or effort.

Another important part of NM's strategy was the continuous search for synergies with other organizations to maximize the impact of their work. At one point, NM joined forces with other NGOs in several projects such as the Career and Entrepreneurship Development Center in Cairo University, in which they partnered with the International Youth foundation and USAID, besides several corporate sponsors. Concurrently, NM had realized that building a long-term developmental organization required the existence of sustainable funds that should be generated from many sources to ensure continuity. NM approached corporations and donor institutions to attract support for their cause, besides building on the usual channel of the individual donors who were the main source of funds for most of the other NGOs in Egypt.

On the other hand, NM started with the ideology that the beneficiaries of the development projects were not simply less-privileged people who are just receiving aid, but also their clients whom they carried out development projects for. Again, this mind set represented a clear step ahead for development and charity organizations in general, as it stressed the importance of getting feedback on all projects from the beneficiaries, designing the projects to meet their real needs, and getting more buy-in from them in the process. Also, since the official establishment of NM, the team worked on hiring professional staff as full time employees to act as the backbone for the organization, ensuring long-term sustainability. However, NM still capitalized on the efforts of the part-time volunteers who can participate each within his or her available time to help whenever needed thus achieving synergy of efforts.

Regarding the application of the social marketing concept, it started by developing a branding for NM amongst the stakeholders, and with the stress on networking. NM also sought to apply innovative means of spreading their vision to

Table 2. Nahdet El Mahrousa core programs (as quoted from the NM organizational profile document)

The Incubator of Innovative Social Enterprises By definition, an incubator is an economic and social development process designed to advise potential start-up projects and through *a comprehensive capacity building and assistance program,* help them to establish and accelerate their growth and success. Nahdet El Mahrousa has initiated the first Incubator for Innovative Social Enterprises in the world that it now aims to document and spread throughout Egypt and the region. The Incubator focuses on creating a continuous pipeline of development projects that can evolve in their own independent institutions or in the form of independent national programs. This approach has a strong multiplier effect and is highly adaptable to the needs of the environment.
NM Fellowships for Social Entrepreneurs The program aims at providing a vehicle to host, develop and support social entrepreneurs as they define, pilot and implement their ideas into operating programs that support the development of Egypt. It provides a competitive and organized way of attracting social entrepreneurs/project leaders to NM and is designed in a way to ensure their commitment by evaluating progress through the rigorous project cycle. The program allows the social entrepreneur to spend 6-12 months (renewable) on full-time basis to develop their idea into a full business plan, pilot the program, fundraise/mobilize resources, create and lead a volunteer team from NM members, creating partnerships, and once funding is available, start hiring full time staff to carry on the day-to-day implementation.
Social Innovation Starts with YOU! Nahdet el Mahrousa and Yahoo! Maktoob have partnered to spearhead an unprecedented online campaign called "Social Innovation Starts with YOU" to encourage social entrepreneurship among young Egyptian professionals and young Egyptians at large. In the social Innovation competition, launching in June (2010), Nahdet el Mahrousa and Yahoo! will invite individuals from across Egypt to be the next social entrepreneurs of the year by developing new ideas in the fields of education, health, environment, and a wildcard category. Funding and technical assistance will be provided to the selected projects whether start-up social enterprises or existing social enterprises in need of support for scaling-up.
Career and Entrepreneurship Development Office (CEDO) In 2006 Nahdet El Mahrousa, in collaboration with other partners such as the International Youth Foundation, USAID and other Egyptian corporate sponsor, has established the first comprehensive *Career Development and Entrepreneurship Center* in Egypt's largest university; Cairo University. During this short period the CEDO was able to train more than 6,000 students, to facilitate the employment of more than 100 graduates, to provide career advising and entrepreneurship services to a broad base of students, and to provide a positive recruitment avenue that meets the needs of Egyptian companies for well-trained talent. This success is manifested in the growing demand for expanding CEDO: Cairo University requested NM to replicate CEDO in six more faculties; Bibliotheca Alexandrina requested its replication in Alexandria; and the Young Arab Leaders requested the replication regionally in other Arab countries.
Young Innovators' Awards (YIA) Nahdet el Mahrousa incubated the Young Innovators' Awards (YIA) program in 2004 with the mission of stimulating the culture of R&D in Egypt. The program aims to positively impact the scientific culture in Egypt in three ways: by supporting research and development activities; empowering and developing scientists, engineers and researchers; and creating linkages between university research and industrial applications. The YIA program achieves these goals by providing young Egyptian scientists, engineers, and researchers with financial support, traineeships, and professional opportunities to engage in R&D at the undergraduate, masters and doctoral levels. Over the past years, the program has grown to cover all national Egyptian universities, including all 58 faculties of Engineering, Agriculture and Sciences, and has implemented partnership with numerous businesses, government agencies, and educational institutions. To-date, more than 1,000 young scientists, engineers and researchers in these universities have received the YIA awards or scholarships to support their graduate education
Nama'a for Sustainable Development Nama'a is a summer crash course combining both theoretical series of lectures on development and citizenship as well as field visits to a selected number of Egyptian graduates. The program is affecting the lives of hundreds of youth, ranging from program participants, program members, and university students.
Misriyati (My Egyptian Identity) Program The program focuses on promoting the values of tolerance, peace and diversity among young Egyptians through an innovative curriculum. The project has an established curriculum and teaching methodology. At the end of each cycle of workshops, participants are requested to brainstorm on means of contributing to their communities and spreading those.
Community Leaders Association (CLA) With the aim to build social leaders through a unique intensive program, the CLA is a civic education program for high school and university students. The program combines experiential learning, community service, discussion and exposure to diversity of ideas and models.

Continued on next page

Table 2. continued

Egyptian Expatriates Development (EED) The EED project was inspired by the idea of the TOKTEN program. It has historically been known as the 'UNDP: Transfer of Knowledge through Expatriate Nationals' (UNDP: TOKTEN), which has been a success in several other countries. By providing the opportunity for experts to transfer some of their expertise back to their home countries, TOKTEN helps in reversing "brain drain". It further develops a sense of belonging among nationals living abroad; especially those who have not been able to contribute to their countries' development, by helping them re-connect productively with their countries. The EED works on matching the qualifications, expertise and knowledge of Egyptian Expatriates with the needs for Egypt Development, particularly in the area of investment, technology and trade. The project is both demand and supply driven. It is demand-driven since Egypt needs to increase its Foreign Direct Investment as well as require International knowledge to empower and develop its local investment, technology and trade environment; while at the same time it is supply driven since Egyptian Expatriates possess Expertise in these sectors who want to find opportunities for investment in Egypt as a means of re-establishing themselves in their hometown as well as contribute to Egypt development.
Egyptian Education & Employment Alliance (EEEA) EEEA was initiated in 2006 as a partnership between the International Youth Foundation, USAID and Nahdet El Mahrousa, as the Egyptian Education and Employment Alliance. During the past period, the initiative has shown great success in partnering with Egypt's public sector (Ministry of Higher Education and the National Youth Council) to directly reach youth with needed services to empower them and prepare them for the job market. The initiative succeeded in establishing *6 "one-stop shop" centers:* 2 in the largest universities in Egypt – Cairo and Ein Shams Universities targeting university students, and 4 in *4 youth centers* – in Cairo, Fayoum and Minya targeting marginalized and underprivileged youth. The one-stop shop centers serve youth in different areas: economic empowerment and skills development, business and social entrepreneurship training and incubation, and career counseling and matching. More than 15,000 university students and 5,500 underprivileged youth benefited from the offices services in securing jobs, soft skills training, internships, and many started their own projects.
Cilantro Café Community Program (January 2005 - December 2007) NM partnered with Cilantro Cafe in an effort to reach their daily customers (consisting of 6,000 youth per day). The program aimed to engage Cilantro's customers in socially responsible activities by publicizing current socially responsibly events, stories about youth, volunteer opportunities, etc... In collaboration with other NGOs, private sector entities and cultural institutions this program disseminated culture and contributed to the alleviation of many social challenges in the community.

supporters through partnerships with organizations such as Cilantro Cafe, with whom they developed a bi-monthly publication that reached all Cilantro customers. Creating awareness for its projects inside universities by simple publications and organizing lectures was another tool that expanded their presence in the minds of their youth target audience. However, NM did not resort to employing mass media tools such as television and outdoor advertising, as applied by other large NGOs like Resala and Misr El Khair, rather depended mainly on below the line media to build its model.

EVOLUTION OF YIA PROGRAM

The first year of operation of the YIA program gave out 10 awards, each worth LE 3,000, and it was all given to students at the Telecommunications Section of the Faculty of Engineering at Cairo University, in order to have a significant impact in its launch year. In coordination with NM, professors endorsed the program and told the students about it, in addition, posters and flyers were distributed with the consent of the university administration. But despite this, students were reluctant to participate as they knew little about NM, which was in the beginning, and the awards was a new idea to Egyptian students. Therefore, NM raised the value of the award value to LE 4,000 to attract students, however they still had concerns, all this changed when a group of students who had the highest academic achievements decided to participate. This group started a wave of positive word of mouth about the project and set a role model for other students to follow. By the end of the first year, 30 students participated in the program, with six awards given, which were completely funded by individual donors.

Corporations starting funding YIA during its second year as the program expanded to the

Mechanical Engineering Faculty at Cairo University. NM team had agreed with one company to sponsor several awards, besides getting another set of individual donations to increase the number of benefiting students. Also, NM hired two young graduates to act as program coordinators to ensure sustainability and continuous growth of YIA, as the level of details required full time management, which is very hard to be covered by volunteers. That year, YIA reached 50 students in just one university, and offered ten awards. By the third year of operation, the number of awards increased to almost 40 awards, reaching almost 200 students in six universities. This growth came as a result of increasing the number of corporate donors besides growing the individual donor participation (See Table 3).

Table 3. YIA partners (based on NM website) organizations and corporations supporting the YIA program

Industrial Modernization Centre
Challenger Limited
Mobinil
Procter & Gamble
DuPont

In addition to the growth in the number of awards, the third year was regarded by the YIA team at NM as a success in terms of organization as well, since they had received all the donations early in the summer, which enabled them to approach the universities at the beginning of the academic year. This gave enough time to promote the program and attract students, then organize the lecture series, and receive a large number of proposals.

The turning point came in the fourth year of YIA, when a single institution came on board as a partner to the project, raising the available budget to a level that enabled them to reach 22 Faculties of Engineering in 18 universities around Egypt. This partnership was extended to the following year enabling the addition of internship and scholarship programs for the top students. Thus, YIA was then a program that encouraged research at graduation year, gave internship opportunities, then scholarships and financial support for students who pursued postgraduate studies. In numbers, YIA's achievements were over two million Egyptian pounds spent on students in five years a motivating tool to instill the research and development culture in their minds and hearts. On the support side, the YIA team started to focus on managing the relation with the large institution that represented the main donor of the program, particularly that this institution promised to provide large ongoing funds to the program to further develop it and increase its scope. However, this focus also resulted in less activity done in the direction of pooling the support of other corporations or institutions, thus the contribution of all other donors, both corporate and individual, fell below 20 percent of the total funds.

Figure 2. Examples of awareness posters used by NM for the YIA program

THE FUTURE OF THE "YOUNG INNOVATORS AWARDS" PROGRAM

During these five years, the promotion used for by NM to attract students to the YIA was simply posters and leaflets distributed on campus announcing the different program details (see Figure 2). Yet, it has always been apparent for the YIA team that each year; students came on board due to the positive word of mouth generated by the participation of the students in the preceding year. This again stressed the need to monitor the feedback of the participating students at the end of each year and incorporate it in the program as needed to ensure continuous improvement.

However, at the beginning of the sixth year, the managing board of the main supporter of YIA, who now represented more than 80 percent of the total funds of the program, informed NM that they will not continue to support the program in its current format. They had decided that it was time for them to direct their funds to tackle other development issues such as fostering the spirit of entrepreneurship in Egypt, and that research and development, which is the main essence and mission of YIA, is now out of their focus. At this point NM did not have an alternative for these funds, and they had already started the primary work of coordinating with the universities for the upcoming round of YIA. El Shawarby, El Zarkani and their team started to negotiate with their main donor institution to maintain its support, so as not to affect the continuity of the program, as stopping the program at this stage threatened to diminish all the positive effect that had started to evolve with students. Also, stopping the program would hurt the credibility of NM as they had started the coordination with universities and presented a direct blow to the sustainable image that they have strived to build through all their projects since establishment. However, the negotiations were not successful, and the team had to face the reality of losing over eighty percent of the funds they needed to run the program, not to mention that the corporations that provided the remaining funds have not been approached yet to verify their readiness to continue support in the year of 2010 as well.

El Shawarby called for a crisis meeting with the members of the board, besides the program director El Zarkani, to decide on the next steps for the YIA program. As he waited for the team to gather, El Shawarby hoped that they would find an alternative source of funding for the YIA, and evade all possible drawbacks of stopping the program. Yet he knew that it would not be an easy task, as sources of funds in Egypt for long term oriented projects are usually scarcer than these directed to charity, and that they do not have the luxury of time to collect funds in the usual manner. Would they stop the program this year to give more time to attracting support for coming years. Or would they continue this year and focus on attracting the support of another large institution to make up for the lost amount of funds. Or would they try to generate new models for funding that can support the YIA in 2010 and the years to come.

Interviewee list

- Mr. Almoataz Bellah Mohamed, Head of Marketing and Advertising at Resalla NGO.
- Mr. Ehab Abdou, Founder and member of board of Directors of Nahdet El Mahrousa.
- Mr. Ihab Medhat, directing manager of the center of information and decision support of NGOs in Egypt
- Mr. Hany Amin, Founding member for Better World NGO.
- Mr. Loay El-Shawarby, Chairman of the board of directors of Nahdet El Mahrousa NGO.
- Mr. Mohamed El Zarkani, YIA program director at Nahdet El Mahrousa NGO.
- Mr. Sherif Salem, Senior Brand Manager at Misr El Khair NGO.

Interview Guide for NM organization

- Can you describe how you use Marketing at Nahdet El Mahrousa? What goals does Marketing achieve for you?
- What are the best marketing tools used before? What were less successful?
- What are the marketing tools that can be shared with other NGOs?
- What were the success factors for NM?
- What were the main landmarks for the YIA program? How was marketing used to promote and expand this project?
- What is needed from different stakeholders (such as Government- public – media – beneficiaries) to facilitate the growth of the NGOs?

REFERENCES

Atia, M. (2008). Arab Republic of Egypt. In Ibrahim, B. L., & Sherif, D. H. (Eds.), *From charity to social change: Trends in Arab philanthropy* (pp. 23–42). Cairo, Egypt: The American University in Cairo Press.

Bellamy, H., Salit, R., & Bell, L. (1997). *Social marketing resource manual: A guide for state nutrition education networks*. Washington, DC: Health Systems Research Inc.

CIA. (2010). *The world fact book, Egypt profile*. Retrieved on 10 August, 2010, from https://www.cia.gov/library/publications/the-world-factbook/geos/eg.html

Dann, S. (2009). Redefining social marketing with contemporary commercial marketing definitions. *Journal of Business Research, 63*, 147–153. doi:10.1016/j.jbusres.2009.02.013

Elliott, R. G., Unsworth, D. A., Gomel, M. K., Saunders, J. B., & Mira, M. (1994). Social marketing: Conceptual and pragmatic observations from a current Australian campaign. *Journal of Marketing Management, 10*, 581–591. doi:10.1080/0267257X.1994.9964306

SIES College of Management Studies. (2010). *Marketing strategies used by NGOs*. Idea Research Paper Series. Retrieved on 26 January, 2010, from http://www.karmayog.org/general/upload/182/Marketing%20strategies%20used%20by%20NGOs.pdf

Wells, R. (2001). Ensuring NGO independence in the new funding environment. *Development in Practice, 11*(1), 73–77.

Chapter 15
Honda Power Products: Ensuring the Future of a Leading Brand in a Turbulent Market

Noha Ismail
American University in Cairo (AUC), Egypt

EXECUTIVE SUMMARY

The International Commercial and Industrial Investment Company, S.A.E (ICII) is a trading company specialized in high-end power products and construction equipment. Honda power products accounts for almost 25% percent of the company's sales. Since the introduction of Chinese products into the Egyptian market, Honda sales have been increasing, however at a decreasing rate. ICII is facing a number of challenges related to Honda's decreasing market share. The main challenges are configuring a marketing strategy to ensure its viability in a turbulent market and selecting growth alternative that ensures its sustainability in light of the changing market conditions.

Ahmed El Sayad, CEO of the International Commercial and Industrial Investment Company, S.A.E (ICII), a member of El Sayad Group, picked up the phone and called for an emergency meeting with his sales manager, Fathy Mahmoud, after reviewing the latest report of the company's performance for the year 2007. "There is something we could do to stop losing market share. The Chinese products are flooding the market with low-priced low-quality products," said El Sayad.

"But we are making good money and our annual profits are increasing," was Mahmoud's reply.

"This should not be our only concern; we have a reputation and a position in the market that we have to protect. I am calling for an urgent meeting now to find a solution for this," said El

DOI: 10.4018/978-1-60960-583-4.ch015

Sayad who upon putting down the phone started thinking, "This company has a legacy that we need to preserve," Looking back at how this business group, which was established by his grandfather, has started and has rapidly became the leader of the power products' market in Egypt.

ORGANIZATIONAL BACKGROUND

El Sayad Group

El Sayad group was established by Awad El Sayad as a medium size family business in 1935. Since then, El Sayad Group had a huge impact on both commercial and industrial sectors in Egypt. It has grown significantly through directly investing in companies which were completely owned by El Sayad family or as anchor investors in privatized, private and non-governmental organizations.

The business group has started out with the department store "Tredco El Sayad" which sells home appliances and electronic equipments, but there were also some side business in exports and imports. After the adoption of the open-door policy in Egypt by President Mohamed Anwar El Sadat, in the seventies, the group found an opportunity in this new economic climate. As a result, they expanded in their marketing and distribution plans. They also succeeded to become the exclusive agent of numerous reputable firms that supply the Egyptian and Arab markets with equipments and machinery. Among these accomplishments was becoming the sole distributor of the Honda power products. In the following years the group invested heavily in privatizing several giant manufacturing firms such as fertilizers, chemicals, cables, textile and construction, a way to ensure diversification of investment and minimizing risks. As a result, the group became, over the past 20 years, one of the biggest business entities in Egypt. Due to globalization, and to further ensure their growth and sustainability, the group started expanding outside Egypt in several Arab countries and established its first subsidiary in Syria: "El Sayad Trading-SYRIA."

The International Commercial and Industrial Investment Co. S.A.E.(ICII), a subsidiary of El-Sayad group, was established in 1987 as a limited liability company to handle all the import business sector for the Group. ICII built a trustful name and worked on its market position by increasing market share of its products year after year. It succeeded in becoming the agent of many worldwide brands such as:

- Honda for Power Equipment. (Japan).
- Honda Marine.
- NSM Saccardo.
- Leroy Somer.
- Markon Sawafuji.
- Passap for knitting machines (Switzerland).
- Landini for deep well pumps (Italy).
- Exen for construction equipment (Japan).
- Visa for big size generators (Italy).
- Komatsu Power for construction equipments.

The Honda department represents a major part of ICII's operations. In the year 2007, The Honda power products' department constituted almost 24 percent of the total number of employees, 24 percent of the company's total sales and 23 percent of its total value of imports (see Figures 1, 2, 3).

Honda

The Honda name has always been renowned for delivering products with dedication and excellence while focusing on performance and innovation to exceed customers' expectations. Honda is now producing diversified products such as cars, including the Civic, which sold around one million cars over the world as well as the Formula 1 car. It also manufactures motorcycles, engines, and power equipment. Honda has always been heavily investing in research and development, and has

Figure 1. Number of employees (©2010 El Sayad Group, Egypt, used with permission)

	2006	2007
TOTAL COMPANY	98	105
HONDA	25	27

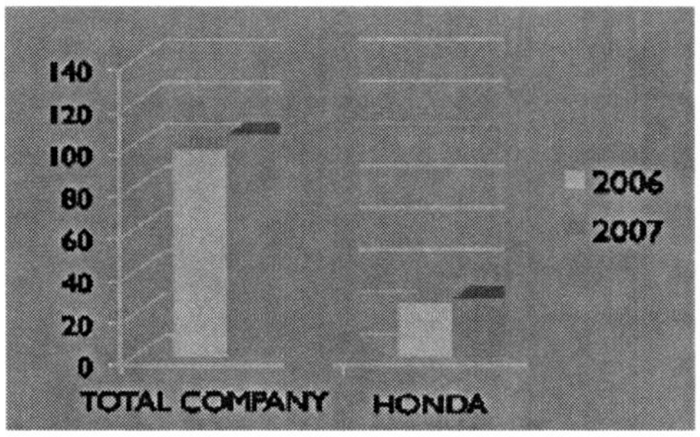

now developed the famous robot Asimo to serve in the future as spare parts of human organs.

According to Honda's official website, Soichiro Honda, the founder of the Honda Company, hoped to create products to better serve people working in their homes and workplaces. As a result, Honda power products started in the year 1953 with a vision to "improve the quality of life". Honda uses superior technology and innovative ideas to manufacture its products. These products include tillers, portable generators, outboard engines, water pumps, lawn mowers, snow throwers, power carrier, electric four-wheel scooter and a household compact cogeneration unit. In 2008, the cumulative production of the Honda power products has reached 85 million units, manufactured in nine countries, 11 plants and sold in 156 countries to 5.5 million customers.

MARKET ANALYSIS

Egypt is situated in a region that has witnessed throughout history much political instability. Although Egypt's economic performance was affected during times of wars and political instability, Egypt has always managed to sustain its international trade successfully. Egypt's main trading partners are the United States, Italy, France, Greece, Germany, the United Kingdom, Syria, Spain, Saudi Arabia, China and Japan. The major types of goods imported are wheat, meat, flour, machinery and automobiles. The major types of goods exported are petroleum, natural Gas, cotton and cotton textiles as well as aluminium

Figure 2. Company sales (©2010 El Sayad Group, Egypt, used with permission)

	2005	2006	2007
TOTAL COMPANY	34,760,931	42,570,704	52,143,925
HONDA	6,626,734	8,593,024	12,318,012
SHARE	19%	20%	24%

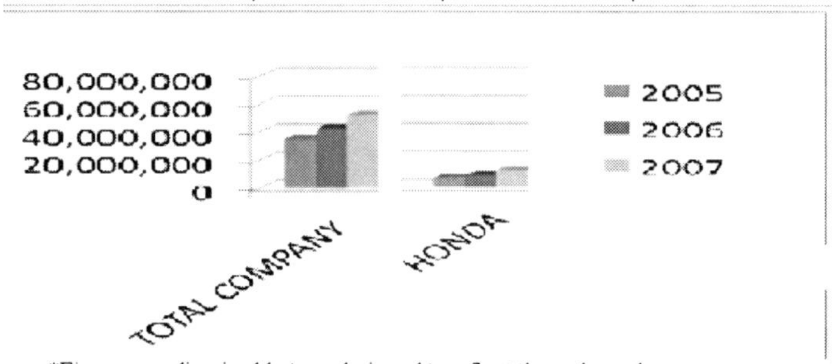

*Figures are disguised but are designed to reflect the real numbers

Figure 3. Import figures (©2010 El Sayad Group, Egypt, used with permission)

Import Figures in USD	2005	2006	2007
TOTAL COMPANY	22,291,978	30,002,030	46,285,686
HONDA	4,868,645	6,410,578	10,467,321
SHARE	22%	21%	23%

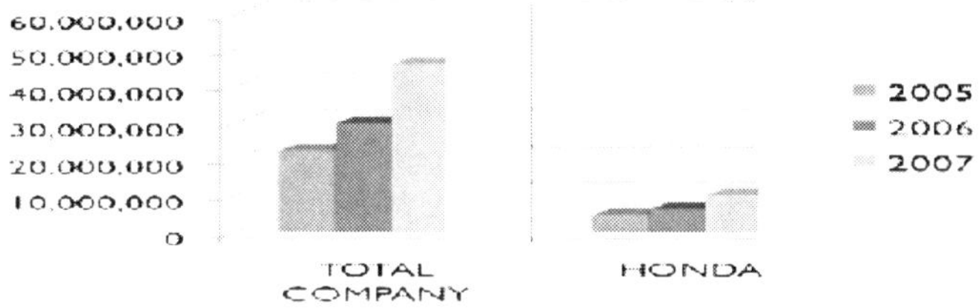

*Figures are disguised but are designed to reflect the real numbers

products. Furthermore, Egypt is a member of several African, Mediterranean and Arabic trade blocs. Since the early 1990s, Egypt has witnessed a significant increase in the purchasing power, especially for consumer goods, due to several governmental initiatives such as decreasing external debt, controlling inflation and deficits and encouraging privatization. Imported brands were always preferred to local ones because consumers felt that international products were of higher quality than the locally manufactured ones. During the period from 1990 to 2000 the GDP per capita increased from $640 to$1450, whereas private consumption per capita rose from $460 to $1100. Starting the year 2000, the Egyptian purchasing power declined due to the fall of the Egyptian pound against the American Dollar. This was reflected in the Egyptian economic growth which reached to 2.7 percent from an average of 5.4 percent from 1996 up until 2000. Consequently, the GDP per capita decreased to $990 and private consumption per capita to $720. Due to the decline of the purchasing power and the decrease of disposable income, people preferred to buy low priced products whenever possible. However, the market started to recover by the year 2004 when the Central Bank of Egypt ensured the presence of foreign currency reserve and when the government officials implemented cuts in tariffs. As a result, imports, consumer demand and economic growth have increased sharply. Since then, the quality of the locally produced products has increased; but there was always a preference for imported products ("Egypt: market profile" 2005).

The Power Products Market

The power products' market in Egypt has always been providing top quality products to customers interested in Japanese and European brands, which are renowned for their durability and efficiency. High end products were dominating the distributors' stores and consisted about 90 percent of their inventory and were sold at a relatively high price. To increase their sales, distributors allocated a minimal profit margin in order to avoid further increase of the selling price. In the late 1990s, the power products' market in Egypt started to change gradually where Chinese products were first introduced to the stores with a price 75 percent less than the average prices available in the market. The Chinese products were all similar with the same specifications. There was no comparative advantage that would differentiate one product over the other. In the following years, more and more Chinese products were introduced until the year 2005 when the market changed dramatically as distributors replaced the high-end products with much cheaper ones. The low-priced Chinese products allowed distributors to allocate triple the profit margin they got from selling high-end goods. The sales of both low-end brands and the remaining high end brands were increasing. For Honda Egypt, the total sales increased but at the same time it was losing market share to the Chinese competitors: in 2007, the Honda annual sales increased whereas the total market sales was booming (see Figures 2, 3, 4 for the annual increase in Honda sales and the total market sales). Honda could not catch up with the Product Life Cycle (PLC) of the market: the market was in the growth stage; however, Honda showed signs of maturity. At the growth stage, markets witness severe competition using appealing promotional strategies, fierce distribution, a strong sales force and strategies for product differentiation (Thietart, &Vivas 1984; Kikuchi 2010). *"Honda was the company's star; it was the market leader of a growing market,"* recalled El Sayad. *"The fear is that it would turn into a problem child,"* he said. The products that are considered the star of their company's portfolio are profit generators. They are also the main pool of their company's investment: companies usually invest heavily in stars in order to preserve their market share and prevent them from turning into cash cows (Nutton, 2006). In Honda's case, the market is still growing but due to the entry of many competitors, Honda being the star, started losing market share which indicated that it was indeed becoming a problem child.

Competition

Prior to 2005, Honda competitors fell in the category of the high end products offering high quality service. These brands included Japanese brands such as Elemax, Kawazaki and Robin. Lambardini, an Italian brand was also competing fiercely. During 2005, many of these brands started fading away and were substituted with the Chinese products. By 2006, the brands Elemax and Kawazaki were completely out of the market. Robin products were still existing but with minimal presence. The Honda products were affected as well; however, the company's management adopted a strategy to increase the dealer's profitability to the maximum in order to encourage them to keep the Honda products in stores. In many occasions, dealers would earn more profit from selling a generator than what ICII itself would earn. Since then, Honda's competitors were Chinese made, low in price, low in quality and do not offer after sale service nor any warranty, a feature that Honda is most renowned for and presented its comparative advantage among the high end products.(See Figure 5 for a comparison of the Honda prices vs. a Chinese competitor). The Chinese competitors included brands such as Kama, Kipor and ATP. Due to the success Chinese products have made in the Egyptian markets, several dealers became the Original Equipment Manufacturers (OEM) of some of the Chinese names but branded them differently. All these activities further expanded the market and increased competition. The market was 10 percent high-end products and 90 percent Chinese products.

Consumer Behaviour

The power product's market in Egypt is very broad and includes various segments of the population. However, Honda cannot target all these segments at once. Some factors are used to divide the market into "manageable segments" that are similar in lifestyle and/or demographics (Quinn, 2009).The power product's customer is mainly between the B+ and A classes: the low tier and the high tier. From Egypt's total population of 70 million, about two million households are considered middle class or wealthier ("Egypt: market

Figure 4. (a) Market evolution, (b) Sales history (©2010 El Sayad Group, Egypt, used with permission)

(a)

In Units	2005	2006	2007
Generators	8700	9600	10500
Water Pumps	9000	10500	12000
Tillers	200	240	300
Lawn Mowers	2200	2500	2900
Riding Mowers	75	100	120
Bruch Cutters	250	280	340
Sprayers	12000	14000	17000
construction equipment	11000	12000	14000
Engines	7000	8000	9000
Out Boards Marine	80	100	120
Others	13000	15000	17000
Total	63505	72320	83280

Figures are disguised but are designed to reflect the real numbers

(b)

In Units	2005	2006	2007
Generators	1800	2600	2860
Water Pumps	1200	1650	1760
Tillers	120	129	147
Lawn Mowers	1270	1560	1760
Riding Mowers	25	42	54
Bruch Cutters	40	49	56
Sprayers	2000	2300	2640
construction equipment	1400	1780	1970
Engines	6500	6870	7540
Out Boards Marine	60	67	75
Others	450	560	670
Total	14865	17607	19532

*Figures are disguised but are designed to reflect the real numbers

profile," 2005). The low tier is price sensitive and not quality oriented, unlike the high tier who cares more about specifications like the noise and the quality of the electricity generated. The high tier customers represented a small portion of the market, and those were the ones who stayed loyal to the Honda products because Honda offers the best quality of electricity among the other brands. However, after the invasion of the Chinese products, the market itself was growing to include new customers who were lured by the low prices of the products available and who otherwise would not have been interested in buying the product. Nevertheless, people were still complaining from the Chinese products because of their low durability. So far, there were no brands to target the mid-tier by offering good quality products, after sale service and reasonable prices. Also, there were no locally manufactured products present to compete in the market.

Honda's Customer profile included three different segments, these are end consumers, construction companies, and communication companies. Each one of these segments used a different product for specific purposes. End consumers, ranging from B+ to A class, bought generators that provide backup for electricity. They installed the generator in their homes and buildings so when there is a power cuts the generator would produce electricity as a substitute for the main electricity

Figure 5. Price comparison (©2010 El Sayad Group, Egypt, used with permission)

		HONDA CBU	KAMA CHINESE
GENERATORS	MODEL	EP2500 CX	KM2500
GENERATORS	OUTPUT	2.4 KVA	2.4 KVA
GENERATORS	PRICE	4000	1050
GENERATORS	MODEL	EP6500 CX	KG6500
GENERATORS	OUTPUT	5.5 KVA	5.5 KVA
GENERATORS	PRICE	8300	3800
GENERATORS	MODEL	EM10000	KGE10000
GENERATORS	OUTPUT	9 KVA	9 KVA
GENERATORS	PRICE	25000	10500
GENERATORS	MODEL	ET12000	KGT12500
GENERATORS	OUTPUT	10.5 KVA	10.5 KVA
GENERATORS	PRICE	27000	11000
WATER PUMPS	MODEL	WB20 XT	WP20
WATER PUMPS	TYPE	2 " PUMP	2 " PUMP
WATER PUMPS	PRICE	2450	750
WATER PUMPS	MODEL	WB30 XT	WP30
WATER PUMPS	TYPE	3 " PUMP	3 " PUMP
WATER PUMPS	PRICE	2700	800

source. Construction companies used construction equipment, water pumps and generators as well. They used all these products as to provide their construction sites with the electricity and water needed to proceed with their on-site work. Honda supplied renowned construction companies in Egypt such as Hassan Allam Construction, Egyptian Contracting Company (Mokhtar Ibrahim), Alexandria Construction Company (Member of Talaat Mostafa Group), Orascom Construction, and the Arab Contractors (Osman Ahmed Osman & Co.). Communication and telecommunication companies such as Mobinil, Vodafone, and TE Data also used the Honda generators in their facilities. Internet Companies relied on the generator as their main source of electricity because their facilities were located in the desert were access to electricity is limited. Due to the sensitivity of their equipment and their operations, internet companies cannot risk a power cut. Therefore, they used the Honda generators because they are professional and reliable.

MARKETING STRATEGY

Brand Positioning

Reputation is defined by marketers as being the "collective impression held by stakeholders of how a company manages its intangible assets" (Kossovsky, 2010). ICII has built a reputation throughout the years of being the leader in supplying power products in Egypt. El Sayad group has always focused on good quality, after sale service, maintenance and warranty. The reputation it built throughout the years is one of the main pillars that kept this group successful till this day, the reason why ICII tries to protect its position in the market by maintaining the high level of products and service it offers to its customers. El Sayad group is sustaining a growing reputation through its continued market-focused strategies, integrated investments, and customer satisfaction. Specifically, the Honda products are very well reputable for their high quality and efficiency. Furthermore, Honda power products are considered the Rolls Royce among the power products due to the quality of electricity it generates and the services it offers. Consistent to their image, Honda Egypt positions its after sales service as being fast, efficient and durable.

Product Strategy

Honda Egypt power products include generators, water pumps, tillers, lawn mowers, riding mowers, brush cutter, sprayers, and outboard marine engines. In order to be consistent with their positioning strategy, ICII focused on after sale service and offered a two year warranty. ICII have five service centres that make overhauling, maintenance, coupling and assembly. ICII takes pride in being able to reach customers anywhere

Figure 6. Numbers of dealers (©2010 El Sayad Group, Egypt, used with permission)

	2004	2005	2006	2007	Estimated 2008	Estimated 2009	Estimated 2010	Estimated 2011
Number of Dealers	38	46	57	57	65	59	65	73

in Egypt and provide them with original spare parts as soon as possible: 98 percent of the spare parts could be available at the nearest dealer within 24 hours from their order. Spare parts could still exist even 15 years after the model is out of production. In addition, new service centers were being opened while conducting continuous service campaigns especially in Alexandria, North Coast, and the city of Sharm El Sheikh on the Red Sea. The company also launched a new project called Mobi – Serve: it is an "on call" vehicle that can reach customers anywhere within 24 to 48 hours to offer immediate technical service support.

Pricing Strategy

Honda Egypt adopted a Cost plus Pricing Strategy with an average of 30 percent profit margin. In order to enter the country, a Honda generator -CIF arriving port- bears extra costs besides the unit's cost. These extra costs include five percent customs, 10 percent sales tax, and three percent clearance expenses (See Figure 7 for the cost breakdown). Being a prestige product, Honda power products depicts a backward bending demand curve where the demand –up to a certain point- increases with the increase in price because people feel that the more they pay the better quality they get(Kumcu, & McClure, 2003).

For every company, the terms of payment are different. Companies that deal with ICII for the first time will have to pay the full amount of the purchase by an internal letter of credit or a certified check. Companies that have a history of trade with ICII have more convenient terms of payment: they are offered to pay the full amount of the purchase within a period of 90 to 120 days.

Distribution Strategy

El Sayad Trading – Misr is marketing all its products through a massive dealers' network through the whole country. They are covering almost every major city in Egypt through a wide network of almost 60 dealers while targeting to reach 75 dealers by the year 2011. (See Figure 6 for the number of dealers)

Advertising and Promotional Strategy

El Sayad believes that marketing a business is one of the most important tools that can help their business grow. Their promotion strategies are both B2B and B2C. The maximized number of dealers is one tool they use to advertise for their goods. In order to further promote the Honda products, they participated in several events such as the International Boat Show in Egypt in 2006 and 2007. Public events are useful for the Honda brand image for many reasons. It guarantees a high level of exposure for the Honda name due to the large number of visitors who attend these events reaching thousands of visitors per day. It also ensures targeting the desired target markets who would be especially interested in these products. In addition, public relation activities, corporate advertising using mediums like television, newspaper or magazines, are some of the ways ICII is planning to use to promote their business in the near future. New showrooms will be opened in premium locations to ensure maximum exposure of the Honda logo. By 2010, they will have three new showrooms and a service centre opened in Hurghada on the Red Sea and another showroom in the New Cairo district.

The selling process for end consumers is usually simple and typical. Consumers who are interested in buying a Honda product usually go to one of the showrooms and buy the product that satisfies their needs. For corporate selling, the process is more complex. If a company is interested in a Honda product, it sends ICII a request via fax or email to buy a specific product; then ICII replies back with a quotation. Once the quotation is accepted by the company, it submits to ICII a purchase order with details of the requested product and the quantity required.

THE FUTURE OF ICII AS A MARKET LEADER

In the maturity stage, many products –like Honda power products in Egypt- become less demanded due to the introduction of new technologies and/or the development of new market trends. In this stage, companies strive to revive their products. Several strategies could be implemented in order to boost the product's sales such as adopting a new product design, use a contract manufacturing or outsource some of the specialized processes ("Product life cycles," 2008). For ICII, other alternatives are available to grow the total company's portfolio.

ICII could blend with the new market trend and start importing other Chinese products to compete with the already existing ones. This will create a diversified portfolio of products, by which ICII could target both the high tier and low tier. Like all Chinese products available in the market, ICII will not provide its customers with warranty or service.

El Sayad expressed his concern during the emergency meeting, *"I fear that this option would jeopardize the company's image and might lead to losing our loyal A class customers."*

Like all companies, ICII's reputation-linked assets form almost 70 percent of its value (Kossovsky, 2010), a value that ICII cannot afford to lose especially that it forms its competitive advantage among the other companies.

After experiencing the low quality of the Chinese products, customers expressed their willingness for better quality products that would provide them with after sales service. *"Of course there is always the option of manufacturing. We can become an OEM of the Honda power products*," suggested El Sayad. *"We can locally manufacture the body of the products but having a Honda engine inside. That way we will offer the same quality. But what about the price?"* he noted. *"We need to know at what price we can manufacture a local generator with a Honda engine,"* El Sayad said.

On this point, Eng. Hanna, the service centres' manager, said, *"We can provide you with a cost breakdown of a generator prototype that we can manufacture in our service centre. It could be the equivalent of the Honda generator EP2500CX and containing also the same engine"* (See Figure 7 the cost breakdown).

ICII's service centres provide services such as coupling and assembly. These service centres represent a good base for a production plant especially that the process of coupling an engine with an alternator or a water pump is similar to the manufacturing process. The advantage of being an OEM is that products can be offered at the market with lower prices because operating costs are reduced and because the "distribution channels are more streamlined". However, products bought from OEMs could be considered by customers as being "not generic" and could be perceived of lower quality (Conte Sr., 2005). *"But wouldn't this cause the cannibalization of the Honda prod-*

Figure 7. Cost breakdown (©2010 El Sayad Group, Egypt, used with permission)

Generator Model	Equivalent to the "EP2500 CXE"
OUTPUT	2.4 KVA
Alternator Model	ES80 C
Engine Model	GX160 VHB Honda
Landed Cost Alternators	750
CIF Cost Engine	830.5
Frame	150
TANK	0
MUFFLER	0
LOCAL EXTRAS	20
Carton	30
Labor Cost	50

ucts and decrease its sales?" said Mahmoud. Cannibalization causes the newly manufactured product to replace the already existing one: The newly manufactured product will decrease the sales of the Honda products especially that the new product can be offered at a lower price (Atasu, Guide, Jr, & Van Wassenhove, 2010).

Expanding into a new business line like for example importing low tier Chinese motor cycles could satisfy the demand of this segment of the market without harming the Honda Power Products image. It can promote diversification, minimize risk and ensure presence in the market. *"This is a valid option but there is still much more opportunity in the Egyptian power product's market especially that it is still in the growth stage and has not reached maturity yet," said El Sayad, who continued,* "May be we should adopt several strategies together in order to make a strong comeback to the market and satisfy the needs of the different parties. I think now we have a clear vision of the different alternatives we can adopt. I have to make a decision by the end of this month on how to proceed. To make up my mind, I need by tomorrow answers for the following:

1. What would be the effect on ICII's image and legacy if we import Chinese products with no maintenance, no after-sale service nor warranty?
2. If we import Chinese products, what would be our competitive advantage that would lead us to significantly increase our market share and strongly compete with the already existing Chinese brands?
3. If we become OEM for Honda, at what price could we offer our products while providing the same Honda quality?
4. What are the pros and cons of each strategy?
5. As the market is in the growth stage, which strategy should the company adopt?
6. On the long run, when the market reached maturity, what should ICII do?

REFERENCES

Atasu, A., Guide, V. Jr, Daniel, R., & Van Wassenhove, L. N. (2010). So what if remanufacturing cannibalizes my new product sales? *California Management Review*, *52*(2), 56–57.

Caribbean Business Magazine. (2008, March 20). Product life cycles can determine the need for contract manufacturing. *Carribean Business*, 28.

Conte, M. Sr. (2005). Are OEM parts of greater value to end users than generic parts? *Foodservice Equipment & Supplies*, *58*(1), 29.

Fumiaki, K. (2010). Influence of product life cycle stage on consideration set size: The case of think products. *Marketing Review*, *10*(1), 48.

Kossovsky, N. (2010). Reputation leadership. *Leadership Excellence*, *27*(5), 7.

Kumcu, E., & McClure, J. (2003). Explaining prestige pricing: An alternative to back-bending demand. *Marketing Education Review*, *13*(1), 49.

Nutton, S. E. (2006). Management accounting-business strategy. *Financial Management*, 45.

Online, E. I. U. (2005). Egypt: Market profile. *Consumer Goods Forecast World*, 116-117.

Quinn, L. (2009). Market segmentation in managerial practice: A qualitative examination. *Journal of Marketing Management*, *25*(3/4), 254.

Thietart, R. A., & Vivas, R. (1984). An empirical investigation of success strategies for business along the product life cycle. *Management Science*, *30*(12), 1405. doi:10.1287/mnsc.30.12.1405

Section 6
Operations Management

Successful marketing starts with value creation, a joint responsibility of production/operations and marketing management. The coordination and integration of these silo business functions is often achieved through the design of business processes including demand management, demand fulfillment, customer service operation, to name a few. The first case, "Spinning Off the Supply Chain," examines the operation of a business in the food service industry. It demonstrates the importance of sound supply chain management practices for an entrepreneurial small business faced with surge in the growth of the business that strained its operational capabilities. The second case, "Kohler Sales Forecasting," explores options to improve sales forecasts for the distribution operation in Egypt of a producer of sanitary equipment. The old forecasting method, which was based on historical sales driven mainly by large construction projects in the Gulf countries, was no longer adequate. Alternative SKU-Project-Country sales forecasting models are considered by the Regional Managers.

Chapter 16
Mona El Fadly:
Spinning Off the Supply Chain

Menna Kamel
Strategist and Business Development Specialist, Egypt

Ali Awni
American University in Cairo (AUC), Egypt

EXECUTIVE SUMMARY

This case examines a business in the food catering industry and demonstrates the importance of supply chain practices even to an entrepreneur's small business. The business is legally registered as 'El Yosr Food Corner' and has been operating in Egypt since 1997. It provides standardized as well as customized home-made oriental dishes at competitive prices. By 2009, the surge in the growth of the business had strained the company's operational capabilities in various ways. Furthermore, the business had encountered a number of hitches as a result of inefficiencies in supply chain management. Menna Reda, El Yosr's consultant, was called in to advise the enterprise owner and managing director, Mona El Fadly, of the proper course of action to address these challenges.

INTRODUCTION

In October 2009, Mona El Fadly, the owner and managing director of El Yosr Food Corner, a privately owned food catering business in Cairo, Egypt, swiftly grabbed her records of purchase orders made to 'Sawaris supermarket'. As she flipped through the dozens of daily receipts, trains of thoughts ran through her mind. The business had been experiencing some difficulties over the past few months, from surges in demand to a mismanaged business-supplier relationship.

As El Fadly jotted down the last item in a customer's phone order, Menna Reda, El Yosr's consultant and an El Yosr customer, arrived at the company and their meeting was about to start. Reda had volunteered to work on this assignment; after the business's high-pressure operations had sparked her attention. Indeed, stress was very much a part of the atmosphere at El Yosr, so much so

DOI: 10.4018/978-1-60960-583-4.ch016

that El Fadly's kitchen operations might well be mistaken for an emergency surgery in a hospital.

Over the past couple of months, Reda learned during the meeting, El Fadly's business had witnessed a set of unfortunate events. The business had delivered three late orders - in fact, over three hours late each. El Fadly had also received a customer complaint regarding a batch of rock-like biscuits. The stuffed biscuits in question were considered the business's flagship brand in Maadi, a suburb of Cairo. The occasional unavailability of critical ingredients at her suppliers' retail stores added to the frustration, to say the least. In the past, the company had handled a much smaller number of orders and operated on a narrower scale. Today, with the ever- increasing items on the menu, the limited storage areas and the need to maintain strict freshness standards, something had to be done concerning business-supplier collaboration, and specifically, collaboration with El Yosr retail suppliers such as 'Sawaris supermarket'.

A few hours later, Reda came out of the company and smelled the warm breeze of *kofta* being grilled in the outdoor area of the company premises. As she walked away, she mentally reviewed the notes she had taken during the meeting, looking for answers to the two vital questions plaguing El Yosr: Could the company grow further with the current processes in place? Or had the company "outgrown" its existing processes?

ORGANIZATIONAL BACKGROUND

El Yosr Food Corner Overview

A mother of three and, for years, a dedicated housewife, Mona El Fadly lived in Maadi, a quiet neighborhood of Cairo, Egypt. As an Egyptian woman whose Middle Eastern culture was characterized by warmth and collectivism, El Fadly enjoyed an active social life. She was also a talented cook, a skill she put to use in her voluntary activities within the community, as well as socially. On holidays and special occasions, friends and neighbors regularly exchanged gifts in the form of cooked meals, and her own culinary skills had not passed unnoticed. In 1993, the peace and quiet of El Fadly's existence was shaken when friends and family urged her to turn her talent into a money-making activity, instead of engaging solely in the old time tradition of caring for her children and serving the community.

The year 1997 marked the beginning of El Fadly's success story. She started her own home-based catering service, cooking two to three times a week at her convenience. She sold *kahk* (Middle Eastern biscuits associated with *Eid El Fitr*, a major Islamic feast), petits fours, tuna cakes and a variety of other desserts, as well as club sandwiches. By 1998, she already had three assistants working full-time, from 8:00 am to 5:30 pm. Customers picked up their orders from her house.

As the business expanded, El Fadly began to realize her home could not continue to double up as her workshop. So in 2000, El Fadly moved her business to a small independent apartment in Maadi that accommodated five assistants and a delivery man. Between the years 2000 and 2003, El Fadly's business experienced two other moves within the neighborhood. In addition to space restrictions as the business continued to grow, El Fadly also had to deal with complaints about the business being in a residential building – the smell of food and the constant flow of people in and out of the apartment irritated some of the neighbors.

Finally, in 2003, El Fadly moved the business to the ground floor of a building owned by her family - an ideal solution. She suffered no more complaints from neighbors; she had her own garden, a private entrance and plenty of parking space; and she could also care closely for her mother, who lived in the same building and was very sick during the last year of her life.

El Fadly had only advertised twice since her business had started up: in the Yellow Pages and in a magazine distributed to the Maadi community. But unlike any other neighborhood in

Greater Cairo, Maadi had an unmatched network of people; it was a real grapevine. So, hardly any of her customers had come through these ads. Those who had contacted her through the advertisements were mostly companies trying to sell her their IT services, insecticides or design materials. In essence, El Fadly's business had evolved through personal recommendations and word of mouth that extended even beyond the geographical boundaries of Maadi.

Products, Customers and Competition

El Fadly specialized in producing homemade food. She offered three food categories on her menu: appetizers, hot dishes and desserts (see Figures 1, 2 and Table 1). The appetizers were a combination of finely picked fresh salads and Middle Eastern starters, such as *kobeba* (stuffed meat) and *sambousak* (stuffed pastry). The hot dishes she served were a variety of well-known Middle Eastern and international cuisine recipes based on poultry, beef, veal, turkey, fish, vegetables and/or rice, to name a few, as well as recipes of El Fadly's own creation. Desserts on her menu included date soufflé, an all-time favorite with most of her customers, and a variety of cakes.

The menu distributed to El Fadly's customers was just a short list of the dozens of items she produced. A more detailed list of the items she offered, along with photos of the dishes, was available on the business's website. In total, El Fadly offered 19 salads, 16 starters, 27 beef or veal plates, 28 white meat plates, 7 fish plates, 21 pasta and rice plates, any kind of vegetable *tagen* or *tajin* (stew cooked in an earthenware casserole), and 20 desserts. These items came in four different sizes: small, medium, large and a special size for parties and events – not to mention custom-made orders.

Customers were mainly females who would personally recommend El Fadly to their friends and acquaintances. El Fadly's business was known to her customers as Mona El Fadly and not "El Yosr Food Corner," which in time served only as

Figure 1. Full menu (© 2010 Mona El Fadly. Used with permission)

Figure 2. Abridged menu (© 2010 Mona El Fadly. Used with permission)

Table 1. Company menu

Appetizers
Salads: Fattoush, tabboula, beans, hommos, tehena, Caesar salad
Sambousak: Cheese, beef, spinach, mixed
Spring rolls: Vegetables, shrimps, chicken, mombar, kobeba
Chicken
Sheesh tawook
Stuffed chicken with rice
Chicken Sharkaseya
Beef
Fatet shawerma
Alexandrian liver
Kofta Dawood Pasha
Fish
Fried shrimps
Fish with tehena
Pasta
Lasagna
Béchamel pasta
Desserts
Cakes: Chocolate, carrot, orange
Date soufflé
Om Ali
Basbousa

the business's legally registered name. Even her business cards were titled Mona El Fadly (see Figure 3). El Fadly offered food catering services to households and for special events such as baby showers, engagements and weddings, as well as events and exhibitions organized by universities and embassies.

The competition El Fadly faced was not fierce, but it was still there, mainly represented by restaurant chains that offered food catering as their second line of business. Other housewives who had transformed their cooking talent into a business also provided a similar service. And the community organization she volunteered at in itself represented competition. Located in Maadi, just 500 meters away from El Fadly's business, the organization was part of a mosque, where well-off women volunteered their time to teach crochet, Qur'an, cooking, and computer skills, among a range of other skills. The kitchen division in the organization had been established by El Fadly long ago and eventually came to be oper-

Figure 3. El Fadly's personal business card (© 2010 Mona El Fadly. Used with permission)

ated by people who had been personally taught cooking and packaging by El Fadly.

The Unique Selling Proposition

El Fadly was not a restaurant, a fast-food pickup place or an event planner. People came to El Fadly for three reasons. As one of her customer's put it: "She provides me with homemade food with no kitchen hassle, made according to my specifications, and I know for a fact that the food will be ready and on time for my 20-person gathering today, even though I just made the order yesterday."

The business's core competencies rested on three pillars: *customization*, *reliability* and *competitive prices*. The kitchen had the ability to cater to a customer's exact needs. Besides the standard items on the menu, El Yosr could produce a customer's variation of an existing recipe, or a new dish altogether. This high level of customization was coupled with reliable service. Customers expected El Fadly to accept their orders even at short notice. Officially, orders were only accepted 36 hours prior to the requested delivery time. However, due to the personal relationship between El Fadly and her customers, orders were almost always accepted. 'Our savior' or 'our rescuer' were words often used by customers to describe El Fadly. To top it all, El Fadly provided her services at reasonable prices.

Culture and Values

El Yosr had an implicit but strong business culture. The company's values were not printed and displayed on any of the walls of the premises, but they were deeply shared by those who chose to work with El Fadly. The business stood on unique principles, some of which were hard to find in business or management cultures, but could be found in cultures that were closely tied to religion and fate. Such was the case at El Yosr, which was guided by the belief in the existence of a divine force in this universe.

There were five basic principles that governed the business's operations:

"Faster Than Light"

The statement 'faster than light' highlighted the importance of speed to El Fadly's business. El Fadly accompanied almost every request she directed at her employees with this phrase, to impress upon them the urgency of producing a delicious meal in as short a time as possible, so that they could cope with the various other orders for the day.

"Flexibility to the Nth Degree"

At El Fadly's, flexibility was essential in every aspect of service delivery, from flexibility in cooking, to flexibility in packing the meals, to flexibility in delivery. El Fadly had almost never said 'no' to a customer's request. The customer's own recipes were accepted no matter how bizarre and impossible they seemed. Likewise, depending on the customer's needs, food could be packed in the customer's serving dishes, the business's own fancy set or even in disposable aluminum plates as individual meals for a big event. If the business's set was used, customers were expected to return the dishes to El Yosr's premises at their convenience. Flexibility in time and method of delivery was just another form of the same principle; customers could either pick up their orders or have them delivered to their doorstep.

"Adding the Homemade Touch"

El Fadly's food resembled homemade food in every way, from the taste of each dish to the packaging and display of the final order. Likewise, El Fadly's serving dishes resembled a typical household's set, so even when customers did not use their own serving plates, the guests believed that their hostess had cooked the delicious and professional looking dishes herself. Cooking skills and capabilities were a matter of pride among some of the women in El Fadly's community. The fact that the food was prepared by El Fadly was only revealed to the hostess's most intimate friends at the gathering, who would later follow suit when hosting their own gatherings.

"The Customer Is Always Right"

As old as this principle may seem, it was often repeated by El Fadly to her employees. Unlike other company values, this one occasionally met with staff resistance. This was especially evident when employees were late in delivering an order because they suspected the customer had deliberately set an earlier delivery time than necessary to guard against a possible one to two hour delay by El Yosr. Since they believed they were meeting the customer's real needs, the employees were sure that the arrival of the order after the requested delivery time would not create a negative image of the quality of El Fadly's service.

El Fadly's usual response to such a statement was: "I am not concerned with the fact that the customer might be over or underestimating the time needed. All we should focus on is delivering the packages at the exact time the customer requested." Meanwhile, El Fadly always advised her customers to set a delivery time that would allow the food to be served hot to the guests, or to be heated up in such a way as not to affect the quality of the food.

Other forms of resistance appeared if the business received a customer complaint. When this happened, the employees tended to come up with excuses and blame the customer instead. Because of this, El Fadly and her direct assistant always handled any complaints themselves.

"Ethics Above Everything"

Business ethics and personal ethics were of extreme importance to the company and to El Fadly, in particular. She prioritized ethics over business profitability, and honesty above ROI (Return on Investment). Unethical competitive intelligence practices were rejected by El Fadly. Tips to chefs that were received before an order was delivered were returned immediately and late deliveries were compensated.

El Fadly was a hardworking woman. She was not troubled when the end of a month approached without their being even midway to covering monthly expenditure. She had faith and confidence, and it worked for her. Typically, before such a month came to a close, she would unexpectedly receive an order for a huge wedding or at least two exhibitions. Some people called it luck; but she believed she was blessed.

The Business Operations

On a regular day, El Fadly was up and at her desk between 9:00 am and 10:00 am, ready to revise the daily checklist with a physical count of all stock in place. This process clarified what items were on hand and what needed to be ordered to ensure a suitable stock of safe items (products always in demand) and semi-cooked items (work in progress). After she had accomplished this task, El Fadly would start her daily routine of receiving orders, procuring raw materials and overseeing staff.

Order Taking

Customers interacted with the business in three main ways: through phone calls, by visiting the business's premises and/or through the company website. However, orders were only taken by phone or at the premises. The business had two phone numbers: El Fadly's personal cell phone and the office number, both of which were used for order taking. Officially, orders had to be made during working hours (from 8:30 am to 5:30 pm) and 36 hours ahead of delivery time. But in actual practice, customers called El Fadly at any time of the day or night and sometimes made orders only a few hours ahead of delivery time. They were always certain their orders would be taken. Occasionally, customers would visit the business premises to deliver their serving dishes, discuss and agree on details regarding the planned event and the quantities to be delivered, or sample some of the dishes on the menu.

The frequency of the orders and, thus, the nature of demand, was another story altogether (see Table 2). Demand was very seasonal, yet unpredictable, with many surges, especially during Ramadan, the Muslim holy month and El Fadly's most profitable month of the year (see Table 3). The business received two distinct types of orders, set-menu or standardized orders, and customized orders. Predicting the recipes and ingredients that would be needed was hardest in the case of customized orders, since no particular pattern of demand could be identified.

Table 2. The nature of demand

Month	Description of Demand
January	**Uncertain**
February	**Low** **Possible reasons**: A typical customer would have consumed his/her money in expenses related to school fees, private lessons and the mid year vacation
March	**High** **Possible reasons**: Demand associated with various Mother's day exhibitions.
April	**Moderate** **Possible reasons**: Demand associated with occasional weddings.
May-June	**High** **Possible reasons**: Demand associated with university events, where El Fadly provides food catering to university students & professors during oral examination period.
July	**Low** **Possible reasons**: Customers experience decreased expenditure during the period of secondary education's final examination, and demand is largely by weddings during the month
August	**Uncertain** **Possible reasons**: Customers travel for summer vacations and weddings remain the main source of income during this month
September-October	**Moderate** **Possible reasons**: Weddings demand driven period
November-December	**Moderate** **Possible reasons**: Parents celebrate their children's birthdays during a regular school year and before the mid year vacation

(Regardless of the typical nature of demand during these twelve months, the month of Ramadan experiences above average demand. Ramadan is considered El Fadly's most profitable month of the year.)

Over time, as the business had grown, so had the number of orders El Fadly received on her personal cell phone. Her family had begged her not to take calls after working hours and to spend some uninterrupted time with them. Eventually, El Fadly had bought another phone for strictly personal and family use. Nevertheless, she continued to be bombarded with orders on her business phone line while dining at night with her family and could never fight the urge to take the call.

Customers preferred to call El Fadly rather than a staff member, for two reasons. The first was that most of El Fadly's customers were her friends and acquaintances who appreciated the personal aspect of El Fadly's business. The second was because El Fadly always had good advice to give - about the type of food to be served for a particular occasion, the appropriate quantities to serve relative to the number of people invited, and other suggestions of the kind. El Fadly could even be categorized as an events consultant or planner, due to the range of value-added services she provided her customers at no extra cost. Such services included making agreements with wholesalers to provide customers with plates, table sets and chairs, especially for engagements, weddings and big birthday parties.

Administrative Tasks

Once an order arrived, a form detailing the client's name, address, delivery time, and the exact order description was filled and three carbon copies automatically made and distributed internally. A copy went instantly to the kitchen's head chef, El Fadly's direct assistant and El Fadly herself, for the purposes of actual operations and cooking, follow up, and management control of business operations respectively. At this preliminary stage, two more tasks were undertaken: transportation arrangements for final order delivery and the pick up of serving dishes from customers (if customers wished to use their own serving platters).

Table 3. The Holy Month of Ramadan

Ramadan is the ninth month of the lunar, Islamic (*Hijri*) calendar**. During this sacred month, Muslims engage in religious rituals and acts of worship. Most notably, they practice abstinence, fasting from dawn to sunset. Fasting Muslims have two main meals: *sohour* and *iftar*. *Sohour* takes place before dawn to prepare fasters for the next fasting day, while *iftar* celebrates the completion of a day of abstinence, when Muslims break their fast by eating and drinking upon the call to sunset prayer. The month of Ramadan is one in which Muslims also practice charity and perform good deeds. One of the most common acts of charity during Ramadan is to provide meals for *iftar* or *sohour* to poor and underprivileged members of the community. Some Muslims put up special food shelters that can serve dozens of underprivileged fasters during *iftar*.
In addition to the religious practices associated with Ramadan, the month in Egypt is a festive one. Families, friends and acquaintances gather over *iftar* or *sohour* to celebrate this holy month, and invitations to meals are exchanged all month round. People generally stay up late in acts of worship till *sohour*. At the end of Ramadan, people celebrate three days of *Eid El Fitr*, which they spend in prayer and in visits to relatives and friends. *Kahk*, a cookie associated with *Eid El Fitr*, is generally offered to guests or hosts during that period.
El Fadly is kept especially busy during this month, not only with family gatherings and social events over *iftar* and *sohour*, but also with the preparation of packed meals to be distributed before *iftar* among the poor on the street or in slum areas, or delivered to her customers' special food shelters.
** The lunar calendar has an 11-12 day offset from the Gregorian calendar, and accordingly, over the years, coincides with different Gregorian months.

Kitchen Operations

Upon receiving an order, the head chef would assign different tasks to staff members. Depending on the order, these typically included cutting the meat, marinating the chicken, heating the pan, lighting the charcoal grill, stir frying the vegetables, rolling the sandwiches and icing the cake.

Regardless of the orders on hand, one or two cooks would be engaged in the preparation of semi-cooked food (i.e. work in progress). *Kobeba*, for example, was one of the popular items on the menu that could be stored in the form of a precooked meal. At any given time, El Fadly had to have 200 units of *kobeba* in stock. The cooks would prepare the *kobeba*, freeze it and then fry or bake it on demand (see Figure 4). In general, this "postponement" strategy was applied to all pastries, because they could retain their freshness in a frozen form, which reduced preparation lead time substantially.

To match supply with demand, El Fadly cooked a few standard items everyday, even before orders were made. Items such as rice, for example, enjoyed a pattern of demand that was more predictable than others. Almost every order delivered to customers was served with rice.

Meanwhile, El Fadly would record more orders from customers, instruct her staff to redo a few of the sandwich rolls that were not up to standard, and along with this, would answer general inquiries from staff regarding the specific details of the order, or give her approval of the final look of the dish.

When an order was ready, El Fadly would test the quality of the product and add her final artistic touches, spreading out the sauce in her own special way and garnishing the plate with bell pepper and a lemon butterfly. Almost all orders were instantly passed along to the delivery stage, after they had been personally tested by El Fadly. As for the few that were redirected to the kitchen, they were fixed or redone, and the cook in charge instructed of the mistake.

Delivery to the Customer

The delivery phase started when the order was packaged and placed in the trunk of a taxi or in the customer's car. At this point, the order was crossed out as 'met' on the business's records. Usually, delivery to the customer, which was restricted to Cairo, Giza, Helwan and 6th of October – in short, Greater Cairo - was made through El Fadly's network of taxi drivers. Since these taxi drivers worked with El Fadly on an individual and as-needed basis, they were sometimes unavailable. As a result, El Fadly had begun to consider other alternatives.

El Fadly had discussed the option of buying her own fleet of cars, because unlike other food businesses, she could not transport her products by motorcycle due to the large size of the orders and serving plates, and because of the use of sauce in most of her recipes. El Fadly believed that buying a fleet of cars would solve the problems of occasional

Figure 4. Kitchen operations: Kobeba (© 2010 Mona El Fadly. Used with permission)

unavailability of taxi drivers and late deliveries. This alternative would undeniably allow El Fadly to have greater control over the delivery and distribution phase. But Reda had warned El Fadly of the implications of such a decision.

The business's latest incident of late delivery had occurred one month before the meeting with Reda. El Fadly had been asked to deliver a large order to a customer's party in 6th of October city by 1 pm. Although the order was out of the kitchen and in the taxis' trunks on time, it arrived three hours late to a disappointed customer and a limited number of guests. The other guests had already left. El Fadly had been deeply upset by how events had unfolded and had refused to receive any payment from this customer. In the midst of her tears, she received a call from a close acquaintance who had referred the customer to El Fadly. "Mona, I know that this was an exception to your flawless service, and we appreciate your concern, but you cannot refuse to take your money," the lady had insisted. But El Fadly had remained firm.

El Fadly stopped using the services of the head driver responsible for the delay, especially after she discovered that the reason behind the delay was his refusal to ask for directions or to call El Fadly to report the delay. This incident highlighted the problem of accountability. It became evident that the delivery system in place only holds individual drivers accountable. It does not hold a specific business entity or employee in charge accountable, a matter that could cause further problems as the business continued to grow.

THE SUPPLY SIDE OF THE SUPPLY CHAIN

Inventory and Stock

El Fadly had three storage rooms. Two of the storage rooms were fully equipped with customized freezing and refrigeration equipment that enabled the business to store safe items, such as raw meat and minced meat, and any precooked items. Additionally, El Fadly stored dry items such as sugar, rice and oil. The amount stored per item was usually equivalent to one week's consumption, and it was held in inventory for a maximum of two weeks. If an item was close to the two-week expiry limit, it was removed from the storage area to the kitchen, where it was transformed into a finished good that was given away to people in need of food, rather than sold.

The Business's Suppliers

The business dealt with three types of suppliers: butchers, wholesalers and retail supermarkets (see Figure 5). These included 6-7 butchers, only a few wholesalers and 4-5 retail supermarkets.

Butchers provided El Fadly with all types of raw meat, both white and red. The wholesalers provided El Fadly with bulk purchases, especially herbs, spices, oil, sugar, nuts and chocolates. Retail supermarkets provided El Fadly with all types of commodities, whether locally produced or imported. El Fadly kept records of her pur-

Figure 5. The supply chain

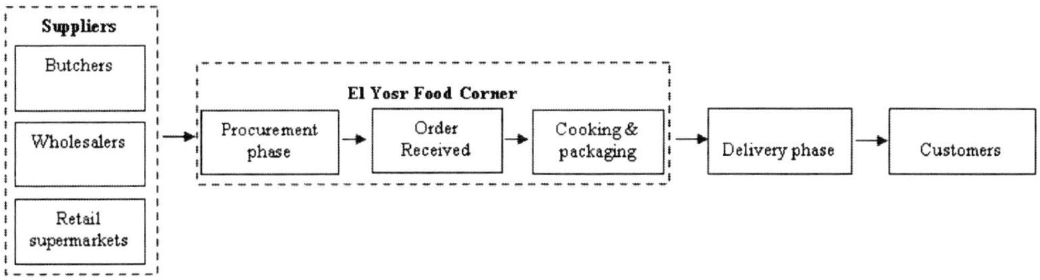

chases on a daily basis using a manual paper-based recording system. The system was effective but not as efficient as computerized recording systems. Moreover, due to the lack of a computerized system, the company could not utilize any analytical tools.

Payment arrangements differed from one type of supplier to the other. Butchers received their payments once every two to three days. Wholesalers had a more relaxed credit system whereby El Fadly paid over a period of one month. Payment was made upon delivery of the product, regardless of the quality of items delivered. Supermarkets received their cash payments upon purchase. Apart from Sawaris supermarket, which offered El Fadly a discount, all other supermarkets dealt with El Fadly as an ordinary customer. The discount was negligible compared to the revenue generated for the supermarkets by El Fadly's business alone.

The degree of collaboration between El Fadly and the butchers was high. The butchers were very accommodating about delivering large quantities to her doorstep and delivering on time. They were also very flexible about delivery hours, responding to requests sometimes as late as 1:00 am or 2:00 am during high seasons. Moreover, they were quick to make recommendations to El Fadly when they received cattle yielding good quality meat. Wholesalers, on the other hand, supported El Fadly only by delivering her orders to her doorstep. Retail supermarkets exhibited minimal collaboration. Unlike the butchers and wholesalers, they did not deliver. El Fadly had to send a staff member to retail outlets to carry out the shopping. On average, El Fadly's staff made around 12 visits per day to the supermarkets.

The Procurement Strategy

A periodic ordering system was applied to materials procured from butchers and wholesalers, the period varying from one season to the other, especially with regard to orders from butchers. In the case of supermarkets, on the other hand, purchases were made on a continuous basis. El Fadly bought stock items like cheese and milk as the need arose. Items tended to be purchased for every couple of customer orders. This enabled El Fadly to provide fresh food, save on storage costs and avoid overstocking perishable goods. However, it also contributed to the high frequency of daily visits by staff to the supermarkets, and when a retail supermarket was out of stock of a certain item, shortages occurred and El Fadly's employees ended up spending more time hunting for the item elsewhere.

Commenting on the nature of the relationship between El Fadly and her suppliers, Reda had explained to El Fadly during their meeting that:

The continuous ordering system certainly eliminates any "artificial" surges due to ordering method, but it needs a high level of coordination between your business and your suppliers. I also noticed that the power in the channel of procurement is a bit distorted. El Yosr Food Corner is a key client for any retail supermarket, and the fact that you have not approached your suppliers for a formal agreement explains the low discount rate and the fact that you have to bear the full burden of absorbing any increase in the prices of raw materials. Your record of large purchases should have grabbed the attention of the retail chains and prompted them to approach you as a partner, rather than an ordinary...

Before Reda had had a chance to complete the sentence, El Fadly had interrupted:

I should speak to them. Sawaris's previous branch manager was very keen to maintain regular contact with me. He handled my orders with special care and checked regularly to make sure my needs were being met. I believe he realized the importance of my business to his monthly sales report, but now with a new manager in place, we are back to square one: no collaboration.

CONCLUSION

Faced with a next-year business plan that included opening the second El Fadly branch in just a few months, Reda had to think fast of recommendations to present to El Fadly at their next meeting. While the proper management of the various components of the supply chain was, to Reda's way of thinking, a top priority, the stress El Fadly was always under made Reda question the load of work an entrepreneur like El Fadly should be handling.

As she analyzed the business situation, she knew her recommendations would have to fit El Yosr's business culture - a culture combining a business/profit making orientation with a people/humanitarian one.

At the end of their meeting, El Fadly had pointed out that:

Many people have suggested that I use a computerized system to solve the challenges we face. I cannot, because the budget cannot cover these capital expenditures and my staff is not qualified to use computer software.

Reda was not concerned with the adoption of new technology. Rather, her attention was focused on the actual operations. "If something is not done about procurement, quality testing and delivery to the customer, the business might die from growth," she pondered as she reviewed her notes (see Table 4).

Table 4. Reda's notes

While concepts of operations strategy and supply chain management are mostly applied to larger organizations, Reda believed that many of these widely known concepts could be applied to El Fadly's business. Below are a number of concepts she jotted down as they crossed her mind:
10/2009
Postponement strategy: Entails "the ability of a supply chain to delay product differentiation or customization until closer to the time the product is sold." (Chopra, & Meindl, 2007)
Supplier relationship management: Is concerned with building and retaining relationships between a company and its suppliers, who are at the upstream side of the supply chain. (Chopra, & Meindl, 2007)
Functional products: Products characterized by a long product lifecycle and stable demand. (Lee, 2002)
Innovative products: Products characterized by a short lifecycle, high innovation and unpredictable demand. (Lee, 2002)
Bullwhip effect: Constitutes "amplified fluctuations in demand" (Narayanan, & Raman, 2004)

REFERENCES

Chopra, S., & Meindl, P. (2007). *Supply chain management: Strategy, planning & operations*. (pp. 328, 491). Upper Saddle River, NJ: Pearson Education, Inc.

Lee, H. L. (2002). Aligning supply chain strategies with product uncertainties. *California Management Review Reprint Series*, *44*(3), 105–119.

Narayanan, V. G., & Raman, A. (2004). Aligning incentives in supply chains. The 21st-century supply chain. *Harvard Business Review*, 94–102.

Chapter 17
KOHLER®:
Forecasting for Project-Based Market

Ali Awni
American University in Cairo (AUC), Egypt

Mohamed Nada
Kohler Co., Egypt

EXECUTIVE SUMMARY

A newly appointed Middle East regional marketing manager for a major sanitary ware producer is exploring options to improve sales forecasts. The old forecasting method, which was based on historical sales from distributors' retail stores, performed very poorly. Regional sales were driven mainly by large construction projects in the Gulf countries. A new approach that explicitly considers the status of each project and the stock-keeping units (SKUs) demanded shows promise.

INTRODUCTION

In late 2008, Mohammed Nada joined Kohler Co., a leader in bathroom and kitchen sanitary ware products, as the company's Regional Marketing Manager stationed in Dubai. One of Mr. Nada's main responsibilities was to prepare the company's periodical regional sales forecast in cooperation with the Supply Chain Group in Paris, France. The forecast was used to determine the quantities of the components and raw materials to be purchased, and the production plan required to ensure that the ordered products were delivered on time.

DOI: 10.4018/978-1-60960-583-4.ch017

Kohler Co. was experiencing good growth in sales, mainly from construction projects in the Gulf countries. In one case, the demand for one slow-moving product from one project alone was equivalent to 12 years' worth of the demand for this product in Europe.

The old forecasting approach relied on historical demand at the company's retail stores. This approach produced poor results when applied to Gulf sales. It resulted in tremendous pressure related to the procurement of components and the production of final products to ensure that project orders were met on time.

Top management was very concerned about the large forecast errors at the stock-keeping unit (SKU) level and the resulting impact on purchasing and production. A new forecasting approach had to be developed that explicitly reflected the needs of the main demand driver in the region: construction projects.

COMPANY BACKGROUND

Kohler Co. is one of America's oldest and largest privately held companies. Kohler Co. has a global presence, with 30,000 associates, 51 plants worldwide, and a diverse portfolio of leading brands in plumbing, engines and power generation systems, fine furniture, hospitality and world-class golf destinations.

Kohler Co. is a recognized leader in kitchen and bath products. The company offers a diverse collection of products that continually sets new standards in design, technology, craftsmanship, and innovation, covering a broad price range.

Kohler Co. owns two brands for sanitary ware: Kohler, a brand based in the United States (US), produced and manufactured in facilities across the US, China, India, and Thailand; and Jacob Delafon, a French brand with manufacturing facilities in France, Spain, Morocco, and Egypt. In the 1980s, Kohler acquired Jacob Delafon to improve its position in markets where it had a weak presence. Jacob Delafon's production facilities and sales operations were retained.

PRODUCT LINES

Kohler and Jacob Delafon offer customers a diverse range of bathroom products. The following eight product categories/lines are offered:

Ceramics: These are products made from vitreous china or fireclay material. In a bathroom, a complete set of ceramic products would be a toilet, toilet seat, bidet and washbasin. Figure 1 presents

Figure 1. Formilia product model/range

an example of the ceramics product category, namely the Formilia product range. Figure 2 lists some of the SKUs within the range.

Faucets/brassware: Faucets are products made from brass, providing water within the bathroom in washbasins, bidets and showers. A full set of brassware products would be a washbasin mixer, bath and shower mixer, and a bidet mixer. Figure 3 provides a list of SKUs under the "Purist," faucet category/line.

Acrylics: These refer to bathtubs made from different kinds of acrylic materials, and come in different shapes, sizes, and designs. Figure 4 shows acrylic bathtubs from the product model/range Odeon Up.

Cast iron: Cast iron products, which are used for decorative purposes, are made from galvanized iron to give an antique and precious look.

Shower panels: Shower panels are manufactured from acrylic material. Shower doors made from glass or plastic form enclosures around the

Figure 2. The Formilia, model/range consists of several SKUs

Kohler SKU	Product Picture	Product Description
4448K		P Trap pan (64 x 36 cm). Comfort height : 41 cm. Supplied with softclose themoset seat 6472K, metal hinges. Invisible fixing set included. Low flush 4 or 6l.
4461K		Independant back - to wall vario pan (54 x 36 cm). Comfort height : 41 cm. Supplied with a soft close seat 6472K with metal hinges. Invisible fixing set included. 4 or 6L.
5008K		Wall hung bidet (54 x 36 cm). 1 tap hole, with overflow cover E4061.
4147K		Self supporting vanity top (100 x 46 cm) double basin. 1 hole per basin. Can be installed on Formilia furniture
4151K		Self supporting semi recessed vanity top (100 x 41 cm). 1 hole left. Can be installed on Formilia furniture
4146K		Self supporting vanity top (60 x 46 cm), right basin, 1 tap hole.
4147K		Self supporting vanity top (60 x 46 cm), left basin, 1 tap hole.
5095K		Double basin self-supporting vanity top (100 x 46 cm). 1 tap hole per basin. Can be installed on Formilia furniture.
5092K		Self-supporting vanity top (60 x 46 cm). 1 tap hole. Can be installed on Formilia furniture.
5090K		Self-supporting vanity top (80 x 46 cm) 1 tap hole. Can be installed on Formilia furniture.
4172K		Self supporting vanity top (120 x 46 cm). 1 tap hole left, 1 tap hole right. Can be installed on Formilia furniture.

Figure 3. Purist product model/range with three different SKUs

Kohler SKU	Product Picture	Product Description
14594D-3-CP	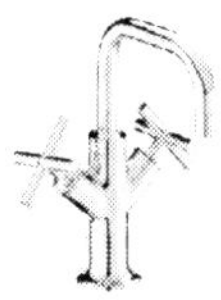	Purist washbasin 2 handle mixer chrome
14595D-3-CP	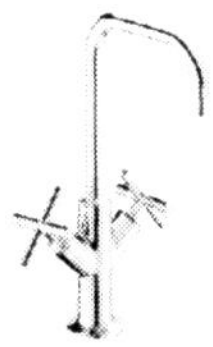	Purist washbasin tall 2 holes mixer ch
14596D-3-CP	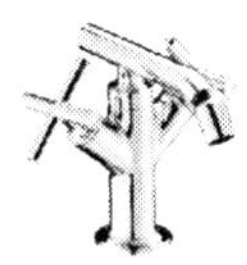	Purist bidet 2 handle mixer, chrome

Figure 4. Odeon UP acrylic bathtubs product category/line

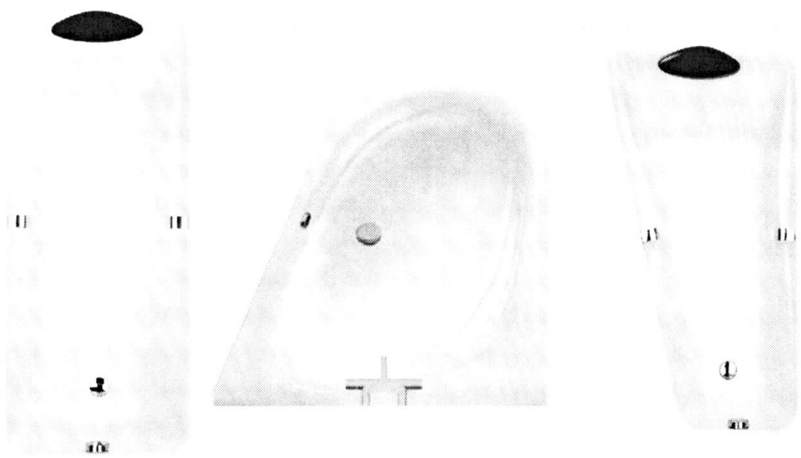

shower panels in walk-in baths, which are square and flat on the ground. Figure 5 shows some of the shower panels and doors available within the Kohler range.

Cabinetry: Cabinets complete the look of the bathroom. Usually made of wood, they are typically placed under the washbasin and around the bathroom for storage. Mirrors are also a part of this range, as mirror enclosures are used for storage as well. Figure 6 shows a list of SKUs under the cabinetry product category/line "Odeon Up."

Accessories: Ranging from towel bars and rings to toilet paper holders and soap dispensers, Kohler's accessories are all brassware items that complete the feel of the bathroom. Figure 7 shows some of these accessories.

Figure 5. Shower panels and doors product category/line

Flight tray product model/range

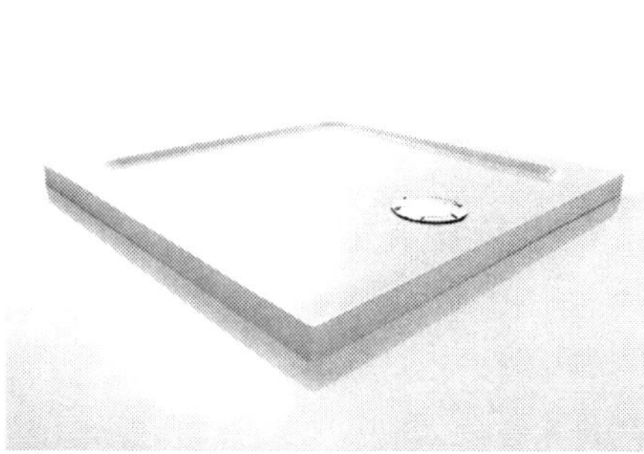

Flight tray product model/range

Quadrant product model/range

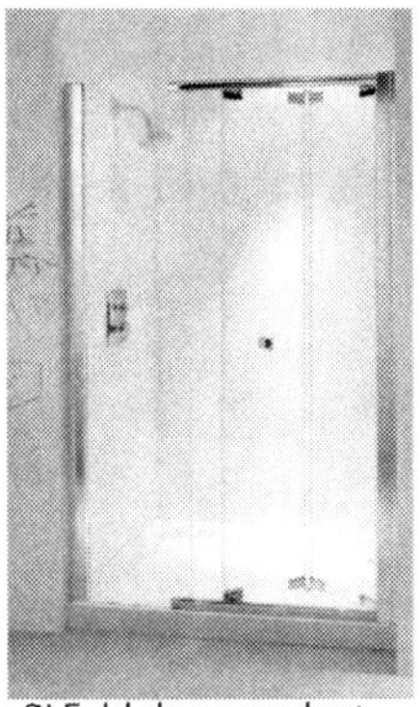

Bi Fold door product model/range

Sliding door product model/range

Pivot door product model/range

Figure 6. Odeon Up product model/range which falls under the cabinetry product category/line with three different SKUs

Kohler SKU	Product Picture	Product Description
4041K	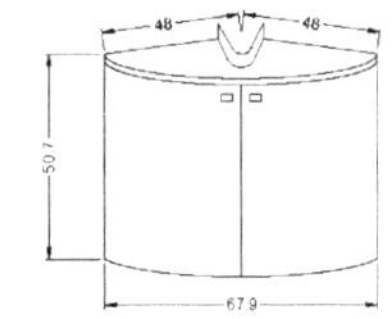	Corner base unit under corner lavatory
4029W	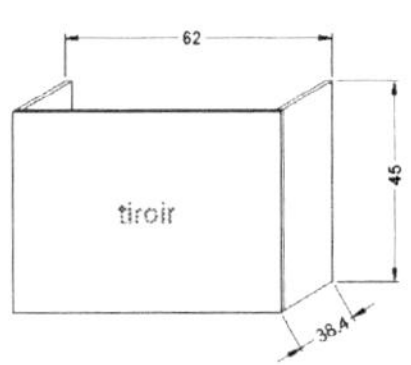	Base unit under vanity
4049W	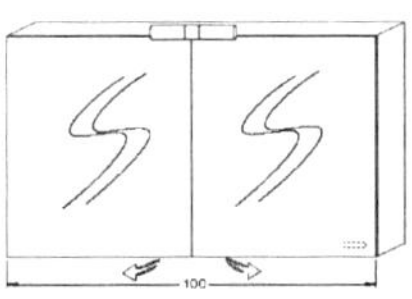	Mirrored cabinet L100, double mirror

Figure 7. Accessories product category/line

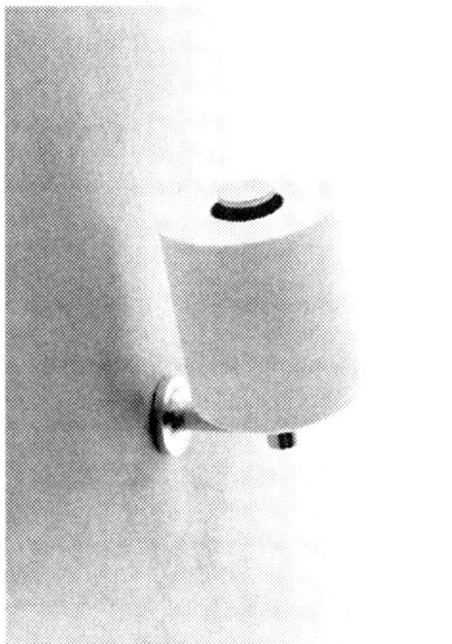

Toilet paper holder

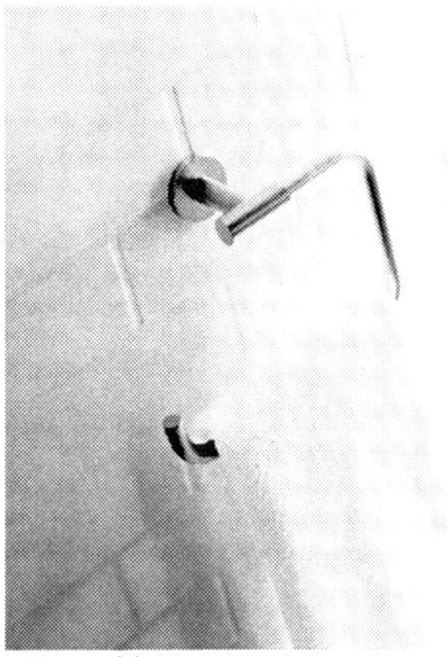

Towel hanger

KOHLER CO. IN THE MIDDLE EAST

Kohler Co. recognizes the Middle East as one of the fastest growing regions in the world. Kohler Co.'s products are available in ten countries of the region: the United Arab Emirates (UAE), the Kingdom of Saudi Arabia (KSA), Qatar, Oman, Bahrain, Kuwait, Lebanon, Jordan, Syria, and Egypt. Each country has distributors/agents that partner with Kohler Co. on a local level to sell products produced by the manufacturing facilities of Kohler and Jacob Delafon around the world. Prior to the acquisition of Jacob Delafon, separate distributors existed for each brand in each country. After the acquisition, in countries where two distributors existed, one was assigned for each brand; otherwise, distributors began selling both brands. Table 1 shows a list of Kohler's distributors in the Middle East. Each distributor is responsible for sales in their area by committing to targets with top management at the beginning of every year. Targets are achieved by selling products from the existing Kohler / Jacob Delafon range.

The Middle East has two types of markets: project-based markets and retail-based markets. In Gulf countries, the project sector accounts for 85% to 90% of the value of sales, while the retail sector accounts for 10% to 15% of the sales value. In countries like Egypt and Lebanon, the contributions of the project and retail sectors are completely reversed: the retail sector accounts for more than 80% of the total sales value and the project sector accounts for 20%.

RETAIL-BASED MARKETS IN THE MIDDLE EAST

In Egypt, Lebanon, Jordan, and Syria, most of the local residents purchase residential units and furnish them separately (on their own). This entails buying most of the furnishing materials on a retail basis. Numerous sanitary ware companies display their products in showrooms with the aim of maximizing their distribution and visibility. Customers furnishing their units visit the showrooms of distributors to choose products to their taste and in accordance with the design needs of their homes. Sanitary ware companies such as Kohler Co. rely on their distributors in those countries to generate a continuous pull of products from customers' demand. Such demand is affected by seasonality and other trends that affect the construction market. The overall steady increase in population in these countries sustains an ever-increasing demand in this type of market.

Sales in retails-based markets depend heavily on factors such as product price, design, advertis-

Table 1. Middle East distributors' list

Country	Distributor Name	Kohler Distributor	JD Distributor
United Arab Emirates	Al Hashimiya Building Materials	Yes	
	Al Ghandi Building Material Co. L.L.C.		Yes
Saudi Arabia	Technical Agencies Co. Ltd	Yes	Yes
	Ibrahim M. Al Najran Sanitary Ware Specialist	Yes	Yes
Qatar	Khalid Corporation W.L.L.	Yes	
	Shebib & Ali Al Attiya Co.		Yes
Oman	Al Ansari Trading Enterprise L.L.C.	Yes	
	Al Mutawaa Trading Co. L.L.C.	Yes	Yes
Bahrain	Elames	Yes	Yes
Jordan	Shehadeh	Yes	Yes
Kuwait	Abdul Aziz Ibrahim Al Rumaih & Co. L.L.	Yes	
Lebanon	Wadih Jreissati et Fils Sanitary Wares & Ceramic Tiles	Yes	Yes
	Geachan Group	Yes	Yes
Egypt	Home Fashion	Yes	
Syria	Damask Rose		Yes

ing and quality. Usually local suppliers dominate the market due to their very competitive prices and extensive distribution networks.

PROJECT-BASED MARKETS IN THE MIDDLE EAST

In the UAE, KSA, Qatar, Bahrain, Oman, and Kuwait, projects dominate the construction business. This is due to the fact that most of the populations residing in these countries are expatriates who do not purchase their units but, rather, rent them for the duration of their stay in the country. Most of these units, therefore, are developed and owned by real estate companies that invest in building residential towers, high-rise buildings, compounds, villas, and commercial towers to satisfy market demand.

Sanitary ware is procured through a tendering process within the construction project. A different set of players, other than the resident/owner in the retail sector, are involved in the buying process. In this case, consultants, contractors, developers, architects, and designers are the decision makers. Residents come into the units when they are completely built and have no say in the choice of the sanitary ware installed.

Depending on the decision maker, a completely different set of buying criteria applies to the project sector. For developers, architects, and designers, the most prestigious brands would be installed to boost the value and design of their projects. For consultants, product quality and technical specifications would be the decisive factor, while for contractors, price is the most important factor, affecting their ability to maximize their profits from the project.

INITIAL FORECASTING METHODOLOGY

The product forecast for the Middle East is developed by the local team and sent to Paris, France for consolidation with the forecasts for the other markets in the EMEA (Europe, Middle East, and Africa) region. Forecasting methodologies employed by Kohler Co. in the EMEA are influenced

Table 2. Forecast in retail-based market

PATIO	Article Code	%		Jan	Feb	Mar	Apr	May	June	July	Aug	Sept	Oct	Nov	Déc
Wall hung bowl	E4187	56.96%	0	524	635	758	498	496	464	0	0	0	0	0	0
Pack P trap	E4192	0.24%	0	2	3	3	2	2	2	0	0	0	0	0	0
Pack S trap	E4193	30.58%	0	281	341	407	268	266	249	0	0	0	0	0	0
Washbasin 60	E4159	12.22%	0	112	136	163	107	106	100	0	0	0	0	0	0
Washbasin 55	E4158	0.00%	0	0	0	0	0	0	0	0	0	0	0	0	0

by the retail-based orientation of France, the hub country of the region.

For the Middle East, forecasting is conducted on a rolling nine-month horizon. This forecast is used to plan sales, purchasing, production, and distribution. Each month, an update takes place to review the numbers and take into consideration any changes in the coming period.

Under the old system, an Excel sheet was created with a list of all products in each category on the leftmost column of the sheet, with columns corresponding to sale history and forecasts for 12 months. This sheet would show seasonality and trends in sales. The table was further broken down by stock keeping unit (SKU). Each family of products consists of several SKUs. For example, in the faucets category the full set of SKUs would be the washbasin mixer, bath and shower mixer, and bidet mixer. Each SKU had to be forecasted independently and the figures inserted into the table. Every product model/range in every product category/line had to go through the same process, a process that was time consuming and led to inaccuracies. Table 2 provides a simple example of what the outcome looked like.

As the table shows, the Patio model/range is formed of five SKUs, the wall hung bowl, P-trap, S-trap, 60 cm wash basin, and 55 cm washbasin. Each SKU is referred to using an article code and description. Percentages in the third column are calculated based on previous sales history. So, for example, if the Middle East market sold 10,000 pieces of Patio, the breakdown would be 5696 pcs of E4187, 3058 pcs of E4193, and 1222 pcs of E4159. Based on these numbers, a forecast was conducted for the following year and, to a great extent, the figures in the following month had to have the same split.

INITIAL FORECASTING PERFORMANCE FOR PROJECT-BASED MARKETS

The initial forecasting approach worked well in retail-based markets like Egypt and Lebanon, where a monthly forecast could be constructed based on sales history and anticipated sales. These countries' sales values, however, represented too small a percentage of the total sales value of the region to have an effect on the total quantities reflected in the forecast. The bulk of the sales value in the Middle East region comes from the project-based markets of the Gulf. Applying this forecasting methodology led to poor quality forecasts for project-based markets and eventually to insufficient product availability, or, in some cases, to over-production due to accounting for a project that never materialized. This was a problem for the sales people, because it was difficult to predict when a project would materialize and - when it did - what quantities of each SKU would be sold. A project that was supposed to materialize into an order starting January could shift all the way to end of Q2 starting in June, and the purchase order would not come in until then. Adding to that, predicting which SKUs would be sold under each product was difficult, because in the end, once a quotation was provided, not all SKUs would be purchased from the same supplier; only one SKU might be purchased, or maybe all SKUs.

Because of these problems, a whole new system for project-based market forecasting had to be developed, to enable the team to produce more accurate figures.

ORDERING IN PROJECTS: THE TENDERING PROCESS

When a project is in the planning phase, the owner will visit a consultant to ask for initial sketches and layouts of the project. Several design firms are contacted during this phase and several designs are supplied to the owner. Designs are reviewed, along with the budget estimates for the project, and a shortlist of designs is created. A single designer/consultant from the shortlist wins the contract for the project. This designer/consultant starts to work on the design of the project; the designs for all civil, mechanical, electrical, and other engineering works are developed and detailed to the highest level.

Sales people from various companies are invited by the owner, consultant or contractor to participate in supplying the project. This invitation is made at various points in the project's life.

The most favorable scenario for the sales people is when they are invited to participate by the owner. This usually happens when a good relationship exists between the owner and the sales people. As the owner is the key decision maker who decides what product is to be installed in the project, confidence that this project will result in a firm purchase order is very high. The second-best favorable scenario, from the perspective of the sales people, is when the invitation comes from the consultant, who is the decision maker in this scenario. The focus is on product quality, performance, durability, warranty and specifications. This different set of criteria tends to lower the confidence level of the sales people, as there are numerous suppliers that could be eligible. The least favorable scenario is when the invitation comes from the contractor. In this scenario, a completely different set of criteria for selecting a supplier is used: price, lead time for delivery, and discounts. Confidence that this project will result in a firm purchase order in this scenario is usually low, as many other suppliers would be involved in the bidding process and a price war would occur. In any of these cases, only when a purchase order is released will the supplier feel completely confident that an order has been secured.

Approaches made by sales people are very different as the project progresses through its different phases: concept, design, and implementation. As mentioned above, the strongest position a supplier can have is when the owner decides that the company's products are to be used in the project. This could happen in the concept phase - at the beginning of the whole process - and it becomes just a matter of time until the purchase order comes in. In that sense, sales people get to sell the product more easily, at a much higher confidence level.

The second favorable scenario is the design phase, where designers/consultants go to preferred suppliers that can assist with the design of the project. This is a great opportunity for all sales people, if they have no strong relationships with the owner, since they enter from the beginning of the project. Their products are introduced in the specification document and they become the benchmark to measure up against in the project. In this scenario, sales people have a very strong relationship with the consultant and their knowledge is used as a source of information for all new and existing products.

Once the design is complete and the specification document is produced and issued by the designer/consultant, several contractors bid for the project contract, moving the project into the implementation phase. Usually the bidder with the lowest offer wins the contract. Once the project commences and the contractor starts work, contact is made with all suppliers, requesting them to submit their quotations for the supply of the specified items. Usually, it is the product specified in the specification document that is purchased and supplied for installation. However, during the course of quotation submission and review, competitors could provide better quality products, better prices, or more efficient lead times for the supply of products to site, giving them a competitive edge. This process involves a great deal of negotiation between the contractor and the various suppliers. This is the least favorable scenario. In this phase, relationships with the contractor play a strong role in winning the contract for the supply of project items. Suppliers provide samples of their products in the form of mockups of actual running bathrooms, enabling the owner and consultant to see the product physically and perhaps even functioning.

Depending on several factors, the outcome of the above three scenarios could vary tremendously. Ideally, the owner would have the power to force both the consultant and contractor to purchase from a specific supplier and, in that case, sales people need to be on good terms with the owner. But under scenario two, the owner is not involved in the decision making or is unaware of the details of the project, and the consultant would call the shots. In this case, the consultant, who is the decision maker, has to be on good terms with the sales people, who would be a source of information on all new products in the market. They could also provide the consultant with useful information and perhaps tools to aid in the design process. This would always help in the decision-making process. Under the third scenario, where the contractor is the decision maker, it is best for the sales person to have direct contact with the contractor to be able to compete within the project.

As Mr. Nada discussed the peculiarities of the project-based market with the Supply Chain Group in France, he pointed out that the Gulf countries of the Middle East were mainly a project-based market where orders typically involved large volumes and very challenging lead times. The company had never experienced order volumes of such sizes outside of the Gulf. Responding to these high volume orders was a challenge for all departments within the company and for Kohler Europe manufacturing facilities. The inventory of purchased parts had to be limited to the project's needs for one to two months to control working capital and ensure better cash flow/control. Purchased components had varying lead times. To ensure proper scheduling of procurements and deliveries, orders had to be known ahead of time to ensure delivery to customers on schedule. Other components needed to be manufactured at various facilities around the world. For faucets and ceramics, assembled products had to be shipped back to the central warehouse in Passel, France, and then shipped on to various parts of the world.

THE NEW FORECASTING METHODLOGY

The meeting between Mr. Nada and the Supply Chain Group in France led to the development and implementation of a new system of forecasting. Under the new system, all quotations are collected from the different sales people around the region. They are all sent to the demand review person in the Supply Chain Group in France. This person analyzes each project separately, and then incorporates all order quantities on one sheet. The sheet is broken down by customer name and currently active projects. Each project is identified by a name. All ordered SKUs and their corresponding quantities are listed. Each project is given a confidence level (a percentage) that indicates the likelihood that the project will actually materialize into an order (how close the sales team is to getting the project) in order to plan production needs and delivery time. The requested delivery time is also included. This identifies the anticipated time the project will be delivered to the customer. More details are added to the sheet, such as the total number of SKUs, total volume required for the project, and quotation date. These are also indicators that can, in some cases, help to identify the situation of a project, e.g., if it has been pending for too long, or if there are several SKUs as options, or if all SKUs are part of the product selection for the project.

This process is carried out on a monthly basis, in order to ensure the validity and accuracy of the data. All projects are reviewed at the SKU level, with the confidence level and delivery request time. Once the above process is finalized, all SKUs are grouped together and placed on one sheet, providing an overview of the forecasted demand. See Table 3 for an example.

As shown in Table 4 below, each product line is broken down into a monthly forecast, using historical data as a trend setter, and considering seasonality and other factors. The second column in the table shows the total amount of each product line mentioned in the financial plan. This is the target number set in the annual sales plan for the product line. These numbers are used because they are the only set of data that would give a full picture for the year. Quotations sent by the Area Managers show quantities in each cell corresponding to each month. So if an order is anticipated in October, the quantity in the quotation is placed in the October cell. This gives a new total on the right hand black column. Both totals are compared to one another in the farthest right column to check for deviations per product family. At the bottom of the sheet, a monthly total of all SKUs to be produced is provided. This again is measured against the financial plan figures to show deviations per month. Usually, the total figures for the forecast and the financial plan should equal each other or at least come close to each other. In this case, we have two figures, forecast = 42,671 units and financial plan = 40,036 units.

Once this sheet is prepared, the Supply Chain Group can start communicating with the different production facilities around the world. All components should be available in order for production to commence. The above sheet provides a guideline for the procurement and production departments, as well as all other departments, on future needs. Usually, availability depends on the demand for the product. If the product is in high demand, producing it in high quantities is no problem, as the product will be sold anyway. However, if it is a low-demand product, it would be a great risk to produce the product without having a 100% confirmed order.

Each product line has a selling trend. This is always measured and compared to the historical data. An example would be a Singulier Face Plate. This product has average sales rate of 15 to 20 pieces per month in all countries in Europe. A project comes in from Dubai and orders 2500 pieces - equivalent to 12 years of demand in Europe for this product. There are no components ready for this kind of demand, no inventory of critical items, and the purchasing department has to start work on providing the needed supplies. This order has to be met immediately to satisfy the customer. If no quantity is forecasted, a lead time of five to six months is quoted to the customer. Manufacturing in Europe commences with a lead time of 2 – 3 weeks. Then the parts are shipped to China, which takes about 5 – 6 weeks. The lead time from China is 10 weeks: 4 weeks for production and 6 weeks for shipping back to Europe. So in total, it would take about 17 – 20 weeks to prepare this product alone. Shipment to the customer takes about 2 -3 weeks. If the forecast is provided beforehand, a good 8 weeks are saved because preparations start early. In some cases, China ships directly to the Middle East in order to cut down the shipping time from a total of 8 weeks to only 2 weeks. But this only happens for very large shipments. Kohler US requires an 18-month forecast to be able to guide the finances of the company in the right direction. Since the Middle East falls under the Kohler Europe entity, a six-month rolling forecast to guide production

Table 3. Monthly project report

PROJECT LIST	SKU	%	Quantity	Delivery Request	Quotation
AL ANSARI					
SBG PLAZA AT GHUBRAH	7	70%	13371	1St Term 2010	11.05.09
	19760D-cp		2113		
	19763D-cp		2067		
	18019D-cp		1495		
	19542D		2067		
	12798D-4-cp		1495		
	10746D-cp		2067		
	882D-4		2067		
AL MUTAWAA					
MURIYA	4	50%	3000	Q2 2010	08.03.09
	E660Y-CP		900		
	E662Y-CP		900		
	E664Y-CP		600		
	E16540Y-CP		600		
AEB Project - Egypt Mixers	6	90%	443	1St Term 2010	09.02.09
	E72051Y CP		141		
	E71076Y CP		65		
	NARCISSE		77		
	E72240Y CP		92		
	E16572Y CP		56		
	E71241Y CP		12		
MOD SHIFA HOSPITAL	7	90%	56	1St Term 2010	30.03.09
	E 73240-cp		1		
	E72240-cp		17		
	E72250-cp		28		
	E12798-4-cp		4		
	E882-NF		2		
	E75142-CP		2		
	E14331-CP		2		

in Europe to satisfy customers in the Middle East has been agreed on.

CONCLUSION AND WAY FORWARD

After using the new method of forecasting for a few months, several improvements have been observed. A better set of information has been provided to the Supply Chain Group in France, enabling them to view what is happening in terms of sales in the Middle East. Through this information, communication between the teams has improved and a cooperative plan has been implemented; every month, a call is sent out for the review of each quotation, including each and

Table 4. Forecasting for project-based market

	Fin Plan	Middle East- Forecast												Forecast	Comparison
Product Line	**Total**	**01.2010**	**02.2010**	**03.2010**	**04.2010**	**05.2010**	**06.2010**	**07.2010**	**08.2010**	**09.2010**	**10.2010**	**11.2010**	**12.2010**	**Total**	**Forecast**
		0.05	0.05	0.12	0.15	0.09	0.11	0.07	0.07	0.06	0.07	0.11	0.04		
Total/ Months	**40036**	**1977**	**2124**	**4816**	**6148**	**3753**	**4300**	**2916**	**2832**	**2381**	**2798**	**4351**	**1640**	**Forecast**	**Vs Fin Plan**
Candide	**1750**		**8**	211	269	164	188	127	124	104	122	190	72	**1579**	100.00%
Carafe	**0**	**4**		**20**	0	0	0	0	0	0	0	0	0	**24**	100.00%
Ceramic Faucet-Bol	**26**			3	4	2	3	2	2	2	2	3	1	**23**	-10.24%
Clairette	**10**			1	2	1	1	1	1	1	1	1	0	**9**	-10.24%
Clip (Dec 2009)	**0**	**67**	**180**	**1**	0	0	0	0	0	0	0	0	0	**248**	100.00%
Forte Traditional-1H	**0**	**20**		**11**	**7**	**176**	0	0	0	0	0	0	0	**214**	100.00%
Forte Traditional-2H	**309**		**35**	37	47	29	33	23	22	18	22	34	13	**312**	1.08%
Galatee	**300**			36	46	28	32	**Out of Brochure**						**142**	-52.50%
Galeo	**625**		**3**	75	96	59	67	46	44	37	44	68	26	**564**	-9.76%
Galeo Cd	**28**		**2**	3	4	3	3	2	2	2	2	3	1	**27**	-3.10%
Ginko (2009)	**0**	**18**	**25**	**12**	0	0	0	0	0	0	0	0	0	**55**	100.00%
Ginko Cd	**0**	**0**	**175**	**246**	0	0	0	0	0	0	0	0	0	**421**	100.00%
Head Shower (Sept 2009)	**100**			12	15	9	11	7	7	6	7	11	4	**90**	-10.24%
Hors Collection	**400**	**612**	**50**	48	61	37	43	29	28	24	28	43	16	**1021**	155.26%
Nateo	**400**		**16**	48	61	37	43	29	28	24	28	43	16	**375**	-6.24%
New Margaux -2008	**0**	**9**	**9**	0	0	0	0	0	0	0	0	0	0	**18**	100.00%
Revival	**1006**	**46**	**89**	121	154	94	108	73	71	60	70	109	41	**1038**	3.18%
Salute/Wave	**1000**		**47**	120	154	94	107	73	71	59	70	109	41	**945**	-5.54%
Product Line Not Account In Fin Plan	+	**8**	**1**	**110**	**81**	**0**	**0**	**0**	**0**	**0**	**0**	**0**	**0**		
Monthly Forecast 2010		**1609**	**2381**	**7692**	**6198**	**3916**	**4291**	**2880**	**2800**	**2322**	**2741**	**4243**	**1600**	**42,671**	
Monthly Fin Plan 2010		**1977**	**2124**	**4816**	**6148**	**3753**	**4300**	**2916**	**2832**	**2381**	**2798**	**4351**	**1640**	**40,036**	
Forecast 2010 Vs Fin Plan (Monthly)		-19%	12%	60%	1%	4%	0%	-1%	-1%	-2%	-2%	-2%	-2%	**7%**	

every SKU within the quotation and the percentage of confidence of project delivery. Integrating the quotation information provided has led to the inclusion of more accurate figures within the SAP system in Europe. A single set of numbers available has also improved communication between remote teams.

Applying this forecast method had led to a drop of 50% in lead time. It has also helped to foresee needs before they occur, thereby ensuring the availability and timely supply of all items required for the manufacture of ordered products.

Another big improvement is evident in a 36% reduction of inventory levels kept in stock to meet the demand from the Middle East. This has led to better cash-flow levels, an important factor in the running costs of the company.

Just-in-time supply of products has also improved, as external suppliers are informed early of needs, allowing them enough time to produce and supply the parts. Sourcing from several parts of the world is one of the challenges at Kohler Co. The new forecasting methodology is expected to improve the efficiency of deliveries between the different manufacturing facilities.

Currently, Mr. Nada, although satisfied with the early success of the approach, believes that the new forecasting method should be run for several months more in order for management to obtain a broader view of the gains the new method has brought about and to identify ways in which the new process can be improved. He believes there can be better ways to account for the status of project progress.

REFERENCES

Chopra, S., & Meindl, P. (2007). *Supply chain management: strategy, planning & operations*. Upper Saddle River, New Jersey, U.S.A: Pearson Education. *Inc.*, *328*, 491.

Smith, C. (December 15, 2000). Improving Supply Chain Sales Forecasting. In J. Mentzer (Ed.), Supply Chain Management (1st ed.). Sage Publications, Inc.

Compilation of References

Ackerman, H., & Van Heden, K. (2002). Vicious and virtuous cycles in ERP implementation: A case Study of interrelations between critical success factors. *European Journal of Information Systems*, *11*, 35–46. doi:10.1057/palgrave/ejis/3000418

Afif, A., Aziz, H., & Mohsen, M. (2010). *Class discussion and project*.

Alkin, K., & Okay, E. (2008). *The process of alignment with Basel II by SMEs in Turkey and recommendations* (pp.68, 74). (Istanbul Chamber of Trade, Publication No: 2008-4).

Alter, S. (1980). *Decision support systems: Current practice and continuing challenge*. Reading: MA Addison Wiley.

AMR Research (currently part of Gartner inc.). (2005). *Market Analytix Report: ERP 2004-2009*.

Anderson, K. (2009). Ethnographic research: A key to strategy. *Harvard Business Review*, *87*(3), 24.

Antonides, G. (1998). *An attempt at integration of economic and psychological theories of consumption. European Perspectives on Consumer Behavior*. Prentice Hall, Europe.

Atasu, A., Guide, V. Jr, Daniel, R., & Van Wassenhove, L. N. (2010). So what if remanufacturing cannibalizes my new product sales? *California Management Review*, *52*(2), 56–57.

Atia, M. (2008). Arab Republic of Egypt. In Ibrahim, B. L., & Sherif, D. H. (Eds.), *From charity to social change: Trends in Arab philanthropy* (pp. 23–42). Cairo, Egypt: The American University in Cairo Press.

Avison, D., Jones, J., Powell, P., & Wilson, D. (2004). Using and validating the strategic alignment model. *The Journal of Strategic Information Systems*, *13*(3), 223–246.

Ballantine, J., Levy, M., & Powell, P. (1998). Evaluating information systems in small and medium-sized enterprises: Issues and evidence. *European Journal of Information Systems*, *7*(4), 241–251. doi:10.1057/palgrave.ejis.3000307

Bancroft, N. (1996). *Implementing SAP R/3*. Greenwich, CT: Manning Publication Co.

Barker, J. (2005). Show time. *Sales & Marketing Management, 157*(26).

Bellamy, H., Salit, R., & Bell, L. (1997). *Social marketing resource manual: A guide for state nutrition education networks*. Washington, DC: Health Systems Research Inc.

Bergeron, F., & Raymond, L. (1995). The contribution of IT to the bottom line: A contingency perspective of strategic dimensions. *Proceedings of the 16th International Conference on Information Systems*, Amsterdam, 167-181.

Bingham, D. (1999). *Food and beverage companies need to integrate information enterprise-wide*. Beverage Online.

Bingi, P. (1999). Critical issues affecting an ERP implementation. *Information Systems Management*, *16*, 7–14. doi:10.1201/1078/43197.16.3.19990601/31310.2

Brazel, J. F., & Dang, L. (2008). The effect of ERP system implementations on the management of earnings and earnings release dates. *Journal of Information Systems*, *22*(2), 1–21. doi:10.2308/jis.2008.22.2.1

Burn, J. M., & Szeto, C. (2000). A comparison of the views of business and IT management on success factors for strategic alignment. *Information & Management*, *37*(4), 197–216.

Burns, J., Ezzamel, M., & Scapens, R. W. (2003). *The challenge of management accounting change: Behavioural and cultural aspects of change management*. London, UK: CIMA Publications.

Burns, J., & Scapens, R. (2000). Conceptualising management accounting change: An institutional framework. *Management Accounting Research*, *11*(1), 3–25.

Capital Market Authority. (2008). *The Egyptian standards on auditing, limited review and other assurance services*. The Capital Market Authority.

Caribbean Business Magazine. (2008, March 20). Product life cycles can determine the need for contract manufacturing. *Carribean Business*, 28.

Cash, J. I., Eccles, R. G., Nohria, N., & Nolan, R. L. (1994). *Building the information-age organization: Structure, Control, and Information Technologies*. Boston, MA: Richard D. Irwin.

Chan, Y. E. (2002). Why haven't we mastered alignment? The importance of the informal organization structure. *MIS Quarterly Executive*, *1*(2), 97–112.

Chan, Y. E., Huff, S. L., Barclay, D. W., & Copeland, D. G. (1997). Business strategic orientation, information systems strategic orientation and strategic alignment. *Information Systems Research*, *8*(2), 125–150.

Chan, Y. E., Huff, S. L., & Copeland, D. G. (1998). Assessing realized information systems strategy. *The Journal of Strategic Information Systems*, *6*(4), 273–298.

Chatterjee, D., Grewal, R., & Sambamurthy, V. (2002). Shaping up for e-commerce: Institution enablers of the organizational assimilation of Web technologies. *Management Information Systems Quarterly*, *26*(2), 65. doi:10.2307/4132321

Chesher, M. (1999). *Electronic commerce and business communications*. London, UK: Springer-Verlag London Limited.

Chopra, S., & Meindl, P. (2007). *Supply chain management: Strategy, planning & operations*. (pp. 328, 491). Upper Saddle River, NJ: Pearson Education, Inc.

Chou, D., Tripuramully, H., & Chou, A. (2005). BI and ERP integration. *Information Management & Computer Security*, *13*(5), 340–349. doi:10.1108/09685220510627241

CIA. (2010). *The world fact book, Egypt profile*. Retrieved on 10 August, 2010, from https://www.cia.gov/library/publications/the-world-factbook/geos/eg.html

Ciborra, C. (2000). *From control to drift*. Oxford, UK: Oxford University Press.

Ciborra, C., & Hanseth, O. (1998). From tool to Gestell. Agendas for managing information infrastructures. *Information Technology & People*, *11*(4), 305–327. doi:10.1108/09593849810246129

Commercial International Brokerage Company. (n.d.). *IPO valuation report*.

Conte, M. Sr. (2005). Are OEM parts of greater value to end users than generic parts? *Foodservice Equipment & Supplies*, *58*(1), 29.

Cooper, R. (1989). You need a new cost system when…. *Harvard Business Review*, (Jan-Feb): 77–82.

Cooper, R., & Kaplan, R. S. (1988). How cost accounting systematically distorts product costs. *Management Accounting Quarterly*, 20-27. London.

CRM2day. (2004). *Business intelligence*. Retrieved from www.crm2day.com/bi

D'Aveni, R. (1995). Coping with hypercompetition: Utilizing the new 7S's framework. *The Academy of Management Executive*, *9*(3), 45–57.

Daft, R. (2007). *Understanding the theory and design of organizations*. Thomson South-Western.

Dann, S. (2009). Redefining social marketing with contemporary commercial marketing definitions. *Journal of Business Research*, *63*, 147–153. doi:10.1016/j.jbusres.2009.02.013

Data monitor. (2001). *Business intelligence from data to profit*. Retrieved from www.researchandmarkets.com

Davenport, T. (1998). Putting the enterprise into the enterprise system. *Harvard Business Review, 76*(4), 121–131.

De Mooij, M. (2003). Convergence and divergence in consumer behavior: Implications for global advertising. *International Journal of Advertising, 22*(2), 183–202.

DeLone, W., & McLean, E. (1992). Information systems success: The quest for the dependable variable. *Information Systems Research, 3*(1), 60–95. doi:10.1287/isre.3.1.60

DeLone, W., & McLean, E. (2003). The DeLone and McLean Model of Information Systems success: A ten-year update. *Journal of Management Information Systems, 19*(4), 9–30.

Ding, D., & Chen, J. (2007). Supply chain coordination with contracts game between complementary suppliers. *International Journal of Information Technology & Decision Making, 6*(1), 163–175. doi:10.1142/S0219622007002332

Donnelly, J. H. (1970). Marketing notes and communications: Attitudes toward culture and approach to international advertising. *Journal of Marketing*, 60–63.

Downing, C. E., Field, J. M., & Ritzman, L. P. (2003). The value of outsourcing: a field study. *Information Systems Management, 20*, 86–91. doi:10.1201/1078/43203.20.1.20031201/40088.11

Drucker, P. (2006). *Classic Drucker*. Harvard Business School Publishing Corporation.

Drucker, P. (1998). The next information revolution. *Forbes*. Retrieved from www.forbes.com

Durisin, B., Calabretta, G., & Parmeggiani, V. (2010). The intellectual structure of product innovation research: A bibliometric study of the journal of product innovation management, 1984-2004. *Journal of Product Innovation Management, 27*(3), 437–451. doi:10.1111/j.1540-5885.2010.00726.x

Earl, M. J. (1989). *Management strategies for Information Technology*. Upper Saddle River, NJ: Prentice Hall.

Eisingerich, A., & Rubera, G. (2010). Drivers of brand commitment: A cross national investigation. *Journal of International Marketing, 8*(2), 64–65. doi:10.1509/jimk.18.2.64

El Mekawy, M., Rusu, L., & Haseeb, N. A. (2009). Business-IT alignment: An evaluation of strategic alignment models. *Communications in Computer and Information Science, 49*, 447-455. Berlin /Heidelberg, Germany: Springer Verlag.

Elliott, R. G., Unsworth, D. A., Gomel, M. K., Saunders, J. B., & Mira, M. (1994). Social marketing: Conceptual and pragmatic observations from a current Australian campaign. *Journal of Marketing Management, 10*, 581–591. doi:10.1080/0267257X.1994.9964306

Fan, M., Stallaert, J., & Whinston, A. (2000). The adoption and design methodologies of component-based enterprise systems. *European Journal of Information Systems, 9*, 25–35. doi:10.1057/palgrave.ejis.3000343

Fan, M. (2000). The adoption and design methodologies of component-based enterprise systems. *European Journal of Information Systems, 9*, 25–35. doi:10.1057/palgrave.ejis.3000343

Fleck, J. (1994). Learning by trying: The implementation of configurational technology. *Research Policy, 23*, 637–652. doi:10.1016/0048-7333(94)90014-0

Francalanci, C. (2001). Predicting the implementation effort of ERP projects: Empirical evidences on SAP R/3. *Journal of Information Technology, 16*(1), 33–48. doi:10.1080/02683960010035943

Fryling, M. (2005). *ERP implementation dynamics*. Information Science and Policy University at Albany. State University of New York.

Frynas, J., Mellahi, K., & Pigman, G. (2006). First mover advantages in international business and firm-specific political resources. *Strategic Management Journal, 27*(4), 324. doi:10.1002/smj.519

Fumiaki, K. (2010). Influence of product life cycle stage on consideration set size: The case of think products. *Marketing Review, 10*(1), 48.

Gable, G., van Den Heever, R., Erlank, S., & Scott, J. (2001). Large packaged application software maintenance: A research framework. *Journal of Software Maintenance and Evolution: Research and Practice, 13*(6), 351–371. doi:10.1002/smr.237

Gable, G., et al. (2002). Enterprise resources planning systems impacts: A Delphi study of Australian public sector. *Proceedings of the sixth Australasian Conference of Information Systems (PACIS 2002),* 2-4 September 2002, Tokyo, Japan.

Gable, G., et al. (2003, December). *Enterprise systems success: A measurement model.* Paper presented at twenty-fourth International Conference on Information Systems, 14-17, Seattle, USA.

Ghosh, J. (2007). *Understanding financial instruments: A guide to IAS 32, IAS 39 and IFRS 7.* CCH-a Wolters Kluwer Business.

Hamilton, W. (1932). Institutions. In Seligman, E. R. A., & Johnson, A. (Eds.), *Encyclopedia of social science* (pp. 560–595).

Hammer, M., & Champy, J. (1994). *Reengineering the corporation: A manifesto for business revolution.* USA: Harper Business Press.

Hardy, C. (1996). Understanding power: Bringing about strategic change. *British Journal of Management, 7,* 3–16.

Henderson, J. C., & Venkatraman, N. (1993). Strategic alignment: Leveraging Information Technology for transforming organizations. *IBM Systems Journal, 32*(1), 4–16.

Holsapple, C., & Whinston, A. B. (1996). *Decision support systems: A knowledge based approach.* Minneapolis, MN: West Publishing.

Horngren, C. T., Bhimani, A., Foster, G., & Datar, S. M. (1999). *Management and cost accounting.* London, UK: Prentice-Hall Europe.

Hu, Q., & Huang, C. D. (2006). Using the Balanced Scorecard to achieve sustained IT-business alignment: A case study. *Communications of AIS, 17*(8), 181–204.

Huff, S. L., Maher, P. M., & Munro, M. C. (2006). Information Technology and the board of directors: Is there an IT attention deficit? *MIS Quarterly Executive, 5*(2), 55–68.

Ifinedo, P. (2006a). Extending the Gable et al. enterprise systems success measurement model: A preliminary study. *Journal of Information Technology Management, 17*(1), 14-33.

Ifinedo, P., & Nahar, N. (2007). ERP system success: An empirical analysis of how two organizational stakeholder groups prioritize and evaluate relevant measures. *Enterprise Information Systems, 1,* 25–48. doi:10.1080/17517570601088539

Ifinedo, P. (2007). Investigating the relationships among ERP systems success dimensions: A structural equation model. *Issues in Information Systems, 8*(2).

International Accounting Standards Board. (2009). *International financial reporting standards (IFRS)-official pronouncements as issued at 1 January 2009.* IASB.

Kallinikos, J. (2004). Deconstructing information packages: Organizational and behavioral implications of ERP systems. *Information Technology & People, 17,* 8–30. doi:10.1108/09593840410522152

Kamaladevi, B. (2010). Customer experience management in retailing. *Business Intelligence Journal, 3*(1), 37–54.

Kaplan, R. K., & Norton, D. P. (2001). *The strategy focused organization: How balanced scorecard companies thrive in the new business environment.* Boston, MA: Harvard Business School Press.

Kasapi, A. (1999). *Mastering credit derivatives.* Prentice Hall.

Kearns, G. S., & Sabherwal, R. (2007). Strategic alignment between business and Information Technology: A knowledge-based view of behaviours, outcome and consequences. *Journal of Management Information Systems, 23*(3), 129–162.

Keskin, E. (2008). *Access to financing for SME's in the EU and Turkey.* REX/264 EU-Turkey Joint Consultative Committee, 25th meeting of the EU-Turkey Joint Consultative Committee Paris, France, 18-19 November, 2008.

King, W. R., & Grover, V. (1991). The strategic use of information resources: An exploratory study. *IEEE Transactions on Engineering Management, 38*(4), 293–305.

Kolb., R., & Overdahl, J. (2003). *Financial derivatives.* Wiley & Sons, Inc.

Kossovsky, N. (2010). Reputation leadership. *Leadership Excellence, 27*(5), 7.

Krumbholz, M. (2000). Implementing enterprise resource planning packages in different corporate and national cultures. *Journal of Information Technology*, *15*(4), 267–280. doi:10.1080/02683960010008962

Kumar, K., & Van Hillegersberg, J. (2000). ERP: Experience and evolution. *Communications of the ACM*, *43*, 23–26.

Kumar, V., Maheshwari, B., & Kumar, U. (2001). An investigation of critical management issues in ERP implementation: Empirical evidences from Canadian organizations. *Technovation*, *23*(10).

Kumcu, E., & McClure, J. (2003). Explaining prestige pricing: An alternative to back-bending demand. *Marketing Education Review*, *13*(1), 49.

Laudon, K. C., & Laudon, J. P. (2004). *Management Information Systems: Managing the digital firm*. New Jersey: Pearson Education, Inc.

Lee, Z., & Lee, J. (2000). An ERP implementation study for a knowledge transfer perspective. *Journal of Information Technology*, *15*(4), 281–288. doi:10.1080/02683960010009060

Lee, H. L. (2002). Aligning supply chain strategies with product uncertainties. *California Management Review Reprint Series*, *44*(3), 105–119.

Levitt, T. (1983). The globalization of markets. *Harvard Business Review*, 92–102.

Light, B. (2001). The maintenance implications of the customization of ERP software. *Journal of Software Maintenance and Evolution: Research and Practice*, *13*(6), 415–429. doi:10.1002/smr.240

Luftman, J. (2000). Assessing business-IT alignment maturity. *Communications of AIS*, *4*(14), 1–50.

Luftman, J., & Ben-Zvi, T. (2010). Key issues for IT executives 2009: Difficult economy's impact on IT. *MIS Quarterly Executive*, *9*(1), 49–59.

Luftman, J., & Kempaiah, R. (2008). Key issues for IT executives 2007. *MIS Quarterly Executive*, *7*(2), 99–112.

Luftman, J., Kempaiah, R., & Rigoni, E. H. (2009). Key issues for IT executives 2008. *MIS Quarterly Executive*, *8*(3), 151–159.

Luftman, J. N., Bullen, C. V., Liao, D., Nash, E., & Neumann, C. (2004). *Managing the Information Technology resource: Leadership in the information age*. Upper Saddle River, NJ: Pearson Education Inc.

Luthans, F., & Doh, J. P. (2009). *International management, culture, strategy, and behavior*. McGraw Hill.

Lycett, M., & Paul, R. J. (1999). Information Systems development: A perspective on the challenge of evolutionary complexity. *European Journal of Information Systems*, *8*, 127–135. doi:10.1057/palgrave.ejis.3000315

Lyne, R. S., & Friedman, A. L. (1997). Activity-based techniques and the death of the beancounter. *European Accounting Review*, *6*(1), 2–20.

Madapusi, A., & Kuo, C. (2007). Assessing data and information quality in ERP systems. *Proceedings of the Decision Sciences Institute Annual Meeting*, Arizona.

Madapusi, A., Kuo, C., & White, R. (2007). A critical factors approach to ERP information quality and decision quality. *Proceedings of the Decision Sciences Institute Annual Meeting,* Arizona.

Management, V. B. (n.d.). *Business dictionary/management dictionary*. Retrieved from http://www.12manage.com/methods_value_based_management.html

Maridive & Oil Services. (2009). *Correspondences between management, auditors and the Egyptian capital market authority*. Maridive & Oil Services.

Markus, M., & Robey, D. (1988). Information Technology and organizational change: Causal structure in theory and research. *Management Science*, *34*, 583–598. doi:10.1287/mnsc.34.5.583

Markus, M., & Tanis, C. (2001b). The enterprise system experience – from adoption to success. In Zmud, R. (Ed.), *Framing the domains of IT management: Projecting the future through the past* (pp. 173–207). Cincinnati, OH: Pinnflex Educational Resources.

Mathews, S. (1998). The changing role of the management accountant: And its implications for qualification development. *Management Accounting*, *76*(8), 68–69.

McCracken, G. (1989). Culture and consumer behavior: An anthropological perspective. *Journal of the Market Research Society. Market Research Society*, *32*(1), 56–73.

McDonald, k., et al. (2002). *Mastering SAP business information warehouse*. Canada: Wiley Publishing.

McFarlan, F. W., McKenney, J. L., & Pyburn, P. (1983). The information archipelago - plotting a course. *Harvard Business Review*, (January-February): 145–156.

McKeen, J. D., & Smith, H. A. (2009). *IT strategy in action*. Upper Saddle River, NJ: Pearson Education Inc.

Mensching, J., & Corbitt, G. (2004). EPR data archiving- a critical analysis. *Journal of Enterprise Information Management*, *17*(2), 131–141. doi:10.1108/17410390410518772

Meredith, B. H. (2010). Where does growth really come from? *NZ Business*, *24*(1), 63.

Moon, Y. B. (2007). Enterprise Resource Planning (ERP): A review of the literature. *International Journal of Management and Enterprise Development*, *4*(3), 235–264. doi:10.1504/IJMED.2007.012679

Nah, F. H., Faja, S., & Cata, T. (2001). Characteristics of ERP software maintenance: A multi-cause study. *Journal of Software Maintenance and Evolution: Research and Practice*, *13*(6), 339–414. doi:10.1002/smr.239

Narayanan, V. G., & Raman, A. (2004). Aligning incentives in supply chains. The 21st-century supply chain. *Harvard Business Review*, 94–102.

Nicolaou, A., & Bhattacharya, S. (2007). Organizational performance effects of ERP systems usage: The impact of post-implementation changes. *International Journal of Accounting Information Systems*, *7*(1), 18–35. doi:10.1016/j.accinf.2005.12.002

Nicolaou, A. (2004). *ERP system implementation drivers of post-implementation success*. Decision Support in an Uncertain and Complex World: The IFIP TC8/WG8.3 International Conference, 2004, (pp. 589-597).

Nolan, R. (1979). Managing the crisis in data processing. *Harvard Business Review*, *57*(2), 115–126.

Nutton, S. E. (2006). Management accounting-business strategy. *Financial Management*, 45.

O'Leary, D. (2002). *Enterprise resource planning systems: System lifecycle, electronic commerce, and risk*. Cambridge, UK: Cambridge University Press.

Olszak, C., & Ziemba, E. (2007). Approach to building and implementing business intelligence system. *Interdisciplinary Journal of Information, Knowledge, and Management*, *2*, 135–148.

Olszak, C., & Ziemba, E., (2006). Business intelligence systems in the holistic infrastructure development - supporting decision-making in organizations. *Interdisciplinary Journal of Information, Knowledge, and Management, 1*.

Online, E. I. U. (2005). Egypt: Market profile. *Consumer Goods Forecast World*, 116-117.

Parr, A., & Schanks, G. (2000). A model of ERP project implementation. *Journal of Information Technology*, *15*(4), 289–304. doi:10.1080/02683960010009051

Pearlson, K. E., & Saunders, C. S. (2009). *Strategic management of Information Systems* (4th ed.). Asia: John Wiley & Sons.

Peppard, J., & Ward, J. (2004). Beyond strategic information systems: Towards an IS capability. *The Journal of Strategic Information Systems*, *13*(2), 167–194.

Porter, M. (1980). *Competitive strategy*. New York, NY: Free Press.

Porter, M. E., & Millar, V. E. (1985). How information gives you competitive advantage. *Harvard Business Review*, (July-August): 149–160.

Ptak, C., & Schragenheim, E. (2000). *ERP: Tools, techniques and applications for integrating the supply chain*. London, UK: Series on Resources Management, St Lucie Press/APICS.

Quinn, L. (2009). Market segmentation in managerial practice: A qualitative examination. *Journal of Marketing Management*, *25*(3/4), 254.

Rasmussen, N., Goldy, P., & Solli, P. (2002). *Financial business intelligence: Trends, technology, software selection and implementation*. New York, NY: Wiley.

Reich, B. H., & Benbasat, I. (2000). Factors that influence the social dimension of alignment between business and Information Technology objectives. *Management Information Systems Quarterly*, *24*(1), 84–113.

Robey, D., & Boudreau, M. (1999). Accounting for the contradictory organizational consequences of information technology. *Information Systems Research*, *10*, 167–185. doi:10.1287/isre.10.2.167

Rusu, L., & El Mekawy, M. (2009). The strategic role of IT: A case study in two Swedish retail companies. In D'Atri, A., & Saccà, D. (Eds.), *Information Systems: People, organizations, institutions, and technologies* (pp. 559–567). Berlin/Heidelberg, Germany: Springer-Verlag.

Sawyer, S., & Southwick, R. (2002). Temporal issues in information and communication technology enabled organizational change. *The Information Society*, *18*, 263–280. doi:10.1080/01972240290075110

Schwalbe, K. (2000). *Information Technology project management*. Cambridge, MA: Course Technology.

Searcy, D. L. (2004). Using activity-based costing to assess channel/customer profitability. *Management Accounting Quarterly*, Winter, 51-60.

Seddon, P. B., Staples, D. S., Patnayakuni, R., & Bowtell, M. J. (1999). Dimensions of Information Systems success. *Communications of the Association for Information Systems*, *2*(3).

Seddon, P. B. (1997). A re-specification and extension of the DeLone and McLean model of IS success. *Information Systems Research*, *18*(3), 240–253. doi:10.1287/isre.8.3.240

Sedera, D., et al. (2002). Enterprise resource planning systems impacts: A Delphi study of Australian public sector organizations. In *Proceedings of the Pacific Asia Conference on Information Systems (PACIS)* (pp. 584-600). Tokyo, Japan.

Sedera, D., et al. (2004). Measuring enterprise systems success: the importance of a multiple stakeholder perspective. In *Proceedings of the 12th European Conference on Information Systems* (pp. 1-13). Turku, Finland.

SIES College of Management Studies. (2010). *Marketing strategies used by NGOs*. Idea Research Paper Series. Retrieved on 26 January, 2010, from http://www.karmayog.org/general/upload/182/Marketing%20strategies%20used%20by%20NGOs.pdf

Silva, L., Figueroa, E., & Reinhart, J. G. (2007). Interpreting IS alignment: A multiple case study in professional organizations. *Information and Organization*, *17*(4), 232–265.

Smith, C. (December 15, 2000). Improving Supply Chain Sales Forecasting. In J. Mentzer (Ed.), Supply Chain Management (1st ed.). Sage Publications, Inc.

Soh, C. (2000). Cultural fits and misfits: Is ERP a universal solution? *Communications of the ACM*, *43*(4), 47–51. doi:10.1145/332051.332070

Spott, D. (2000). Componentizing the enterprise applications packages. *Communications of the ACM*, *43*(4), 63–90. doi:10.1145/332051.332074

Stedman, C. (2002). Maximizing the ERP investment. *Competitive Financial Operations: The CFO Project*, *1*, 1–6.

Stedman, C. (1999, November 1). Failed ERP gamble haunts Hershey. *Computerworld*. Retrieved April 16, 2006, from www.computerworld.com

Suerdem, A. (1993). Social de(re)construction of mass culture: Making (non) sense of consumer behavior. *International Journal of Research in Marketing*, *11*, 423–443.

Support for Environmental Assessment and Management Project. (1999). *Textile sector report, Egypt*. Retrieved on April 25, 2010, from http://www.eeaa.gov.eg/seam/Manuals/TextileSectorReport/Part%20A.PDF

Tang, Z., & Walters, B. (2006). The interplay of strategic management and Information Technology. In Walters, B., & Tang, Z. (Eds.), *IT-enabled strategic management: Increasing returns for the organization* (pp. 1–15). Hershey, PA: Idea Group Publishing.

The Egyptian Exchange. (n.d.). *Homepage*. Retrieved from http://www.egyptse.com

Thietart, R. A., & Vivas, R. (1984). An empirical investigation of success strategies for business along the product life cycle. *Management Science*, *30*(12), 1405. doi:10.1287/mnsc.30.12.1405

Thomas, M. F., & Mackey, J. (2006). Supply chain management: Monitoring strategic partnering contracts with activity-based measures. *Management Accounting Quarterly*, Fall, 1-10.

Thorne, H., & Gurd, B. (1999). Activity-based costing: Improved product costing or activity management? *Advances in Management Accounting*, *8*, 173–194.

Trombley, M. (2003). *Accounting for derivatives and hedging*. McGraw-Hill Irwin.

TUIK- Turkish Statistical Institute. (2003). *General census of industry and establishments*. Retrieved from https://www.tuik.gov.tr

Turban, E., Leidner, D., McLean, E., & Wetherbe, J. (2006). *Information Technology for management. Transforming organizations in the digital economy* (5th ed.). USA: John Wiley & Sons.

Turban, E. (2006). *Information Technology for management: Transforming organizations in the digital economy* (5th ed.). John Wiley & Sons Inc.

Turney, P. B. B. (1992). What an activity-based cost model looks like. *Journal of Cost Management,* Winter, 54-60.

Udo, G. G. (2000). Using analytic hierarchy process to analyze the information technology outsourcing decision. *Industrial Management & Data Systems*, *100*(9), 421–429. doi:10.1108/02635570010358348

Weiss, J. W., & Anderson, D. (2004). Aligning technology and business strategy: Issues & frameworks, a field study of 15 companies. *Proceedings of the 37th Annual Hawaii International Conference on System Sciences* (HICSS'04), January 5-8, 2004, Hilton Waikoloa Village, Island of Hawaii, USA, IEEE Computer Society Press, (pp. 1-10).

Wells, R. (2001). Ensuring NGO independence in the new funding environment. *Development in Practice*, *11*(1), 73–77.

Willcocks, L., & Sykes, R. (2000). The role of the CIO and IT function in ERP. *Communications of the ACM*, *43*, 33–38. doi:10.1145/332051.332065

Wilson, R. M. S., & Chua, W. (1994). *Managerial accounting: Method and meaning* (2nd ed.). London, UK: Chapman and Hall.

Xiong, Y., Su, W., & Lin, T. W. (2008). Activity-based costing popularity in China. *Cost Management,* May/June, 40-48.

Xu, H., Nord, J., Brown, N., & Nord, D. (2002). Data quality issues in implementing an ERP. *Industrial Management & Data Systems*, *102*(1), 47–58. doi:10.1108/02635570210414668

Xu, H. (2002). Data quality issues in implementing an ERP. *Industrial Management & Data Systems*, *102*(1), 47–58. doi:10.1108/02635570210414668

Yen, D. C., Chou, D. C., & Chang, J. (2002). A synergic analysis for Web-based enterprise resource planning system. *Computer Standards & Interfaces*, *24*(4), 337–346. doi:10.1016/S0920-5489(01)00105-2

Yin, R. K. (2003). *Case study research: Design and methods* (3rd ed.). Thousand Oaks, CA: Sage Publications.

Zwass, V. (2003). Electronic commerce and organizational innovation: Aspects and opportunities. *International Journal of Electronic Commerce*, *7*(3), 7–37.

About the Contributors

Adel I. El-Ansary is the Donna L. Harper Professor of Marketing at the University of North Florida. Prior to joining the faculty at the University of North Florida as the First Holder of the Paper and Plastics Educational Research Foundation Eminent Scholar Chair in Wholesaling, he served as Professor and Chairman of Business Administration at the George Washington University, Washington, D.C. Having lectured, consulted, and conducted research in over thirty-five countries across six continents, El-Ansary achieved the status of a global educator. El-Ansary is a Fulbright Scholar. He received the State of Florida University System Professional Excellence Award in 1999 and was named Prime Osborne, III Distinguished Professor in 2002. He is co-author of the leading text-reference books on *E-Marketing, 3rd and 4th editions*, Prentice-Hall, 2003 & 2006 and *Marketing Channels, 1st through 7th edition, Prentice-Hall, 1977 - 2006.* He is a contributor to the *Encyclopedia of Marketing, Encyclopedia of Economics, American Marketing Association Marketing Encyclopedia, the Logistics Handbook*, and over thirty-five contributions to books and conference proceedings. El-Ansary's research and writing contributed eighteen key articles published in major journal including the *Journal of Marketing, Journal of Marketing Research, Journal of Marketing Channels, Journal of Retailing, Journal of the Academy of Marketing Science, Journal of Relationship Marketing, Journal of Macro Marketing, European Business Review, Journal of Personal Selling and Sales Management,* and *International Marketing Review.* El-Ansary was on leave from the University of North Florida 1995-1996 to serve as Chief of Party of International Business and Technical consultants, Inc. in Cairo, Egypt. He was in charge of all aspects of project management for the monitoring and evaluation of the Privatization Program of the Government of Egypt funded through technical assistance provided by the United States Agency for International Development (U.S.AID). El-Ansary served as team leader and project coordinator, implemented, or participated in over twenty government and international organization contracts and assignments including U.S. AID, the World Bank, and the Governments of Egypt, Saudi Arabia, Tunisia, Kuwait, and Qatar. He served on Presidents' Nixon and Ford national Advisory Council for the U.S. Small Business Administration. He served on a sub-Presidential Mission for President Reagan's Caribbean Initiatives. The focus of the mission was on improving food distribution in Central America. El-Ansary completed over sixty national and international consulting assignments and executive development programs for clients including the Jacksonville NFL Jaguars, Volvo Penta, Volvo Car Corporation, Northrop Corporation, Paper Corporation of America, Rotel International, IBM, Aluminum Association, Family Health Foundation of Louisiana, General Electric Information Services, and Saudi Arabian Airlines. He conducted over twenty-five executive briefings nationally and internationally and delivered over fifty speeches at major national and international business and academic conferences. El-Ansary served on the National Advisory Board of U.S. Small Business Administration under Presidents Nixon and Ford, the Board of Director of the International Consultants Foundation, the Global Council of the

American Marketing Association, Founder of the Special Interest Group in Wholesale Distribution and Co-Chairman of the Relationship Marketing Interest Group of the Academic Council of the American Marketing Association, and Member of the Board of Governors of the Academy of Marketing Science.

* * *

Sara Abdallah is at her final stages of the Master's of Philosophy in the Cairo University. She is currently working on a research project on Corporate Internet reporting in developed vs. developing countries. Currently, she is working as a Lecturer of Accounting in the British university in Egypt (BUE). She also works as a Research Assistant in the American University in Cairo (AUC). She contributed to a recent research on corporate governance structures and voluntary disclosure by the top 100 companies listed on the Egyptian Stock Exchange (EGX) that was funded by the Egyptian Financial Supervisory Authority (EFSA) and the American University in Cairo.

Mohamed Omar Ads has been with Danone Egypt for two years managing the Danette brand. Mohamed has a Bachelor degree in Business Administration from the American University in Cairo (AUC), and is currently studying to complete his MBA from the AUC as well. Previously, Mohamed served as regional sales manager in Nestle Egypt after being brand manager in the ice cream category business. He is also active in the field of development through participating with Afaq El Hayah NGO that aims to develop poor villages in Egypt.

Sami Akabawi is a professor of Information Systems in the Management Department, School of Business at the American University in Cairo, Egypt, since 1983. Akabawi has been active participant in the local and regional business community in the capacity of ICT consultant and advisor to many institutions. During his career, he has provided extensive professional consultancy services to many Egyptian and regional industrial and trading organizations for the development, use, and adoption of ICT and information systems within their management and operational business processes. Akabawi's current research interests cover the architecting, design, development, and implementation of ICT infrastructures; adoption and institutionalization of enterprise systems; impacts of the use of ICT artifacts on the human agency's behavior particularly in developing countries environment. He holds a Ph.D. in Computer Science from the City University, London (1977), a Master of Science in Computer Science from London University (1973), and a Bachelor of Science in Industrial Engineering from Cairo University (1967).

Ramazan Aktas is Professor and Chair of Business Administration Department at TOBB University of Economics and Technology. He has over 25 years' experience teaching graduate and undergraduate business courses including financial management, financial analysis, entrepreneurship, and introduction to business. He has taught many seminars to businesspeople on subjects like financial statement analysis, financial mathematics, risk management, SMEs, entrepreneurship, et cetera. He is also the director of the Continuing Education Center of TOBB University of Economics and Technology. His interest areas are corporate finance, financial markets and institutions, investment and portfolio analysis, and SMEs analysis. Prof. Aktas holds a B.S. in Business Administration from Military Academy, Ankara-Turkey, a Master's degree in Middle East Technical University, Ankara-Turkey, and a Ph.D. in Business Administration from Ankara University, Political Science Faculty. He has written 7 books and many articles in business publications.

Ali Awni is an Associate Professor at the Business School, American University in Cairo (AUC) since September 2009. He teaches operations management courses at the undergraduate and MBA level. His areas of research are in applications of operations management in Egypt, and for SMEs in particular, upgrading of operations for Egyptian exporters, and suppliers' selection and evaluation. Prior to joining the AUC, Awni was the Head of the Qualifying Industrial Zones (QIZ) Unit, at the Ministry of Trade & Industry, Government of Egypt. The unit is entrusted with the administration of all the terms of the QIZ trade protocol. Furthermore, the unit acts as a catalyst for the implementation of operational plans to maximize the benefits of the protocol to Egyptian industries, including promotions of FDI and upgrading of export readiness of QIZ companies. Awni also served as an adjunct faculty at the American University in Cairo teaching MBA courses in operations management. Awni was the Partner-in-charge of supply chain consulting services at KPMG Hazem Hassan in Egypt, where he guided and directed the successful completion of various projects in supply chain diagnostics, process design, and performance improvement in operations and business logistics for clients in food, consumer products, industrial, apparel, and pharmaceutical industries. Awni has extensive management consulting, system development, and operations research experience in the USA focusing on supply chain management and business logistics improvements. Ali Awni holds BS in Computer Science & Statistics from Kuwait University, MS in Systems Science from the University of Ottawa, and a Ph.D. in Operations Research from North Carolina State University.

Aliaa Bassiouny holds a BBA as well as an MBA, both with a specialization in finance from the American University in Cairo. She is currently a PhD candidate at ESADE Business School. Ms. Bassiouny has played a variety of roles at AUC. She has delivered several training modules in executive financial training programs as well as teaches undergraduate finance courses. Ms. Bassiouny is also involved with a variety of financial research and has worked as research associate in the finance unit on research papers as well as case studies.

Khaled Dahawy is the Director of MBA programs and an Associate Professor in the Department of Accounting at the American University in Cairo (AUC). He has a PhD (University of North Texas) and MBA (Pennsylvania State University). He is a Certified Public Accountant (CPA) in the State of Illinois, USA, certified from the Egyptian Society for Accountants and Auditors (ESAA), and is certified by the Egyptian Accounting Syndicate. He has several papers and cases published in academic accounting journals and presented at academic and practitioner conferences. His research interests include corporate governance disclosure, disclosure in developing countries, the role of the audit profession in strengthening transparency and disclosure, the use of Information Technology in accounting and the implementation of computerised accounting Information Systems. He teaches financial accounting, international accounting, tax accounting, and auditing. He has extensive practical experience as an expert in the Capital Market Authority (CMA) and has served as a Consultant in many missions with the World Bank and the National Democratic Party (NDP).

Mohamed El Mekawy is a teaching assistant at the Department of Computer and Systems Sciences from Stockholm University. He holds a BSc. in Architectural Engineering from Zagazig University, Egypt, a MSc. in Spatial Planning and an MSc in Engineering and Management of Information Systems both from Royal Institute of Technology (KTH) Stockholm, Sweden. He has a professional experience of over 5 years within the area of Geographical Information Systems by working in different companies in Egypt and Sweden. His research interest is in strategic business-IT alignment and Geographical Information Systems use in crisis management.

Ahu Genis-Gruber is Assistant Professor in Business Administration Department at TOBB University of Economics and Technology where she teaches organizational theory, organizational behavior, management theories, cross cultural management, and human resource management. Her interest areas are international management, cross cultural management, merger and acquisitions, and e-commerce. Dr. Genis-Gruber holds a B.S. in Labor Economics and Industrial Relations from Ankara University, Political Science Faculty, a Master's degree (Mag.rer.soc.oec.) in Social and Economic Sciences from Johannes Kepler University, Linz-Austria and a Ph.D. (Dr.rer.soc.oec.) in Social and Economic Sciences from Johannes Kepler University, Linz-Austria.

Karim Hegazy is executive partner in Crowe Dr. A.M. Hegazy & Co- a member of Crowe Horwath International – Chartered Accountants and Consultants. Karim holds Bachelor degree in Accounting and Finance from Middlesex University – U.K, as well as a Master degree in Accounting and Finance from Brunel University – U.K. Karim speaks fluent German, English, and French languages. His areas of interest for research are financial audit, corporate governance, cost accounting, and financial reporting.

Mohamed Hegazy is Professor of Accounting and Auditing at the Department of Accounting, School of Business, the American University in Cairo. Dr Hegazy holds two Bachelor degrees from Cairo University in Accounting and in Law. He also holds two Master degrees; one in Accounting from Birmingham University, U.K and the other in Knowledge Based Systems (i.e. Expert Systems) from Edinburgh University. He received his PhD in Accounting and Finance from Birmingham University, U.K. His research and teaching interests include financial reporting, auditing, and other assurance services, Information Systems, corporate governance, financial and administrative restructuring, and valuation studies. He published articles, books, chapters in international books, and research papers in international conference proceedings. Hegazy is an active CPA in one of the International Public Firm "Crowe Horwath International."

Heba Hodeeb was born in November 1st, 1983. She graduated with highest honors from the American University in Cairo with major in Business Administration, concentrating in Marketing and a minor in Economics. During her undergraduate studies, she participated as a delegate in the International Student Leadership Conference. After her graduation, she started her career in a multinational beverage company located in Cairo and worked as a Sales Analyst and Project Coordinator for three years. She was then chosen to be an elected pioneer of Mohammed Bin Rashid Al Maktoum scholarship in order to pursue her MBA studies at the American University in Cairo. She is currently married and has children.

Noha Ismail is the Business Development Coordinator at El-Khazindar Business Research and Case Center (KCC) established in the American University in Cairo (AUC). El-Khazindar Business Research and Case Center provides world-class case studies and other educational services offering students outstanding Participant-Centered Learning tools. KCC's services are dedicated to developing top caliber students, connecting businesses and students in the region, and ultimately contributing to the betterment of the society through academic research and practical applications. Mrs. Ismail's role is to lead and implement plans that would ensure the growth of the center and its sustainability. She initiates new activities and programs that would widen the operations of the center and ensures it efficiency. Mrs. Ismail obtained her Bachelor degree of Arts with a concentration of Marketing from the American University in Cairo in 2007, with a GPA of 3.8. She obtained her Thanaweya Amma Degree in 2004, with a score of 99.2%.

Menna Reda Kamel was born in Cairo, Egypt, and received her Bachelor of Business Administration concentration in marketing and a minor in psychology summa cum laude in 2008 from the American University in Cairo (AUC). She then joined the program of Masters in Business Administration at AUC and received her MBA degree with a concentration in finance and operations management in 2010 as the top honor student of her graduating class. Kamel has worked on social marketing projects for the WHO, PAHO, and UNICEF as part of her work at the communications and design agency, which she joined during her Master's program, and for which she is currently holding the position of a strategist and business development specialist. She is also participating in writing a book in the field of business development. Her research interest is in the areas of: supply chain management, distribution channels, social marketing, branding, and development in the Arab world.

Elham Metwally is an Assistant Professor of Strategic Management, Misr International University. She is also an adjunct faculty of Administration of Public Personnel, the American University in Cairo, Egypt. She earned her Doctorate of Business Administration (2009) and Master of Philosophy (2006) with distinction, from Maastricht School of Management, the Netherlands. She earned her Master of Business Administration (2002) and Bachelor of Arts in Economics (1982) with honors from the American University in Cairo. She is a member of the Academy of Management and the National Association of Student Financial Aid Administrators, USA. She is also a member of the Middle East Council for Small Business & Entrepreneurship (MCSBE). Dr. Metwally is also the Associate Director for Scholarships and Budgeting at the American University in Cairo. Earlier, she made more than a dozen years of experience at the Hong Kong and Shanghai Banking Corporation (HSBC).

Nourhan El-Mougi works in the Marketing Research field, passionate of analyzing figures to identify innovative market opportunities. She holds great enthusiasm in helping others learn and grow. She started her career as a Teaching Assistant in Statistics, Calculus and other related topics while working on her MBA degree. She joined TNS Global, Marketing Research Agency, in 2008 for 2 years. In that time, attained TNS Special Award for excellent performance, and was nominated for TNS Research Knowledge Box (TKB) among a group of TNS worldwide nominees. Recently, she joined Vodafone as a Consumer Insight Senior Specialist focusing on the understanding, analysis and opportunity identification of the Consumer segment. Nourhan holds a Bachelor degree in Statistics from Cairo University with grade of Very Good with honors, and an MBA from AUC with GPA 3.52. She is passionate of horse-riding, traveling and embracing new experiences.

Mohammed Nada is the Marketing Manager at Kohler Middle East, based in Dubai, since October 2008. He is responsible for managing assigned products from creation of new products through their removal from the product line for all Kohler and Jacob Delafon faucet markets in the Middle East. He is also responsible for planning and directing the company's short and long range marketing programs. He develops plans and programs, including forecasts, for Middle East marketing programs, pricing, and product line development. Nada's career started at a young age with several internships during his education at AUC. Most of the internships were engineering related working for BMW, Fiat – Hitachi, Caterpillar, and finally PACCAR International. After graduation, he joined CONTRACK, a construction company, in the rotation program for two years. This program introduced him to several departments within the company like costing, contracts, procurement, design, site, et cetera. Following that, he joined Grohe as a projects sales engineer selling products to projects all over Egypt. His role was to enhance the presence of Grohe in the market and to increase market share. During his time in Grohe, he developed with a team of his colleagues in the MBA program a complete IMC (Integrated Marketing Campaign) for the re-launch of Grohe in Egypt. His next stop was an FMCG working as a brand manager for a detergent that was produced locally. Fully fledged campaigns were created and executed with a complete team of junior brand managers and sales coordinators. They were able to push the brand from 3% market share to 6% in one year. Mohammed is a graduate from AUC (American University in Cairo) with a Bachelor's degree in Mechanical Engineering. Bachelor's of Science has been received in 2002 with a double specialization in Industrial Engineering and Materials and Manufacturing. He also holds a Master's in Business Administration from AUC graduated in 2010.

Lazar Rusu is an Associate Professor and Leader of Research Group in IT Management within Information Systems Laboratory from the Department of Computer and Systems Sciences, at Stockholm University, Sweden. He holds a Degree in Electrical Engineering (MSc) from Cluj-Napoca Polytechnic Institute, a Degree in Management (MSc) from Babes-Bolyai University Cluj-Napoca, a PhD in Management from West University of Timisoara, Romania, and a Docent in Information Systems from Royal Institute of Technology (KTH) Stockholm, Sweden. Over his career he has focused mainly in doing research on the management of Information Systems/Information Technology and has over 25 years professional experience in both industrial and academic information technology.

Khaled Samaha is an Assistant Professor in the Department of Accounting at the American University in Cairo (AUC). He received his PhD from Manchester Business School – UK and his MSc from Birmingham Business School - UK. Samaha is a Certified Public Accountant (CPA) from the Egyptian Society for Accountants and Auditors (ESAA), and is certified by the Egyptian Accounting Syndicate. Samaha has extensive practical experience in the practical application of International Financial Reporting Standards (IFRSs) and has recently published four papers about convergence with IAS/IFRS in Egypt in the *Afro Asian Journal of Finance and Accounting (AAJFA)*, *Journal of Current Research in Global Business (JCRGB)*, *International Journal of Accounting and Finance (IJAF)*, and *the International Journal of Accounting, Auditing and Performance Evaluation (IJAAPE)*. He is currently serving as a member on the editorial board of the *Afro Asian Journal of Finance & Accounting* published by Inderscience. Samaha has served as an audit consultant to several companies listed on the Egyptian Stock Exchange, as well as the Ministry of Transport. His research interests include harmonization and compliance with IAS/IFRS in the developing countries, corporate governance disclosure, financial reporting and corporate governance mechanisms, audit procedures and methodologies, financial reporting on the Internet, and the use of modern cost accounting systems.

Ahmed H. Tolba is currently Assistant Professor of Marketing at the Department of Management, School of Business, the American University in Cairo. Also, he is the Director of El-Khazindar Business Research and Case Center (KCC) at AUC. KCC is the first center in the Middle East and North Africa region that focuses on developing world-class refereed local and regional case studies to be used for teaching and training purposes. He was awarded his PhD from The George Washington University in 2006; his MBA and BSc from the American University in Cairo in 1997 and 2001, respectively. He taught a variety of courses at the George Washington University and the American University in Cairo at both undergraduate and MBA levels. Courses he taught include Principles of Marketing, Marketing Research, Advanced Marketing Research, Consumer Behavior, Marketing Management, International Marketing, Marketing Information Systems, Marketing Strategy, and Strategic Brand Management. He conducted a variety of training courses in Marketing for several training institutions, covering the topics of Marketing Management, Marketing Research, Strategic Brand Management, Marketing Strategy, and Integrated Marketing Communications. His clients include Microsoft Egypt, Bank Audi, Heinz Egypt, the Institute of Management Development (IMD) at the American University in Cairo, International Marketing Institute (IMI), and Insight Training in Alexandria, Egypt. His professional experience includes four years at Procter & Gamble Egypt, where he worked on a variety of brands, including Ariel, Tide, Downy, Pampers, Always, Pantene, Pert Plus, Head & Shoulders, Camay, and Zest. Also, he has been responsible for several internal training and development programs, such as leadership, individual effectiveness, and finance for non-finance managers. He also worked as a consultant for several local firms including Wadi Degla, Net Signature, El-Rashad Asset Management, GMC, Taki, and Engineering Consultants Group (ECG), among others. His research focuses on the areas of strategic brand management, brand equity measurement, models, marketing research, global branding, and nation branding. His research has been published in leading academic journals and conferences, such as the Journal of Product and Brand Management, the American Marketing Association (AMA), the Academy of Marketing Science (AMS), Society for Marketing Advances, Academy of Management, Thought Leaders International Conference on Brand Management, Frontiers in Services Conference, Association for Global Business, Middle East Studies Association (MESA) and the Sustainable Development Forum (SDF). He also co-authored the teaching guide of the third edition of the "Strategic Brand Management" book authored by Dr. Kevin Keller (2008). He is currently co-authoring a new Middle East edition of the "Principles of Marketing" book by Philip Kotler and Gary Armstrong.

Eskandar Tooma is an associate professor of finance and holds the British Petroleum endowed chair with the Department of Management at The American University in Cairo. He is a member of the American Economic Association (AEA), the American Finance Association (AFA), and also is the Secretary General of the African Finance Association. Professor Tooma obtained his B.A. in Business from The American University in Cairo and Adelphi University. Dr. Tooma holds two M.S. degrees, the first in Finance and the second in International Economics from Adelphi and Brandeis Universities, respectively. Finally, he holds a Ph.D. in Finance from Brandeis University. Professor Tooma is a specialist in financial economics. His writings focus on volatility dynamics and forecasting in emerging stock markets as well as market microstructure. Subsequent research is in the areas of asset pricing, portfolio theory, and stock market regulations. Currently, he is focusing on research in the area of agent based modelling and stock market simulations as well as writing finance case studies that are used worldwide as teaching aids in both graduate and undergraduate courses. Professor Tooma combines academic experience with practical exposure through assuming a variety of public and private professional posts. He was senior advisor to the Capital Market Authority for 2.5 years, as well as a member of a variety of committees including the EGX30 Index Committee, Market Advancement Committee at the Egyptian Stock Exchange, an advisor and member of the Derivatives and Commodities Exchange Committee with the Ministry of Investments, and an advisor to the Ministry of International Cooperation on Egypt's Debt Swap Experience. Privately, he has advised leading institutions including but not limited to: Citadel Capital, Beltone Financial, EFG-Hermes, AAIB, and Osoul Fund Management. Dr. Tooma is a co-owner and board member of Premium International for Credit Services as well as a board member of Orascom Housing Communities, Orascom Investment Fund, Egyptian Resorts Company, Roward Tourism, and Regina Food Industries, among others. Professor Tooma is currently advising leading real estate and development groups on financial and restructuring issues. He sits on the boards of one of the largest real estate funds in the region and is a financial advisor to Orascom for Hotels and Development (OHD).

Taylor Valore is a Special Projects Officer at the American University in Cairo in the Office of Planning and Administration, where he manages long-range strategic planning and budgeting. Formerly head of product development at RavenPack International, a software company in Spain, Taylor oversaw the development of a high-end analytics service sold to investment banks and hedge funds in partnership with Dow Jones. Taylor is skilled at strategic planning, process development and technology, and project management in multi-cultural organizations both large and small. He holds a BA in Computer Science and International Relations from Carleton College, where he founded *The Lens*, an award-winning, nationally-distributed magazine of politics and culture. He is a certified Project Management Professional and fluent in Spanish.

Mayada A. Youssef is currently an Assistant Professor at the Accounting Department, College of Business & Economics, United Arab Emirates University, U.A.E. She is also a Lecturer (on leave) at the Accounting Department, Faculty of Commerce & Business Administration, Helwan University, Egypt. She earned her Ph.D. in Accounting & Finance from Manchester Business School, Manchester University, Manchester, U.K., in 2005. Her research interests include management accounting change and electronic commerce. She published a number of research papers in this interdisciplinary field of study. Her teaching interests include management accounting, cost accounting, principles of financial accounting, accounting Information Systems, and intermediate accounting. She taught some parts of CIA & CMA programs in UAE University. She was a consultant for Egypt Education Reform Project, Ministry of Education, Egypt, in 2007- 2008.

Index

D

E

F

G

H

I

J

K

L

M

T

U

V

W

Y

CPSIA information can be obtained at www.ICGtesting.com
264416BV00002B/4/P

9 781609 605834